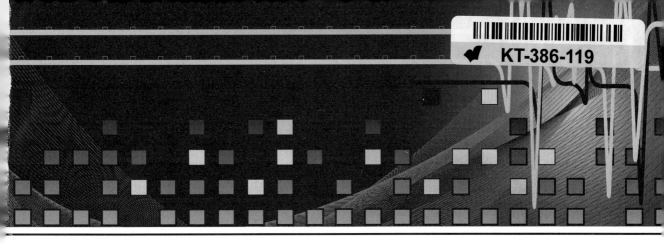

HEALTHCARE HUMAN RESOURCE MANAGEMENT

Third Edition

Walter J. Flynn
Saint Mary's University of Minnesota

Robert L. Mathis
University of Nebraska at Omaha

John H. Jackson
University of Wyoming

Sean R. Valentine
University of North Dakota

CENGAGE
Learning·

Australia • Brazil • Mexico • Singapore • United Kingdom • United States

CENGAGE
Learning®

Healthcare Human Resource Management, 3e
Walter J. Flynn, Robert L. Mathis,
John H. Jackson, Sean R. Valentine

Vice President, General Manager,
Social Science & Qualitative Business:
Erin Joyner

Product Director: Mike Schenk

Product Manager: Michael Roche

Content Developer: Christopher Santos

Product Assistant: Jamie Mack

Marketing Director: Kristen Hurd

Marketing Manager: Emily Horowitz

Marketing Coordinator:
Christopher P. Walz

Art and Cover Direction, Production
Management, and Composition:
Lumina Datamatics, Inc.

Intellectual Property Analyst:
Jennifer Nonenmacher

Project Manager: Amber Hosea

Senior Manufacturing Planner:
Ron Montgomery

Cover Image(s): © Ariel Skelley/Blend
Images/Corbis description:
doctors working in teleconference
©marivlada/Shutterstock
description: vector modern template
for medical treatment company

For product information and technology assistance, contact us at
Cengage Learning Customer & Sales Support, 1-800-354-9706

For permission to use material from this text or product,
submit all requests online at **www.cengage.com/permissions**
Further permissions questions can be emailed to
permissionrequest@cengage.com

Library of Congress Control Number: 2014952096

ISBN-13: 978-1-285-05753-8

Cengage Learning
20 Channel Center Street
Boston, MA 02210
USA

Cengage Learning is a leading provider of customized learning
solutions with office locations around the globe, including Singapore,
the United Kingdom, Australia, Mexico, Brazil, and Japan. Locate your
local office at: **www.cengage.com/global**

Cengage Learning products are represented in Canada by
Nelson Education, Ltd.

To learn more about Cengage Learning Solutions, visit
www.cengage.com

Purchase any of our products at your local college store or at our
preferred online store **www.cengagebrain.com**

Printed in the United States of America
Print Number: 01   Print Year: 2014

BRIEF CONTENTS

Contents

v

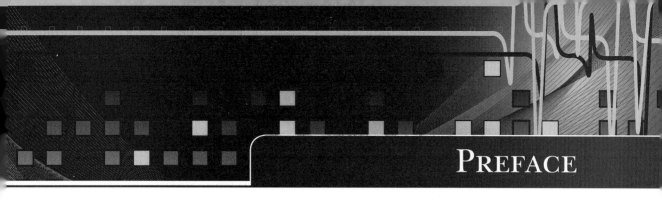

WHY A BOOK ON HEALTHCARE HUMAN RESOURCE MANAGEMENT

As the authors of this textbook, we have long recognized the unique aspects of healthcare human resource management (HRM) and the need for a textbook specifically focused on this area. Collectively, we have experience in healthcare HRM as practitioners, consultants, and professors. In this book, we provide both the HRM student and the practitioner a comprehensive, focused source of information on this important body of knowledge and specialized field of practice.

PRIMARY AUDIENCES FOR THIS BOOK

There are several audiences that will find this book to be a useful resource, including college and university students and faculty members, various HR practitioners in healthcare organizations, and healthcare professionals and managers in numerous fields where HRM issues affect organizational and individual performance.

COLLEGE/UNIVERSITY STUDENTS AND FACULTY MEMBERS

The importance of human relations skills and HRM knowledge for application in the healthcare industry has grown due to the significant recruitment and retention issues that exist for healthcare workers. Graduates of healthcare-related administration/management degree programs must have a solid knowledge base of HRM topics to be successful in their careers. The types of courses that are well suited for this text include:

- Undergraduate courses in human resource management offered to health-care administration majors.
- Undergraduate human resource management courses that emphasize the healthcare industry.
- Graduate-level human resource management courses offered in healthcare administration programs.
- College curriculums for management tracks for degrees in:
  - Nursing
  - Respiratory Care
  - Radiological Technology
  - Allied Health
  - Public Health
  - Health Promotion
- Distance learning programs containing the courses and related to the degrees described above.

HEALTHCARE HR PROFESSIONALS AND HEALTHCARE MANAGEMENT PRACTITIONERS

HR management issues will continue to be a major focus for all individuals with management responsibilities in healthcare organizations. Both the academic and practical experiences of the authors have contributed to the book's balance between the theoretical and the practical aspects of healthcare HR. This balance makes the textbook not only useful for the academic setting, but equally useful as a reference for healthcare leaders and professionals with HR responsibilities. Even highly experienced healthcare HR professionals will find the presentations of both theory and actual healthcare organizational HR practices insightful and informative.

ORGANIZATION OF THIS BOOK

The textbook includes 14 chapters; each chapter discusses a particular HRM topic. Each chapter can be used in instruction as a stand-alone presentation, or in conjunction with the other chapters. Regardless of the approach, this book provides a comprehensive source of information on both theory and practice in healthcare HRM.

Chapter 1 discusses the nature and challenges of healthcare HR management through an overview of the current and future states of the healthcare industry. The chapter also describes the various types of organizations that make up the healthcare industry.

Chapter 2 presents a unique review of the competencies that are important for healthcare HR professionals. The chapter discusses healthcare organizational structures and the placement of HR departments within the organizational structure, and HR budgets and staffing. The Joint Commission on Accreditation of Healthcare Organizations (JCAHO) is also described along with the key quality standards that impact healthcare HRM.

Chapter 3 describes the importance of strategic HRM. The chapter discusses the process and relevance of effective HR planning against the backdrop of the most challenging HRM issues that confront healthcare organizations.

Chapter 4 discusses the legal issues affecting the healthcare workplace, with particular focus on equal employment opportunity regulations and issues. Chapter 5 reviews the importance of job design and analysis as it affects all aspects of HRM in healthcare organizations.

Chapter 6 presents a comprehensive discussion on the critical topics for healthcare organizations of recruitment and selection. The chapter includes a discussion on strategic recruiting and an overview of various recruitment methods that are successful in the healthcare industry.

Chapter 7 explores employee retention, presenting many of the acknowledged "best practices" that are achieving retention results in healthcare organizations. Given both the current state and the anticipated shortage of healthcare workers, employee retention is one of the most important responsibilities that healthcare HR professionals and healthcare managers have.

Chapter 8 provides a comprehensive discussion on training and development in healthcare organizations. The JCAHO standards dealing with orientation and training also are highlighted in the chapter, as they relate to the verification and development of healthcare worker competencies.

Chapter 9 focuses on the topic of performance management. This chapter includes a review of both the theoretical and practical aspects of establishing performance criteria and developing and conducting performance appraisals for healthcare workers.

Chapters 10 and 11 deal with the interrelated healthcare HR management topics of employee and labor relations. Chapter 10 focuses on a variety of concerns that affect how healthcare organizations manage their workers. Chapter 11 deals specifically with the complexities of managing healthcare workers who are covered under collective bargaining agreements.

Chapters 12 and 13 present healthcare compensation, benefits, and variable pay practices. Chapter 12 details the various compensation programs and processes, including executive pay plans, utilized in healthcare organizations. Chapter 13 discusses the benefits and variable pay programs that make up the total compensation provided to healthcare workers.

Chapter 14 describes the safety, health, and security issues in healthcare organizations and how they affect HRM. The safety, health, and security concerns present in healthcare environments are emphasized as part of healthcare HRM.

Textbook Features and Highlights

To enhance the readability and healthcare focus, there are a number of features in the book, including:

Examples Specific to the Healthcare Focus

The healthcare environment is the focus of each HRM topic covered. "Best practice" examples appear throughout the text, enriching the discussion of current theory.

Healthcare HR Insights

Each chapter begins with a "Healthcare HR Insight," which is an example of programs, solutions, and/or initiatives undertaken by various healthcare organizations relevant to the topic covered in the chapter. Special attention has been given by the authors to ensure that healthcare institutions of different types are represented in the Healthcare HR Insights.

Healthcare Reform and HR Practices

Each chapter includes a feature discussing how the Affordable Care Act and other healthcare reform initiatives have and will impact healthcare organizations and HR practices. The Affordable Care Act is the most sweeping legislation of its nature in decades and has far-reaching implications for HR management. Each feature presents a commentary on an aspect of healthcare reform and how it impacts the topic presented in the chapter.

Study Aids

Figures, including illustrations, process maps, charts, and tables, are used throughout the chapters to assist readers in examining the topics discussed.

Glossary: Key Vocabulary and Concepts

Key vocabulary and concepts are contained in the glossary. For ease of reference, these terms also appear in bold print in the text to alert readers that a definition is included in the glossary.

Chapter-Ending Cases

At the end of each chapter, case studies are offered to allow readers to analyze a case scenario that is relevant to the chapter content. The cases describe actual situations that have been experienced by healthcare organizations, but the names have been disguised. The problems and issues to be analyzed are framed by discussion questions at the end of the case.

SUPPLEMENTAL MATERIALS

In order to facilitate and enhance the use of the book by faculty members and instructors, an Instructor's Manual, Test Bank, and PowerPoint slides are available on the instructor support website accessible at www.cengagebrain.com:

Instructor's Manual contents include:

- Chapter outlines
- Instructor notes
- Chapter-Ending Cases include recommended solutions

Test Bank contents include:

- Multiple-choice
- True/False
- Short essay questions

All questions include answers with reference to pages in the text.

ACKNOWLEDGMENTS

There are a number of individuals who assisted the authors in the development of this book and we would like to acknowledge them. Two who deserve special recognition are Kathy Flynn and Kelly Kneflin, who were so supportive and helpful throughout the development of this edition.

Some other individuals whose ideas and assistance were invaluable include Cassie Flynn, Gina Franklin, Chris Nohner, Gina Rens, and Angie Guillaume.

ABOUT THE AUTHORS

Walter J. Flynn, SPHR, MBA

Mr. Flynn was born in Kentucky and currently resides in Minnesota. He is the CEO of the human resources consulting firm of W.J. Flynn and Associates LLC, based in Eagan, Minnesota. His firm specializes in working with healthcare organizations in all areas of human resources management. Mr. Flynn has published numerous articles covering a wide array of HR topics.

Mr. Flynn's education includes an MBA from Xavier University, Cincinnati, Ohio; a BS from Northern Kentucky University; and advanced work in quality management, diversity awareness, and strategic management. In addition, he has attained the Senior Professional Human Resources (SPHR) designation from the Society for Human Resources Management (SHRM).

In addition to his current consulting experience, he has more than 25 years of HR practice and leadership experience, including: Vice President of Human Resources for Cincinnati's Children's Hospital, Personnel Director for the Central Trust Co., and Managing Consultant for R. J. Kemen and Associates. He currently holds a faculty appointment at Saint Mary's University of Minnesota, and has held faculty appointments at the University of Minnesota, University of Cincinnati, Northern Kentucky University, and Thomas More College.

Dr. Robert L. Mathis

Dr. Robert Mathis is a Professor of Management at the University of Nebraska at Omaha (UNO). Born and raised in Texas, he received a BBA and MBA from Texas Tech University and a PhD in management and organization from the University of Colorado. At UNO he received the university's "Excellence in Teaching" award.

Dr. Mathis has coauthored several books and published numerous articles covering a variety of topics over the last 25 years. On the professional level, Dr. Mathis has held numerous national offices in the Society for Human Resource Management and in other professional organizations, including the Academy of Management. He also served as President of the Human Resource Certification Institute (HRCI) and is certified as a Senior Professional in Human Resources (SPHR) by HRCI.

He has had extensive consulting experiences with organizations of all sizes in a variety of areas. Firms assisted have been in the telecommunications, telemarketing, financial, manufacturing, retail, healthcare, and utility industries. He has extensive specialized consulting experience in establishing or revising compensation plans for small- and medium-size firms. Internationally, Dr. Mathis has consulting and training experience with organizations in Australia, Lithuania, Romania, Moldova, and Taiwan.

Dr. John H. Jackson

Dr. John H. Jackson is a Professor of Management at the University of Wyoming. Born in Alaska, he received his BBA and MBA from Texas Tech University. He then worked in the telecommunications industry in human resources management for several years. After leaving that industry, he completed his doctoral studies at the University of Colorado and received his PhD in management and organization.

During his academic career, Dr. Jackson has authored six other college texts and more than 50 articles and papers, including those appearing in *Academy of Management Review, Journal of Management, Human Resources Management,* and *Human Resource Planning.* He has consulted with a variety of organizations on HR and management development matters and served as an expert witness in a number of HR-related cases.

At the University of Wyoming, he served three terms as department head in the Department of Management and Marketing. Dr. Jackson received the university's highest teaching award and worked with two-way interactive television for MBA students. He designed one of the first classes in the nation on "Business, Environment, and Natural Resources." Two of the governors of the state of Wyoming have appointed him to the Wyoming Business Council and the Workforce Development Council. Dr. Jackson is also president of Silverwood Ranches Inc.

Dr. Sean R. Valentine

Dr. Sean R. Valentine is the UND Alumni Leadership and Ethics Professor and Professor of Management at the University of North Dakota. Originally from Texas, he received a BS in management/human resources from Park University, a BS in hotel, restaurant, and tourism management from New Mexico State University, an MBA in business administration from Texas State University, and a DBA in management from Louisiana Tech University. He was employed in the hospitality industry for many years and was an officer in the Army National Guard.

During his academic career, Dr. Valentine has published more than 75 articles in journals such as *Human Resource Management, Human Relations, Human Resource Development Quarterly, Journal of Business Research, Journal of Business Ethics, Journal of Personal Selling & Sales Management, Contemporary Accounting Research,* and *Behavioral Research in Accounting.* His primary research and teaching interests include human resource management, business ethics, and organizational behavior, and he has received numerous awards and other recognition for his work. He has also consulted with a variety of organizations on different business matters.

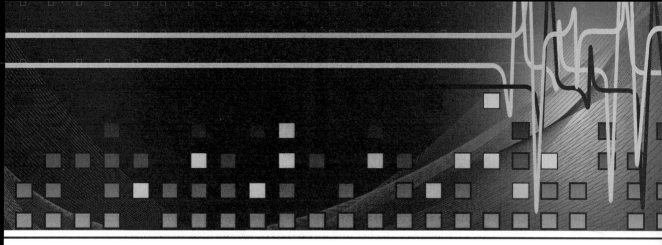

HEALTHCARE HUMAN
RESOURCE MANAGEMENT

The Nature and Challenges of Healthcare HR Management

Learning Objectives

After you have read this chapter, you should be able to:

- Identify the types of healthcare organizations.
- Describe the current and future states of the healthcare industry.
- List and briefly describe human resource management activities.
- Explain the unique aspects of managing human resources in healthcare organizations.
- Discuss several of the human resource challenges existing in healthcare.

HEALTHCARE HR INSIGHTS

The Institute for Healthcare Improvement (IHI), an independent not-for-profit organization based in Cambridge, Massachusetts, is focused on developing strategies for health and healthcare improvement.[1] Consistent with its mission it has developed a framework for healthcare improvement based on optimizing health system performance. It is IHI's belief that new designs must be developed to simultaneously pursue three dimensions, which it calls the "Triple Aim":

Improving the patient experience of care (including quality and satisfaction)

- Improving the health of populations
- Reducing the per capita cost of health care[2]

At the heart of the Triple Aim approach is a fundamental rethinking of how healthcare workers are trained, managed, coached, and compensated in order to pursue the dimensions noted above. Healthcare organizations that adopt this new design must translate these dimensions into HR strategies because ultimately people provide healthcare. Examples include: healthcare worker training and coaching designed to provide them with new skills in customer relations to improve the patient experience. Jobs may need to be redesigned to focus more on primary care versus specialty care to deal with the full continuum of healthcare provision. Healthcare workers may be compensated based on how effectively their organizations deliver high-quality care at the lowest possible price.

Many healthcare organizations have begun to translate the Triple Aim design into high-impact results. The following examples illustrate this approach, including:

- Genesys Health System in Flint, Michigan, worked with its partners Genesee Health Plan and Genesys Physician Hospital Organization to better engage patients in their own care. The combination of a patient-centered medical home and a health navigator who supports patients and providers, and links both with community resources, helps to improve access and appropriate utilization. Genesys says that it is demonstrating 10 to 25 percent lower healthcare costs than competitors, across a diverse population that includes both insured and uninsured patients.

- HealthPartners, based in Minnesota, introduced a program designed around the concepts of consistency (reliable processes), customization (adapting care to individual needs), convenience (improving access), and coordination. Health-Partners calculates that spreading their best practices nationwide would save $2 trillion in 10 years.

- QuadMed, based in Wisconsin, provides employer-sponsored, work site health care, bringing primary healthcare services in-house for employees and dependents, and managing clinics for two other national companies. Thirty- to 90-minute appointments support prevention and wellness; onsite lab, X-ray, and ancillary services offer convenience and coordination; and the result is more spending on primary care and less on hospitalization and pharmacy. QuadMed

(Continued)

spends about 31 percent less to cover QuadGraphics employees than the average Wisconsin company.[3]

Each of these organizations could achieve the successful outcomes noted only by engaging its workforce in the changes necessary to drive the Triple Aim objectives. HR strategic management is critical in achieving these outcomes.

NATURE OF HEALTHCARE ORGANIZATIONS

The healthcare industry is very diverse from an organizational standpoint. The industry includes firms that provide medical care, residential care and treatment, and various forms of therapies and health services.

Healthcare organizations can be divided into several categories. Some of these—such as hospitals—employ hundreds of people in large building complexes. Others—such as home healthcare providers—involve few employees, and the "facility" is wherever the patient is. In between are many organizations that make up the healthcare employment spectrum.

- *Hospitals*—Hospitals provide complete healthcare, ranging from diagnostic services to surgery and continuous nursing care. Hospitals can be small, freestanding rural facilities, or they can be part of a vast, multifacility, geographically dispersed, integrated system. Some hospitals specialize in treatment such as burn care, cancer, or pediatrics, while others are full-service providers.

- *Nursing and Residential Care Facilities*—Nursing facilities provide inpatient nursing, rehabilitation, and health-related personal care to those who need continuous healthcare but do not require hospital services. Other facilities, such as nursing and convalescent homes, help patients who need less assistance but also need special rehabilitation services.

- *Physician Offices and Clinics*—Physicians and surgeons practice individually or in groups of practitioners who have the same or different specialties. Group practice has become the recent trend, including clinics, freestanding emergency care centers, and ambulatory surgical centers.

- *Other Ambulatory Healthcare Services*—Included in this segment are such services as dental, chiropractic, optometric, other specialist, and medical and diagnostic labs.

- *Home Healthcare Care Services*—Skilled nursing or medical care is sometimes provided in the home, under a physician's supervision. Home healthcare services are provided mainly to the elderly and individuals with special needs.

- *Outpatient Care Centers*—Among the establishments in this group are kidney dialysis centers, drug treatment clinics and rehabilitation centers, blood banks, and providers of childbirth preparation classes.

Employment in Healthcare

No matter what form of healthcare or type of facility is involved, employees are needed to deliver care. In the United States, more than 14 million[4] individuals

FIGURE 1-1   Employment in Healthcare

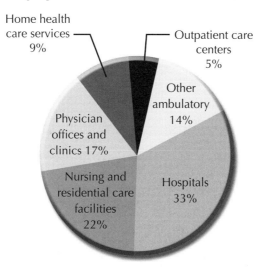

© 2016 Cengage Learning®

are employed in the healthcare industry. The healthcare share of total employment in the United States is approximately 11 percent. The healthcare industry can be characterized as a labor-intensive industry with a wide diversity of position types requiring a broad cross section of skill sets, professional training, and academic preparation. Many healthcare positions require at least four-year college degrees Figure 1-1 shows the composition of healthcare employment by type of organization. Hospitals are by far the largest employers of healthcare workers.[5]

Types of Healthcare Jobs

The delivery of healthcare requires workers in a variety of job categories with different levels of education, training, and experience. In addition to the myriad of medical and clinical positions present in healthcare delivery, there are also significant requirements for workers with skills in the following fields:

- Management and administration
- Legal and compliance services
- Physical plant operations
- Safety and security
- Information technology
- Fund raising and community affairs
- Food and nutritional services

The scope of jobs in healthcare depicted in Figure 1-2 shows a healthcare position hierarchy. It also depicts two other relationships: the levels and the number of positions required in each job category.

FIGURE 1-2 Healthcare Position Hierarchy

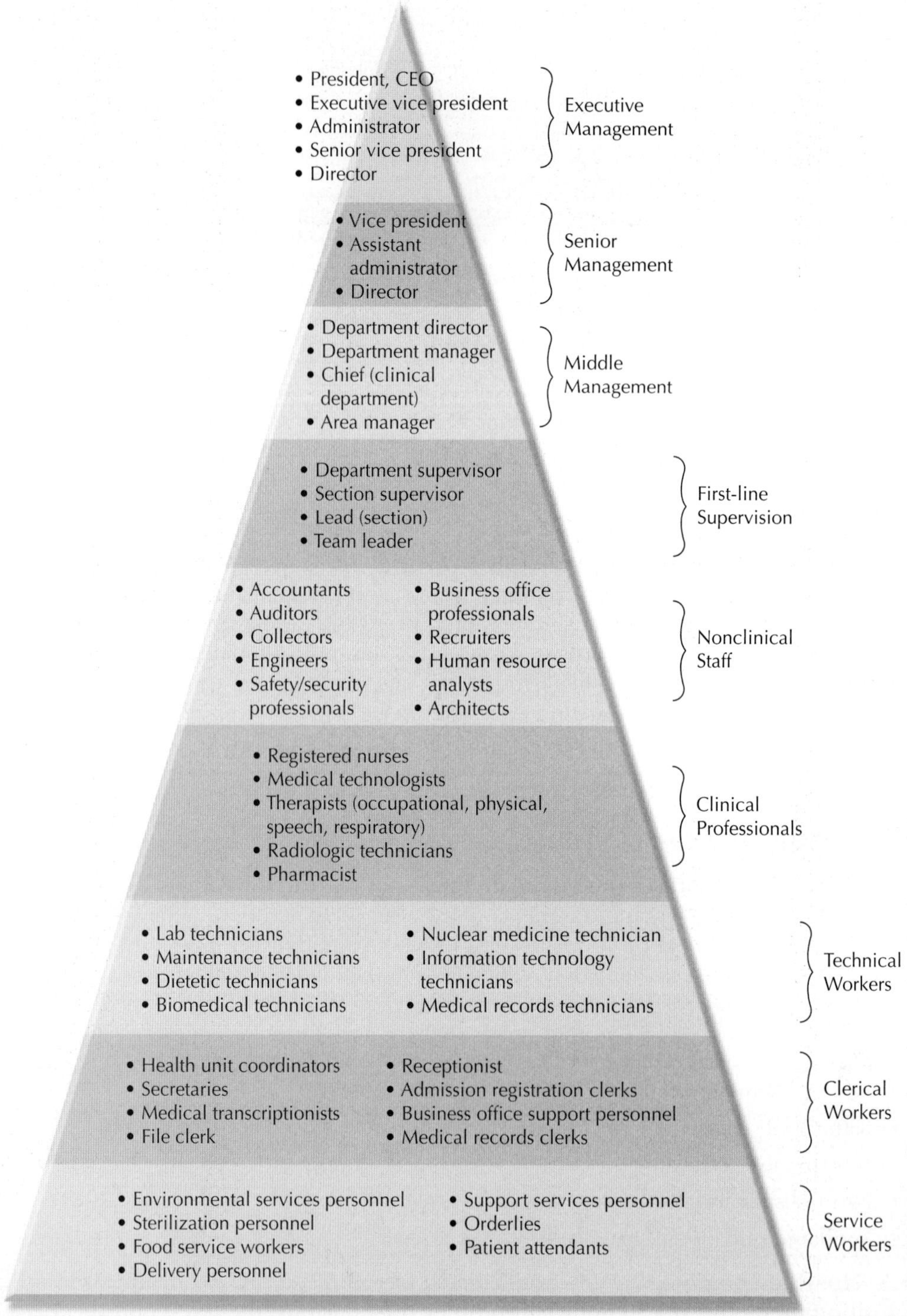

- President, CEO
- Executive vice president
- Administrator
- Senior vice president
- Director

} Executive Management

- Vice president
- Assistant administrator
- Director

} Senior Management

- Department director
- Department manager
- Chief (clinical department)
- Area manager

} Middle Management

- Department supervisor
- Section supervisor
- Lead (section)
- Team leader

} First-line Supervision

- Accountants
- Auditors
- Collectors
- Engineers
- Safety/security professionals
- Business office professionals
- Recruiters
- Human resource analysts
- Architects

} Nonclinical Staff

- Registered nurses
- Medical technologists
- Therapists (occupational, physical, speech, respiratory)
- Radiologic technicians
- Pharmacist

} Clinical Professionals

- Lab technicians
- Maintenance technicians
- Dietetic technicians
- Biomedical technicians
- Nuclear medicine technician
- Information technology technicians
- Medical records technicians

} Technical Workers

- Health unit coordinators
- Secretaries
- Medical transcriptionists
- File clerk
- Receptionist
- Admission registration clerks
- Business office support personnel
- Medical records clerks

} Clerical Workers

- Environmental services personnel
- Sterilization personnel
- Food service workers
- Delivery personnel
- Support services personnel
- Orderlies
- Patient attendants

} Service Workers

© Cengage Learning®

Healthcare Position Hierarchy   It is useful to understand the various levels of positions to appreciate the distribution of power and responsibility within healthcare organizations. Large health systems are especially hierarchical with significant numbers and levels of jobs, while clinics and physician groups have very flat organizational structures with fewer levels. Purposely not depicted in this illustration are physicians, who by definition would fall in the clinical professional category. However, depending on the nature and size of a healthcare organization, physicians could also be associated with any level of executive, senior, or middle management or supervision, and their power associated with their knowledge makes them difficult to classify in a typical managerial position chart.

Distribution of Positions   The graphical depiction of a pyramid is a model for considering the labor requirements of the various levels in a healthcare organization. At the top of the pyramid is executive management, which would represent the fewest number of individuals required across the industry. At the base of the pyramid are service workers, who would represent the category of workers requiring the largest number of individuals.

The Current State of Healthcare

The current state of the delivery of healthcare in the United States is important to the discussion of healthcare human resources (HR) management and how healthcare organizations manage their employees.

The U.S. healthcare system is one of the best in the world. Access to care (although sometimes unevenly distributed) and advances in technology, therapies, and pharmaceuticals continually contribute to a longer and higher quality of life for the U.S. population. Yet certain realities and issues provide a compelling backdrop against which the accomplishments of the healthcare system must be balanced. The following list details some of the key areas for awareness in the environment in which healthcare operates:

- *Technology Driven*—The healthcare system in the United States is very focused on research and innovation in new technology. The adoption of new medical technologies generally creates demand for new services despite the higher costs typically associated with the new technologies.

- *Access to Healthcare Services Is Largely Based on Insurance Coverage*—Although the United States offers some the best healthcare in the world, access to care is largely dependent on whether an individual has health insurance or sufficient resources to pay for healthcare services.

- *Legal Risk Management Affects Practice Behavior*—Because of concerns for the potential of large jury awards due to malpractice lawsuits, healthcare providers engage in what is referred to as "defensive medicine." Effectively, healthcare providers *defensively* prescribe additional diagnostic tests, require excessive follow-up appointments, and maintain an abundant amount of documentation to support medical decisions.[6]

- *Healthcare Worker Shortages*—Currently, certain areas in the United States face shortages of critical healthcare workers, including primary care physicians, nurses, behavioral health and long-term care workers, as well as public health and human service professionals. Moreover, this problem is anticipated to increase in the coming years. More than half of the counties in the United States have no behavioral health worker at all. With the implementation of the Affordable Care Act and the resulting expansion of health insurance coverage, demand for services of primary care professionals will increase substantially.[7]

- *Healthcare Reform Implications*—With the passage of the Patient Protection and Affordable Care Acts in 2010 (collectively known as ACA), there is no question that the healthcare system in the United States has changed and will continue to change. It is less clear that ACA will realize the objectives of higher-value care efficiently provided in the best location at a fair, competitive price.[8]

- *Providing Culturally Competent Care*—The United States' increasing diversity results in a more diverse patient population. Studies indicate that there are significant disparities in how minorities access, receive, and benefit from the nation's healthcare system. There are clear indications that a lack of diversity in the direct providers of care and healthcare management and their lack of sensitivity to cultural differences can produce less positive or even negative healthcare outcomes for racially/ethnically diverse consumers.[9]

The Future of Healthcare

If the best predictor of the future is the recent past, then a review of historical precedents and current political, economic, and environmental developments can be used to provide insights as to the future of healthcare in the United States. Depicted in Figure 1-3 are certain trends and "drivers" of the future of healthcare that can be predicted with a degree of certainty, primarily because they have so much momentum that regardless of unforeseen or catastrophic events it would be difficult to alter their course.

- *Acceleration of Technological Advancements*—Consistent with the "current state of healthcare," innovation in healthcare technology will continue to occur, if not accelerate. In the future state of healthcare, innovations in such areas as imaging, minimally invasive surgery, genetic mapping, and remote monitoring of patients will dramatically impact the delivery of healthcare.[10]

FIGURE 1-3 The Current and Future States of Healthcare

HEALTHCARE	
CURRENT STATE	FUTURE STATE
• Technology driven • Legal risk management affects practice behavior • Healthcare worker shortages • Healthcare reform implications	• Acceleration of technological advancements • Continued financial pressures • More accountability • Demographic changes • Health planning policy initiatives

© 2016 Cengage Learning®

- *Continued Financial Pressures*—The federal government, third-party payers, consumers, and employers will continue to pressure the healthcare industry to stabilize costs. And perhaps as legislated through the ACA, the healthcare industry will provide more value in all aspects of the care delivery continuum for the healthcare dollars being spent.

- *More Accountability*—Federal, state, and local governments, along with employer and consumer groups, are already demanding more accountability from healthcare organizations and individual providers. The future will predictably include a call for more information on the quality of doctors and hospitals. Hospital and physician price information should also be publicly available, as well as information on the actual net cost of any procedure, treatment, or test.

- *Demographic Changes*—The United States is in the midst of a major demographic shift. In the coming decades, people aged 65 and over will make up an increasingly large percentage of the population: the ratio of people aged 65+ to people aged 20–64 will rise by 80 percent. This shift is happening for two reasons: people are living longer, and many couples are choosing to have fewer children and to have those children somewhat later in life.[11] The resulting demographic shift will present the healthcare industry with significant challenges, both to provide healthcare to the aging population and to replace the healthcare workers leaving the workplace due to retirements and poor health.

- *Health Planning Policy Initiatives*—Clearly a critical national agenda item that has impacted the current state of healthcare and will have an important impact on the future of healthcare is the health planning policies concerning access to care. According to the U.S. Department of Health and Human Services' Healthy People 2020 goals and objectives for health promotion and disease prevention, access to health services means the timely use of personal health services to achieve the best health outcomes. It requires three distinct steps:

  1. Gaining entry into the healthcare system
  2. Accessing a healthcare location where needed services are provided
  3. Finding a healthcare provider with whom the patient can communicate and trust[12]

Disparities in access to health services affect individuals and society. Limited access to healthcare impacts people's ability to reach their full potential, negatively affecting their quality of life. Barriers to services include: lack of availability, high cost, and lack of insurance coverage. Healthcare reform as legislated through the ACA as well as other federal, state, and local health planning policies will continue to drive access to healthcare.

HR CHALLENGES IN HEALTHCARE

The current state of healthcare and predictions about the industry require healthcare organizational leaders who can manage in an ever-changing and challenging environment. HR leadership is especially critical because many of the current realities and future eventualities for the healthcare industry have, at their core, significant human resource management implications.

The list of challenges is both daunting and exciting. HR professionals have the opportunity to make contributions to their organizations and to their industry by providing solutions for the most difficult issues and problems the industry faces. Two of the most prominent challenges are the *recruitment and retention* of the correct number of qualified staff and *managing the changes* that affect people.

Recruitment and Retention

The enormous demand for healthcare workers is predicted to increase for a number of key healthcare positions. The ever-increasing need for registered nurses (RNs) has been well-chronicled in the popular media. According to the U.S. Bureau of Labor Statistics Employment Projections 2012–2022, the registered nursing workforce is one of the top occupations in terms of job growth through 2022. It is expected that the number of employed nurses will grow from 2,711,500 in 2012 to 3,238,400 in 2022—an increase of 526,800, or 19.4 percent; 1,052,600 of these openings will be due to growth and replacement needs.[13] However, the recruitment and staffing issues are clearly not exclusive

---

FIGURE 1-4   Projected Growth of Selected Health Professions 2012–2022

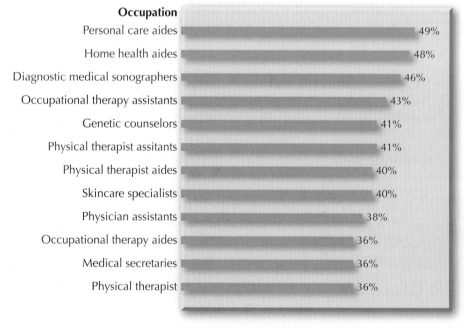

© 2016 Cengage Learning®

to nursing; all healthcare professions have been and will be affected. To further illustrate the magnitude of the growth in health occupations, Figure 1-4 shows the fastest-growing occupations as identified by the *U.S. Bureau of Labor Statistics: Occupational Outlook Handbook* for the period 2012 to 2022—12 out of the top 20 are healthcare positions. Note that many of these positions require a minimum of a two-year associate's degree, and three of the positions—genetic counselor, physician assistant, and physical therapist—require specialized training beyond a four-year bachelor's degree.

HR professionals in all segments of the industry will be faced with the challenge of recruiting and retaining the right number of competent employees for their organizations. The following trends will have a direct impact on the supply of and demand for healthcare workers.

Hospitals, Residential Care, and Rehabilitation Facilities   During the next 15 years, the U.S. healthcare system, particularly inpatient institutions, will face two critical problems related to the healthcare workforce. First and foremost, there will not be enough workers, and second, those who will be available will not have the skills needed in the health system that is emerging. The issues, again, are the demographics of the aging population demanding more care and the overall size of the healthcare delivery system.

The demand for nurses and allied health workers will also be driven by significant growth in three other parts of the healthcare system, as follows.

Ambulatory Care   Healthcare continues to move from inpatient to outpatient or ambulatory care. Thus care providers, which include clinics, physician offices, home health agencies, and freestanding surgery and diagnostic centers, will see requirements for ambulatory care providers expand.

Health Service Businesses   Alternative care delivery is rapidly gaining momentum, creating a variety of health service businesses. Managed care companies, "health concierge" companies, and grocery and drug stores will be looking for individuals with clinical training and a knack for customer service.

Independent Practice   Some healthcare professionals are moving to independent practice to meet the demand for alternative care. High-demand skills include nutrition and weight management, physical therapy, pain management, and personal care combined with therapy. Independent practitioners are utilizing the training they received from hospitals and clinics and establishing fee-for-service businesses marketed directly to the consumer.

The challenge to healthcare HR professionals to recruit and retain competent employees includes dealing with some very compelling issues, among which are the following:

- Attractive career paths have emerged outside of the life sciences, particularly in technology and other service industries, which offer comparable or better wages, friendlier work environments, and greater opportunities for advancement.

FIGURE 1-5 **Major Healthcare HR Change Elements**

- Managing Costs
- Compliance
- Managing diversity and providing culturally competent care
- New technologies
- Employee demands for quality of work life

© 2016 Cengage Learning®

- As career opportunities for women have broadened over the last 50 years, many women who would have historically chosen health careers have pursued other non-health-related career paths.

- The healthcare workplace, due to budget issues, staffing shortage, and increased workloads caused by greater demand and fewer workers, has grown more stressful. This could negatively impact healthcare organizations' ability to attract and retain workers.[14]

Managing Change

The healthcare industry and change have been and are synonymous. Without question, managing the changes that impact the healthcare workplace is one of the most important challenges facing healthcare HR professionals. Figure 1-5 provides an overview of five of the more compelling elements of change impacting the healthcare workplace that have significant HR implications and require HR change management.

Discussion has highlighted the continuous pressure on the cost of healthcare delivery, rapid and constant technology advances, consumers demanding improvement in clinical performance, and other environmental and market forces. These changes have had a significant effect on the management of human resources in healthcare organizations.

Managing Costs In response to cost-containment issues, healthcare organizations have undertaken a seemingly endless stream of budget-cutting initiatives, restructuring to gain efficiencies, curtailment of low-demand or low-margin services, and other initiatives designed to meet cost reduction objectives.

- **HR Implications:** Given the fact that 60 to 70 percent of the total operating costs of most healthcare organizations resides in employee pay and benefits, managing costs almost always means managing the number, skill mix, or wages of employees.

Compliance with Quality Standards With the increasing pressure on the healthcare delivery system to improve clinical performance, performing to quality standards is a critical challenge. Whether meeting the Joint Commission for the Accreditation of Healthcare Organizations (JCAHO) quality standards, responding to third-party payer clinical outcome reviews, or dealing with a state health department audit, healthcare organizations are required to continually improve the quality and responsiveness of their delivery of services.

- **HR Implications:** The tasks of orienting, training, and continually monitoring employees' performance relative to safety, quality, and care standards are critical requirements for HR planning and programming. Inevitably each year, new regulations, standards, or requirements call for updated training, new policies, and other programming to maintain employees' competencies in this critical area.

Managing Diversity and Providing Culturally Competent Care

Healthcare providers must ensure that each person, regardless of race, ethnicity, gender, age, and ability to pay medical bills, receives medical care in a competent, sincere, and equal manner. As the demographics of the United States are changing, so must the organizational response to dealing with difficult diversity issues in the healthcare workplace. Effectively managing these issues not only impacts care delivery, but also the ability of healthcare organizations to recruit and retain a competent, diverse workforce.[15]

- **HR Implications:** HR planning and programming to match provider and patient demographics are virtually unending and continually changing as demographics change.

Preparing Healthcare Workers for New Technologies

New technologies are leading to significant advances in the delivery and quality of services. These advances are also contributing to productivity gains and more cost-effective care. Advances include new drugs, new imaging technologies, genetic mapping and testing, and the transfer of medical information from paper to computer.

- **HR Implications:** As these advances are implemented, healthcare workers must receive orientation and training to effectively and safely operate with new technologies. The skill sets of future healthcare workers must include not only clinical and administrative capabilities but also computer knowledge and related capabilities to use ever-improving healthcare technology.

Quality of Work Life

Healthcare workers, like workers in other industries, are experiencing significant difficulty in juggling work and family responsibilities. However, in healthcare work environments that frequently demand 24 hours a day, 7 days per week coverage, this is especially true. The patients, residents, and clients of healthcare providers require care outside what is considered a "normal" workday of 8:00 A.M. to 5:00 P.M. And even if healthcare workers are not required to do shift work, they are still continually confronted with work and schedule demands that conflict with family and other personal life responsibilities.

- **HR Implications:** HR policy development is required to continually monitor and initiate solutions such as flexible scheduling programs, on-site day care, and other efforts to aid employees in this difficult area.

JOINT COMMISSION ON ACCREDITATION OF HEALTHCARE ORGANIZATIONS

Every industry possesses unique characteristics that affect the management of human resources. This is especially true in the healthcare industry. One of the most unique characteristics of the healthcare industry is that employee errors can potentially result in death or injury to patients, clients, or residents. This characteristic requires healthcare employers to have the highest standards in assuring staff competence, safe practice, ethical treatment, and confidentiality.

JCAHO is an accreditation organization concerned with quality and whose members subscribe to a standards-based review process. Compliance with quality standards as demonstrated through on-site reviews by JCAHO is critical to ensure that the consumers of healthcare are receiving consistent levels of safe, quality care.

HEALTHCARE REFORM AND HR PRACTICES

Healthcare reform as legislated by the Patient Protection and Affordable Care Acts in 2010 (collectively known as ACA) has and will have a significant impact on healthcare delivery in the United States. Clearly reform will impact healthcare HR leaders in two ways: first is the impact on healthcare workers resulting from the number of individuals that will now have access to healthcare by virtue of the fact that they have health insurance. With major coverage expansions taking place in 2014, the Affordable Care Act (ACA) has reduced the uninsured rate substantially.[17] The ACA fills existing gaps in coverage by providing for an expansion of Medicaid for adults with incomes at or below 138 percent of the federal poverty level in states that choose to expand, building on employer-based coverage, and providing premium tax credits to make private insurance more affordable for many with incomes between 100 and 400 percent of the federal poverty level. The net effect of the ACA is providing insurance for up to 26 million more Americans.[16] Clearly that will require more workers, resulting in more demand for healthcare workers.

Second, healthcare organizations will also need to be compliant with the ACA and effectively administer the requirements of the legislation. These requirements include providing employees with timely communications regarding the health reform, assuring that the health insurance offerings are at appropriate levels, and monitoring the various Labor Department, IRS, and Health and Human Services regulations as various aspects of the ACA are implemented over time. It is important that healthcare HR leaders, owners of health organizations, and managers with HR responsibilities are fully aware of these requirements of reform.

JCAHO has "Requirements for Accreditation" for a wide array of healthcare functions and performance areas. These requirements cover such areas as: the environment of care, emergency management, human resources, information management, leadership, life safety, and others. JCAHO expects healthcare providers to use a collaborative and multidisciplinary approach to improve performance, pursue quality initiatives, and develop staff competencies. Many human resource standards are linked to the standards for other departmental and division functions. As an example, staff education is shared among HR and other departments.

Within each of the functional areas in the organization, a number of JCAHO standards deal with the responsibilities of HR management:

- Planning for effective staffing
- Providing competent staff
- Orienting, training, and educating staff
- Evaluating competence and managing performance

Each one of these responsibilities has standards associated with it that include policy, practice, and documentation of compliance requirements. Throughout this text, the JCAHO standards and their impact on HR practices in hospital or medical center facilities will be cited.

THE HR FUNCTION IN HEALTHCARE

The HR management function in healthcare organizations continues to gain prominence relative to the other functional areas of healthcare organizations. This trend has evolved for two critical reasons: First, it is due to the clear need to provide HR support more efficiently and effectively. Second, healthcare HR professionals are increasing their training, skills, understanding, and competency, all of which increase their ability to contribute to their organizations.

HR Management Activities

The central focus for healthcare HR management is to contribute to organizational success. As Figure 1-6 depicts, HR management usually is composed of several groups of interlinked activities. However, the performance of these HR activities is done in the context of a specific organization, which is represented by the inner rings in Figure 1-6. A brief description of the major HR activities follows.

- *HR Planning and Analysis*—Through *HR planning*, managers attempt to anticipate forces that will influence the future supply of and demand for employees. Having a *human resource information system (HRIS)* to provide accurate and timely information for HR planning is crucial.

FIGURE 1-6 HR Management Activities

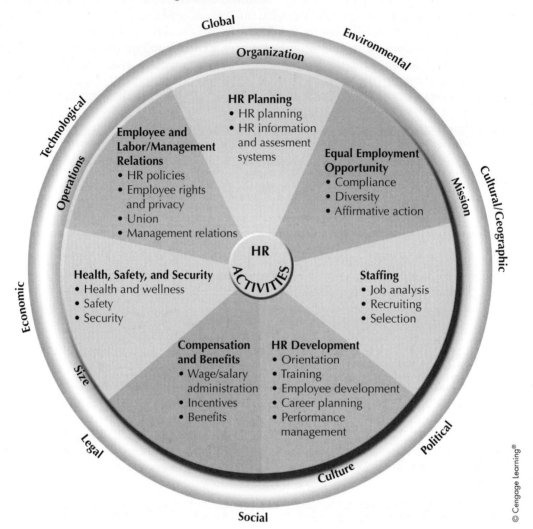

© Cengage Learning®

- *EEO Compliance*—Compliance with equal employment opportunity (EEO) laws and regulations affects all other HR activities. For instance, strategic HR plans must ensure availability of a *diversity* of individuals to meet *affirmative action* requirements. In addition, when recruiting, selecting, and training individuals, all managers must be aware of EEO requirements, including accommodations of individuals with disabilities.

- *Staffing*—The aim of staffing is to provide an adequate supply of qualified individuals to fill the jobs in an organization. By studying what workers do, *job analysis* provides the foundation for the staffing function. From this analysis, *job descriptions* and *job specifications* can be prepared and used to *recruit* applicants for job openings. The *selection process* is then concerned with choosing the most qualified individuals to fill jobs in the organization.

- *HR Development*—Beginning with the *orientation* of new employees, HR training and development also includes *job-skill training.* As jobs evolve and change, ongoing *retraining* is necessary to accommodate technological changes. Encouraging *development* of all employees, including supervisors and managers, is necessary to prepare organizations for future challenges. *Career planning* identifies paths and activities for individual employees as they develop within the organization. Assessing how employees perform their jobs and make improvements is the focus of *performance management.*

- *Compensation and Benefits*—Compensation rewards people for performing organizational work through *pay, incentives,* and *benefits.* Employers must develop and refine their basic *wage* and *salary* systems. Also, *incentive programs* such as gainsharing are growing in usage. Additionally, the rapid increase in the costs of benefits, especially healthcare benefits, will continue to be a major issue.

- *Health, Safety, and Security*—The physical and mental health, safety, and security of employees are vital concerns. The traditional concern for *safety* has focused on eliminating accidents and injuries at work. Additional concerns are *health* issues arising from hazardous work with certain chemicals and newer technologies. Also, workplace *security* has grown in importance, in response to the increasing number of acts of workplace violence.

- *Employee and Labor–Management Relations*—The relationship between managers and their employees must be handled effectively if both the employees and the organization are to prosper together. Whether or not a *union* represents the employees, *employee rights* must be addressed. It is important to develop, communicate, and update *HR policies, procedures,* and *rules* so that managers and employees alike know what is expected.

CASE

At a recent meeting of the board of directors of General City Hospital, the CEO gave his annual "state of the hospital" presentation. Each year the CEO would provide the directors with an in-depth report of the accomplishments, challenges, and key metrics that would give the governing body the information they needed to understand the current state of the hospital. Before the CEO began his report, he warned the directors that this year's report would be very different from past years. He went on to explain that the nature of healthcare was changing rapidly, and new realities required new information and a different view of what was happening at the hospital. Specifically due to healthcare reform, and pressure from insurance companies, government agencies, and consumer groups, General City Hospital needed to change its culture to be even more focused on quality-of-care outcomes, patient satisfaction, and employee satisfaction. As such, he outlined the following:

With regard to accomplishments, he highlighted a number of items, including the completion of construction projects, the attainment of contracts with payers, and the successful implementation of a new electronic medical record. But he showcased the fact that at the end of the fourth quarter, there was a year-over-year improvement in patient satisfaction scores of nearly 10 percent.

With regard to challenges, he noted concern and focused improvement efforts around collections from insurance companies and needed information technology enhancements. However, the challenge that was of most concern was the unfilled vacancies of three physician assistants and four physical therapists that were impacting the hospital's ability to provide timely care to its patients.

Regarding key metrics, he reviewed hospital admissions, length of stay, and outpatient rates—all of which he explained were critical indicators for the directors to acknowledge. Yet the focus of his metrics report was on the following:

- Employee turnover rate for the year
- The level of employee satisfaction
- The number of employees who successfully completed cultural competence training
- The decline in hospital-acquired infection rates
- Coupled with the patient satisfaction scores, initiatives under way for areas that required improvement

The board members were very appreciative of the CEO's report, congratulating him on the importance and value of the information presented.

Questions

1. Why was the CEO's "state of the hospital" report so unique?
2. Describe the HR elements of the CEO's report and why these elements are so important in today's healthcare environment.

END NOTES

1. See *http://www.ihi.org/about/pages /default.aspx* for more information.
2. See *http://www.ihi.org/offerings/Initiatives/ TripleAim/Pages/ImprovementStories .aspx* for more information.
3. *http://www.ihi.org/offerings/Initiatives/ TripleAim/Pages/default.aspx.*
4. U.S. Department of Labor, Bureau of Labor Statistics data, 2014.
5. Ibid.
6. Adapted from Leiyu Shi and Douglas A. Singh, *Essentials of the U.S. Health Care System,* 3rd ed. (Burlington, MA: Jones and Bartlett Learning, 2013), 10–12.
7. See *http://www.hhs.gov/strategic-plan/ goal5.html* for more information.
8. J. Silvers, "The Affordable Care Act: Objectives and Likely Results in an Imperfect World," *Annals of Family Practice* (September/October 2013), 402–405.
9. Carol Keehan, "Culturally Competent Care," *Journal of Healthcare Management* (July/August 2013), 250–252.
10. Shi and Singh, *Essentials of the U.S. Health Care System,* 353.
11. Laura B. Shrestha and Elayne J. Heisler, *The Changing Demographic Profile of the United States,* Congressional Research Service (March 31, 2011), 23–24.
12. See *http://www.healthypeople.gov /2020/topicsobjectives2020/overview .aspx?topicid=1* for more information.

13. See *http://www.bls.gov/news.release /ecopro.t06.htm* for more information.

14. "Are Health Care and Hospital Workers Most Stressed?," *EHS Today* (July 2013), 10.

15. See *http://minorityhealth.hhs.gov* 2014 for more information.

16. G. Kenney et al., "State and Local Coverage Changes under Full Implementation of the Affordable Care Act," Kaiser Family Foundation and The Urban Institute, 2013, available at: *http:// www.kff.org/report-section/state -and-local-coverage-changes-under-full -implementation-of-the-affordable -care-act-report/*.

17. Shi and Singh, Essentials of the U.S. Health Care System, 339.

HEALTHCARE HR COMPETENCIES, STRUCTURES, AND QUALITY STANDARDS

Learning Objectives

After you have read this chapter, you should be able to:

- Define the competencies required for healthcare HR professionals.

- Describe the importance of attaining HR management credentials.

- Explain the relationship between the type of healthcare organization and the level of senior HR position.

- Discuss how the healthcare industry compares to other industries in terms of HR staffing and expenditures.

- Explain the importance of successful HR programs to the delivery of safe, competent healthcare.

HEALTHCARE HR INSIGHTS

Effective HR management is critical to the success of healthcare organizations. Whether the HR leader is a corporate vice president of human resources for a multihospital healthcare system or an HR manager for a 65-bed skilled nursing facility, they are able to contribute strategically only if they understand how their organization works and develop HR programs and policies that support the "business" of the organization.

In David Ulrich's book *HR from the Outside In: Six Competencies for the Future of Human Resources*, he postulates that a primary challenge for HR going forward is to turn external business trends and stakeholder expectations into internal HR practices and actions. Healthcare HR professionals who understand and focus on the external business trends and stakeholder expectations will clearly be more credible "business partners" with their management colleagues and more effective in meeting the needs of the employees.[1]

An excellent example of HR leadership understanding external business trends and stakeholder expectations and turning them into internal HR practices and actions is at Seattle Children's Hospital. Steven Hurwitz, vice president of human resources, describes not only how his department must support the daily operational needs of his organization, but to truly be relevant, the HR program also focuses on the key strategic areas of workforce planning and succession planning.

Cognizant of the labor shortages that loom on the 5- to 20-year horizon due to the retirement of baby boomers, lower birth rates, and increased demand for health services, Hurwitz and his team have been engaged in comprehensive workplace planning over the last two years that has achieved notable results—evidence of which was the successful staffing of a new ambulatory surgery center.

Succession planning is another focus area of HR strategic planning at Seattle Children's. From a national perspective, a large percentage of healthcare executives will be exiting the workforce in the next five years. Seattle Children's will be similarly impacted. As such, HR leadership, working closely with senior leadership, developed a comprehensive succession plan for the board's approval. It included a timeline of readiness and a development plan. In both areas of strategic planning, Hurwitz and his HR team focused on the external business trends and stakeholder expectations impacting the organization and developed strategic solutions.[2]

To fulfill their mission, healthcare organizations must have competent HR leaders, effective HR structures and programs, and an understanding of the relationship between the delivery of quality care and effective HR policies and practices, especially given the nature of rapid change in healthcare. This chapter will provide an overview of these areas and establish the framework for how HR activities are managed.

COMPETENCIES FOR HEALTHCARE HR

Research, study, and discussion of HR management competencies have been extensive and far ranging. For example, the general HR literature tends to refer to competencies through the acronyms SKAs or KSAs, sometimes referred to as skills, knowledge, and abilities. Practical definitions include a cluster of related knowledge, skills, and attitudes that impact a major part of an HR professional's job. As an example, there is a need for well-developed communication skills that include the ability to counsel employees, as well as make professional presentations to large audiences.

The Society of Human Resources Management (SHRM) has developed an HR Success Competency Model. The model comprises nine competencies: one technical competency and eight behavioral competencies. Human resource expertise is the fundamental requirement for HR professionals, while the eight behavioral competencies reflect the way through which an HR professional leverages his or her technical competence. SHRM's competency model includes the following areas:[3]

- Human Resource Expertise
- Ethical
- Relationship Management
- Communication
- Consultation
- Global and Cultural Effectiveness
- Organization Leadership and Navigation
- Critical Evaluation
- Business Acumen

Leadership Competencies and Emotional Intelligence

Closely related to the management and HR competencies previously described are specific behavioral competencies that can also be identified as contributors to the success of healthcare and organizational leaders. As Figure 2-1 depicts, Warren Bennis describes four leadership competencies that are critical to the success of organizations. These leadership competencies include management of attention, management of meaning, management of trust, and management of self.

- *Management of attention*—the ability to articulate a set of intentions or a vision in order to achieve an outcome, goal, or direction.
- *Management of meaning*—the ability to make dreams apparent to others and to align people with them. Leaders must communicate their vision.
- *Management of trust*—the main determinant of trust is reliability or constancy. Effective leaders must be aware of what they stand for.

FIGURE 2-1 **Four Core Competencies Critical to High-Performing HR Leaders**

- *Management of self*—knowing one's skills and deploying them effectively. Without self-management, leaders and managers can do more harm than good.[4]

Emotional intelligence is another critical set of HR management skills equally relevant to the successful contribution of healthcare HR professionals to their organization. *Emotional intelligence* is defined as proficiencies in intrapersonal and interpersonal skills in the areas of self-awareness, self-control, self-motivation, social awareness, and social skills as shown in Figure 2-2.[5]

A common theme in the skill sets and competencies of effective healthcare HR professionals are strong interpersonal communications. The nature of healthcare requires HR professionals to be effective communicators in one-on-one interviews, in small-group discussions and meetings, and in presentations to large groups. Being socially aware and having the ability to treat people with respect and dignity and to communicate effectively with them is

FIGURE 2-2 **Emotional Intelligence**

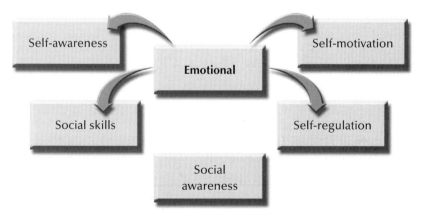

also a critical component of emotional intelligence. As an example, an HR manager in a busy dental practice must deal with employment and employee situations involving diverse applicants and employees. In order to be effective, she must be competent in recognizing and dealing with their unique communication needs.

HR professionals typically have a great deal of organizational power because of the nature of their responsibilities and the scope of their authority. They regularly make decisions that can affect the lives, careers, and financial well-being of others. For instance, a typical duty for an employment manager at a hospital is determining who, out of a number of qualified applicants for an open position, is referred to the department head for final consideration. The power to reject or further consider a particular candidate should be used objectively and fairly. Self-regulation as a part of emotional intelligence is important to ensure that HR professionals make appropriate decisions that are consistent with effective management of people, as well as with HR policy and practice.

HR Management Certifications

One of the characteristics of a professional field is having a means to acknowledge or certify the knowledge and competence of members of the profession. The most well-known certification program for HR generalists is administered by the Human Resource Certification Institute (HRCI). Figure 2-3 describes the credential levels and the criteria that must be met to achieve the various HRCI designations. Studying and preparing for the exams is an excellent opportunity to increase the HR knowledge base of a healthcare HR professional. Just as accounting professionals pursue CPAs, HR professionals should consider pursuing certification through HRCI or other certification organizations to document their HR knowledge.[6]

Other HR Certifications   Additional certification programs for HR specialists and generalists are sponsored by various other organizations. For specialists, some well-known programs include the following:

- Certified Compensation Professionals (CCP), sponsored by the WorldatWork Association
- Certified Employee Benefits Specialist (CEBS), sponsored by the International Foundation of Employee Benefits Plans
- Certified Benefits Professional (CBP), sponsored by the WorldatWork Association
- Certified Performance Technologist (CPT), sponsored by the International Society for Performance Improvement
- Certified Safety Professional (CSP), sponsored by the Board of Certified Safety Professionals

FIGURE 2-3   Understanding Eligibility Requirements By Exam

PHR® (/our-programs/our-hr-certifications/phr) ELIGIBILITY REQUIREMENTS

- A minimum of 1 year experience in an exempt-level (professional) HR position (/exam-preparation/experience-and- education/understanding-exempt-level-experience) with a Master's degree or higher, OR
- A minimum of 2 years of experience in an exempt-level (professional) HR position with a Bachelor's degree, OR
- A minimum of 4 years of experience in an exempt-level (professional) HR position with less than a Bachelor's degree

SPHR® (/our-programs/our-hr-certifications/sphr) ELIGIBILITY REQUIREMENTS

- A minimum of 4 years experience in an exempt-level (professional) HR position (/exam-preparation/experience-and-education/understanding-exempt-level-experience) with a Master's degree or higher, OR
- A minimum of 5 years of experience in an exempt-level (professional) HR position with a Bachelor's degree, OR
- A minimum of 7 years of experience in an exempt-level (professional) HR position with less than a Bachelor's degree

GPHR® (/our-programs/our-hr-certifications/ gphr) ELIGIBILITY REQUIREMENTS

- A minimum of 2 years of global experience in an exempt-level (professional) HR position (/exam-preparation/experience-and-education/understanding-exempt-level-experience) with a Master's degree or higher, OR
- A minimum of 3 years of experience (with 2 of the 3 being global HR experience) in an exempt-level (professional) HR position with a Bachelor's degree, OR
- A minimum of 4 years of experience (with 2 of the 4 being global HR experience) in an exempt-level (professional) HR position with less than a Bachelor's degree

HRMP (/our-programs/our-hr-certifications/ hrmp) ELIGIBILITY REQUIREMENTS

- A minimum of 4 years of professional-level experience in an HR position with a Master's degree or global equivalent, OR
- A minimum of 5 year of professional-level experience in an HR position with a Bachelor's degree or global equivalent, OR
- A minimum of 7 years of professional-level experience in an HR position with less than a Bachelor's degree or global equivalent, OR
- Please note, the HRMP is only available to candidates outside of the United States. HRMP candidates also must demonstrate knowledge of local employment law (/exam-preparation/experience-and-education/knowledae-of-local-emplovment-laws) as a part of exam eligibility requirements

- Occupational Health and Safety Technologist (OHST), given by the American Board of Industrial Hygiene and the Board of Certified Safety Professionals
- Certified Outsourcing Professional (COP), provided by the International Association of Outsourcing Professionals

HR Departments and Healthcare Organizational Charts

Consistent with the wide variety of titles and levels of responsibilities corresponding to the differences in the sizes and types of healthcare organizations, the actual organizational placement of healthcare HR departments varies widely. A trend is emerging in healthcare wherein the HR leader reports directly to the CEO due to the importance of the HR issues facing healthcare organizations. A reporting relationship of this nature is designed to provide more access and better flow of communications between the two. In addition, if HR leaders report directly to the CEO, they will typically be considered a part of the senior leadership team and participate in broader organizational decision making, as well as have more access to their counterparts in other senior leadership positions with the so-called seat at the table of decision making.

Figure 2-4 depicts the organizational chart of a 60-doctor specialty practice with freestanding clinics and more than 200 employees, located in Minneapolis, Minnesota. It shows how the HR function might report in a healthcare organization. As depicted on the chart, the human resources director reports directly to the CEO and is at the same organizational level as other key leadership positions.

Measuring Healthcare HR Management

Another way to evaluate the strategic importance of HR in healthcare organizations is to statistically evaluate their organizational influence. Statistical analysis and comparisons are useful to understanding the broader context of the overall healthcare industry's commitment to HR.

Staffing Ratios and Budgets   HR activities, budgets, and staffing are regularly surveyed by the Bureau of National Affairs (BNA) Bloomberg. BNA has surveyed and reported on HR staffing levels over the past several years. Figure 2-5 depicts the BNA comparisons of the healthcare HR staffing ratios with other industries. Notice that for all industries, the median ratio of HR department staff to total employee headcount is 1.3 HR staff members for every 100 employees in an organization. For healthcare employers surveyed, the median is 0.7 HR staff members per 100 employees.[7]

Taken at face value, these statistics might suggest a lesser HR commitment across the board by healthcare organizations compared to nonhealthcare organizations. However, as noted earlier in the chapter, the healthcare industry varies both in size of organizations and in how healthcare is provided. This variety makes it difficult to capture who in a healthcare organization is performing HR duties. As an example, in a large medical center there is typically a full complement of HR leaders and specialists to handle the total continuum of HR activities. These individuals would be easily accounted for in the BNA survey data. In contrast, in a small rural nursing home the HR function might be the

FIGURE 2-4   Specialty Physician Practice Organizational Chart

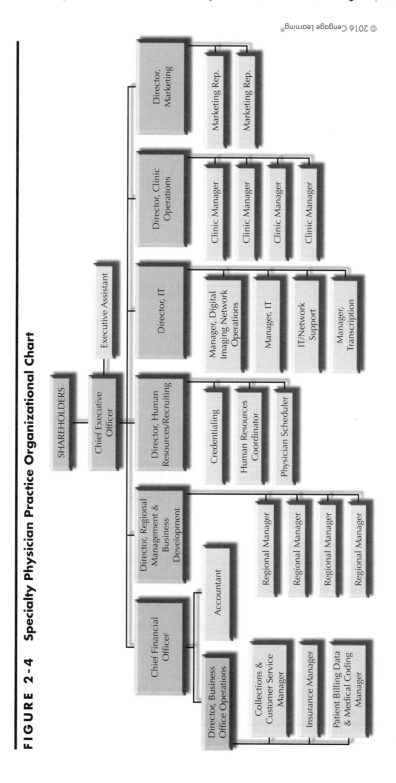

FIGURE 2-5   HR Staff Rations By Industry (HR staff for 100 employees)

	MEDIAN
ALL EMPLOYERS	1.3
Information Services, Telecommunications and Data Processing	2.2
Finance, Insurance, Banking and Real Estate	1.5
Government	1.4
Education	1.0
Healthcare	0.7

© 2016 Cengage Learning®

responsibility of an assistant administrator who "wears many hats," including HR. That individual would most likely not be recorded in a BNA survey as an HR staff member, nor would that person's salary be accounted for as an HR expenditure.

Measuring Effectiveness of Human Resources

There are many ways of measuring the qualitative and quantitative impact of the HR practices in a healthcare organization, and many challenges associated with doing so. Return on investment (ROI) is a common measure used by financial professionals to assess the value of an investment. For example, if a hospital invests $20,000 for a supervisory training program, what does it gain in better patient satisfaction scores, lower legal costs, higher employee productivity, and lower employee turnover? The benefits of HR practices are not always immediately visible, which is what makes measuring HR's impact such a challenge. However, successful efforts can usually be made to assess HR practices.

A long-standing myth perpetuates the notion that one cannot really measure the value of HR practices. That myth has hurt HR's credibility because it suggests that either HR efforts do not add value or they are too far removed from business results to matter. That notion is, of course, untrue. HR, like all other functions, must be evaluated by considering the results of its actions and the value it adds to the organization. Unfortunately, the perceptions of managers and employees in many organizations are mixed because HR has not historically measured and documented its contributions or communicated those results. Further, accounting practices treat expenditures on human capital and talent development as expenses rather than capital investments. This practice encourages top management to view employees as consumers of capital rather than as a long-term investment.

People-related costs are typically not only the largest expense but also the most controllable expense in healthcare organizations. Effective management of these costs can make a positive difference in the survival of a healthcare organization. Collecting and analyzing HR information can pinpoint waste and improper allocation of human resources. It is important that HR managers understand financial and operational measures that drive the business and relate decisions to key performance indicators (KPIs). Metrics, benchmarking, and balanced scorecards can help the organization track HR performance and measure the value of HR practices.[8]

HR Metrics

HR metrics are specific measures of HR practices. They are performance indicators of some element of HR, for example, turnover rate. Metrics are typically used to assess the HR practices and results within the organization over time. A metric can be developed using costs, quantity, quality, timeliness, and other designated goals. Metrics can be developed to track both HR efficiency and effectiveness. A pioneer in developing HR measurements, Jac Fitz-Enz, has identified a wide range of HR metrics. A number of key HR metrics are shown in Figure 2-6.[9]

HR and line managers collect and share the data needed to track performance. Data to track these measures come from several sources within the organization. Financial data are required to determine costs for various HR activities and performance, and turnover data can be found in HR and operations records. The real value in using metrics is not in the collection and reporting of the results—it is the analysis and the interpretation of the data that can lead to improvements in human capital utilization.[10] Information and historical data are reviewed and studied to determine the reasons for current performance levels and to learn how to improve these levels in the future.

Metrics and software have been combined to make analysis easier, but it is still an evolving area. *Analytics* can simply be a way to report certain metrics or a sophisticated predictive modeling designed to answer "what if" questions about

FIGURE 2-6   Key HR Metrics

HR Staff and Expenses	Staffing
• HR-to-employee ratio • Total HR staff • HR expenses per FTE	• Number of positions filled • Time to fill • Cost per hire • Annual turnover rate

Compensation	Training
• Annual wage and salary increases • Payroll as a percentage of operating expenses • Benefit costs as a percentage of payroll	• Hours of training per employee • Total costs for training • Percentage of employees participating in tuition reimbursement program

Retention and Quality	Development
• Average tenure of employees • Percentage of new hires retained for 90 days • Performance quality of employees in first year	• Positions filled internally • Percentage of employees with career plan

© Cengage Learning®

HR variables.[11] A definition of **HR analytics** that considers both extremes is as follows: HR analytics is an evidence-based approach to making HR decisions on the basis of quantitative tools and models.[12]

HR Analytics

Unlike financial reporting, there is not yet a standard for the implementation and reporting of HR measures.[13] This lack of consistency in HR reporting makes it difficult to evaluate a specific healthcare organization and then to compare HR practices across organizations.[14] The following characteristics should be considered when developing HR metrics and analytics:

- Accurate data can be collected.
- Measures are linked to strategic and operational objectives.
- Calculations can be clearly understood.
- Measures provide information valued by executives.
- Results can be compared both externally and internally.
- Measurement data drive HR management efforts.

Benchmarking

Benchmarking is the process of comparing the business metrics and outcomes to an industry standard or best practice. In other words, the organization compares itself to "best-in-class" organizations that demonstrate excellence for a specific process. Benchmarking is focused on external practices that a healthcare organization can use to improve its own processes and practices.[15] When implementing benchmarking, managers should be careful to find organizations with similar contexts, cultures, operations, and size.[16] Practices that would work effectively in a hospital of 500 employees might not transfer very well to an academic medical center with more than 5,000 employees. The organization should study and choose benchmarks that relate well to its size, staffing characteristics, and type of care provided. Benchmarking of this nature will have the greatest impact on the organizational performance.

Balanced Scorecard

One effective approach to measuring strategic performance of healthcare organizations, including their HR practices, is to use the balanced scorecard. The **balanced scorecard** is a framework organizations use to report on a diverse set of performance measures. Organizations that did not use a balanced scorecard recognized that focusing strictly on financial measures only limited their view.[17] The balanced scorecard balances financial and nonfinancial measures so that managers focus on long-term drivers of performance and organizational sustainability. As shown in Figure 2-7, the balanced scorecard measures performance in four areas:

- *Financial Measures*—Traditional financial measures such as profit and loss, operating margins, utilization of capital, return on investment, and return on assets are needed to ensure that the organization manages its bottom line effectively.

FIGURE 2-7   Balanced Scorecard Framework

© 2016 Cengage Learning®

- *Internal Business Processes*—Product and service quality, efficiency and productivity, conformance with standards, and cycle times can be measured to ensure that the operation runs smoothly and efficiently.

- *Patient Relations*—Patient satisfaction, loyalty, and retention are important to ensure that the organization is meeting the expectations of patients and clients and can depend on repeat business.

- *Learning and Growth Activities*—Employee training and development, mentoring programs, succession planning, and knowledge creation and sharing provide the necessary talent and human capital pool to ensure the future of the organization.

Organizational results in each of these areas determine if a healthcare organization is progressing toward its strategic objectives. For example, organizations have recognized that when employee engagement survey results show a decline in employee satisfaction, several months later there are declines in patient loyalty and retention.[18] Further, investing money in employee leadership development training can be linked to lower employee turnover and reduced time to hire managers from outside the organization.

A variety of organizations claim to use a balanced scorecard approach. The Mayo Clinic has used this approach to align performance measures with their organizational strategy. Using the balanced scorecard requires spending considerable time and effort to identify the appropriate HR measures in each of the four areas mentioned earlier and how they tie to strategic organizational success. The balanced scorecard should align with company goals and focus on results.[19]

Human Capital Effectiveness Measures

HR measures outcomes that traditional accounting does not account for. Human capital often provides both the biggest value and the biggest cost to organizations; therefore many metrics reflect people-related *costs*. Measuring the *benefits* of human capital is more challenging but equally important. Assessing the value of human capital demonstrates the importance of effective HR practices to maintain a high-quality workforce.[20]

As noted previously, human capital refers to the collective value of the competencies, knowledge, and skills of the employees in the organization. This capital is the renewable source of creativity and innovativeness in the organization but is not reflected in its financial statements.

Revenue per employee is a basic measure of human capital effectiveness. The formula is Revenue/Head Count (full-time employee equivalents). It is a measure of employee productivity and shows the revenue generated by each full-time employee. This measure is commonly used in government reporting (see Bureau of Labor Statistics [BLS]) as well as by organizations to track productivity over time. If revenues increase but employee head count remains constant, productivity would increase.

Many financial measures can be tracked and reported to show the contribution human capital makes to organizational results.[21] Without such measures, it would be difficult to know what is going on in the organization, identify performance gaps, and provide feedback. Managers should require the same level of rigor in measuring HR practices as they do for other functions in the organization. Regardless of the time and effort placed on HR measurement and HR metrics, the most important consideration is that HR effectiveness and efficiency must be measured regularly for managers to know how HR practices affect organizational success.[22]

HR and Quality Patient Care

Another consideration in establishing the framework for effectively managing the healthcare HR function is understanding the linkage between quality patient care delivery and HR programs. The process of ensuring healthcare consumers in the United States that a particular provider of care is competent and safe takes many forms. It includes governmental oversight through the Medicare reimbursement program; local, county, and state health department oversight; independent agencies who supply quality review information on health insurance plans and their preferred providers; and quality review organizations that perform comprehensive standard-based assessments of their subscribing members.[23]

Competitive Position   Healthcare organizations are experiencing significant change in response to ever-increasing costs, technology advances, and recruitment and retention issues. To ensure quality care and organizational viability, healthcare organizations must hire and retain a competent workforce.

Providing high-quality healthcare and achieving a competitive position in their respective marketplaces are clearly linked for healthcare providers. Business and industry groups have required that health plans disclose quality-of-care information on providers and evaluate the effectiveness of a provider's care in certain disease categories and care modalities. The pressure from the healthcare plans on the providers to disclose outcome information, consumer satisfaction information, and other metrics of safe patient care is having a significant impact on the healthcare industry at every level of delivery—from sole practitioner physicians to multistate integrated healthcare systems.

JOINT COMMISSION (JCAHO) AND HEALTHCARE MANAGEMENT

The dominant quality review organization for hospitals, long-term care and assisted living facilities, clinical laboratories, ambulatory care organizations, behavioral healthcare organizations, and home care agencies is the Joint Commission on Accreditation of Healthcare Organizations (JCAHO). The JCAHO accredits more than 15,000 healthcare organizations in the United States. In this section is a review of how the JCAHO quality standards have affected HR programming and how healthcare organizations meet those standards.

JCAHO Process

The JCAHO surveys healthcare organizations in a broad range of administrative and clinical functions. Under each of these functions is a series of standards that must be defined and operationalized by the healthcare organizations that subscribe to JCAHO. The standards are action statements that provide specific expectations for quality achievement on a detailed basis within each function. JCAHO reviewers survey healthcare organizations to determine their accomplishment on the various standards for all of the functions. An organization that attains a satisfactory survey receives accreditation from the JCAHO. Accreditation carries with it an indication that within the functions surveyed, the organization is substantially meeting the standards. Also, JCAHO survey data are critically reviewed by insurance companies, healthcare oversight groups, and individual consumers of healthcare.

Methodology of JCAHO Review   The JCAHO surveyors attempt to be as comprehensive in their review of an organization's attainment of quality as possible. They consider a variety of data points as evidence of quality and performance to determine the organization's accomplishment on a particular standard. Sources of evidence of performance for HR standards include the following:

- Interviews with staff members, department directors, and senior managers
- Performance evaluations or competency assessment processes
- Employee personnel records and file documentation
- Organizational and departmental policies and procedures
- Staff development plans and education records
- Committee reports and meeting minutes
- Description of licensure, certificates, and credential verifications

Due to the importance JCAHO has placed on the HR standards, HR professionals typically play key roles in the preparation for a JCAHO survey and in the actual on-site review.

The JCAHO's statement on the HR function indicates that through its Management of Human Resources, Improving Organization Performance (PI),

FIGURE 2-8 **JCAHO Requirements for HR**

- Defining staff qualifications & performance expectations
- Providing adequate numbers of competent staff
- Ongoing assessments of staff competence
- Orienting, training, and educating staff

Healthcare Leaders' HR Responsibilities

© 2016 Cengage Learning®

Leadership (LD), and other accreditation standards, the JCAHO helps healthcare organizations take a systematic approach to addressing staffing needs.[24] Figure 2-8 depicts the HR leadership responsibilities. The JCAHO's statement on HR management notes that the broad goals of the HR function are to identify and provide the right number of competent staff to meet the needs of the patients, clients, or residents served by the healthcare provider. As indicated in Figure 2-8, healthcare leaders are responsible for the following broad processes to fulfill this goal:

- *Planning*—This defines the qualifications, competencies, and staffing necessary to fulfill the provider's mission.

- *Providing Competent Staff*—The staff includes both employees of the organization and those contracted to provide service or care. Applicants' credentials must be assessed and confirmed prior to employment or service delivery.

- *Assessing, Maintaining, and Improving Staff Competence*—This includes ongoing periodic competence assessment and performance evaluation of staff to ensure the continuing ability of staff to perform.

- *Promoting Self-Development and Learning*—Leaders encourage self-development and continued learning.

JCAHO HR Standards and Serious Adverse Events

HR standards are not the exclusive domain of HR professionals in healthcare organizations. The JCAHO evaluates the extent to which these standards are met through a multidisciplinary approach. As such, HR professionals and operational managers must work collaboratively to meet the standards. These standards serve as a valuable set of guiding principles for HR policy and practice for healthcare organizations that are reviewed by JCAHO. Healthcare HR professionals play a very key role in ensuring the delivery of safe, competent healthcare by developing programming to meet these standards and by documenting performance to the standards.

The Role of HR Issues in Serious Adverse Events   Since the mid-1990s, JCAHO has been collecting data on serious adverse events in the healthcare setting; these are also referred to as *sentinel events*. A sentinel event is further defined as an unexpected occurrence involving death, or serious physical or psychological injury, or the risk thereof. The term *sentinel* is used by JCAHO because it signals the need for immediate reporting, investigation, and remediation to ensure that there is no further occurrence.

By studying the root causes of sentinel events, the JCAHO has been able to provide valuable information designed to help prevent the circumstances that lead to such events. Thousands of such events have been closely studied and evaluated, and HR and management-related issues have consistently played a major role in the causation of sentinel events. The top three categories reported for 2013 include:

- *Human Factors*—such as inappropriate staffing levels, lack of appropriate staff orientation, in-service education or competency assessment, poor staff and resident supervision, and other (e.g., rushing, fatigue, distraction, complacency, bias)
- *Communications*—poor or inadequate oral, written, or electronic communications among staff, with/among physicians, with administration, and/or with the patient or family
- *Leadership*—poor or inadequate organizational planning, poor community relations, lack of service availability, inadequate priority setting, poor resource allocation, lack of leadership collaboration, inadequate policies and procedures, noncompliance with policies and procedures, lack of performance improvement, and poor nursing leadership[25]

Throughout this book, JCAHO standards and how they impact the HR function in healthcare organizations will be brought into the discussion. For those organizations that do not subscribe to JCAHO, these standards can still provide a useful template for how quality standards apply to all HR management within healthcare organizations.

HEALTHCARE REFORM AND HR PRACTICES

The current health reform environment requires healthcare HR and non-HR leaders to dramatically rethink the way they lead their organizations. Essentially, healthcare leaders must offer an accelerated value proposition to the people and communities they serve.

At the heart of healthcare reform is a switch from a fee-for-service to value-based payment structure. This switch will require extraordinary leadership from healthcare organizations to be successful. Sally Jeffcoat, FACHE, president and CEO of Idaho-based Saint Alphonsus Health system, describes the leadership imperatives Alphonsus Health utilized to move her organization forward to deal with the changes driven by healthcare reform. These include:

1. Clarity of Vision, Strategic Direction, and Brand: This required a "deep dive" with Saint Alphonsus's executive team, board, and medical staff to achieve clarity, direction, and brand development.

2. Alignment of Talent and Team: Healthcare leaders need to work differently with their colleagues to deliver a future of highest quality of care and value-based reimbursement. This resulted in realignment positions, clearly defined skill sets related to value-based reimbursement, and changes in leadership positions.

3. Innovation and Collaboration: Saint Alphonsus required its executives to think about problems differently and to solve them creatively. This change in approach had a significant impact on the organization's culture—with executive leadership acting as role models for employee innovation supported with the appropriate rewards.

(Continued)

4. System Performance Improvement Rigor: Saint Alphonsus trained more than 1,000 employees in lean management principles, deployed project management throughout the system, and infused significant energy into improving quality and reducing waste.

5. Leadership Development Succession: Saint Alphonsus devoted significant resources to the development of a succession pool and developing future leaders. In addition, they have implemented a physician leadership academy to enhance clinical integration and encourage physician leadership and governance.

6. Movement to a Community of Leaders: Saint Alphonsus supports a philosophy that leadership is all about the team, and a community of leaders is more important than ever. Jeffcoat indicates that "we have to go from individual silos to a collection of team members that can deliver the future we envision."[26]

Leadership imperatives of this nature that are necessitated by healthcare reform have significant HR leadership implications, including the development of innovative HR approaches to recruitment and selection, compensation, and employee communications.

CASE

Adult and Pediatric Primary Care (APPC), a five-doctor clinic with 40 employees and two offices, is a financially viable, growing organization with an expanding patient base. The practice is five years old, started by two physicians who left a larger group with a goal to provide high-quality care. At the time they started, they hired an experienced medical office manager, a front-desk receptionist, and two medical assistants. Over the past five years, they have added more physicians and staff as patient volumes grew. The physician owners are very cautious about adding cost to the operation, always making sure that patient revenues could appropriately cover their overhead.

At a recent practice meeting that included the physician owners and the office manager, the agenda included a discussion point about adding a human resources professional to the administrative team. The office manager indicated that she was spending a significant amount of her time dealing with HR-related duties at the expense of her other duties, such as billing management, vendor negotiations, and shopping for an electronic medical records system. Although she felt that she was skilled at hiring and training, she did not feel her competencies included, at the level necessary, the other areas of HR such as legal compliance, performance management, and benefits and compensation management. Consequently, she was recommending hiring an individual with those skills. The physician owners generally agreed with her recommendation but voiced concern about the additional expense of adding a non-revenue-producing staff member and wanted more detail as to what an HR professional would do for a practice their size. The meeting was adjourned without making a final decision regarding adding the HR staff member pending more research by the office manager on the specific duties the HR professional would perform and a cost–benefit analysis on the position.

Questions

1. Describe the potential value a human resources professional could bring to APPC.

2. What are the key human resources qualifications and competencies APPC should look for in a human resources professional if they choose to hire someone in that capacity?

END NOTES

1. D. Ulrich, W. Brockbank, J. Younger, and M. Ulrich, *HR from the Outside In: The Next Era of Human Resources Transformation* (New York: McGraw-Hill, 2012), 41.

2. S. Hurwitz, "Key Human Resource Strategies within a Healthcare Organization," *Washington Healthcare News* (June 21, 2012), 1–2.

3. See *http://www.shrm.org/hrcompetencies/pages/model.aspx* for more information.

4. W. Bennis, "Leadership Competencies," *Leadership Excellence* (February 2010), 20.

5. Daniel Goleman, "The Focused Leader," *Harvard Business Review* 91, no. 12 (December 2013), 50–60.

6. See *http://www.hrci.org/exam-preparation* for more information.

7. "HR Staff Ratios for 2013 by Industry," BNA-Bloomberg, 2013.

8. Beth Tootell et al., "Metric: HRM's Holy Grail? A New Zealand Case Study," *Human Resource Management Journal* 19 (2009), 375–391.

9. "Human Capital Benchmarking Study," Society for Human Resource Management, *http://www.shrm.org*.

10. D. Robb, "Creating Metrics for Senior Management," *HR Magazine* (December 2011), 109–111.

11. Allison Rossett, "Metrics Matters," *T & D* 64 (March 2010), 65–69.

12. Laurie Bassi, "Raging Debates in HR Analytics," *People and Strategy* 34 (2011), 14–18.

13. Special Report on HR Metrics, a Supplement to HRfocus (July 2010).

14. Robert Grossman, "Disclosing HR Metrics: How Much Information Is Too Much?," *HR Magazine* (March 2013), 48–52.

15. Eric Krell, "Measuring the True Value of Your Services," *HR Magazine* (September 2010), 99–103.

16. Jeremy Shapiro, "Benchmarking the Benchmarks," *HR Magazine* (April 2010), 43–46.

17. Meena Chavan, "The Balanced Scorecard: A New Challenge," *Journal of Management Development* 28 (2009), 393–406.

18. P. Lencioni, "Stooping to Greatness," *Businessweek.com* [serial online] (December 13, 2010), 6.

19. Robert S. Kaplan et al., "Managing Alliances with the Balanced Scorecard," *Harvard Business Review* (January–February 2010), 115–126.

20. Stephen Gates and Pascal Langevin, "Human Capital Measures, Strategy, and Performance," *Accounting, Auditing, and Accountability* 23 (2010), 111–132.

21. Frank DiBernardino, "The Missing Link: Measuring and Managing Financial Performance of the Human Capital Investment," *People and Strategy* 34 (2011), 44–47.

22. Alexis A. Fink, "New Trends in Human Capital Research and Analytics," *People and Strategy* 33 (2010), 14–21.

23. Michael Ewing, "The Patient-Centered Medical Home Solution to the Cost–Quality Conundrum," *Journal of Healthcare Management* (July/August 2013), 258–266.

24. Bruce Buckley, "JCAHO to Zero In on Staffing Effectiveness," *Drug Topics.modernmedicine.com*, June 17, 2012.

25. See *http://www.jointcommission.org/assets/1/18/Root_Causes_by_Event_Type_2004- 2Q2013.pdf*.

26. Marisa Paulson, "A New Spirit of Service," *Healthcare Executive* (November/December 2013), 76–79.

3

STRATEGIC HR MANAGEMENT

Learning Objectives

After you have read this chapter you should be able to:

- Describe why a strategic view of human resources (HR) is important.

- Discuss HR as an organizational core competency.

- Explain how healthcare HR planning contributes to the attainment of organizational strategies and objectives.

- Define HR planning in healthcare organizations.

- Identify three HR management challenges found in healthcare organizations.

HEALTHCARE HR INSIGHTS

Southern Ohio Medical Center, located in Portsmouth, Ohio, has been consistently recognized as one of the best places to work in America according to *Fortune* magazine.[1] *Fortune* annually acknowledges "100 Best Companies to Work For." The magazine looks at a wide spectrum of U.S. companies, including healthcare organizations. Other healthcare organizations that have made the list include the Mayo Health system, St. Jude Hospital, and Baptist Health South Florida.

The designation as one of the country's best places to work has significant strategic human resources management implications. As an example, *Fortune* cited Southern Ohio Medical Center's support for employees aiming to improve their education as one of the reasons for the high ranking, noting: "This regional health care system pays 100% of tuition for employees seeking to advance their education and pursue a degree in the medical field."[2] The president and CEO of Southern Ohio Medical Center, Randy Arnett, acknowledged the designation, remarking about the linkage between providing outstanding care to their patients and also caring deeply about their employees. Southern Ohio Medical Center employees are proud to work for a medical provider that has won numerous awards for patient care, a fact that is reflected in its average tenure. Nearly 20 percent of the staff has worked there for more than 20 years.[3]

Achieving high employee productivity and morale, low turnover, and satisfied patients does not happen by accident in healthcare organizations. It is incumbent upon healthcare HR professionals to provide leadership in the planning and execution of strategies to achieve these key HR accomplishments.

Many factors determine whether or not an organization will be successful. Effectiveness, efficiency, and the ability to adapt to changes in the market, as well as other issues, are involved. Adept management will decide where the organization needs to go and how to get there, and then regularly evaluate to see if it is on track. Strategic objectives, the external environment, internal business processes, and determining how effectiveness will be measured and defined should all be addressed in the strategic management process.

HR management is (or should be) involved with all of these. For example, how can effective HR help improve productivity in an assisted living facility or dental practice? How can it enhance innovativeness in a medical center? These kinds of questions are indicative of strategic thinking.[4]

Strategic HR management maximizes the effectiveness of employees and results in the achievement of an organizational mission and a competitive advantage in the market. This advantage may occur through the HR department's formal contributions to organization-wide planning efforts, or by simply being knowledgeable about issues facing the organization and being prepared to make effective HR-related recommendations.

MANAGEMENT OF HUMAN ASSETS IN ORGANIZATIONS

Healthcare organizations must manage four types of assets in their search for success:

- *Physical*—Buildings, land, furniture, computers, vehicles, equipment, etc.
- *Financial*—Cash, financial resources, financial securities, etc.
- *Intangible*—Specialized research capabilities, patents, information systems, designs, operating processes, etc.
- *Human*—Individuals with talents, capabilities, experience, professional expertise, relationships, etc.

All these assets are crucial to varying degrees. However, human assets are the "glue" that holds all the other assets together and guides their use to achieve organizational goals and results. Certainly, the doctors, nurses, receptionists, technical professionals, and other employees at a dental clinic or medical center allow all the other assets of their organization to be used to provide client or patient services. By recognizing the importance of human assets, healthcare organizations are increasingly emphasizing the human capital.

Human Capital and HR

Human capital is not the people in organizations—it is what those people bring and contribute to organizational success.[5] **Human capital** is the collective value of the capabilities, knowledge, skills, life experiences, and motivation in an organization's workforce.

Sometimes it is called *intellectual capital* to reflect the thinking, knowledge, creativity, and decision making that people in organizations contribute. For example, an academic medical complex like the University of Minnesota Medical Center (UMMC) has significant intellectual capital, including technical and research employees who create new biomedical devices, formulate pharmaceuticals that can be patented, and develop new software for specialized therapeutic uses. All these organizational contributions indicate the value of UMMC's human capital.[6]

Human Resource as a Core Competency

The development and implementation of specific strategies must be based on the areas of strength in an organization. Referred to as *core competencies*, these strengths are the foundation for creating a competitive advantage for an organization. A **core competency** is a unique capability that creates high value and at which a healthcare organization excels.

Many healthcare organizations have identified that their HR practices differentiate them from their competitors, and that HR is a key determinant of competitive advantage. Recognizing this, organizations as diverse as Baptist Health South Florida, Cincinnati's Children's Hospital, and The Everett Clinic have focused on human resources as having special strategic value for their respective organizations.

The same can be true with small companies as well. For example, an internal medicine clinic with two doctors and a nurse practitioner located in a large urban center such as Chicago or New York City can have a strong patient following because their patients can develop a close professional rapport with the providers, which can improve communications about their medical needs. This same type of close patient–doctor relationship may not be able to be achieved in larger, more complex clinic settings where the patients may be seen by different doctors each time.

Certainly, many healthcare organizations have attempted to showcase their human capital as differentiating them from their competitors.[7] Many healthcare organizations through their marketing efforts have emphasized some special competency of their employees or the expertise and credentials of their clinical providers. As an example, a plastic surgery practice in California advertises in an airline magazine that their doctors and staff are internationally recognized for their face lift surgical expertise, clearly focusing on its human resources as providing special strategic value for their organization.

The people in an organization become a core competency through the HR activities of attracting and retaining employees with unique professional and technical capabilities, investing in training and development of those employees, and compensating them in ways that retain them and keep them competitive with their counterparts in other organizations. For example, academic health centers have attracted patient referrals because they emphasize leading-edge technology and very accomplished academic physicians skilled in diagnosing and treating the most difficult cases. They emphasize their staff members as an advantage. Figure 3-1 shows some possible areas where human resources might become part of a core competency.

FIGURE 3-1   **Examples of Healthcare Human Resource Areas for Core Competencies**

© 2016 Cengage Learning®

Organizational Culture

The ability of a healthcare organization to use its human capital as a core competency depends at least partly on the organizational culture that is operating.[8] **Organizational culture** consists of the shared values and beliefs that give members of an organization meaning and provide them with rules for behavior. These values are inherent in the ways organizations and their members view themselves, define opportunities, and plan strategies. Much as personality shapes an individual, organizational culture shapes its members' responses and defines what an organization can or is willing to do.

The culture of an organization is seen in the norms of expected behaviors, values, philosophies, rituals, and symbols used by its employees. Culture evolves over a period of time. Only if an organization has a history in which people have shared experiences for years does a culture stabilize.[9] As an example, a dental clinic that has existed for less than two years probably has not yet developed a stable culture.

Culture is important because it tells people how to behave (or not to behave). It is relatively constant and enduring over time. New employees, including physicians, learn the culture from senior employees; hence, the rules of behavior are perpetuated. These rules may or may not be beneficial, so culture can either facilitate or limit performance.

Managers must consider the culture of the organization before implementing HR practices. Otherwise, excellent ideas can be negated by a culture that is incompatible. In one culture, external events might be seen as threatening, whereas in another culture the same changes are challenges requiring immediate responses. The latter type of culture can be a source of competitive advantage.

Organizational culture can be seen as the "climate" of the firm that employees, managers, customers, and others experience. This culture affects service and quality, organizational productivity, and financial results. From a critical perspective, it is the culture of the firm, as viewed by its employees, that affects the attraction and retention of competent workers. Alignment of the organizational culture with what management is trying to accomplish determines whether human capital can indeed be a core competency.

HR MANAGEMENT ROLES

If a healthcare organization has a formal HR department/function, there are typically three different roles the HR professionals in that department might play in the organization. Which of the roles predominates or whether all three roles are performed depends on what management wants HR to do and what competencies the HR staff has demonstrated. The potential mix of roles is shown in Figure 3-2.

- *Administrative*—Focusing on clerical administration and record keeping, including essential legal paperwork and policy implementation

FIGURE 3-2   The Changing Nature of HR Management Roles

- *Operational and Employee Advocate*—Managing most HR activities in keeping with the strategies and operations that have been identified by management and serving as employee "champion" for employee issues and concerns
- *Strategic*—Helping to define the business strategy relative to human capital and its contribution to organizational results

While the administrative role traditionally has been the dominant role for healthcare HR professionals (including payroll professionals), the emphasis on the operational and employee advocate role is growing in many healthcare organizations, especially large clinics, hospitals, and medical centers. The strategic role requires the ability and orientation to contribute to strategic decisions and recognition by upper management of those skills.[10] This practice is less common but reportedly growing.

Administrative Role for Human Resource

The administrative role of HR management has been heavily oriented to processing information and record keeping. This role has given HR management in some organizations the reputation of being staffed by people who primarily tell managers and employees what *cannot* be done, usually because of some policy or problem from the past. If limited to the administrative role, HR staff are primarily clerical and lower-level administrative aides to the organization. Two major shifts driving the transformation of the administrative role are greater use of technology and outsourcing.

Technology and Administrative Human Resource   More HR functions are being performed electronically or are being done using web-based technology. Technology has changed most HR activities, from employment applications and employee benefits enrollment to e-learning. There will always be a record-keeping responsibility. It can, however, be done electronically or outsourced.

Outsourcing Administrative Human Resource   Some HR administrative functions can be outsourced to vendors. This outsourcing of HR administrative activities has grown dramatically in HR areas such as employee assistance (counseling), retirement planning, benefits administration, payroll services, and outplacement services. The primary reasons why HR functions are outsourced are to save money on HR staffing and to take advantage of specialized vendor expertise and technology.

Operational and Employee Advocate Role for Human Resource

HR has been viewed as the "employee advocate" in some healthcare organizations. As the voice for employee concerns, HR professionals traditionally may serve as "company morale officers," but they spend considerable time on HR "crisis management," dealing with employee problems that are work related. As an example, HR generalists at a long-term care facility may spend a considerable portion of their efforts on overseeing both the nursing home's and the employees' compliance with Family and Medical Leave Act requirements.

The employee advocacy role helps ensure fair and equitable treatment for employees regardless of personal background or circumstances. Sometimes, when dealing with an HR issue that places an employee at odds with a manager, there is a difficult balancing of priorities required by HR professionals between what is best for the organization and what is best for a particular employee. Consequently, sometimes the HR advocate role may create conflict with operating managers. However, without the HR advocate role, employers could face even more lawsuits and regulatory complaints than they do now.[11]

The operational role requires HR professionals to cooperate with various departmental and operating managers and supervisors to identify and implement needed programs and policies in the organization. As an example, at a large urban hospital the director of nursing suggested that the HR recruiters set up tours for area high school students to encourage the students to consider careers in health care. The implementation of the tours has proven to be an excellent program that has resulted in many students choosing academic programs leading to healthcare-related careers.

Compliance with equal employment opportunity (EEO) and other laws is ensured, employment applications are processed, current openings are filled through interviews, supervisors are trained, safety problems are resolved, and wage and benefit questions are answered. These efforts require making certain that HR operations carry out the strategies of the organization.

Strategic Role for Human Resources

The strategic role means that HR is proactive in addressing business realities, focusing on future business needs, and understanding how the need for human capital fits into those plans and needs. Historically, HR may not help formulate strategies for the organization as a whole; rather it may merely carry them out. But HR management can become a strategic contributor to the "business" success of a healthcare organization, because even not-for-profit organizations, such as an Indian Health Service clinic or a county-run mental health provider, must manage their human resources in a businesslike manner.

Part of the strategy for HR should be knowing what the true cost of human capital is for the employer. For example, in some situations it costs twice a key employee's annual salary to replace her if she leaves. These costs may even be higher for hard-to-fill healthcare professional positions such as physical therapists or MRI technicians. Turnover is something HR can help control, and if it is successful in saving the organization money with good retention and talent management strategies, those may be important contributions to the bottom line of organizational performance.

The role of HR as a *strategic business partner* is often described as "having a seat at the table," and contributing to the strategic direction and success of the organization. That means HR is involved in *devising* strategy in addition to *implementing* strategy. That contribution requires financial expertise and results, not just employee engagement concerns or administrative efficiencies.[12] A significant concern is whether healthcare HR professionals are equipped to help plan and meet financial and other non-HR requirements.

Some examples of areas where strategic contributions can be made by HR are:

- Conducting workforce planning to anticipate the retirement of employees at all levels and identify workforce expansion in organizational strategic plans
- Instituting HR management systems to reduce administrative time, equipment, and staff costs with technology
- Identifying organizational training opportunities that will more than pay back the costs
- Evaluating mergers and acquisitions for organizational "compatibility," structural changes, and staffing needs

HUMAN RESOURCES AND STRATEGY

Regardless of which specific strategies are adopted for guiding a healthcare organization, having the right people will be necessary to make the overall strategies work. If a strategy requires worker skills that are currently not available in the organization, it will take time to find and hire people with those skills. Strategic HR management (HRM) provides input for organizational strategic planning and develops specific HR initiatives to help achieve the organizational goals. While it seems important to consider HR in the overall organizational strategy, estimates are that only 30 percent of HR professionals are full strategic partners. Their primary role remains one of providing input to top management.[13]

Although administrative and legally mandated tasks are important, HR's strategic contribution can also add value to the organization by improving the performance of the business. Some businesses are highly dependent on human capital for a competitive advantage; others are less so. For example, the productivity of an imaging center depends as much on the effectiveness of the imaging equipment (MRI, CT, etc.) as it does on human resources. However, every business strategy must be carried out by people, so human capital always has an impact on business success.

Strategic HR management refers to the use of HR management practices to gain or keep a competitive advantage. Talent acquisition, deployment, development, and reward are all strategic HRM approaches that can impact the organization's ability to achieve its strategic objectives.[14]

An important element of strategic HRM is to develop processes in the organization that help align individual employee performance with the organizational strategic objectives.[15] When employees understand the relevant priorities, they can better contribute by applying their skills to advance the strategic goals. Employees who understand the big picture can better make decisions that will contribute to achieving the objectives of the firm.[16] HRM practices that facilitate this include talent development and reward systems that channel employee efforts toward the bottom line.

Requirements for Human Resource Contribution to Strategy

Specific HR management strategies obviously depend on the strategies and plans of the company.[17] Figure 3-3 depicts how HR strategy is developed, implemented, and measured. To contribute in the strategic planning process, HR professionals provide their perspective and expertise to operating managers by doing the following:

- *Understanding the Business*—Knowing the financials and key drivers of business success is important to understanding the need for certain strategies.
- *Focusing on the Key Business Goals*—Programs that have the greatest relevance to business objectives should get priority.
- *Knowing What to Measure*—Metrics are a vital part of assessing success, which means picking those measures that directly relate to the business goals.
- *Preparing for the Future*—Strategic thinking requires preparing for the future, not focusing on the past—except as a predictor of the future.

For example, when a 50-bed hospital with five clinics decided to hire its own doctors to staff its clinics instead of relying on contracted physicians from another health center, HR's strategy had to change to match the organizational strategy. The HR group devised a plan to do so and as a result its mission

FIGURE 3-3 **HR Strategy Development, Implementation, and Measurement**

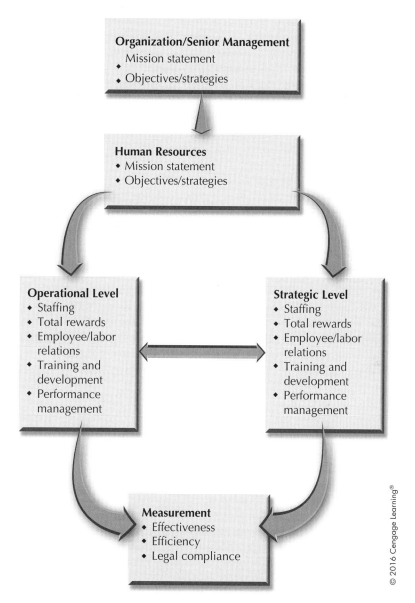

© 2016 Cengage Learning®

required a more active role in driving the business, supporting management in recruiting physicians, and delivering a broader array of HR services. This required retraining the HR staff and initiating a wide range of measures to monitor progress. The organization's strategy changed, and HR's strategy had to change too.

HUMAN RESOURCE PLANNING

Human resource planning is the process of analyzing and identifying the need for and availability of people so that the organization can meet its strategic objectives. The focus of HR planning is to ensure that the organization has the *right number of people* with the *right capabilities*, at the *right times*, and in the *right places*. In HR planning, an organization must consider the availability and allocation of people to jobs over long periods of time, not just for the next month or even the next year.[18]

HR plans can include several approaches. Actions may include shifting employees to other jobs in the organization, laying off employees or otherwise cutting back the number of employees, retraining current employees, and/or increasing the number of employees in certain areas. Factors to consider include the current employees' knowledge, skills, and abilities (KSAs) and the expected vacancies resulting from retirements, promotions, transfers, and discharges. To do this, HR professionals must work with executives and managers.[19]

Human Resources Planning Process

The steps in the HR planning process are shown in Figure 3-4. Notice that the process begins with considering the organizational plans and the environmental analysis that went into developing strategies. The figure includes an environmental analysis to identify the situation in which HR is operating. Strengths, weaknesses, opportunities, and threats are considered. Then the possible *available workforce* is evaluated by identifying both the external and internal workforce.

Once those assessments are complete, forecasts must be developed to determine both the demand for and supply of human resources. Management then formulates HR staffing plans and actions to address imbalances, both short term and long term. Specific strategies may be developed to fill vacancies or deal with surplus employees. For example, a strategy might be to fill 50 percent of the expected vacancies in the billing office by training employees in lower-level jobs and promoting them.

Finally, HR plans are developed to provide specific direction for the management of HR activities related to employee recruiting, selection, and retention. The most telling evidence of successful HR planning is a consistent alignment of the availabilities and capabilities of human resources with the needs of the organization over time.[20]

Environmental Analysis

Before the managers in a healthcare organization can begin strategic planning, they study and assess the dynamics of the environment in which they operate to better understand how these conditions might affect their plans. The process of **environmental scanning** helps to pinpoint strengths, weaknesses, opportunities,

FIGURE 3-4   HR Planning Process

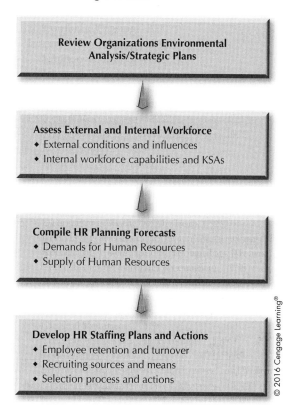

© 2016 Cengage Learning®

and threats that the organization will face during the planning horizon. Whether this is done or not at the organizational level, it should be conducted at the HR planning level.[21]

The external environment includes many economic, political, and competitive forces that will shape the future. For HR the internal environment includes the quality and quantity of talent, the organizational culture, and the talent pipeline and leadership bench strength. Figure 3-5 shows the HR elements of a SWOT (**S**trengths, **W**eaknesses, **O**pportunities, and **T**hreats) analysis that are part of the environmental analysis.

Opportunities and threats emerge from the external environment and can impact the outcomes for the organization. Many of these forces are not within the organization's control but must be considered in the scanning process because they can affect the business. Dealing with uncertainty in the external environment is an important skill for planners. The external environmental scan includes an assessment of economic conditions, legislative/political influences, workforce composition and work patterns, demographic changes, and geographic and competitive issues.

FIGURE 3-5 **HR Elements of a SWOT Analysis**

Strengths
- Intellectual capital
- Loyal, committed employees
- Innovative, adaptive employees
- High-performance practices

Weaknesses
- Lack of skilled employees
- Lack of leadership pipeline
- Outdated talent management practices

Opportunities
- Market position
- Unexplored markets
- Global expansion
- Technology advances

Threats
- Legal mandates and restrictions
- Competitor power
- Economic uncertainty
- Talent shortage

© 2016 Cengage Learning®

PLANNING FOR EXTERNAL WORKFORCE AVAILABILITY

If a home healthcare agency plans to double its number of patients from 100 to 200 in a three-year period, the agency must also identify how many and what types of new employees will be needed to staff the expanded number of patients. Those new employees will probably have to come from outside the current pool of employees. Several specific factors that affect that external pool of potential employees are highlighted next.

Economic and Governmental Factors

The general economic cycles of recession and boom affect HR planning. Factors such as interest rates, inflation, and economic decline or growth affect the availability of workers and should be considered when organizational and HR plans and objectives are formulated. There is a considerable difference between finding qualified applicants in a 4 percent unemployment market and finding them in a 9 percent unemployment market. This is especially true for healthcare employers due to the education and training that is required for many healthcare positions.

A broad array of government regulations affects the labor supply and therefore HR planning. As a result, HR planning must be done by individuals who understand the legal requirements of various government regulations. Pension provisions and Social Security legislation may change retirement patterns and funding options. Elimination or expansion of tax benefits for job-training expenses might alter some job-training activities associated with workforce expansion. In summary, healthcare organizations must consider a wide variety of economic factors and government policies, regulations, and laws during the HR planning process, focusing on specific ones that affect the company.

Geographic and Competitive Evaluations

When making HR plans, healthcare employers must consider a number of geographic and competitive concerns. The *net migration* into a particular region is important. For example, in the past decade, the populations of some U.S. cities in the South, Southwest, and West have grown rapidly and have provided sources of labor. However, areas in the Northeast and Midwest have experienced declining populations or net outmigration. This affects the number of people available to be hired.[22]

Direct competitors are another important external force in HR planning. Failure to consider the competitive labor market and to offer pay scales and benefits comparable with those of organizations in the same categories of care provision and geographic location may cost a healthcare organization dearly in the long run. Even during the recent downturn in the economy, healthcare wages remained relatively strong in comparison to other industries. Healthcare employers were required to maintain competitive wages to retain skilled workers.[23]

Changes in the Conditions of Work

Changes in the composition of the workforce, combined with the varied work patterns of the healthcare environment, have created healthcare workplaces and organizations that are very different from those of the past. The traditional work schedule, in which employees work full-time, 8 hours a day, five days a week at the employer's place of operations, is in transition. Healthcare organizations have been leaders in implementing many different possibilities for change: the four-day, 40-hour week; the four-day, 32-hour week; the 12-hour shift, three days a week; and flexible scheduling.

The healthcare industry has also been especially aggressive in adopting approaches to flexibility in staffing, especially as part of its recruitment and retention efforts. Changes of this nature must be considered in HR planning. Also, a growing number of healthcare employers are allowing workers to use different working arrangements. Some employees work partly at home and partly at an office, sharing office space with other *office nomads*. As an example, many hospitals, clinics, and physician practices have all or part of their medical transcription work performed by employees who work out of their homes. *Telecommuting* is the process of working via electronic computing and telecommunications equipment.

Other employees have *virtual offices*: their offices are wherever they are, whenever they are there. An office for a home healthcare nurse could be an unoccupied treatment room, a conference room, or even his or her car. The shift to such arrangements means that work is done anywhere, anytime, and that people are judged more on results than on "putting in time." Greater trust, less direct supervision, and more self-scheduling are all job characteristics of those with virtual offices and other less traditional arrangements.

Changing Workforce Considerations

Significant changes in the workforce must be considered when examining the outside workforce for HR planning. Shifts in the composition of the workforce, combined with the use of different work patterns, have created workplaces and organizations in healthcare that are notably different from those of just a decade ago.

When assessing these factors, it is important to analyze how they affect the current and future availability of healthcare workers with specific capabilities and experiences. For instance, in a number of industries, the median age of highly specialized professionals is more than 50 years, and the supply of potential replacements with adequate education and experiences is not sufficient to replace such employees as they retire. As a case in point, there is a predicted shortfall of a serious nature in the number of physicians across all specialties, including primary care, starting in 2015 and continuing well into the next two decades. The shortage by 2025 is predicted to be more than 130,000 physicians. Among other factors, this shortage is directly associated with the number of physician retirements that will occur over the next decade.[24]

PLANNING FOR INTERNAL WORKFORCE AVAILABILITY

Analyzing the jobs that will need to be done and the capabilities of people who are currently available in the organization to do them is the next part of HR planning. The needs of the organization must be compared against the existing labor supply, as well as the potential labor supply available outside the organization.

Current and Future Jobs Audit

The starting point for evaluating internal workforce strengths and weaknesses is an audit of the jobs that need to be done in the organization. A comprehensive analysis of all current jobs provides a basis for forecasting what jobs will need to be done in the future. Much of the data required for the audit should be available from existing staffing and organizational databases. The following are key questions that are addressed during the internal jobs assessment:

- What jobs exist now and how essential is each job?
- How many individuals are performing each job?
- What are the reporting relationships of jobs?
- What are the vital KSAs (knowledge, skills, and abilities) needed in the jobs?

- What jobs will be needed to implement future organizational strategies?
- What are the characteristics of those anticipated jobs?

Employee and Organizational Capabilities Inventory

As HR planners gain an understanding of the current and future jobs that will be necessary to carry out organizational plans, they can conduct a detailed audit of current employees and their capabilities. The basic data on employees should be available in the HR records in the organization.

An inventory of organizational skills and capabilities may consider a number of elements. Especially important are:

- Individual employee demographics (age, length of service in the organization, time in present job)
- Individual career progression (jobs held, time in each job, education and training levels, promotions or other job changes, pay rates)
- Individual performance data (work accomplishment, growth in skills, working relationships)

Managers and HR staff members can gather data on individual employees and aggregate details into a profile of the current organizational workforce. This profile may reveal many of the current strengths and deficiencies of people in the organization.

Human Resource Information Systems   Electronic data management has simplified the task of analyzing vast amounts of data. The use of human resource information systems (HRISs) can be invaluable in HR management, from payroll processing to record retention. An HRIS is an integrated system designed to provide information used in HR decision making. An HRIS has many uses in an organization.[25] The most basic is the automation of payroll and benefit activities. With an HRIS, employees' time records are entered into the system, and the appropriate deductions and other individual adjustments are reflected in the final paychecks. As a result of HRIS development and implementation in many organizations, several payroll functions are being transferred from accounting departments to HR departments. Another common use of HRIS is EEO/affirmative action tracking.

The dramatic increase in the use of the Internet is raising possibilities and concerns for HR professionals, particularly when establishing an HRIS. Use of web-based information systems has allowed HR departments in healthcare organizations to become more administratively efficient and to be able to deal with more strategic and longer-term HR planning issues.

Two issues of concern for HR are *security* and *privacy of the HRIS*. Controls must be built into the system to restrict indiscriminate access to HRIS data on employees. For instance, health insurance claims might identify someone who has undergone psychiatric counseling or treatment for alcoholism, and access to such information must be limited both for employee privacy reasons and for compliance with Health Insurance Portability and Accountability Act (HIPAA) requirements. Likewise, performance appraisal ratings of employees must be guarded.

FORECASTING HR SUPPLY AND DEMAND

Forecasting uses information from the past and present to predict expected future conditions. When forecasting future HR conditions, the forecast comes from workforce availability and requirements. Projections for the future are, of course, subject to error. Changes in the conditions on which the projections are based might even completely invalidate them, which is the chance forecasters take. Fortunately, experienced people usually are able to forecast with enough accuracy to positively affect long-range organizational planning. Figure 3-6 depicts the process of HR forecasting.

Forecasting

Approaches to forecasting human resource needs range from a manager's best guess to a rigorous and complex computer simulation of the labor force.[26]

FIGURE 3-6   HR Forecasting

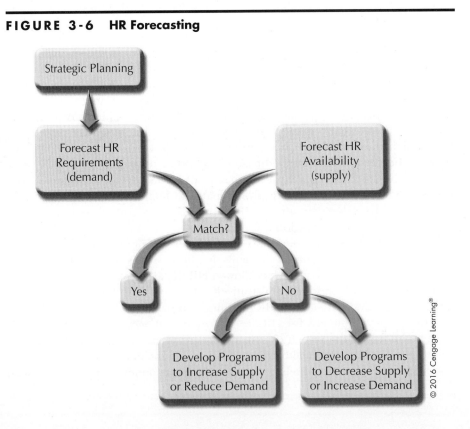

© 2016 Cengage Learning®

Simple assumptions might be sufficient in certain instances, but complex models might be necessary for others. HR forecasting should be done over three planning periods: *short range, intermediate,* and *long range.* The most commonly used planning period is short range, usually a period of six months to one year. This level of planning is routine in many healthcare organizations because very few assumptions about the future are necessary for such short-range plans. Also, in many healthcare organizations, a six-month to one-year period typically corresponds with a budget cycle, which requires some level of forecasting to establish or project payroll and benefit expense budgets.

Demand versus Supply of Human Resources   Forecasting the number of people needed can be done using two frameworks. One approach considers specific openings that are likely to occur and uses that information as the basis for planning. The openings (or demands) are created when employees leave positions because of promotions, transfers, or terminations. The analysis always begins with the top positions in the organization, because from those there can be no promotions to a higher level.

Once the need for human resources has been forecasted, then availability or supply must be identified. Forecasting the availability of human resources considers both external and internal supplies. The external supply of potential employees available to the organization must be estimated. Here are some of the factors that may be considered:

- Individuals entering and leaving the workforce
- Individuals graduating from schools and colleges
- Economic forecasts for the next few years
- Technological developments and shifts
- Government regulations and pressures
- Circumstances affecting persons entering and leaving the workforce

ELEMENTS OF SUCCESSFUL HR PLANNING

There are several critical success factors to HR planning in healthcare organizations. The HR plan should be strategically aligned, purposeful, measurable, and documented. Each of these areas is discussed next.

The HR plan must be aligned with the broader organizational strategies and objectives. This requires HR leaders to be fully knowledgeable and involved in the strategic management of the organization to ensure that the HR plan will be developed in a manner that will meet organizational objectives. As an example, many large surgical specialty practices have found that owning and operating same-day surgery facilities is an excellent source of revenue, especially with declining reimbursement payments. The strategic decision by the surgeons to operate a same-day surgery center must be supported by an HR plan that would include the staffing, compensation, and employee relations of surgical nurses and technicians for the facility. The success and viability of the surgery center would, in large part, be dependent on the successful implementation of the HR plan.

The HR plan must be developed so that there is no ambiguity about its purpose and what it is to accomplish. In implementing and sustaining the elements of an HR plan, it is important that it is developed in such a way that progress can be tracked.

Referencing the same-day surgery clinic example, the HR plan component for staffing the facility should include trigger points relating to patient volumes. As the facility increases the number of surgeries performed, the employment, orientation, and training of new staff must be appropriately identified and sequenced to ensure that staffing levels and competencies correspond to the growth in the patient care delivery needs of the facility.

The HR plan should be written and updated annually. HR leaders should be responsible for presenting the plan to the other executives and board of directors. Periodic updates regarding the progress of the plan should also be provided. In the surgery center example, the implementation of the staffing component of the HR plan would carry significant costs that should be discussed with and agreed to by the board.

Key Inputs to the Healthcare HR Strategic Plan A strategic plan cannot be created in a vacuum. For the HR plan to be useful, it must take into account a number of important internal and external organizational inputs. A look at each of these areas from Figure 3-7 follows:

- *Organizational Mission*—The purest definition of mission is answering the question, "Why does the organization exist?" Healthcare organizations rarely struggle with this question; in fact, one of the true strengths of a healthcare provider is the clarity of its care delivery mission. An example of a healthcare organizational mission statement is Children's Healthcare of Atlanta: "To enhance the lives of children through excellence in patient care, research and education."[27]

- *Organizational Objectives and Strategies*—In many instances, organizational objectives and strategies include significant HR considerations, especially regarding workforce planning, executive and management staffing, and compensation. The HR plan should cover the regular and routine HR aspects of supporting organizational functioning such as staffing and employee relations. It should also consider new initiatives or objectives of the organization, such as in the example of a hospital opening a new nursing unit for oncology patients, the HR needs of which would include staffing, compensation, and employee orientation and training for the unit.

- *Environmental Assessment*—As detailed earlier in the chapter, evaluating the environment is extremely important to the management of healthcare human resources. The HR plan must fully and comprehensively consider external environmental issues and opportunities, such as other healthcare

FIGURE 3-7   Inputs to Healthcare HR Strategic Plan

© 2016 Cengage Learning®

organizations that may be expanding or downsizing, which could potentially affect the supply of healthcare workers.

- *Organizational Resources and Capabilities*—The HR plan must consider the volume or productivity requirements of the organization. For instance, measurement of patient census, patient days, admissions, and average length of stay is used in developing staffing plans in order to match human resources with organizational capabilities.

- *Financial Realities*—Financial decisions, including budgetary allocations and capital expenditures, affect every aspect of HR management. The HR plan must be financially realistic, while maintaining consistent levels of support for such HR activities as staffing, compensation, and benefit administration. Financial resources needed for new human resources initiatives, such as the upgrade of the HR information system, must also be considered.

- *Considering the Plans of Other Functional Areas*—Effective HR planning should be both supportive of and compatible with the planning of all the other functional areas within the organization, such as patient care, surgery, or finance. The actual development of the HR plan should be in line with the development of the plans for the other areas.

HEALTHCARE REFORM AND HR PRACTICES

The impact of healthcare reform on healthcare organizations, even as the federal and state governments struggle to finalize regulations and fully implement all phases of the ACA legislation, has been far reaching. Potentially the biggest impact will be in the anticipated change to a fee-for-service payment system to a capitated model, at the heart of which is the predetermined payment for the provision of care to a defined group of patients. This new payment system will require all healthcare providers to maximize the quality, efficiency, safety, and patient satisfaction of the care provided.

Joseph R. Swedish, president and CEO of Trinity Health in Novi, Michigan, shared his organization's strategic planning for dealing with ACA against the backdrop of these new realities. He identified the need to transform his organization to be competitive in an evolving consumer-centric environment. He notes that the only way to deal with these rapid changes is through careful and purposeful planning.

Trinity Health's planning includes a focus on patient quality and safety utilizing what they described as the "Seven C's": culture, consolidation, consistency, coordination, cost, collaboration, and consumerism. Trinity Health's end goal is to provide better and safer care at a price consistent with the demands of the marketplace. The HR strategic planning and execution implications to Trinity Health's organizational planning are significant. Key focus areas will include recruiting individuals with strong customer service skills, developing training programs to support better and safer care initiatives, and culture building to sustain Trinity Health's organization change.[28]

HR MANAGEMENT CHALLENGES

The environment faced by HR management is challenging because changes are occurring rapidly across a wide range of issues. The following sections describe some of these challenges.

A Changing Workforce

The U.S. workforce is more diverse racially and ethnically, more women are in it than ever before, and the average age of its members is increasing. As a result of these demographic shifts, HR management in healthcare organizations has had to adapt to a more varied labor force both externally and internally. The changing workforce has raised employer concerns and requires more attention to resolve these concerns.[29]

Racial/Ethnic Diversity Racial and ethnic minorities account for a growing percentage of the overall labor force, with the percentage of Hispanics roughly equal to or greater than the percentage of African Americans. Immigrants will continue to expand that growth. An increasing number of individuals character-ize themselves as *multiracial,* suggesting that the American "melting pot" is blur-ring racial and ethnic identities.

Racial/ethnic differences have also created greater cultural diversity because of the accompanying differences in traditions, languages, religious practices, and so on. For example, global events have increased employers' attention to individuals who are Muslim, and more awareness of and accommodation for Islamic religious beliefs and practices have become a common concern.

Gender in the Workforce   Women constitute about 50 percent of the U.S. workforce, but they may be a majority in certain occupations. It is not unusual for healthcare organizations to have a workforce that is 80 percent or more female. Additionally, numerous women workers are single, separated, divorced, or wid-owed, and are "primary" income earners. A growing number of U.S. households include "domestic partners," who are committed to each other though not mar-ried, and who may be of the same or the opposite sex.

For many workers in the United States, balancing the demands of family and work is a significant challenge. Although that balancing has always been a concern, the increased number of working women and dual-career couples has resulted in greater tension for many workers, both male and female. Employers have had to respond to work–family concerns to retain employees. Responses have included greater use of job sharing, the establishment of child-care ser-vices, increased flexibility in hours, and work–life programs.

Aging Workforce   In the United States during the second decade of the twenty-first century, a significant number of experienced employees will be retir-ing, changing to part-time work, or otherwise shifting their employment. Replac-ing the experience and talents of longer-service workers is a challenge facing employers in all industries. This loss of longer-service workers is frequently referred to as a "brain drain," because of the capabilities and experience of these workers. As discussed earlier in this chapter, this is a reality for physicians. Employers are having to develop programs to retain them, have them mentor and transfer knowledge to younger employees, and find ways for them to con-tinue contributing in limited ways.[30]

Growth in Contingent Workforce   *Contingent workers* (temporary workers, independent contractors, leased employees, and part-timers) represent about one-fourth of the U.S. workforce.[31] Many employers operate with a core group of regular employees who have critical skills, and then expand and shrink the workforce by using contingent workers.

The number of contingent workers has grown for many reasons. One reason is the economic factor. Temporary workers are used to replace full-time employ-ees, and many contingent workers are paid less and/or receive fewer benefits than regular employees. For instance, omitting contingent workers from health-care benefits saves some firms 20 to 40 percent in labor costs.[32]

Another reason for the increased use of contingent workers is that it may reduce legal liability for some employers. As more employment-related lawsuits are filed, employers have become more wary about adding regular full-time employees. By using contract workers, employers may reduce many legal issues regarding selection, discrimination, benefits, discipline, and termination.

CASE

Sharonville Community Medical Center (SCMC) is a 25-bed hospital located in a rural area of the Midwest. It is 75 miles away from the closest large city and serves a geographic region with a population base of approximately 14,000 people. SCMC employs 200 employees, 40 of whom are in nursing positions, including 14 RNs and 26 LPNs.

SCMS's board of trustees is made up of various community and business leaders who are concerned about the hospital's future. As a community hospital, its operating and capital budget is supported through a small tax levy. Due to excellent fiscal control and planning, the financial condition of the hospital far exceeds its peer group. However, the board commissioned a study of its workforce and was alarmed by the following findings:

- By the year 2015, 66 percent of the current nursing employees will be at retirement age.

- The primary source of nursing candidates has been from individuals with nursing training who live within a 30-mile radius of Sharonville. Eighty percent of the current nursing employees attended Sharonville High School, went away to college for nursing training, and returned to the area to pursue their careers. However, fewer recent graduates of Sharonville High School are entering nursing school. Those that do are not returning to Sharonville as others before them did.
- SCMC does not have a current workforce replacement plan in place to deal with the nursing employee attrition expected over the next decade.

Questions

1. Define the role of HR in dealing with this critical workforce planning issue.
2. Apply the HR planning process in addressing this issue.

END NOTES

1. Milton Moskowitz, "The 100 Best Companies to Work For," *Fortune* (February 4, 2013), 85–96.
2. *http://money.cnn.com/magazines/fortune/bestcompanies/2013/snapshots*.
3. *http://www.somc.org/news/somc-named-fortunes-18th-best-place-to-work/*.
4. Annamarie Lang, "Create a Learning Journey," *Training* (November/December 2013), 58.
5. Martin Dewhurst et al., "Redesigning Knowledge Work," *Harvard Business Review* (January/February 2013), 58–64.
6. *http://www.uofmmedicalcenter.org/Research/index.htm*.
7. Thomas Davenport et al., "Competing on Talent Analytics," *Harvard Business Review* (October 2010), 52–58.
8. Robert E. Ployhart et al., "The Consequences of Human Resource Stocks and Flows: A Longitudinal Exam of Unit Service Orientation and Unit Effectiveness," *Academy of Management Journal* 52 (2007), 996–1015; Katherine Tyler, "Diagnosing Cultural Health," *HR Magazine* (August 2011), 52–53.

9. Carol Morrison, "The Four Ps of High Performance," *Human Resource Executive Online* (June 16, 2011), 1–4; Peter Cappelli, "Creating a Performance Culture," *Human Resource Executive Online* (September 12, 2010).

10. E. Edward Stark and Francis L. Jeffries, "Part II: Leadership, Social Capital, and Personality: Social Capital via Leader–Member Exchanges: An Avenue to Human Capital?," *Current Topics in Management* (2011), 117–136.

11. Harry J. Van Buren III et al., "Strategic Human Resource Management and the Decline of Employee Focus," *Human Resource Management Review* 21 (September 2011), 209–219.

12. Jennifer Schramm, "Under Pressure," *HR Magazine* (April 2011), 104.

13. E. E. Lawler III and J. W. Boudreau, "What Makes HR a Strategic Partner?," CEO (Center for Effective Organizations) publication G09-01 (555), 1–23, 9.

14. Katrina Pritchard, "Becoming an HR Strategic Partner: Tales of Transition," *Human Resource Management Journal* 20 (2010), 175–187.

15. Susan R. Mersinger, "Thinking Strategically," *Human Resource Executive Online* (May 16, 2011), 1–2.

16. Dave Ulrich et al., "The Role of Strategy Architect in the Strategic HR Organization," *People and Strategy* 32 (2009), 24–31.

17. Mark L. Legnick-Hall et al., "Strategic Human Resource Management: The Evolution of the Field," *Human Resource Management Review* 19 (2009), 64–85.

18. Steven Balsam et al., "The Impact of Firm Strategy on Performance Measures Used in Executive Compensation," *Journal of Business Research* 64 (2011), 187–193.

19. Van Buren et al., "Strategic HRM and the Decline of Employee Focus."

20. Paul F. Buller and G. M. McEvoy, "Strategy, HRM, and Performance: Sharpening the Line of Sight," *Human Resource Management Review* 22 (March 2012), 43–56.

21. Don Ruse et al., "How Strategic Workforce Planning Can Help You Thrive," *Workspan* (December 2009), 26–32.

22. U.S. Census Bureau Population Division, "U.S. Population Projections," *http://www.census.gov.*

23. Virgil Dickson, "Partners in Health," *Modern Healthcare* (December 23, 2013), 16.

24. Charlotte Huff, "Location, Location, Location," *Trustee* (January 2012), 8–12.

25. "Recruiting Software: Total Package or Best of Breed?," *Workforce Management* 6 (June 2013), 26.

26. Tom Stamer, "A Strategic Workforce Planning Officer?," *Human Resource Executive Online* (June 5, 2012), 1–7.

27. *http://www.choa.org/Menus/Documents/Aboutus/StandardsOfConduct.pdf.*

28. Joseph Swedish, "Clinical Integration: The Foundation of Our Future," *H&HN: Hospitals & Health Networks* (May 2012), 64.

29. Marlene Prost, "When the End Is in Sight," *Human Resource Executive Online* (July 1, 2010), 1–5.

30. John Dumay and Jim Rooney, "Dealing with an Aging Workforce," *Journal of Human Resource Costing and Accounting* 15 (2011), 174–195.

31. Michael O'Brien, "A Temp's Perspective," *Human Resource Executive Online* (February 1, 2009), 1.

32. Jennifer Taylor Arnold, "Managing a Nontraditional Workforce," *HR Magazine* (August 2010), 75–77.

4 LEGAL ISSUES AFFECTING THE HEALTHCARE WORKPLACE

Learning Objectives

After you have read this chapter, you should be able to:

- Describe the major laws affecting the healthcare workplace.

- Define what are lawful and unlawful preemployment inquiries.

- Discuss the components of an affirmative action plan.

- Describe the steps to take in responding to an equal employment opportunity (EEO) complaint.

- Identify the important elements of a sexual harassment prevention program.

- Compare and contrast legal responsibilities and ethics.

HEALTHCARE HR INSIGHTS

In the largest single-employee verdict awarded in U.S. history, the plaintiff Ani Chopourian was awarded $168 million (note: the jury verdict was later reduced to $82 million). In her suit against Catholic Healthcare West, the jury decided that Chopourian had been the victim of sexual harassment and being defamed as a whistleblower when she brought her complaints to management. The facts of the case are very disturbing. As revealed through testimony, Ms. Chopourian was tormented and sexually harassed by surgeons and the medical staff in the surgery center at Catholic Healthcare West's Mercy General over a two-year period of time. The harassment even included being stuck by a needle. During this time she made 18 written complaints to the human resources department about the harassment and other violations of policy. After the verdict, Mercy General Hospital continues to deny the charges and is appealing the verdict.[1]

Regardless of Mercy General Hospital's success with an appeal, the hospital has already spent considerable time and resources on this case. Further, these types of cases impact the reputation and even the morale of the organization as the news of the verdict is communicated by the media.

HR professionals, when confronted with serious allegations of harassment, can significantly mitigate the risks associated with these cases by conducting prompt, effective investigations. Once the facts are learned the appropriate action can be taken.[2]

Healthcare HR professionals face many concerns beyond sexual harassment when ensuring equal treatment of all employees and compliance with numerous equal employment laws. Ensuring equal opportunity and fair treatment in the healthcare workplace is the responsibility of every healthcare leader who makes employment-related decisions. HR professionals in healthcare firms shoulder a significant portion of the responsibility due to their role in the organization. Consequently, HR practitioners must be extremely knowledgeable about the laws that impact the workplace so they can provide leadership, compliance oversight, and consultation to the managers and staff.

EQUAL EMPLOYMENT OPPORTUNITY

Equal employment opportunity is a broad-reaching concept that essentially requires employers to make **status-blind** employment decisions. Status-blind decisions are made without regard to applicants' personal characteristics (i.e., age, sex, race, and so on). Most employers are required to comply with equal employment opportunity laws. Affirmative action means that an employer takes proactive measures when considering women and minorities for employment. The objective of affirmative action plans is to compensate for past patterns of discrimination. Federal contractors are required to implement and maintain affirmative action plans.[3]

The following bases for protection have been identified by various federal, state, and local laws:

- Race, ethnicity, origin, color (African Americans, Hispanic Americans, Native Americans, Asian Americans)
- Sex/gender (women, including those who are pregnant)
- Age (individuals over age 40)
- Individuals with disabilities (physical or mental)
- Military experience (Vietnam-era veterans)
- Religion (special beliefs and practices)
- Marital status (some states)
- Sexual orientation (some states and cities)

These categories are considered protected characteristics under EEO laws and regulations. All workers are provided equal protection; the laws do not favor some groups over others. For example, both men and women can file charges on the basis of alleged sex discrimination.

Sources of Regulation and Enforcement

The employment relationship is governed by a wide variety of regulations. All three branches of government have played a role in shaping these laws. Federal statutes enacted by Congress form the backbone of the regulatory environment. State and city governments also enact laws governing activity within their domains. The courts interpret these laws and rule on cases. Case law helps employers to understand how laws are applied and what they must do to comply. Executive orders are issued by the president of the United States to help government departments and agencies manage their operations.

Government agencies responsible for enforcing laws issue guidelines and rules to provide details on how the law will be implemented. Employers then use these guidelines to meet their obligations in complying with the laws.

The two main enforcement bodies for EEO are the Equal Employment Opportunity Commission (EEOC) and the U.S. Department of Labor (DOL) (in particular, the Office of Federal Contract Compliance Programs [OFCCP]). The EEOC enforces employment laws for employers in both private and public workplaces. The DOL has broad enforcement power and oversees compliance with many employment-related laws. The OFCCP enforces employment requirements set out by executive orders for federal contractors and subcontractors. Many states have enforcement agencies to ensure compliance with state employment laws. Compliance can become complex for companies that operate in multiple states.

Discrimination remains a concern as the U.S. workforce, including the healthcare workforce, becomes more diverse. Charges filed with the EEOC continue to rise.[4] Over the past 15 years, the total number of charges has increased nearly 24 percent. While race and sex have historically represented the highest percentages of complaints, in recent years charges of retaliation have become the most common. Historically, the EEOC has found "no reasonable cause" in about two-thirds of those claims. The remaining one-third are settled, withdrawn, or pursued by the EEOC. The EEOC has also been held accountable for filing lawsuits against employers without properly investigating the charges and has been forced to reimburse those employers' legal costs.[5]

Major Employment Laws

Numerous federal, state, and local laws address EEO concerns. Figure 4-1 presents an overview of the major laws, regulations, and concepts. They are discussed in more detail in the remainder of this chapter.

FIGURE 4-1 Major Federal Equal Employment Opportunity Laws and Regulations

Act	Year	Key Provisions	Covered Employees
		Broad-Based Discrimination	
Title VII, Civil Rights Act of 1964	1964	Prohibits discrimination in employment on basis of race, color, religion, sex, or national origin	Employers with 15+ employees
Executive Orders 11246 and 11375	1965 1967	Require federal contractors and subcontractors to eliminate employment discrimination and prior discrimination through affirmative action	Federal contractors with 50+ employees and a government contract of $500,000 or more
Civil Rights Act of 1991	1991	Overturns several past Supreme Court decisions and changes damage claims provisions	Employers with 15+ employees
Congressional Accountability Act	1995	Extends EEO and Civil Rights Act provisions to U.S. congressional staff	U.S. Congress
		Military Status	
Vietnam Era Veterans' Readjustment Assistance Act	1974	Prohibits discriminations against Vietnam era veterans by federal contractors and the U.S. government and requires affirmative action	
Uniformed Services Employment and Reemployment Rights Act	1994	Protects members of the uniformed services from discrimination in employment and provides for reinstatement to their job upon return from active duty.	All employers
		National Origin Discrimination	
Immigration Reform and Control Act	1986 1990 1996	Establishes penalties for employers who knowingly hire illegal aliens; prohibits employment discrimination on the basis of national origin or citizenship.	Employers with 15+ employees

Equal Employment Opportunity Concepts

Court decisions and administrative rulings have helped to define several basic EEO concepts. The four key concepts discussed next (see Figure 4-2) help to clarify key EEO ideas that lead to fair treatment and nondiscriminatory employment decisions.

Business Necessity and Job Relatedness A **business necessity** is a practice necessary for safe and efficient organizational operations, such as restricting healthcare workers from sporting beards that might obstruct the wearing of a surgical mask even though the facial hair may be required by the worker's religion. Business necessity has been the subject of numerous court cases. Educational requirements are often decided on the basis of business necessity. However, an employer that requires a minimum level of education, such as a high school diploma, must be able to defend the requirement as essential to the performance of the job (job related), which may be difficult. For instance, equating a high school diploma with the possession of math or reading abilities is considered questionable.

Employers are expected to use job-related employment practices. The use of criminal background checks and credit reports in the selection process has come under fire because it often results in disparate impact on minority applicants. The EEOC issued guidelines regarding such use of criminal history. Essentially, the EEOC reiterated that the nature of the job sought by the applicant is a major determining factor in whether or not a criminal conviction is job related. Healthcare organizations must seek a balance between their obligations to provide a safe working environment and to ensure equal employment opportunity.

Bona Fide Occupational Qualification Employers may discriminate on the basis of sex, religion, or national origin if the characteristic can be justified as a bona fide occupational qualification reasonably necessary to the normal operation of the particular business or enterprise. Thus, a **bona fide occupational**

FIGURE 4-2   EEO Concepts

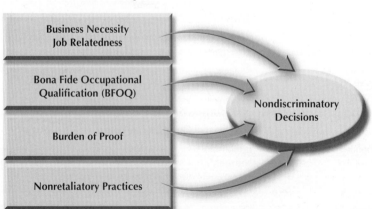

qualification (BFOQ) provides a legitimate reason why an employer can exclude persons on otherwise illegal bases of consideration. The application of a BFOQ is very narrowly determined, and a healthcare employer seeking to justify hiring on this basis is advised to obtain prior authorization from the EEOC.

What constitutes a BFOQ has been subject to different interpretations in various courts. Legal uses of BFOQs have been found for hiring women as attendants to be present when a male obstetrician is conducting a gynecologic exam but not for hiring only female prison guards in a women's prison.[6]

Disparate Treatment and Disparate Impact It would seem that the motives or intentions of the employer might enter into the determination of whether discrimination has occurred. However, the outcome of the employer's actions, not the intent, is considered by the regulatory agencies or courts when deciding if illegal discrimination has occurred. Two concepts used to activate this principle are *disparate treatment* and *disparate impact.*

Disparate treatment occurs when protected-class members are treated differently from others. For example, if female applicants must take a special skills test not given to male applicants, then disparate treatment may be occurring. If disparate treatment has occurred, the courts generally have said that intentional discrimination exists.

Disparate impact occurs when there is substantial underrepresentation of protected-class members as a result of employment decisions that work to their disadvantage. The landmark case that established the importance of disparate impact as a legal foundation of EEO law is *Griggs v. Duke Power* (1971).[7] The decision of the U.S. Supreme Court established two major points:

1. It is not enough to show a lack of discriminatory intent if the employment tool results in a disparate impact that discriminates against one group more than another or continues a past pattern of discrimination.

2. The employer has the burden of proving that an employment requirement is directly job related as a "business necessity." Consequently, the intelligence test and high school diploma requirements of Duke Power were ruled not to be related to the job.

Therefore, employers covered by Title VII must be able to document through numerical calculations and statistical analyses of the workforce that disparate treatment and disparate impact have not occurred.

Burden of Proof When a legal issue regarding unlawful discrimination is raised, the **burden of proof** must be satisfied to file a suit against an employer and establish that unlawful discrimination has occurred. The plaintiff charging discrimination must establish a *prima facie* case of discrimination through either factual or statistical evidence. The prima facie case means that sufficient evidence is provided to the court to support the case and allow the plaintiff to continue with the claim. The burden then shifts to the employer, who must provide a legitimate, nondiscriminatory reason for the decision. The plaintiff then must show either that the employer's reason was a pretext for discrimination or that there is an alternative selection technique that would not result in discrimination. The plaintiff maintains the final burden of proving that an employment decision was the result of unlawful discrimination.[8]

Nonretaliatory Practices   Employers are prohibited from retaliating against individuals who file discrimination charges. **Retaliation** occurs when employers take punitive actions against individuals who exercise their legal rights. Retaliation claims now constitute the highest percentage of charges filed with the EEOC because they can be added to all antidiscrimination charges, and a wide range of workplace decisions might be interpreted as retaliatory. An important aspect of retaliation charges is that the charging party may lose the case on the basis of discrimination but still win if the employer took punitive action against him or her.

To prevent charges of retaliation, the following actions are recommended for employers:[9]

- Create and disseminate an antiretaliation policy.
- Train supervisors on what retaliation is and what is not appropriate.
- Review all performance evaluation and discipline records to ensure consistency and accuracy.
- Conduct a thorough internal investigation of any claims and document the results.
- Take appropriate action when any retaliation occurs.

Organizations that use a proactive approach may reduce the number of lawsuits and possible fines.

ELEMENTS OF EEO COMPLIANCE

Based on the scope of EEO laws and regulations and the potential of significant monetary awards for violations, healthcare organizations must develop effective and responsive compliance policies and practices.

EEO Policy Statement

All healthcare employers should have a written EEO policy statement. This policy should be widely communicated by posting it on bulletin boards, printing it in employee handbooks, reproducing it in organizational newsletters, and reinforcing it in training programs. The contents of the policy should clearly state the organizational commitment to equal employment and incorporate the listing of the appropriate protected classes.

EEO Records

All employers with 15 or more employees are required to keep certain records that can be requested by the EEOC, OFCCP, or other state and local enforcement agencies. Under various laws, employers also are required to post an "officially approved notice" in a prominent place where employees can see it. This notice states that the employer is an equal opportunity employer and does not discriminate.

EEO Records Retention   All employment records must be maintained as required by the EEOC. Required records include application forms and records concerning hiring, promotion, demotion, transfer, layoff, termination, rates of pay or other terms of compensation, and selection for training and apprenticeship. Even application forms or test papers completed by unsuccessful applicants may be requested. The length of time documents must be kept varies, but generally *three years is recommended as a minimum*. Complete records are necessary to enable an employer to respond should a charge of discrimination be made.

Annual Reporting Form   The basic report that must be filed with the EEOC is the annual report form EEO–1. The following employers must file this report:

- All employers with 100 or more employees, except state and local governments
- Subsidiaries of other companies where total employees equal 100 or more
- Federal contractors with at least 50 employees and contracts of $50,000 or more
- Financial institutions with at least 50 employees in which government funds are held or saving bonds are issued

The form requires employment data by job category, classified according to various protected classes.

Applicant Flow Data   Under EEO laws and regulations, employers may be required to show that they do not discriminate in the recruiting and selection of members of protected classes. Because collection of racial data on application forms and other preemployment records is not permitted, the EEOC allows employers to use a "visual" survey or a separate *applicant flow form* that is not used in the selection process. This form is filled out voluntarily by the *applicant*, and the data must be maintained separately from other selection-related materials. These analyses may be useful in showing whether an employer has underutilized a protected class because of an inadequate applicant flow of protected class members, in spite of special efforts to recruit them. Also, these data are reported as part of affirmative action plans that are filed with the OFCCP.

Preemployment versus After-Hire Inquiries   Figure 4-3 lists preemployment inquiries and identifies whether they may or may not be discriminatory. The following list further identifies circumstances that permit or prohibit certain preemployment inquiries:

- Employers acting under bona fide affirmative action programs or acting under orders of equal employment law enforcement agencies of federal, state, or local governments may make some of the prohibited inquiries to the extent that the inquiries are required by such programs or orders.
- Employers having federal defense contracts are exempt to the extent that certain inquiries are required by federal law for security purposes.

FIGURE 4-3 **Lawful and Unlawful Preemployment Inquiries**

INQUIRES BEFORE HIRING	LAWFUL	UNLAWFUL
1. Name	Name	Inquiry into any title which indicates race, color, religion, sex, national origin, handicap or ancestry
2. Address	Inquiry into place and length of current address	Inquiry into foreign address that would indicate national origin
3. Age	• Requiring proof of age in form of work permit issued by school authorities • Requiring proof of age by birth certificate or otherwise after hiring	Requiring birth certificate or baptismal record before hiring
4. Birthplace or National Origin		• Any inquiry into place of birth • Any inquiry into place of birth of parents, grandparents, or spouse
5. Race or Color		Any inquiry that would indicate race or color
6. Sex		Any inquiry that would indicate sex
7. Religion-Creed		• Any inquiry that would indicate or identify religious denomination or custom • Telling applicant of any religious identity or preference of the employer • Requesting religious leaders' recommendation/reference
8. Physical Limitations (requirements)	Inquiries necessary to determine applicant's ability to substantially perform job related functions and to determine accommodations, if any	Disease diagnosis Receipt of worker's compensation
9. Citizenship	• Whether a U.S. Citizen • Whether applicant can legally work in the United States	If native-born or naturalized Whether parents or spouse are native-born or naturalized Proof of citizenship before offer
10. Photographs		Requiring photographs before hiring

(Continued)

FIGURE 4-3   Lawful and Unlawful Preemployment Inquiries (Continued)

INQUIRES BEFORE HIRING	LAWFUL	UNLAWFUL
11. Arrests and Convictions	Inquiries into *conviction* of specific crimes related to the job for which the applicant applied	• Any inquiry which would reveal arrests without convictions • Convictions unrelated to the job responsibilities
12. Education	• Inquiry into nature and extent of academic, professional, or vocational training • Inquiry into language skills such as reading and writing of foreign languages, if job related	• Any inquiry asking specifically the nationality or racial or religious affiliation of a school • Inquiry as to what mother tongue is or how foreign language ability was acquired
13. Relatives	Names of relatives already employed by employer	Any inquiry about a relative that would be unlawful if made about the applicant
14. Organizations	Inquiry into organization memberships and offices held, excluding any organization, the name or character of which indicates the race, color, religion, sex, national origin, handicap or ancestry of its members	Inquiry into *all* clubs and organizations where membership is held
15. Military Service	• Inquiry into service in U.S. Armed Forces when such service is a qualification for the job • Requiring military discharge certificate after being hired	• Inquiry into military service in armed service of any country but United States • Requesting military service records • Type of discharge
16. Work Schedule	Inquiry into willingness to work required work schedule	Any inquiry into willingness to work any particular religious holiday
17. Other Qualifications	Any question required to reveal qualifications for the job applied for	Any non-job related inquiry which may reveal information permitting unlawful discrimination
18. References	General, personal, and work references not relating to race, color, religion, sex, national origin, handicap or ancestry	Request references specifically from any persons who might reflect race, color, religion, sex, national origin, handicap, or ancestry of applicant

Once an employer tells an applicant he or she is hired (the "point of hire"), inquiries that were prohibited earlier may be made. After hiring, medical examination forms, group insurance cards, and other enrollment cards containing inquiries related directly or indirectly to sex, age, or other bases may be requested. Photographs or other evidence of race, religion, or national origin also may be requested after hire for legal, compliance, and workplace security, but not before. Such data should be maintained in a separate personnel records system in order to avoid their use when managers and supervisors make appraisal, discipline, termination, or promotion decisions.

Civil Rights Act of 1964, Title VII

Although the very first civil rights act was passed in 1866, it was not until passage of the Civil Rights Act of 1964 that the keystone of antidiscrimination employment legislation was put into place. Title VII, the employment section of the Civil Rights Act of 1964, details the legal protections provided to applicants and employees and defines prohibited employment practices. Title VII is the foundation on which all other workplace nondiscrimination legislation rests.

Title VII of the Civil Rights Act states that it is illegal for an employer to:

- fail or refuse to hire or discharge any individual, or otherwise discriminate against any individual with respect to his compensation, terms, conditions, or privileges of employment because of such individual's race, color, religion, sex, or national origin, or
- limit, segregate, or classify his employees or applicants for employment in any way that would deprive or tend to deprive any individual of employment opportunities or otherwise adversely affect his status as an employee because of such individual's race, color, religion, sex, or national origin.

Title VII Coverage   Title VII, as amended by the Equal Employment Opportunity Act of 1972, covers most employers in the United States. Any organization meeting one of the following criteria must comply with rules and regulations that specific government agencies have established to administer the act:

- All private employers of 15 or more employees
- All educational institutions, public and private
- State and local governments
- Public and private employment agencies
- Labor unions with 15 or more members
- Joint labor–management committees for apprenticeships and training

Title VII has been the basis for several extensions of EEO law. For example, in 1980 the EEOC interpreted the law to include sexual harassment. Further, a number of concepts identified in Title VII are the foundation for court decisions, regulations, and other laws discussed elsewhere in this chapter. Most healthcare employers fall under one or more of these criteria.

Civil Rights Act of 1991

In response to several Supreme Court decisions during the 1980s, Congress amended the Civil Rights Act of 1964 to strengthen legal protection for employees, provide for jury trials, and allow for damages payable to successful plaintiffs in employment discrimination cases.[10]

The Civil Rights Act of 1991 requires that employers show that an employment practice is job related for the position and consistent with *business necessity*. The act clarifies that plaintiffs bringing discrimination charges must identify the particular employer practice being challenged and must show that protected status played *some role in their treatment*. For employers, this means that an individual's race, color, religion, sex, or national origin *must play no role* in their employment practices. The act allows people who have been targets of intentional discrimination based on sex, religion, or disability to receive both compensatory and punitive damages.

Executive Orders 11246, 11375, and 11478

Several important executive orders have been issued by the U.S. president that affect the employment practices of federal contractors and subcontractors. The OFCCP in the U.S. Department of Labor is responsible for overseeing federal contractor operations and ensuring that unlawful discrimination does not occur. Executive Orders 11246, 11375, and 11478 require federal contractors to take **affirmative action** to compensate for historical discrimination against women, minorities, and handicapped individuals. The concept of affirmative action is not without controversy. Supporters offer many reasons why affirmative action is important, while opponents argue firmly against it. Individuals can consider both sides in the debate and compare those positions with their personal views of affirmative action.

Many healthcare organizations receive federal monies for research or directly contract with the federal government to provide services. Consequently, these organizations must comply with the executive orders governing affirmative action.

Affirmative Action Program (AAP)

Federal contractors are required to develop and maintain a written **affirmative action program (AAP)** that outlines proactive steps the organization will take to attract and hire members of underrepresented groups. Figure 4-4 illustrates the components of an affirmative action plan. This data-driven program includes analysis of the composition of company's current workforce with a comparison to the availability of workers in the labor market. The overall objective of the AAP is to have the company's workforce demographics reflect as closely as possible the demographics in the labor market from which workers are recruited. The contents of an AAP and the

FIGURE 4-4 Components of an Affirmative Action Plan (AAP)

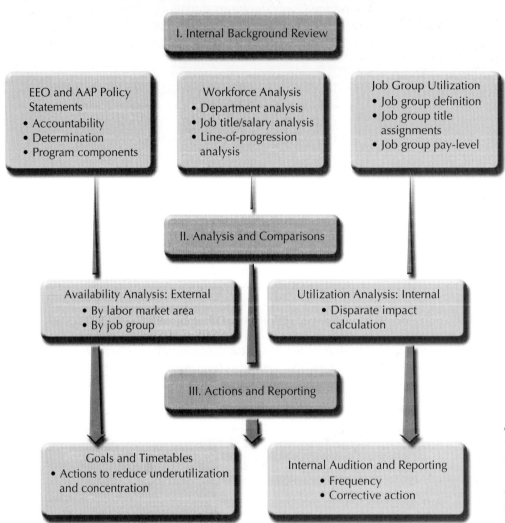

policies flowing from it must be available for review by managers and supervisors within the organization. The AAP is reviewed by the OFCCP and subject to periodic audits to ensure compliance. In addition to an extensive workforce analysis, the AAP includes goals, timetables, and good faith efforts to reduce and prevent employment discrimination against historically disadvantaged groups. Organizations implement outreach programs, targeted recruiting, and training programs to recruit and advance women and minorities. Affirmative action plans vary in length; some are long and require extensive staff time to prepare.

Managing Racial and Ethnic Discrimination Issues

The original purpose of the Civil Rights Act of 1964 was to address race discrimination in the United States. This concern continues to be important today, and employers must be aware of potential HR issues that are based on race, national origin, and citizenship to take appropriate actions.

Charges of racial discrimination continue to make up one-third of all complaints filed with the EEOC. Employment discrimination can occur in numerous ways, from refusal to hire someone because of his or her race/ethnicity to the questions asked in a selection interview. All employment inquiries and decisions should be based on job-related factors and not personal characteristics. Sometimes racial discrimination is very subtle. For example, some healthcare organizations have set artificially high educational requirements for supervisory positions, thus precluding talented workers, including women and minorities, without degrees from those promotional opportunities. Further, the use of employee referral programs can lead to a more homogenous workforce as employees are more likely to refer people of the same demographic background as themselves. One solution is to use *anonymous application procedures* in which names and other identifying characteristics of the applicants are deleted from candidate documents. Decision makers in the hiring process are presented only with credentials and job-relevant information. This procedure, while controversial, may level the playing field and reduce the possibility of bias in selection.[11]

Racial/Ethnic Harassment   Racial/ethnic harassment is such a concern that the EEOC has issued guidelines on it. It is recommended that employers adopt policies against harassment of any type, including ethnic jokes, vulgar epithets, racial slurs, and physical actions.

Sex/Gender Discrimination Laws and Regulations

The inclusion of sex as a basis for protected status in Title VII of the 1964 Civil Rights Act has led to additional areas of legal protection, and a number of laws and regulations now address discrimination based on sex or gender.

Pregnancy Discrimination

The Pregnancy Discrimination Act (PDA) of 1978 amended Title VII to require that employers treat maternity leave the same as other personal or medical leaves. Closely related to the PDA is the Family and Medical Leave Act (FMLA) of 1993, which requires that qualified individuals be given up to 12 weeks of unpaid family leave and also requires that those taking family leave be allowed to return to jobs. The FMLA applies to both men and women. Provisions of the Affordable Care Act (2010) allow for break time and a private place for nursing mothers to express breast milk for one year after the birth of a child.[12]

These laws are especially important in the healthcare industry in that approximately 75 percent of healthcare practitioners and related technical employees are female.[13] In the absence of these laws, many healthcare employers would probably provide similar protections for their female employees to support them and maintain their employment. However, these laws provide a framework by which HR policies and practices can be developed and followed.

Discrimination may occur because of employer perceptions of pregnancy affecting the employee's job performance and attendance, or from questions related to pregnancy or child-care plans asked during an employment interview. A Milwaukee medical-staffing company was fined for terminating a woman who had just given birth. The owner made offensive comments about her pregnancy and fired her when she took maternity leave. Discrimination can occur if a pregnant applicant is not hired or is transferred or terminated. Courts have generally ruled that the PDA requires employers to treat pregnant employees the same as nonpregnant employees with similar abilities or inabilities. Employers have a right to maintain performance standards and expectations of pregnant employees but should be cautious to use the same standards for nonpregnant employees and employees with other medical conditions. In *McFee v. Nursing Care Management of America* (2010), terminating a pregnant employee for excessive absenteeism was deemed lawful because the PDA does not require preferential treatment in such cases, but only similar treatment to employees with non-pregnancy-related disabilities.[14] A careful review of FMLA policy decisions is important to prevent discrimination claims under the PDA for attendance issues.

Fears about higher health insurance costs and possible birth defects caused by damage sustained during pregnancy lead some employers to reassign women from hazardous jobs to lower-paying, less hazardous jobs. Such reproductive and fetal protection policies have been ruled unlawful.[15]

Equal Pay and Pay Equity

The Equal Pay Act of 1963 requires employers to pay similar wage rates for similar work without regard to gender. A *common core of tasks* must be similar, but tasks performed only intermittently or infrequently do not make jobs different enough to justify significantly different wages. Differences in pay between men and women in the same jobs are permitted because of:

1. Differences in seniority
2. Differences in performance
3. Differences in quality and/or quantity of production
4. Factors other than sex, such as skill, effort, and working conditions

In response to a procedural issue in pursuit of a fair pay claim, Congress enacted the Lilly Ledbetter Fair Pay Act in 2009, which eliminates the statute of limitations for employees who file pay discrimination claims under the Equal Pay Act. Each paycheck is essentially considered a new act of discrimination. Lawmakers recognized that because pay information is often secret, it might take months or even years for an employee to discover the inequity. The successful plaintiff can recover up to two years of back pay.

Pay equity is the idea that pay for jobs requiring comparable levels of knowledge, skill, and ability should be similar, even if actual duties differ significantly. This theory has also been called *comparable worth* in earlier cases. Some state laws mandate pay equity for public-sector employees. However, U.S. federal courts generally have ruled that the existence of pay differences between the different jobs held by women and men is not sufficient to prove that illegal discrimination has occurred.

A major reason for the pay equity idea is the continuing gap between the earnings of women and men. In 1980, women on average earned 60 percent of what men earned. By 2010, their earnings had risen to 80 percent of the average man.[16] Several reasons have been given for this gender pay gap such as the fact that women take more time off during their childbearing years, which makes it difficult to remain even with their male counterparts. Persistent, widespread stereotypes, such as the notion that men are more productive than women, may unconsciously influence behavior and manager decisions, leading to lower merit pay.

The number of female physicians has grown rapidly over the last two decades, effectively representing 22 percent of the total number of physicians. However, with regard to pay, according to data published by the Medical Group Management Association (MGMA) in 2010, male physicians still outpaced female physicians in almost every reported specialty. In some cases, the salary difference was minor. In other cases, the discrepancy was substantial: male gastroenterologists earned $120,000 more a year than female gastroenterologists.[17]

Managing Sex/Gender Issues

The influx of women into the workforce has had major social, economic, and organizational consequences. The percentage of women in the total U.S. civilian workforce has increased dramatically since 1950, to almost 50 percent today and, as noted above, even higher in healthcare. During the last economic downturn, unemployed workers were more likely to be male because the industries hit hardest in the recession tended to employ more men—construction and manufacturing. Women, on the other hand, are primarily employed in management and professional occupations and less likely to be employed in operations, transportation, or construction occupations.[18]

The growth in the number of women in the workforce has led to more sex/gender issues related to jobs and careers. Since women bear children and traditionally have a primary role in raising children, issues of work–life balance can emerge, especially in healthcare occupations heavily populated with women, such as registered nurses and X-ray techs. Respect for employees' lives outside of the workplace can pay off in terms of attracting and retaining high-quality talent. Healthcare organizations can offer a range of options to help employees achieve satisfaction in both their work and personal lives. Glassdoor.com reports in its second annual list of the Top 25 Companies for Work–Life Balance that organizations on the list have many of the following features:

- Support from senior leadership
- Flexible hours
- Telecommuting options

- Compressed workweeks
- Family-friendly work environments
- Generous paid time off
- On-site cafeteria
- On-site fitness center

Healthcare employers have historically been creative in providing flexible hours and compressed workweeks. This is especially the case for individuals employed in hard-to-fill positions such as physical therapists.

Employees at different career stages and with different household structures may seek different elements to help balance work and family obligations. For example, single employees value flexible work arrangements but not a work–family culture, while parents value the work–family culture and supervisors' social support. Organizations considering implementing work–family balance programs have a wide range of choices and benefit most from customizing to their specific culture rather than adopting a one-size-fits-all approach.[19]

Glass Ceiling For years, women's groups have alleged that women in workplaces encounter a **glass ceiling**, which refers to discriminatory practices that have prevented women and other minority-status employees from advancing to executive-level jobs. Despite the fact that organizations with greater gender diversity enjoy better financial performance than those with less diversity, women still hold a small percentage of top leadership jobs in corporations. Only 41 of the Fortune 1000 companies are led by a female CEO. In organizations where diversity is seen as strategically important, a higher percentage of C-level executives are women.

Women have tended to advance to senior management in a limited number of support or staff areas, such as HR and corporate communications. The healthcare industry offers somewhat of a paradox in this regard, in that women have achieved gains in some important areas, yet remain behind in one significant area. Although women comprise 73 percent of medical and health services managers, only 18 percent of hospital CEOs are women.[20]

Limits that keep women from progressing only in certain fields have been referred to as "glass walls" or "glass elevators." These limitations are seen as being tied to organizational, cultural, and leadership issues.

Breaking the Glass A number of employers have recognized that breaking the glass, whether ceilings, walls, or elevators, is good business for both women and racial minorities. Some of the most common means used to "break the glass" are as follows:

- Establish formal mentoring programs for women and members of racial/ethnic minorities.
- Provide opportunities for career rotation into operations, marketing, and sales for individuals who have shown talent in accounting, HR, and other areas.

- Increase the memberships of top management and boards of directors to include women and individuals of color.

- Establish clear goals for retention and progression of women and minorities and hold managers accountable for achieving these goals.

- Allow for alternative work arrangements for employees, particularly those balancing work–family responsibilities.

SEXUAL HARASSMENT

Healthcare employers are consistently challenged to provide a workplace free from sexual harassment. The very nature of healthcare delivery and the occupational need to discuss the body and body functions lends itself to discussions among physicians, employees, and patients that sometimes blur the lines of appropriate speech and conduct.

Nearly 25 percent of women report having been harassed at work during their careers. This widespread problem is a form of sex discrimination under Title VII. The Equal Employment Opportunity Commission has issued guidelines designed to curtail sexual harassment. **Sexual harassment** is unwelcome verbal, visual, or physical conduct of a sexual nature that is severe and affects working conditions or creates a hostile work environment. Sexual harassment can occur between a boss and a subordinate, among coworkers, and when nonemployees have business contacts with employees. (See Figure 4-5.)

Most of the sexual harassment charges filed involve harassment of women by men. However, more than 10 percent of claims were filed by men claiming

FIGURE 4-5   Potential Sexual Harassers

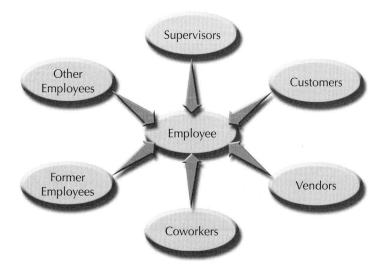

© 2016 Cengage Learning®

they were sexually harassed. Interestingly, women almost universally report that they were harassed by a male, while males report an equal percentage of male and female harassers. Most claims of harassment go unreported as victims are reluctant to speak out for fear of retribution. Supervisors are the most frequent harassers, but coworkers and even subordinates have also been involved in these incidents.[21]

Types of Sexual Harassment

Two basic types of sexual harassment have been defined by EEOC regulations and a number of court cases. Figure 4-6 shows the two types and how they differ. They are defined as follows:

1. **Quid pro quo** is harassment in which employment outcomes are linked to granting sexual favors.
2. **Hostile environment** harassment exists when an individual's work performance or psychological well-being is unreasonably affected by intimidating or offensive working conditions.

In quid pro quo harassment, an employee may be promised a promotion, a special raise, or a desirable work assignment, but only if the employee grants some sexual favors to the supervisor. Since supervisors are agents of the company, the company always bears liability for quid pro quo harassment.

The second type, hostile environment harassment, may include actions such as commenting on appearance or attire, telling jokes that are suggestive or sexual in nature, allowing revealing photos and posters to be displayed, or making continual requests to get together after work. These actions can lead to the creation of a hostile work environment. If the employer has taken appropriate steps to prevent sexual harassment, it may be possible to offer an affirmative defense and prevail in a lawsuit.

FIGURE 4-6   Types of Sexual Harassment

Quid pro quo Harassment	Hostile Environment Harassment
• Perpetrated by employee's superior	• Perpetrated by employee's superior, coworkers, and/or third parties
• Employment decisions hinge on whether an employee provides sexual favors	• Pervasive, unwanted sexual comments, pictures, jokes, and/or other derogatory events create a dysfunctional workplace
• Company is liable	• Company may be liable if it cannot offer an affirmative defense

© 2016 Cengage Learning®

Preventing Sexual Harassment

A proactive prevention approach is the most effective way to reduce sexual harassment in the workplace. If the workplace culture fosters harassment, and if policies and practices do not inhibit harassment, healthcare employers should reevaluate and solve the problem before lawsuits follow.

Healthcare organizations may avoid liability if they take reasonable care to prohibit sexual harassment, the so-called affirmative defense. Important elements of the affirmative defense include the following:

- Establish a sexual harassment policy.
- Communicate the policy regularly.
- Train employees and managers on avoiding sexual harassment.
- Investigate and take action when complaints are voiced.

Effective training to prevent sexual harassment ideally includes instruction for employees and supervisors on what constitutes sexual harassment and how to handle an incident. Role plays can be especially effective during the training, particularly when accompanied by timely feedback and opportunities for practice. Evaluating the effectiveness of the training is important to ensure that the training is transferred back to the workplace. Training HR staff in proper investigation techniques is also advised to ensure that a prompt, impartial review of all complaints occurs.[22]

DISABILITY DISCRIMINATION

Several federal laws have been enacted to advance the employment of disabled individuals and to reduce discrimination based on disability. These laws and regulations affect employment matters as well as public accessibility for individuals with disabilities. Despite these attempts to open the workplace to disabled individuals, unemployment among the disabled population has consistently exceeded the overall unemployment rate, particularly during economic downturns.[23]

Rehabilitation Act

The earliest law regarding disabled individuals was passed in 1973 and applied only to federal contractors. The Rehabilitation Act defined many of the terms and concepts incorporated into subsequent laws and provided for equal employment opportunity for disabled workers and applicants. The act went further and required that federal contractors take affirmative action to employ disabled workers. A section of the contractor's AAP is devoted to steps taken to promote the employment of disabled persons.[24]

Americans with Disabilities Act

Two decades after passage of the first law prohibiting discrimination against disabled individuals, the Americans with Disabilities Act (ADA) was enacted in 1990. This act applies to private employers, employment agencies, and labor unions with 15 or more employees and is enforced by the EEOC. State government employees are not covered by the ADA, which means that they cannot sue in federal courts for relief and damages. However, they may still bring suits under state laws in state courts. Many of the concepts and definitions included in the ADA were based on the Rehabilitation Act.

Amendments to the ADA

In 2009, Congress passed amendments to the ADA, which overruled several key cases and regulations and reflected the original intent of the ADA. The effect was to significantly broaden the definition of disabled individuals to include anyone with a physical or mental impairment that substantially limits one or more major life activities *without* regard for the ameliorative effects of mitigating measures such as medication, prosthetics, hearing aids, and so on. This establishes a very low threshold for establishing whether an individual is "disabled."

Who Is Disabled?   A three-pronged test is used to determine whether or not an individual meets the definition as "disabled." A person must meet one of the following three conditions as stated in the ADA and modified by the Americans with Disabilities Act Amendments Act (ADAAA):

1. He or she has a physical or mental impairment that substantially limits him or her in some major life activities.
2. He or she has a record of such an impairment.
3. He or she is regarded as having such an impairment.

   A person is considered disabled even if any corrective measures are used to reduce the impact of the disability, such as a wheelchair or medication. The only exception is ordinary eyeglasses or contact lenses. Major life activities include not just visible activities like seeing, breathing, and walking but internal bodily functions such as neurological, immune, endocrine, and normal cell growth. The definition of *disabled* no longer rests on the individual's inability to *do* something, but on his or her medical condition, whether or not it limits functioning. This expanded definition of *disabled* now encompasses a much larger percentage of workers, meaning that employers are likely to encounter situations that require action.

Mental Disabilities   A growing area of concern to employers under the ADAAA is individuals with mental disabilities. A mental disability is defined by the EEOC as "any mental or psychological disorder, such as an intellectual disability, organic brain syndrome, emotional or mental illness, and specific learning disabilities." Employers may find that accommodating for mental disabilities is more difficult and that maintaining effective performance standards is a challenge. In healthcare organizations, the assessment of whether an individual with a mental disability is able to perform a particular job, especially if it includes providing direct patient care, must be based on documented sound medical information. Assuming that someone with a disability is unable to perform patient care would be a violation of that individual's right under ADAAA.

More ADA complaints are being filed by individuals who have or claim to have mental disabilities. Two of the top seven disabilities most frequently cited in EEOC claims for disability discrimination are mental disabilities: depression, and anxiety disorder. The cases that have been filed have ranged from individuals with a medical history of paranoid schizophrenia or clinical depression to individuals who claim that job stress has affected their marriage or sex life. Regardless of the type of employees' claims, it is important to treat mental disabilities in the same way as physical disabilities. Obtain medical verification of worker limitations and engage in an interactive process to establish a reasonable accommodation.

Employees Who Develop Disabilities   For many employers, the impact of the ADA has been the greatest when handling employees who develop disabilities, not when dealing with applicants who already have disabilities. As the workforce ages, it is likely that more employees will develop disabilities. For instance, a medical assistant in a clinic who suffers a serious leg injury in a car accident away from work may request reasonable accommodation.

Employers should be prepared to respond to accommodation requests from employees whose contribution to the organization has been satisfactory before they became disabled and who now require accommodations to continue working. Handled inappropriately, these individuals are likely to file either ADA complaints with the EEOC or private lawsuits.

Employees sometimes can be shifted to other jobs where their disabilities do not affect them as much. For instance, a warehouse firm might transfer the injured stock worker to a purchasing inventory job inside so that climbing and lifting are unnecessary. But the problem for employers is what to do with the next worker who develops problems if an alternative job within the organization is not available. Even if the accommodations are just for one employee, the reactions of coworkers must be considered.

ADA and Job Requirements

Discrimination is prohibited against individuals with disabilities who can perform the **essential job functions**—the fundamental job duties—of the employment positions that those individuals hold or desire. These functions do not include marginal functions of the position. For example, an essential function for the job of hospital orderly is to transport patients. A marginal function of that job would be restocking crash carts. The EEOC provides guidelines to help employers determine which job functions are essential. Figure 4-7 lists the criteria recommended by the EEOC.

For a qualified person with a disability, an employer must make a **reasonable accommodation**, which is a modification to a job or work environment that gives that individual an equal employment opportunity to perform. EEOC guidelines encourage employers and individuals to work together to determine what the appropriate reasonable accommodations are, rather than employers alone making those judgments. Under the ADAAA, the focus has shifted from determining whether or not an individual is disabled to an emphasis on finding ways to

FIGURE 4-7 **Determining if a Job Function is Essential**

A Job Function May Be Considered Essential for Any of Several Reasons, Including but Not Limited to the Following:

1. The function may be essential because the reason the position exists is to perform that function.
2. The function may be essential because there is a limited number of employees available who can perform the job function.
3. The function may be highly specialized so that the job incumbent is hired for that expertise or ability to perform the particular function.

A Job Function May Be Considered Essential for Any of Several Reasons, Including but Not Limited to the Following:

1. The employer's judgment as to which functions are essential.
2. Written job descriptions prepared before advertising or interviewing applicants for the job.
3. The amount of time spent on the job performing the function.
4. The consequences of not requiring the incumbent to perform the function.
5. The terms of a collective bargaining agreement.
6. The work experience of past incumbents in the job.
7. The current work experience of incumbents in similar jobs.

Adapted from Part 1630 Regulations to Implement the Equal Employment Provisions of the Americans with Disabilities Act

accommodate that individual in the workplace. The process of determining a reasonable accommodation is expected to be interactive, with the disabled individual as an active participant in the process. Many options may be considered, but in the end the employer has the authority to select the accommodation to be implemented.

Reasonable accommodation is limited to actions that do not place an undue hardship on an employer. An **undue hardship** is a significant difficulty or expense imposed on an employer in making an accommodation for individuals with disabilities. The ADA offers only general guidelines in determining when an accommodation becomes unreasonable and will place undue hardship on an employer. The determination of undue hardship is made on a case-by-case basis. Undue hardship might stem from financial requirements to scheduling options or facilities modifications. What might be reasonable for a large hospital might be an undue hardship for a smaller dental office with fewer resources.

The key to making reasonable accommodations is identifying the essential job functions and then determining which accommodations are reasonable so that the individual can perform the core job duties. Architectural barriers should not prohibit disabled individuals' access to work areas or restrooms.

Appropriate work tasks must be assigned or modified to allow the individual to perform them effectively. This may mean modifying jobs or work area layouts or providing assistive devices or special equipment. Work hours and break schedules may be adjusted. Fortunately for employers, most accommodations needed are relatively inexpensive. Free assistance is readily available from the Job Accommodation Network's online resource center.[25]

Since most organizations are covered, employers under the ADA will likely have a plan in place before an accommodation is requested, which can save time and simplify the process.[26]

The following steps can facilitate this process:

- Define essential functions in advance.
- Handle all requests for accommodation properly.
- Work with the HR staff to explore various options for accommodation.
- Interact with the employee with good faith and documentation.
- Know and follow the reasonable accommodation rules.

ADA Restrictions and Medical Information   The ADA includes restrictions on obtaining and retaining medically related information on applicants and employees. Restrictions include prohibiting employers from rejecting individuals because of a disability and from asking job applicants any question about current or past medical history until a conditional job offer is made. Also, the ADA prohibits the use of preemployment medical exams, except for drug tests, until a job has been conditionally offered. An additional requirement of the ADA is that all medical information be maintained in files separated from the general personnel files. Medical files must be stored in a secure location, and only individuals with a "need to know" should be granted access to these files.

Claims of Disability Discrimination

During the decade prior to the enactment of the ADAAA, approximately 16,000 disability discrimination claims were filed with the EEOC each year. In 2010 and 2011, that number skyrocketed to more 25,000 claims per year, representing a 17 percent increase in the historical average. Experts attribute this increase to the changes made in the definition of "disabled" under the ADAAA. Prior to the ADAAA, employers won 90 percent of the challenges regarding whether or not an individual was qualified as "disabled." Now that argument is essentially moot and companies no longer aggressively work to disqualify the person from that status.

Claims of discrimination are more common at the lower levels of organizations. However, the CEO of a home furnishings retailer filed charges of disability discrimination claiming that the board of directors perceived her to be disabled based upon a recent diagnosis of breast cancer and terminated her employment. This example shows that *being regarded* as disabled qualifies an individual for protection under the law whether or not the person shows any outward impairment or requests an accommodation. This is an example of the second prong of the definition of "disabled individual" and sends a note of caution that treating someone as if he or she is disabled does in fact grant him or her coverage under the law. In fact, "regarded as" claims represent the highest percentage of claims filed in ADA charges.[27]

Genetic Bias Regulations

Related to medical disabilities is the emerging area of workplace genetic bias. As medical research has revealed the human genome, medical tests have been developed that can identify an individual's genetic markers for various diseases. Whether these tests should be used and how they are used can raise ethical issues.

Genetic Information Nondiscrimination Act Congress passed the Genetic Information Nondiscrimination Act (GINA) in 2009 to limit the use of genetic information by health insurance plans and to prohibit employment discrimination on the basis of this information. Employers are prohibited from collecting genetic information or making employment decisions on the basis of genetic information. "Genetic information" includes information about genetic tests of the employee or family members and family medical history. GINA allows exceptions for employees who wish to *voluntarily* participate in a wellness program and when employers need medical certification to determine eligibility for FMLA. Coordinating compliance policies for GINA, ADA, HIPAA, and leave policies can reduce confusion and liability.[28]

AGE DISCRIMINATION LAWS

The population of the United States is aging. On the one hand, this change means that as older workers with a lifetime of experiences and skills retire, healthcare organizations face significant challenges in replacing them with workers with the capabilities and work ethic that characterize the many mature workers in the United States. On the other hand, many older people will remain in the workforce beyond traditional retirement age because of longer life spans, improvements in health, and financial shortfalls in their savings portfolios, leading to a greater possibility of bias and discrimination.[29]

Age Discrimination in Employment Act

The Age Discrimination in Employment Act (ADEA) of 1967, amended in 1978 and 1986, prohibits discrimination in terms, conditions, or privileges of employment against all individuals of age 40 or older working for employers having 20 or more workers. However, state employees may not sue state government employers in federal courts because the ADEA is a federal law. Age discrimination charges consistently represent 20 to 25 percent of all discrimination charges filed with the EEOC.

Older Workers Benefit Protection Act

This law is an amendment to the ADEA and protects employees when they sign liability waivers for age discrimination in exchange for severance packages during reductions in force. Workers over the age of 40 are entitled to receive complete accurate information on the available benefits, a list of all workers impacted in the reduction, and several weeks to decide whether or not to accept severance benefits in exchange for a waiver to not sue the employer.[30] This act ensures that older workers are not compelled or pressured into waiving their rights under the ADEA. Procedures for laying off older workers require legal oversight and a strict protocol to ensure compliance.

Managing Age Discrimination

One issue that has led to age discrimination charges is labeling older workers as "overqualified" for jobs or promotions. In a number of cases, courts have ruled that the term *overqualified* may have been used as a code word for workers being too old, thus causing them not to be considered for employment. Also, selection and promotion practices must be "age neutral."

To counter significant staffing difficulties, some healthcare employers recruit older people to return to the workforce through the use of part-time and other attractive scheduling options. During the past decade, the number of older workers holding part-time jobs has increased. It is likely that the number of older workers interested in working part-time will continue to grow.

A strategy used by healthcare employers to retain the talents of older workers for a period of time is **phased retirement**, whereby employees gradually reduce their workloads and pay levels. This option is growing in use as a way to allow older workers with significant knowledge and experience to have more personal flexibility, while the organizations retain them for their valuable capabilities. As an example, an urgent care center rehired retired doctors to cover hard-to-fill weekend shifts. The retired doctors work only a few hours per week, make a good wage, and are still able to enjoy their retirement. This arrangement is a win-win for both the center and the doctors.

RELIGION AND SPIRITUALITY IN THE WORKPLACE

Title VII of the Civil Rights Act prohibits discrimination on the basis of religion. The increasing religious diversity in the workforce has put greater emphasis on religious considerations in workplaces. Faith-based schools and institutions can use religion as a BFOQ for employment practices on a limited scale. Also, employers must make reasonable accommodation efforts regarding an employee's religious beliefs unless they create an undue hardship for the employer.

Religious diversity in the United States is also reflected in the workplace. The wide range of beliefs and practices may evolve as immigrant populations bring with them not only cultural but also religious diversity to the nation and workplaces.

Religious discrimination can take many forms, from hostile remarks to refusal to hire individuals from different faiths. Problems can also arise because of conflicts between employer policies and employee religious practices such as dress and appearance. Some religions have standards about appropriate attire for women or shaving or hair length for men. Generally, employers are encouraged to make exceptions to dress code policies unless public image is so critical that it represents a business necessity. Deferring to customer preferences in making these determinations is risky and may lead to charges of unlawful discrimination. Healthcare employers are on firmer ground when worker safety is involved and the employer refuses to modify its dress or appearance policies.

Managing Religious Diversity

The EEOC recommends that employers consider the following reasonable accommodations for employees' religious beliefs and practices:

- Scheduling changes, voluntary substitutes, and shift swaps
- Changing an employee's job tasks or providing a lateral transfer
- Making an exception to dress and grooming rules
- Accommodations relating to payment of union dues or agency fees
- Accommodating prayer, proselytizing, and other forms of religious expression

Another issue concerns religious expression. In the last several years, employees in several cases have sued employers for prohibiting them from expressing their religious beliefs at work. In other cases, employers have had to take action because of the complaints by workers that employees were aggressively "pushing" their religious views at work, thus creating a "hostile environment."

MANAGING OTHER DISCRIMINATION ISSUES

A number of other factors, such as national origin/immigration, language, military status, and appearance and weight, might lead to unlawful discrimination. In addition to the Title VII protections, a number of federal laws have been enacted to address these forms of discrimination. Many of these laws were passed in response to improper decisions by companies that resulted in unfair treatment of applicants or employees.

Immigration Reform and Control Acts

The United States is home to 40 million foreign-born residents, primarily from Latin America and Asia. This number includes people living in the United States both legally and illegally. Modern-day immigrants are blending in as rapidly as those from previous generations.[31] The influx of immigrants has led to extensive political, social, and employment-related debates. The Immigration Reform and Control Act (IRCA), enacted in 1986, requires employers to verify the employment status of all employees, while not discriminating because of national origin or ethnic background. Employers may not knowingly hire unauthorized aliens for employment in the United States.

Regardless of company size, every employer must comply with the provisions of the act. High-profile Immigration and Customs Enforcement (ICE) raids on employers since January 2009 have led to audits of 7,500 employers and imposition of $100 million in penalties.[32] Employers ignore these obligations at their own peril. Within the first three days of employment, each employee must complete an Employment Eligibility Verification (commonly called an I-9) form and provide documents proving that they are legally authorized to work in the United States.

The E-verify federal database instantly verifies the employment eligibility of employees. Federal contractors are required to use the system as are employers in a number of states where it has been mandated. Other employers may use the system to check and verify employees' legal status.[33]

Visa Requirements   Various revisions to the IRCA changed some of the restrictions on the entry of immigrants to work in U.S. organizations, particularly organizations with high-technology and other "scarce skill" areas. More immigrants with specific skills have been allowed legal entry, and categories for entry visas were revised. Among the most common visas encountered by employers are the B1 for business visitors, H-1B for professional or specialized workers, and L-1 for intracompany transfers. Academic medical centers and other medical research organizations are significant employers of immigrant workers with scarce skills. Foreign-trained medical doctors, PhD scientists, and other skilled healthcare workers are frequently sponsored by these organizations to work in the United States.

Military Status Protections

The employment rights of military veterans and reservists have been addressed in several laws. The two most important laws are the Vietnam Era Veterans Readjustment Assistance Act of 1974 and the Uniformed Services Employment and Reemployment Rights Act (USERRA) of 1994. Under the latter, employees are required to notify their employers of military service obligations. Employers must give employees serving in the military leave-of-absence protections under USERRA.

With the use of reserves and National Guard troops abroad, the provisions of USERRA have had more impact on employers. This act does not require employers to pay employees while they are on military leave, but many firms voluntarily provide additional compensation to bridge the gap between military pay and regular pay. Uniformed military personnel are provided up to five years of active-duty service leave during which the employer must hold their job. Requirements regarding benefits, disabilities, and reemployment are covered in the act as well.

EEOC Investigation Process

When a discrimination complaint is received by the EEOC or a similar agency, it must be processed. To handle the growing number of complaints, the EEOC has instituted a system that categorizes complaints into three categories: *priority, needing further investigation,* and *immediate dismissal.* If the EEOC decides to pursue a complaint, it uses the process outlined here. In certain cases where a complaint is filed with both the EEOC and the state civil rights agency, the EEOC may request the state agency to investigate first. However, regardless of the state agency's findings, the EEOC may continue its involvement in the investigation.

Compliance Investigative Stages   In a typical situation, an EEO complaint goes through several stages before the compliance process is completed. First, the charges are filed by an individual, a group of individuals, or their representative. A charge must be filed within 180 days of when the alleged discriminatory action occurred. Then the EEOC staff reviews the specifics of the charge to determine if it has *jurisdiction,* which means that the agency is authorized to investigate that type of charge. If jurisdiction exists, a notice of the charge must be served on the employer within 10 days after the filing; the employer is asked to respond. Following the charge notification, the EEOC's major effort turns to investigating the complaint.

During the investigation, the EEOC may interview the complainant(s), other employees, company managers, and supervisors. Also, it can request additional records and documents from the employer. Assuming that sufficient cause is found that alleged discrimination occurred, the next stage involves mediation efforts by the agency and the employer. **Mediation** is a dispute resolution process in which a trained mediator assists the parties in reaching a negotiated settlement. The EEOC has found that use of mediation has reduced its backlog of EEO complaints and has resulted in faster resolution of complaints.

If the employer agrees that discrimination has occurred and accepts the proposed settlement, then the employer posts a notice of relief within the company and takes the agreed-on actions. If the employer objects to the charge and rejects conciliation, the EEOC can file suit or issue a **right-to-sue letter** to the complainant. The letter notifies the complainant that he or she has 90 days in which to file a personal suit in federal court.

In the court litigation stage, a legal trial takes place in the appropriate state or federal court. At that point, both sides retain lawyers and rely on the court to render a decision. The Civil Rights Act of 1991 provides for *jury trials* in most EEO cases. If either party disagrees with the court ruling, either can file appeals with a higher court. The U.S. Supreme Court becomes the ultimate adjudication body.

Employer Responses to EEO Complaints

The general steps in responding effectively to an EEO complaint are outlined in Figure 4-8 and are crucial for effective HR management. Employers who vigorously investigate their employees' discrimination complaints before they are taken to outside agencies can control many problems and expenses associated with EEO complaints. An internal employee complaint system and prompt, thorough responses to problem situations are essential tools in reducing EEO charges and in remedying illegal discriminatory actions.

FIGURE 4-8   Stages in Responding to EEO Complaints

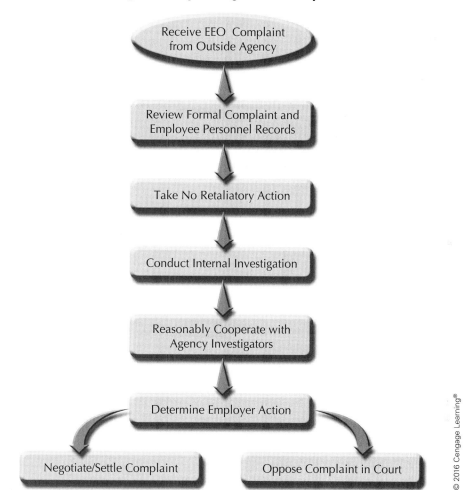

© 2016 Cengage Learning®

DIVERSITY AND CULTURAL COMPETENCE TRAINING

Traditional diversity training has a number of different goals. One prevalent goal is to minimize discrimination and harassment lawsuits. Other goals focus on improving acceptance and understanding of people with different backgrounds, experiences, capabilities, and lifestyles. Employees are encouraged to recognize, evaluate, and appreciate differences. In healthcare organizations, the focus of diversity training and awareness has been on a concept referred to as **cultural competence**.

ETHICS AND THE LAW

For HR professionals, there are ethical ways in which they should act relative to a given HR issue. However, determining ethical actions is not always easy. Just complying with the laws does not guarantee ethical behavior. Business ethicists argue that laws and ethics intersect, as depicted, but are not the same.

Dealing with discrimination in the healthcare workplace is clearly not just a legal issue. Healthcare employers can make legally correct decisions relative to employment promotion, pay increases, or other employment actions and yet violate ethical standards.

Although many large medical centers and university-based health organizations that receive federal funding must have an AAP and commit to pursuing affirmative action in attracting and recruiting qualified minority applicants, it is difficult to determine true compliance with that requirement. Organizations can merely go through the motions of affirmative action and focus on the documentation aspects of an AAP to prepare for OFCCP audits, or they can truly be very aggressive in efforts that produce results, whereby the numbers of protected group members are significantly increased.

Laws and regulations cannot cover every situation that HR professionals will face. Instead, healthcare HR professionals must also be guided by values and personal behavior codes of conduct that represent fairness and equal treatment.

Cultural competence is a set of congruent behaviors, attitudes, and policies that come together in a system, in an agency, or among professionals that enables effective work in cross-cultural situations. "Culture" refers to patterns of behavior that include the language, communications, customs, beliefs, values, and institutions of racial, ethnic, religious, or social groups. "Competence" implies having the capacity to function effectively as an individual and an organization within the context of the cultural beliefs, behaviors, and needs presented by the patient. Cultural competence is one of the main ingredients in closing the disparities gap in health care. It is the way patients and doctors can come together and talk about health concerns without cultural differences hindering the conversation, but instead enhancing it. Quite simply, healthcare services that are respectful of and responsive to the health beliefs, practices, and cultural and linguistic needs of diverse patients can help bring about positive health outcomes.

Culture and language may influence:

- Health, healing, and wellness belief systems
- How illness, disease, and their causes are perceived, by both by the patient/consumer and healthcare providers

- The behaviors of patients/consumers who are seeking healthcare and their attitudes toward healthcare providers
- The delivery of services by the provider, who looks at the world through his or her own limited set of values, which can compromise access for patients from other cultures

The increasing population growth of racial and ethnic communities and linguistic groups, each with its own cultural traits and health profiles, presents a challenge to the healthcare delivery service industry in this country. The provider and the patient each bring their individual learned patterns of language and culture to the healthcare experience, which must be transcended to achieve equal access and quality healthcare.[34]

Through *cultural competence* training, healthcare organizations hope to build greater understanding of the differences among people. This type of training helps all participants to see and accept the differences in people with widely varying cultural backgrounds.

CASE

Marshall Ambulatory Surgery Center (MASC) has historically had a strong culture of patient care excellence and employee commitment. Two surgeons from the community started MASC 20 years ago and have continued to own and operate the center since then. A few weeks ago they brought in another surgeon as a partner. The new surgeon, although outstanding from a technical perspective, is not especially concerned about his bedside manner with patients or with encouraging employee engagement and commitment. In fact, he has already received numerous patient complaints about his communication style, and the nursing staff is growing weary of his rude and aggressive approach to them.

Things have recently escalated with regard to the new surgeon's approach with the nursing staff. During a routine case, a patient developed an unanticipated bleed, and the surgeon became very annoyed and began shouting at the scrub nurse and throwing instruments. The bleeding was eventually stopped and the surgery was successfully completed. Once the patient was stable and moved to the recovery room, the scrub nurse left the OR and went directly to the nursing supervisor to file a complaint against the surgeon based on his actions during the surgery. The nursing supervisor, upon hearing about the events that just occurred, defended the surgeon and informed the nurse that she was overreacting and basically refused to take the complaint further. The scrub nurse was shocked by her supervisor's response, and as she completed her shift, she contemplated whether she would continue to work for MASC and whether she should contact an attorney to discuss her rights in this situation.

Questions

1. What type of claim could the scrub nurse bring against MASC and the surgeon?
2. How should have the nursing supervisor responded to the scrub nurse?

END NOTES

1. Enjoli Francis, "$168 Million Awarded in California Sex Harassment Suit," ABC News (March 2, 2012).
2. Christopher Duke, "Avoiding Legal Liability for Employee Discrimination Claims," HRfocus Special Report: Workplace Investigations (January 2013).
3. "Office of Federal Contract Compliance Programs: Facts on Executive Order 11246—Affirmative Action" (January 2002), *http://www.dol.gov/ofccp/regs/compliance/aa.htm.*
4. Kevin McGowan, "Retaliation Charges Were Most Common in Record-Breaking FY 2011, BNA Bulletin to Management" (January 31, 2012), *http://www.bna.com/retaliation-charges-common.*
5. Tom Starner, "Bias Claims on the Rise," *Human Resource Executive* (January/February, 2011), 145; Andrew McIlvaine, "It's Pay-Up Time for the EEOC," *Human Resource Executive* (October 16, 2011), 10.
6. *Breiner v. Nevada Dept. of Corrections*, No. 09-15568 (E.D. Nev., July 8, 2010).
7. *Griggs v. Duke Power Co.*, 401 U.S. 424 (1971).
8. *Dunlap v. Tennessee Valley Authority*, No. 07-5381 (E.D. Tenn., March 28, 2008); *Rowe v. Cleveland Pneumatic Co.*, 690 F.2d 88 (1982).
9. Jamie Prenkert, "Handle with Care: Avoiding and Managing Retaliation Claims," *Business Horizons* (May 2012), 1.
10. "U.S. Equal Employment Opportunity Commission: Title I—Federal Civil Rights Remedies, Damages in Cases of International Discrimination" (2012), *http://www.eeoc.gov/laws/statutes/cra-1991.cfm.*
11. Olaf Aslund and Oskar Nordstrom Skans, "Do Anonymous Job Application Procedures Level the Playing Field?," *Industrial and Labor Relations Review* 65 (2012), 82–107.
12. "U.S. Department of Labor, WHD: Break Time for Nursing Mothers" (2010), *http://www.dol.gov/whd/nursingmothers.*
13. *http://www.bls.gov/cps/cpsaat11.pdf.*
14. Mary-Kathryn Zachary, "Pregnancy Discrimination–Avoiding and Defending Lawsuits," *Supervision* (August 2010), 23–26; Kjersten Whittington, "Mothers of Invention: Gender, Motherhood, and New Dimensions of Productivity in the Science Profession," *Work and Occupations* (August 2011), 417–456; "Milwaukee Company Pays for Firing New Mother," Associated Press (March 3, 2012); *McFee v. Nursing Care Management of America*, No. 2009-0756 (E.D. Ohio, June 22, 2010).
15. *UAW v. Johnson Controls, Inc.*, 499 US 187 (1991); Mark Valarie, "The Flip Side of Fetal Protection Policies: Compensating Children Injured through Parental Exposure to Reproductive Hazards in the Workplace," *Golden Gate University Law Review*, vol. 22 (1992), *http://digitalcommons.law.ggu.edu/ggulrev/vol22/iss3/4.*
16. C. J. Weinberger and P. J. Kuhn, "Changing Levels or Changing Slopes? The Narrowing of the Gender Earnings Gap 1959–1999," *Industrial and Labor Relations Review* 63 (2010), 384–406; A. Manning and F. Saidi, "Understanding the Gender Pay Gap: What's Competition Got to Do with It?," *Industrial and Labor Relations Review* 63 (2010), 681–698; Stephen Benard, "Why His Merit Raise Is Bigger than Hers," *Harvard Business Review* (April 2012).
17. Rachel Fields, "Male Physicians Still Out-Earn Female Physicians in Almost Every Specialty," *Becker's Hospital Review* (March 31, 2011), *http://www.beckershospitalreview.com/compensation-issues.*
18. "U.S. Department of Labor: Women in the Labor Force in 2010" (2011), *http://www.dol.gov/wb/factsheets/Qf-laborforce-10.htm.*
19. Jacquelyn Smith, "The Top 25 Companies for Work–Life Balance," *Forbes* (August 10, 2012); Colette Darcy, Alma McCarthy, Jimmy Hill, and Geraldine Grady, "Work–Life Balance: One Size Fits All? An Exploratory Analysis of the Differential Effects of Career Stage," *European Management Journal* (April 2012), 111–120; Jing Wang and

Anil Verma, "Explaining Organizational Responsiveness to Work–Life Balance Issues: The Role of Business Strategy and High-Performance Work Systems," *Human Resource Management* (May/June 2012), 407–432; Lieke ten Brummelhuis and Tanja van der Lippe, "Effective Work–Life Balance Support for Various Household Structures," *Human Resource Management* (March/April 2010), 173–193.

20. Molly Gamble, "Women Make Up 73% of Healthcare Managers but Only 18% of Hospital CEOs" (July 27, 2012), *http://www.beckershospitalreview.com/ hospital-management-administration.*

21. Scott Clement, "Quarter of Women Report Being Harassed in Workplace," *Denver Post* (November 17, 2011), 8A; "Sexual Harassment Statistics in the Workplace" (2012), *http://www.sexualharassmentlaw-firms .com/Sexual-Harassment-statis-tics.cfm.*

22. "Model Discrimination and Harassment Policy," Ceridian Abstracts, 1–3, *http:// www.hrcompliance.ceridian.com*; Elissa Perry, Carol Kulik, and Marina Field, "Sexual Harassment Training: Recommendations to Address Gaps between the Practitioner and Research Literatures," *Human Re-source Management* 48 (September/October 2009), 817–837; Christina Stoneburner, "Want an Easy and Cost-Effective Defense to Employment Discrimination Claims? Provide Harassment Training for Your Employees," *Employee Benefit News* (November 22, 2011).

23. H. Stephen Kaye, "The Impact of the 2007–09 Recession on Workers with Disabilities," *Monthly Labor Review* (October 2010), 19–34.

24. "Fact Sheet: Your Rights Under Section 504 of the Rehabilitation Act," *Department of Health and Human Services* (June 2006).

25. Job Accommodation Network, *http:// askjan.org.*

26. Matthew Brodsky, "Disability Flexibility," *Human Resource Executive Online* (September 2, 2011); Jonathan Segal, "ADA Game Changer," *HR Magazine* (June 2010), 121–126.

27. Jared Shelly, "Discrimination Deluge," *Human Resource Executive Online* (April 1, 2011); Jared Shelly, "Disability Discrimina-tion Rises," *Human Resource Executive Online* (February 24, 2011); Joann Lublin and Saabira Chaudhur, "Ex-CEO Says Cancer Led to Her Ouster," *Wall Street Journal* (August 4/5, 2012).

28. Allen Smith, "Coordinate GINA Compliance with Leave, ADA, and HIPAA Policies" (June 30, 2008), *http://www. shrm.org/legalissues*; Susan Hauser, "Sin-cerely Yours, GINA," *Workforce Management* (July 2011), 16–22.

29. MitraToossi, "Labor Force Projections to 2018: Older Workers Staying More Active," *Monthly Labor Review* (November 2009), 30–51; Peter Cappelli and Bill Novelli, *Managing the Older Worker: How to Prepare for the New Organizational Order* (Boston, MA: Harvard Business Press, 2010).

30. Richard Posthuma and Michael Campion, "Age Stereotypes in the Workplace: Common Stereotypes, Moderators, and Future Research Directions," *Journal of Management* (February 2009), 158–188.

31. Miriam Jordan, "Immigrants Are Still Fitting in," *Wall Street Journal* (November 14, 2011), A5.

32. Miriam Jordan, "Fresh Raids Target Illegal Hiring," *Wall Street Journal* (May 3, 2012), A2; Miriam Jordan, "Chipotle Faces Inquiry on Hiring," *Wall Street Journal* (May 23, 2012), B3.

33. "U.S. Citizenship and Immigration Services" (2012), *http://www.uscis.gov/ portal/site/uscis*; D. Savino, "Immigration Policies and Regulations Continue to Create Uncertainty for Both Employers and Employees," *Employment Relations Today* (Fall 2009), 57–68.

34. *http://minorityhealth.hhs.gov/templates/ browse.aspx?lvl=2&lvlID=11.*

5 JOB DESIGN AND ANALYSIS

Learning Objectives

After you have read this chapter, you should be able to:

- Explain the relationship between performance and job design.

- Describe the importance and typical uses of job analysis.

- List the common methods of job analysis.

- Identify the stages of the job analysis process.

- Define the elements of job descriptions and job specifications.

- Explain the relationship of Joint Commission on Accreditation of Healthcare Organizations (JCAHO) standards to job descriptions.

HEALTHCARE HR INSIGHTS

Perhaps one of the most significant changes to the nature and design of healthcare positions over the last half century has been the introduction of electronic medical records (EMRs) or electronic health records (EHRs) in healthcare organizations. Although EHRs have been utilized for many years, the adoption and meaningful use of EHR systems was catalyzed by the federal EHR incentive payment program under the American Recovery and Reinvestment Act launched in 2011 and continuing at a rapid pace.[1] For those healthcare organizations who have adopted EHR systems—including hospitals, medical centers, long-term and residential care centers, and physician offices and clinics—the impact on jobs is significant.

The basic concept of an EHR is to allow the provider (physician, nurse, therapist, etc.) the ability to capture data at the point of care electronically. The implications for the improvement of patient care through the more effective capture, study, and sharing of data are immense.[2] Similarly, the implications for healthcare jobs are far reaching. Examples include:

- A medical center employed more than 50 individuals in its medical records department. The medical records clerks were responsible for maintaining thousands of paper files and charts for patient records. The duties of the job were very manual—pulling files, sorting, lifting, and delivering. As the medical center adopted an EHR system and slowly transitioned away from the paper file, the medical center required fewer medical records clerks and needed to retrain or hire electronic health records technicians with an entirely different skill set.

- When a large specialty group physician practice with 50 physicians adopted a new EHR system, many of the physicians were reluctant to utilize a computer terminal during the time they were spending with their patients. Consequently, the practice hired "scribes" to be present in the treatment room as the physician and patient were interacting to enter data into the EHR.

- Prior to implementing an EHR system, a 60-bed long-term care facility, recognizing that many of its employees were not very "computer literate," provided free computer training courses to its staff. The management of the long-term care facility was concerned that the success of the EHR system implementation would be at risk if the employees were not comfortable with, let alone knowledgeable about, interacting with a computer.

These are just a few examples of the dramatic changes occurring in healthcare today due to the introduction of new technology. As new technology is utilized, healthcare managers and HR professionals must redesign jobs, identifying different work flows and worker competencies. These redesign initiatives require comprehensive job analysis in order to understand the work—the inter- and intradepartmental interactions and communications, the outcomes, and other key aspects of employment.

In addition to the introduction of new technologies, both employees and jobs in healthcare organizations are rapidly changing due to (1) the service delivery expectations of the consumers of healthcare and (2) the pressures to contain costs.[3] Two parts of dealing with those changes are job design and job analysis. Job design is logically arranging tasks and duties in a job to best get work done. A snapshot of what people are doing in their jobs currently is developed through formal job analysis, which aids in the development of job descriptions and job specifications. In addition, the information that comes from job analysis is the foundation for recruitment, selection, training, compensation, and many other HR activities.

ACCOMPLISHING STRATEGIC OBJECTIVES THROUGH JOB DESIGN

Analyzing what employees actually do in their jobs is vital to accomplishing the strategic objectives of healthcare organizations. Job design is depicted in Figure 5-1.

As organizational objectives are planned and implemented, individual departments or functional areas are required to establish objectives that contribute to the accomplishment of the broader organizational objectives. These departmental objectives directly affect job design because the process ultimately outlines the duties and responsibilities that are required to accomplish the departmental objectives. As noted in the Healthcare HR Insight discussion of the impact EHR systems, clearly the decision to adopt this type of system was an organizational aim that impacts on the objectives of many departments and is ultimately implemented through the new or revised job designs of the healthcare workers.

FIGURE 5-1   The Importance of Job Design

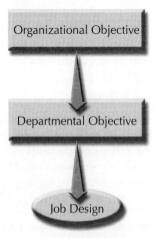

Productivity and Job Design

Job design refers to organizing tasks, duties, and responsibilities into a productive unit of work. It involves job content and the effect of jobs on employees. Identifying the components of a given job is an integral part of job design.

Job design can influence *performance* in many jobs, especially those where employee motivation can make a substantial difference. In healthcare organizations, job design can play an important role in the retention of key clinical employees. As an example, in an effort to improve the retention of physical therapists (PTs), a rehabilitation center eliminated much of the administrative duties from the PT job description, allowing the PTs to spend more time on direct patient care, which is more satisfying work.

Job design changes such as this can also affect *job satisfaction.* Jobs designed to take advantage of important job characteristics are more likely to be positively received by employees. Such characteristics help distinguish between "good" and "bad" jobs. Many approaches to enhancing productivity and quality reflect efforts to expand some of the basic job characteristics.

Person–Job Fit   As depicted in Figure 5-2, person-job fit is a key concept in job analysis. Not everyone would enjoy being an HR manager, an engineer, a nurse, or a receptionist. But some people like and do well at each of these jobs. The **person–job fit** is a simple but important concept of matching characteristics of people with characteristics of jobs.[4]

If a person does not fit a job, theoretically either the person can be changed or replaced or the job can be redesigned. However, though an employer can try to make a "round" person fit a "square" job, it is hard to successfully reshape people. If it is possible to redesign a job, the person–job fit may sometimes be improved more easily.[5] For example, surgery schedulers talk to people all day primarily by phone; an individual who would rather not talk to others may perform better in a position that does not require so much interaction because that part of the surgery scheduler job cannot be changed.

NATURE OF JOB ANALYSIS IN HEALTHCARE ORGANIZATIONS

The most basic building block of HR management, **job analysis**, is a systematic way to gather and analyze information about the content and human requirements of jobs and the context in which jobs are performed. Job analysis involves collecting information on the characteristics of a job that differentiate it from other jobs. Information that can be helpful in making that distinction includes the following:

- Work activities and behaviors
- Interactions with others
- Performance standards
- Financial and budgeting impact
- Equipment and technology used
- Working conditions
- Supervision given and received
- Necessary knowledge, skills, and abilities

FIGURE 5-2   Person-Job Fit

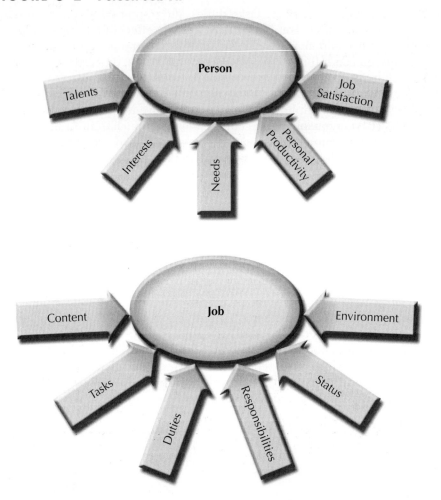

Although the terms *job* and *position* are often used interchangeably, there is a slight difference in emphasis. A **job** is a grouping of common tasks, duties, and responsibilities. A **position** is a job performed by one person. Thus, if there are two people operating sterilization equipment, there are two positions (one for each person) but just one job (sterilization technician).

Task-Based Job Analysis

Job analysis based on what is done on the job focuses on the tasks, duties, and responsibilities performed. A **task** is a distinct, identifiable work activity comprised of motions, whereas a **duty** is a larger work segment comprised of several tasks that are performed by an individual. Since both tasks and duties describe activities, it is not always easy or necessary to distinguish between the two. For example, if one of the employment supervisor's duties is to interview applicants, one task associated with that duty would be asking questions. The **job responsibilities** are obligations to perform certain tasks and duties.

Competency-Based Job Analysis

The **competency approach** to job analysis focuses on the competencies that individuals need to perform jobs rather than focusing on the tasks, duties, and responsibilities that comprise a job. **Competencies** are basic characteristics that can be linked to enhanced performance by individuals or teams. Specific types of competencies include:

- Skill
- Knowledge
- Ability
- Training
- Education
- Licensure, certification, and/or registration

The competency approach also attempts to identify the hidden factors that are often critical to superior performance. For instance, many supervisors talk about employees' attitudes, but they have difficulty identifying what they mean by *attitude*. The competency approach uses some methodologies to help supervisors identify examples of what they mean by appropriate attitude and how those factors affect performance. Examples of common competencies often include the following:

- *General or Generic Competencies*—Characteristics required across all jobs in the organization, such as decision making and problem solving, professionalism and accountability, and customer service
- *Departmental Competencies*—Skills needed to provide care, treatment, or services within a department or unit and that apply to all employees in that department or unit; for example, providing care to residents with dementia on a unit in a skilled nursing home
- *Job-Specific Competencies*—Competencies related to specific tasks, such as performing a specific procedure, and using particular equipment or technology
- *Cultural Competencies*—A set of attitudes, skills, and behaviors that allow an individual to work respectfully and effectively with patients and colleagues in a culturally diverse work environment[6]

As an example of the above, the Institute of Medicine (IOM) outlined five core competencies for healthcare professionals critical to providing high-quality, safe care:

- Working as part of interprofessional teams
- Delivering patient-centered care
- Practicing evidenced-based medicine
- Focusing on quality improvements
- Using information technology[7]

Joint Commission Standards and Job Analysis

The JCAHO recognizes the importance of job design and job analysis in the development of staffing plans and organizational competence systems. Development of employees focuses on enhancing all their needed competencies, rather than preparing them for moving to specific jobs. In this way, they can develop capabilities useful in their jobs as changes occur.

Healthcare organizations that subscribe to the JCAHO standards and review process must establish staffing plans and a competency system. Both staffing plans and a competency system require significant attention to job design and analysis.

The **HR** and **leadership standards** relating to HR planning require the leaders of healthcare organizations to analyze their staffing needs and provide the appropriate types and sufficient number of staff to meet care needs. The HR and leadership standards relating to the establishment of a competency system expect the leaders of an organization to develop and maintain a system that ensures the following:

- Recruitment, employment, and retention of competent healthcare workers
- Ongoing assessment of staff competency
- Ability of the organization to maintain and increase staff knowledge in the performance of their jobs

The foundation for these HR and leadership standards is job design and analysis. Job analysis—discovering how people's jobs are being done—is a critical element of maintaining staff competence, which is done by defining job qualifications, competencies, and performance expectations.

USES OF JOB ANALYSIS

Healthcare HR managers use job analysis as the foundation for a number of HR activities. Job analysis provides an objective basis for hiring, evaluating, training, supervising, and accommodating persons with disabilities, as well as improving the efficiency of the organization. Job analysis or work analysis has grown in importance as the healthcare workforce and jobs have changed.[8]

In some healthcare organizations, job analysis is sometime seen as needless bureaucracy, requiring too much time and effort for the value received. However, failing to do effective and accurate job analysis can negatively impact the HR activities noted above. For instance, not understanding the key requirements and competencies necessary to perform a job can lead to hiring an individual with the wrong skill set or improper training. In addition, effective job analysis, which produces accurate job descriptions, can positively impact employee satisfaction.[9]

It is a logical process to determine the following:

- *Purpose*—The reason for the job
- *Essential Functions*—The job duties that are critical or fundamental to the performance of the job

- *Job Setting*—The work station and conditions where the essential functions are performed
- *Job Qualifications*—The minimal skills an individual must possess to perform the essential functions

The process of analyzing jobs in healthcare organizations requires planning of several factors. As Figure 5-3 indicates, some of these considerations include the analysis of how it is to be done, who provides data, and who conducts the analysis and uses the data so that job descriptions and job specifications can be prepared and reviewed. Once those decisions are made, then several results are linked to a wide range of HR activities. The most fundamental use of job analysis is to provide the information necessary to develop job descriptions and specifications.

FIGURE 5-3   Decisions in the Job Analysis Process

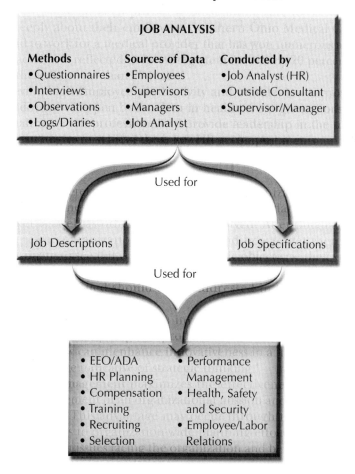

© 2016 Cengage Learning®

In most cases, the job description and job specifications are combined into one document that contains several different sections. A brief overview of each follows next; a more detailed discussion appears later in this chapter.

A **job description** is a document that indicates the tasks, duties, and responsibilities of a job. It identifies what is done, why it is done, where it is done, and—briefly—how it is done.

Performance standards usually flow directly from a job description, telling what the job accomplishes and how performance is measured in key areas of the job description. If employees know what is expected and how performance is to be measured, they have a much better chance of performing satisfactorily.

While the job description describes activities to be done in the job, the **job specification** lists the knowledge, skills, and abilities (KSAs) an individual needs to perform a job satisfactorily. KSAs include education, experience, work skill requirements, personal abilities, and mental and physical requirements. It is important to note that an accurate job specification identifies what KSAs a person needs to do the job, not necessarily what qualifications the current employee possesses.

Job Families, Departments, and Organization Charts

Once all jobs in the organization have been identified, it is often helpful to group the jobs into job families and display them on an organization chart. There are various ways of identifying and grouping job families. A **job family** is a grouping of jobs with similar characteristics. In identifying job families, significant emphasis is placed on measuring the similarity of jobs. A **department** depicts a distinct grouping of organizational responsibilities.

An **organization chart** depicts the relationships among jobs in an organization. Organization charts have traditionally been hierarchical and have shown the reporting relationships for authority and responsibilities. In most organizations, these charts can help clarify who reports to whom.

Job Analysis and HR Activities

The completion of job descriptions and job specifications, based on job analysis, is at the heart of many other HR activities, as Figure 5-4 indicates. But even if legal requirements did not force employers to do job analysis, effective HR management would demand it.

HR Planning   HR planning requires auditing of current jobs. Current job descriptions provide the basic details necessary for this internal assessment, including such items as the jobs available, current number of jobs and positions, and reporting relationships of the jobs/positions. By identifying the functions currently being performed and calculating the time being spent to perform them, managers and HR specialists can redesign jobs to eliminate unnecessary tasks and combine responsibilities where desirable.[10]

FIGURE 5-4   Job Analysis and Other HR Activities

© 2016 Cengage Learning®

Recruiting and Selection   Equal employment opportunity (EEO) guidelines clearly require a sound and comprehensive job analysis to validate recruiting and selection criteria. Without a systematic investigation of a job, an employer may be using requirements that are not specifically job related. Organizations use job analysis to identify job specifications necessary for obtaining qualified employees for anticipated job openings, whether recruited internally or externally.

EEO Compliance   Many aspects of EEO compliance require accurate and verifiable job analysis information. Job analysis is critical in determining the essential functions of a job and deciding what the necessary qualifications are for a job. This information is crucial for use in the selection process in a nondiscriminatory manner.[11]

Compensation   Job analysis information is vital when determining compensation. As part of identifying appropriate compensation, job analysis information is used to determine job content for *internal* comparisons of responsibilities and *external* comparisons with the compensation paid by competing employers. Information from job analysis can be used to give more weight, and therefore more pay, to jobs with more difficult tasks, duties, and responsibilities.

Training and Development   By defining which activities make up a job, the analysis helps the supervisor explain that job to new employees. Information from job descriptions and job specifications can also help in career planning by showing employees what is expected in jobs that they may choose in the future. Job specification information can point out areas in which employees might need to develop in order to further their careers. For organizations that are accredited by JCAHO, this use of job analysis is critical to document what skills are necessary to safely perform the job and then provide the necessary training to the employee.

Performance Appraisal Using performance standards to compare what an employee is supposed to be doing with what the person actually has done, a supervisor can determine the employee's performance level. The **performance appraisal** process should then tie to the job description and performance standards. Developing clear, realistic performance standards can also reduce communication problems in performance appraisal feedback among managers, supervisors, and employees.[12]

Safety and Health Job analysis information is useful in identifying possible job hazards and working conditions associated with jobs. From the information gathered, managers and HR specialists can work together to identify the health and safety equipment needed, specify work methods, and train workers.

Union Relations Where workers are represented by a labor union, job analysis is used in several ways. First, job analysis information may be needed to determine whether the job should be covered by the union agreements. Second, it is common in unionized environments for job descriptions to be very specific about what tasks are and are not covered in a job. Finally, well-written and specific job descriptions can reduce the number of grievances filed by workers.

WORK SCHEDULES AND JOB ANALYSIS

Different work schedules can be part of designing healthcare jobs. The traditional U.S. work schedule of eight hours a day, five days a week, is in transition. Many healthcare jobs by the nature of the work performed require 24-hour-a-day, seven-day-a-week coverage (often called 24/7) on-site at the health facility. However, many healthcare jobs do lend themselves to different schedules or the ability to perform the work someplace other than the health facility. In healthcare and many other industries, workers may work less or more than eight hours at a workplace, and may have additional work at home.[13]

The work schedules associated with healthcare jobs vary as some jobs must be performed during "normal" daily work hours and on weekdays, while others require employees to work nights, weekends, and extended hours. These include shift work, the compressed workweek, part-time schedules, job sharing, and flextime.

Shift Work   A common work schedule design is shift work. Many healthcare organizations, such as hospitals, residential care facilities, and urgent care centers, need 24-hour coverage and therefore typically schedule three 8-hour shifts per day. As an example the shifts might run as follows:

Day or First Shift: 7:00 A.M. to 3:00 P.M.

Evening or Second Shift: 3:00 P.M. to 11:00 P.M.

Night or Third Shift: 11:00 P.M. to 7:00 A.M.

Most healthcare employers provide some form of additional pay, called a *shift differential*, for working the evening or night shifts, since those are typically the most difficult shifts to staff. The shift differential provides an inducement to workers to work those shifts. Some types of shift work have been known to cause difficulties for some employees, such as weariness, irritability, lack of motivation, and illness. However, healthcare facilities with 24/7 staffing requirements do not have much choice in continuing to have evening and night-shift work schedules to cover patient care needs.

Compressed Workweek   Another type of work schedule design is the **compressed workweek**, in which a full week's work is accomplished in fewer than five 8-hour days. Compression usually results in more work hours each day and fewer workdays each week, such as four 10-hour days, or a three-day week with 12-hour shifts. Often the workers who shift to 12-hour schedules do not wish to return to 8-hour schedules because they have four days off each week.

A very popular form of a compressed workweek was pioneered more than 20 years ago by Baylor Health Care System primarily for recruiting and retaining nurses. Its staffing plan is described as follows:

The Baylor Plan provides full-time benefits for working 24 hours during the weekend—at a pay rate comparable to working 36 hours during the week. Full-time nurses can also work three 12-hour, four 10-hour or five 8-hour shifts.[14]

Many healthcare organizations, especially hospitals and medical centers, have adopted programs similar to the Baylor Plan for their nurses and other healthcare professionals.

Part-Time Schedules   Part-time jobs are used when fewer than 40 hours per week are required to do a job. Part-time jobs are attractive to those who may not want to work 40 hours per week—older employees, parents of small children, or students. In some cases, professionals may choose part-time work. Most healthcare employers utilize part-time schedules to cover peak demand times, augment full-time staff at shift change, and provide weekend coverage.

Job Sharing   Another alternative used is **job sharing**, in which two employees perform the work of one full-time job. For instance, a hospital allows two radiological technicians to fill one job, and each individual works every other week.

Such arrangements are beneficial for employees who may not want or be able to work full-time because of family, school, or other reasons. The keys to successful job sharing are that both "job sharers" must coordinate effectively together, and each must be competent in meeting the job requirements.[15]

Flextime In flextime, employees work a set number of hours a day but vary starting and ending times. In another variation, employees may work 30 minutes longer Monday through Thursday, take short lunch breaks, and leave work at 1 P.M. or 2 P.M. on Friday.

Managing Flexible Work

Flexible scheduling allows management to relax some of the traditional "time clock" control of employees, while still covering workloads.[16] In some cases, electronic monitoring may be used. For example, transcriptionists that work for a clinic in rural Iowa are home-based employees and are monitored electronically on the number of pages of dictated notes they complete in a workday.

Flexibility and Work–Life Balance

For many healthcare employees, balancing their work and personal lives is a significant concern. The quality of an employee's personal and family life is improved by flexibility at work, according to 68 percent of HR professionals polled.[17] Most employees, regardless of the industry they work in, do not feel they spend enough time with their families.

Work–life balance may take the form of employer-sponsored programs designed to help employees balance work and personal life. For example, the University of Kentucky allows flexible work arrangements for its employees, so Randy Hines, who works as a mechanic, can meet his kids at the bus stop around 2:40 every day and walk them home. Hines's work begins at 7:30 A.M. and ends at 4 P.M., but he and his supervisor agreed to a schedule that allows him to come in at 6 A.M. and clock out at 2:30 P.M. It saves Hines $400 per month in child care for which the family does not have to pay.[18]

Work–life balance initiatives can improve recruiting and retention by attracting and keeping people who need the flexibility.[19] However, employees may dismiss such programs as window dressing if they are not applied consistently. It is not uncommon to have such policies identified and available but not actually practiced in some organizations.

LEGAL ASPECTS OF JOB ANALYSIS

Permeating the discussion of equal employment laws, regulations, and court cases in preceding chapters is the concept that legal compliance must focus on the jobs that individuals perform. The 1978 Uniform Selection Guidelines[20] make it clear that HR requirements must be tied to specific job-related factors if employers are to defend their actions as a business necessity.

Job Analysis and the Americans with Disabilities Act

One result of the Americans with Disabilities Act (ADA) is increased emphasis by employers on conducting job analyses, as well as developing and maintaining current and accurate job descriptions and job specifications.

The ADA requires that organizations identify the *essential job functions*, which are the fundamental duties of a job. These do not include the marginal functions of the positions. **Marginal job functions** are duties that are part of a job but are incidental or ancillary to the purpose and nature of the job. As covered in Chapter 4, the three major considerations used in determining essential functions and marginal functions are the following:

- Percentage of time spent on tasks
- Frequency of tasks done
- Importance of tasks performed

Job analysis should also identify the physical demands of jobs. For example, the important physical skills and capabilities used on the job of a nursing assistant could include being able to hear well enough to aid patients and doctors. However, hearing might be less essential for a cook in a hospital cafeteria.

Job Analysis and Wage/Hour Regulations   As will be explained in Chapter 12, the federal Fair Labor Standards Act (FLSA) and most state wage/hour laws indicate that the percentage of time employees spend on manual, routine, or clerical duties affects whether they must be paid overtime for hours worked in excess of 40 hours a week. To be exempt from overtime, the employees must perform their primary duties as executive, administrative, professional, computer professional, or outside sales employees. Primary has been interpreted to mean occurring at least 50 percent of the time.

Other legal-compliance efforts, such as those involving workplace safety and health, can also be aided through the data provided by job analysis and job descriptions. It is difficult for a healthcare employer to have a legal staffing system without performing job analysis. Truly, job analysis is the most basic HR activity and the foundation for most other HR efforts.

BEHAVIORAL ASPECTS OF JOB ANALYSIS

Job analysis involves determining what the core job is. A detailed examination of jobs, although necessary, sometimes can be a demanding and disruptive experience for both managers and employees, in part because job analysis can identify the difference between what currently is being performed in a job and what should be done. This is a major issue about job analysis for some employees, but it is not the only concern. Other behavioral factors can affect job analysis.

Current Incumbent Emphasis

A job analysis and the resulting job description and job specifications should not just describe what the person currently in the job does and that person's qualifications. The incumbent may have unique capabilities and the ability to expand the scope of the job to assume more responsibilities, but the employer might have difficulty finding someone exactly like that employee if the person were to leave. Consequently, it is useful to focus on core duties and necessary knowledge, skills, and abilities by determining what the job would be if the incumbent were to quit or be moved to a different job. Focus should be on the *job* and not the incumbent working in the job.[21]

"Inflation" of Jobs and Job Titles

People have a tendency to inflate the importance and significance of their jobs. Since job analysis information is used for compensation purposes, both managers and employees hope that "puffing up" jobs will result in higher pay levels, greater "status" for résumés, and more promotional opportunities.

Inflated job titles also can be used to enhance employees' images without making major job changes or pay adjustments. For instance, the use of the job title of administrative assistant is very popular in healthcare organizations for individuals that function basically as secretaries or clerical support; the title is inflated to provide more prestige to the job, but the individuals employed in this job are typically compensated as secretaries.

An additional concern is the use of offbeat titles. For example, what is a "growth manager," a "chief transformation officer," or "process improvement guru"? What does a "human character manager" really do? These examples illustrate how job titles may be misleading, both inside and outside the place of employment. Best practice would dictate that titles should convey a clear picture of what a job involves.

Employee and Managerial Anxieties

Both employees and managers have concerns about job analysis. The resulting job description is supposed to identify what is done in a job. However, it is difficult to capture all facets of a job in which employees perform a variety of duties and operate with a high degree of independence.

Employee Fears   One concern that employees may have involves the purpose of a detailed investigation of their jobs. Some employees fear that an analysis of their jobs will limit their creativity and flexibility by formalizing their duties. They are also concerned about pay deduction or even layoff as a result of job analysis. However, having accurate, well-communicated job descriptions can assist employees by clarifying their roles, as well as the expectations within those roles. One effective way to handle anxieties is to involve the employees in the revision process.

The content of a job may often reflect the desires and skills of the incumbent employee. For example, in one mental health care facility, an employee promoted to shift supervisor continued to spend considerable time doing direct patient care, rather than supervising employees who provided care. As part of job analysis discussions, the site manager discussed the need for the supervisor to delegate patient care duties to others.

Managerial Straitjacket   Another concern of managers and supervisors is that the job analysis and job descriptions will unrealistically limit managerial flexibility.[22] Since workloads and demands change rapidly, managers and supervisors may elect to move duties to other employees, cross-train employees, and have flexible means available to accomplish work. If job descriptions are written or used restrictively, employees may argue that a change or omission to a job description should limit management's flexibility to require that work. In organizations with unionized workforces, some very restrictive job descriptions may exist.

Because of such difficulties, the final statement in many job descriptions is a miscellaneous clause that consists of a phrase similar to "Performs other duties as needed upon request by immediate supervisor." This statement covers unusual situations in an employee's job. However, duties covered by this phrase cannot be considered essential functions under legal provisions including the Americans with Disabilities Act.

Job Analysis Methods

Job analysis information about what people are doing in their jobs can be gathered in a variety of ways. Traditionally, the most common methods have been (1) observation, (2) interviewing, and (3) questionnaires. However, the expansion of technology has led to computerization and web-based job analysis information resources. Sometimes a combination of these approaches is used depending on the situation and the organization.

Observation

With the observation method, a manager, job analyst, or HR specialist watches an employee performing the job and takes notes to describe the tasks and duties performed. Use of the observation method is limited because many healthcare jobs do not have complete and easily observed job duties or job cycles. Thus, observation may be more effective when analyzing healthcare jobs when used in conjunction with other methods or as a way to verify information.

Work Sampling   One type of observation, work sampling, does not require attention to each detailed action throughout an entire work cycle. This method allows a job analyst to determine the content and pace of a typical workday through statistical sampling of certain actions rather than through continuous observation and timing of all actions. Work sampling is particularly useful for routine and repetitive jobs.

Employee Diary/Log   Another observation method that is relatively popular in healthcare organizations requires employees to "observe" their own performance by keeping a diary/log of their job duties and the time required for each one. Although this approach can generate useful information, it may be burdensome for employees to compile an accurate log. The logging approach can be technology based, reducing some of the problems.

Interviewing

The interview method requires a manager, job analyst, or an HR specialist to talk with the employees performing each job. A standardized interview form is used most often to record the information. Both the employee and the employee's supervisor must be interviewed to obtain complete details on the job.

Sometimes, group or panel interviews are used. A team of subject matter experts (SMEs) who have varying insights about a group of jobs is assembled to provide job analysis information. This option is particularly useful for highly technical or complex jobs, such as a specialized pharmacist. Since the interview method alone can be quite time-consuming, combining it with one of the other methods is common.

Questionnaires

The questionnaire is a widely used method of gathering data on jobs. A survey instrument is developed and given to employees and managers to complete.

The questionnaire method offers a major advantage in that information about a large number of jobs can be collected inexpensively in a relatively short period of time. However, the questionnaire method assumes that employees can accurately analyze and communicate information about their jobs. Using the interview and observation methods in combination with the questionnaire method allows HR professionals to clarify and verify the information gathered in questionnaires.

Computerized Job Analysis

As computer technology has expanded, researchers have developed computerized job analysis systems. An important feature of computerized job analysis sources is the specificity of data that can be gathered. All of this specific data is compiled into a job analysis database. A computerized job analysis system often can reduce the time and effort involved in writing job descriptions. These systems have banks of job duty statements that relate to each of the tasks and scope statements of the questionnaires.

THE JOB ANALYSIS PROCESS

The process of job analysis must be conducted in a logical manner, following appropriate management and professional psychometric practices. Therefore, a multistage process usually is followed, regardless of the job analysis methods used. The stages for a typical job analysis are outlined here, but they may vary with the methods used and the number of jobs included. Figure 5-5 illustrates the basic stages of the process.

FIGURE 5-5   Stages in Job Analysis Process

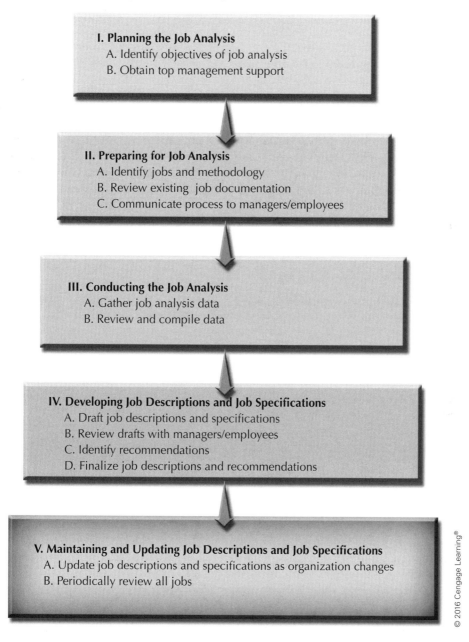

I. Planning the Job Analysis
   A. Identify objectives of job analysis
   B. Obtain top management support

II. Preparing for Job Analysis
   A. Identify jobs and methodology
   B. Review existing job documentation
   C. Communicate process to managers/employees

III. Conducting the Job Analysis
   A. Gather job analysis data
   B. Review and compile data

IV. Developing Job Descriptions and Job Specifications
   A. Draft job descriptions and specifications
   B. Review drafts with managers/employees
   C. Identify recommendations
   D. Finalize job descriptions and recommendations

V. Maintaining and Updating Job Descriptions and Job Specifications
   A. Update job descriptions and specifications as organization changes
   B. Periodically review all jobs

© 2016 Cengage Learning®

Planning

It is crucial that the job analysis process be planned before gathering data from managers and employees. Probably the most important consideration is to identify the objectives of the job analysis. Maybe the main objective is to update job descriptions. Or, it may include revising the compensation programs in the organization based on the outcome. Another objective could be to redesign the jobs in a department or division of the organization or to change the structure in parts of the organization to align it better with new organizational strategies. As cost-containment and staffing issues have required revising strategies and plans, job analysis has proven to be an important tool to aid in implementing new initiatives or reducing staffing costs.

Preparation and Communication

Preparation consists of identifying the jobs under review. Another task in the identification phase is to review existing documentation. Existing job descriptions, organization charts, previous job analysis information, and other industry-related resources all may be useful to review. A crucial step is to communicate and explain the process to managers, affected employees, and other concerned people, such as union stewards. Explanations should address the natural concerns and anxieties people have when someone puts their job under close scrutiny and should anticipate issues likely to arise.

Conducting the Job Analysis

With the preparation completed, the job analysis can be conducted. The methods selected will determine the timeline for the project. Sufficient time should be allotted for obtaining the information from employees and managers. Once details from job analysis have been compiled, they should be sorted by job family and organizational unit. This step allows for comparison of details from similar jobs throughout the organization. The data also should be reviewed for completeness, and follow-up may be needed in the form of additional interviews of managers and employees.

Developing and Maintaining Job Descriptions, Job Specifications, and Performance Standards

The output from the analysis of a job is used to develop a job description, job specifications, and performance standards. Together, they summarize job analysis information into a readable format and provide the basis for legally defensible job-related actions. They also serve individual employees by providing documentation from management that identifies specific job expectations.

Generally, healthcare organizations have found that having managers and employees write job descriptions is not recommended. HR can write them, and when they are finished, they can be distributed by the HR department to managers, supervisors, and employees. It is important that each supervisor or manager review the completed description with individual employees so that there is understanding and agreement on the content that will be linked to performance appraisals, as well as to all other HR activities.

Once job descriptions and specifications have been completed and reviewed by all appropriate individuals, a system must be developed for keeping them current. Otherwise, the entire process, beginning with job analysis, may have to be repeated in several years. Two effective approaches to maintaining the currency

HEALTHCARE REFORM AND HR PRACTICES

Although not a part of the Accountability Care Act (ACA), certain aspects of the Health Insurance Portability and Accountability Act (HIPAA) of 1996 are key to improving healthcare delivery in the United States.[24] Consequently, HIPAA is often thought of in the same manner as the ACA in legislating reforms and improvement in healthcare. Parts of the HIPAA legislation are designed to ensure that all medical records, medical billing, and patient accounts meet certain consistent standards with regard to documentation, handling, and privacy. The federal Department of Health and Human Services' Office for Civil Rights (OCR) is responsible for enforcing the documentation, handling, and privacy of medical information. Violations of the HIPAA privacy and security rules can cost healthcare organizations thousands of dollars in penalties.

A critical aspect of HIPAA compliance is ensuring that healthcare workers who occupationally have contact with health information are handling the information safely and securely. HIPAA has touched many aspects of healthcare HR, including the function of job analysis. As job analysis is conducted, special attention must be paid to the confidentiality requirements of the job being analyzed to ensure that clear specifications and requirements are recorded. Job descriptions that inadequately address HIPAA responsibilities could lead to poor performance or inadequate coverage of the confidentiality (HIPAA) requirements of the job. This could lead to violations of HIPAA regulations.

of job descriptions include updating the description coincidental to an incumbent's performance review and/or prior to the initiation of recruitment activities when a position becomes vacant.

JOB DESCRIPTION COMPONENTS

The ADA focused attention on the importance of well-written job descriptions. Legal compliance requires that they accurately represent the actual jobs. Job titles should be descriptive of job functions performed. There is a real art to writing job descriptions that are sufficiently clear without being overly detailed. A typical job description, such as the one depicted in Figure 5-6, contains several major parts. Overviews of the most common components are presented next.

Identification

The first part of the job description is the identification section, in which the job title, reporting department, relationships, location, and FLSA status

FIGURE 5-6   Sample Job Description

Title: Health Information Clerk		Pay Grade: Nonexempt, Hourly
Department: Medical Records		Date Approved: 1/15/2015
Supervisor: Medical Records Supervisor		

Job Summary: Maintain patients' electronic medical records. Provide electronic files.

Job Accountabilities:

*E/M/NA	%Time	Description
E	35%	Maintains confidentiality of medical records. Controls access to electronic files.
M	30%	Batches patient information into the computer and retrieve patient demographic data.
E	20%	Inputs information such as progress notes, laboratory reports, X-ray results, and correspondence into patient
E	5%	Creates new records.
E	5%	Releases patient information to requesting parties following established confidentiality procedures. Answers patient inquiries for laboratory results.
M	3%	Makes copies of dictated reports and forwards as indicated.
M	2%	Answers telephones and greet patients. Schedules patient appointments.
		Performs other related duties as assigned or requested. The organization reserves the right to add or change duties at any time.

*Select E (Essential), M (Marginal), or NA (Non-Applicable) to denote importance of each job function to position.

© 2016 Cengage Learning®

analysis may be given. Usually, it is advisable to note other information that is useful in tracking jobs and employees through a human resource information system.

General Summary

The second part is the general summary, which is a concise statement of the general responsibilities and components that make the job different from others. One HR specialist has characterized the general summary statement as follows: "In 30 words or less, describe the essence of the job."

FIGURE 5-6   Sample Job Description (*Continued*)

Job Specifications

Skills: Administrative
Understand and apply policies and procedures.
Assemble and organize numerical data.
Answer telephones.

Priortize different projects.
Read handwritten text.

Education and Experience
Minimum education: Less than high school

Preferred experience: 6–12 months

Preferred education:
High School or Equivalent
Preferred field-of-expertise:
Medical records

Physical Requirements

Physical Requirements	Rarely 0–12%	Occasionally 12–33%	Frequently 34–60%	Regularly 67–100%
Seeing—Reading reports, filing				X
Hearing—Communicating with coworkers				X
Standing/walking			X	
Climbing/stooping/kneeling			X	
Lifting/pulling/pushing			X	
Fingering/grasping/feeling— Writing, typing and using telephone			X	

Skills: Computer Software ___**X**___   Scanning Equipment ___**X**___
          Fax ___**X**___

The above statements are intended to describe the general nature and level of work being performed. They are not intended to be construed as an exhaustive list of all responsibilities, duties, and skills required of personnel so classified and do not create an employement contract.

Signatures

Employee: _____ Date: _____

Supervisor: _____ Date: _____

Essential Functions and Duties

The third part of the typical job description lists the essential functions and duties. It contains clear, precise statements on the major tasks, duties, and responsibilities performed. Writing this section is the most time-consuming aspect of preparing job descriptions. The general format for an essential function statement is: (1) *action verb*, (2) *what it applies to*, (3) *how the information is obtained*, (4) *how, why, and how often.*

The language of the ADA has stressed the importance of arranging job duties so that the most essential (in criticality and amount of time spent) are listed first and the supportive or marginal duties are listed later. Within that framework, specific functional duties should be grouped and arranged in some logical pattern. If a job requires an accounting supervisor to prepare several reports, among other functions, statements relating to the preparation of reports should be grouped together. The *miscellaneous clause* typically listed last is included to assure some managerial flexibility.

Job Specifications

The next portion of the job description gives the qualifications needed to perform the job satisfactorily. The job specifications typically are stated as: (1) knowledge, skills, and abilities, (2) education and experience, and (3) physical requirements and working conditions. The components of the job specifications provide information necessary to determine what accommodations might and might not be possible under ADA regulations.

Job specifications can be developed from a variety of information sources. Obviously, the job analysis process provides the primary starting point. But any KSA included must be based on what is really needed to perform a job. Furthermore, the job specifications listed should reflect what is necessary for satisfactory job performance, not what the ideal candidate would have. In light of the ADA, it is crucial that the physical and mental dimensions of each job be clearly identified. If lifting, stooping, standing, walking, climbing, or crawling is required, it should be noted. Also, weights to be lifted should be specified, along with specific visual and hearing requirements of jobs.[23]

Performance Standards and Competencies

Performance standards and competencies can flow directly from the job description and indicate what the job accomplishes and how performance is measured in key areas of the job description. In compliance with JCAHO standards, many healthcare organizations have adopted an approach of combining the job description with performance and competency assessment. The reason for including the performance standards and competencies is clear. If employees know what is expected, how performance is to be measured, and what competencies are required, they have a much better chance of performing satisfactorily. Figure 5-7 shows a job description duty statements and some performance standards used for a central sterile manager in a hospital as an example.

Disclaimer and Approvals

The final section on many job descriptions contains approval signatures by appropriate managers and a legal disclaimer. This disclaimer allows employers to change employees' job duties or request employees to perform duties not listed,

FIGURE 5-7   Sample Job Duty Statements and Performance Standards

Job Title: Central Sterile Manager
Supervisor: Director of Surgical Operations

DUTY	PERFORMANCE STANDARDS
Develop, review, evaluate, and ensure the implementation of a central sterilization process for the surgery department.	• Monitor and forecast workload of department and recommend staffing levels to director to meet workload requirement. • Prepare annual budget for department. • Ensure appropriate review and evaluation of hospital procedures and sterilization equipment as they pertain to infection control.
Identify sterilization problems and outcomes, and document and recommend corrective actions.	• Follow all related departmental policies, procedures, guidelines, and standards in carrying out technical functions. • Perform routine and specialized environmental checks per departmental guidelines. • Ensure new equipment meets standards of sterilization and infection control.

© Cengage Learning®

so that the job description is not viewed as a "contract" between the employer and the employee.

Since healthcare organizations are changing and jobs vary in different organizations, managers and employees alike are finding that designing and analyzing jobs requires greater attention than in the past. Understanding the work done in the organization must be based on the analysis of facts and data, not just the personal perceptions of managers, supervisors, and employees.

CASE

Orange County Pediatric Medical Center (OCPMC) had acquired three physician practices in its service area to broaden its ability to provide primary care. Based on its evaluation of the HR and business practices of the three practices, OCPMC was confident that it could reduce the costs of operations at these practices by consolidating and centralizing business activities. The business activities include accounting and finance, HR, billing, purchasing and materials management, and facilities maintenance. Additionally, the center would be able to spread the general costs of administration over the three facilities.

After nearly six months of operating the three new acquisitions, OCPMC's financial analysis found that very poor budgetary results had occurred. All three practices were over budget by more than 10 percent, and projections were for even larger financial losses. The most significant budgetary issue was labor costs.

In further analyzing the problem, the main issue appeared to be the staffing mix of MDs, RNs, and assistive (nonlicensed) personnel. When the practices were acquired, the staffing mix was a simple combination of MDs and nonlicensed medical assistants. When OCPMC took over the practices, it changed the staffing mix to include RNs. This was consistent with the staffing model at the medical center and the other clinics OCPMC currently owned and operated. The budgetary problem was directly related to the increased expense of the RNs' wages.

OCPMC decided to evaluate the care delivery processes and the skill sets necessary at these clinics to determine if the staffing mix could be changed. The HR department was requested to undertake a job analysis, consider alternative job designs, and make recommendations.

Questions

1. Outline the steps that should be taken to evaluate the work at the practices to determine the appropriate staffing mix.
2. What methods of job analysis would be most effective for this assignment?

END NOTES

1. Joseph Conn, "Gains, Challenges Abound for Healthcare Info Technology," *Modern Healthcare* (December 23, 2013), Supplement, 36.
2. Stephen S. Hau, "An Elegant Solution to Improve Workflow," *Health Management Technology* (December 2013), 20–21.
3. "Prospering by Standardizing Processes and Improving the Patient Experience," *Modern Healthcare* (January 13, 2014), 28–29.
4. James B. Avery et al., "The Additive Value of Positive Psychological Capital in Predicting Work Attitudes and Behavior," *Journal of Management* (2010), 47–62.
5. Rosanna Miguel and Suzanne Miklos, "Individual Executive Assessment: Sufficient Science, Standards and Principles," *Industrial and Organizational Psychology* (2011), 330–333.
6. Joint Commission Resources Inc., "Improving Healthcare Quality and Safety," *Issues in Human Resources for Hospitals* (2004), 21–25.
7. Mari Edlin, "IOM Core Competencies Focus on Collaborative Care," *Managed Healthcare Executive* (December 2013), 48–49.
8. Frederick P. Morgeson and Erich C. Dierdorff, "Work Analysis: From Technique to Theory," *APA Handbook of Industrial and Organizational Psychology* 2 (2011), 3–41.
9. G. Rai, "Job Satisfaction among Long-Term Care Staff: Bureaucracy Isn't Always Bad," *Administration in Social Work* [serial online] (January 2013), 90–99.
10. Hessam Sadatsafavi and John Walewski, "Corporate Sustainability: The Environmental Design and Human Resources Management Interface in Healthcare Settings," *Health Environments Research & Design Journal* (Winter 2013), 98–118.
11. See *http://askjan.org/Erguide/ErGuide.pdf* for more information.
12. Robert E. Lewis, "Accountability Is Key to Effective Performance Appraisal Systems," *Industrial and Organizational Psychology* (June 2011), 173–175.
13. Harriet B. Presser and Brian W. Ward, "Nonstandard Work Schedules over the Life Course: A First Look," *Monthly Labor Review* (July 2011), 3–16.
14. See *http://www.baylorhealth.com/Careers/Career_Fields/Nursing/specialties/Pages/Research.aspx* for more information.
15. Timothy R. Hinkin and J. Bruce Tracey, "What Makes It So Great?," *Cornell Hospitality Quarterly* 51 (March 8, 2010), 158–170.
16. Jim Fickness, "Build Your Company's Flexibility Muscles Now," *Workspan* (May 2011), 72–77; Sayed Sadjady, "Find the Right Balance with Flexibility," *Workspan* (June 2012), 62–66.

17. Stephan Miller, "Flexible Hours in the Ranks," *2010 HR Trendbook*, 16–17.

18. Michael O'Brien, "Balancing Work/Life by the Hour," *Human Resource Executive Online* (July 11, 2011), 1–4.

19. F. Brisco et al., "Memberships Has Its Privileges? Contracting and Access to Jobs that Accommodate Work–Life Needs," *Industrial and Labor Relations Review* 64 (2011), 258–282.

20. See *http://www.gpo.gov/fdsys/pkg/CFR-2011-title29-vol4/xml/CFR-2011-title29-vol4-part1607.xml* for more information.

21. Deb Levine and Lesa Albright, "How Do I Conduct Job Analysis?" *HR Magazine* (November 2010), 21.

22. Jesse Sostrin, "Beyond the Job Description," *Chief Learning Officer* (February 2014), 90.

23. Chad H. Van Iddekinge et al., "An Examination of the Validity and Incremental Value of Needed-at-Entry Ratings," *Applied Psychology: An International Review* 60 (2011), 24–45.

24. See *http://www.hhs.gov/ocr/privacy/hipaa/understanding/index.html* for more information.

6 HEALTHCARE RECRUITMENT AND SELECTION

Learning Objectives

After you have read this chapter, you should be able to:

- Specify the decisions necessary to make as part of a strategic approach to recruitment.

- Describe the methods utilized for both internal and external recruitment.

- Discuss the criteria used to evaluate the effectiveness of organizational recruitment efforts.

- Compare and contrast job performance, selection criteria, and predictors.

- Identify the legal requirements of selection and outline the process.

- Explain the importance of conducting preemployment background investigations.

HEALTHCARE HR INSIGHTS

The landscape for recruiting healthcare professionals is changing rapidly. Hospitals, medical centers, long-term care facilities, physician practices, and clinics are all competing for the same workers. For positions like RNs, primary care providers (MDs, physician assistants, and nurse practitioners), and pharmacists, the competition is fierce. Healthcare HR professionals with recruiting and staffing responsibilities are increasingly challenged to be innovative and resourceful if they are to be effective in their efforts.

One of the challenges to healthcare recruitment is to develop new strategies around recruiting from an ever-increasing diverse workforce. Diversity as represented in many ways, including generational (baby boomers—born 1946 to 1964, Gen X—born 1965 to 1980, and Gen Y—born 1981 to 2000), race and ethnicity, and culture. Healthcare organizations cannot rely on traditional methods of recruitment—such as newsprint ads, word of mouth, or people just walking into the HR department to apply—to access diverse individuals. Among the efforts that have proven successful for attracting a diverse applicant flow are:

- Posting ads on social media (Facebook, LinkedIn, and Twitter) is effective for recruiting younger medical professionals.
- Reward mentoring by managers and medical professionals of minority students in health careers.
- Commit to training students with varying levels of academic refinement.
- Attend job fairs that specifically reach out to various minority groups.[1]

These and other innovative recruiting efforts may require more time and higher costs to implement versus the more traditional methods noted above. However, given the realities of the healthcare workforce, to be successful in attracting and employing healthcare workers there are few alternatives.

The Healthcare HR Insight illustrates that healthcare HR professionals must keep focused on dealing with staffing issues. The healthcare labor market is extremely cyclical. Regardless of the availability of specific types of healthcare workers, innovative recruitment and retention strategies will continue to be important, even if there is a temporary lull in staffing shortages and requirements. There is no better time to restrategize and improve processes than when some accomplishment has occurred and the press of immediate action subsides.

RECRUITING AND LABOR MARKETS

Labor Market Components

Several means of identifying labor markets exist. One useful approach is to take a broad view of the labor markets and then narrow them down to specific recruiting sources. The broadest labor market component and measure is the **labor force population**, which is made up of all individuals who are available for selection if all possible recruitment strategies are used.

The **applicant population** is a subset of the labor force population that is available for selection if a particular recruiting approach is used. This population can be broad or narrow depending on the jobs needing to be filled and the approaches used by the employer. For example, if a pharmacy chain is recruiting pharmacists for multiple geographic locations, the recruiting methods may involve a broad range of approaches and sources, such as contacting professional associations, attending conventions, utilizing general and specialized websites, using recruiting consulting firms, and offering recruitment incentives to existing employees.

However, a small hospital in a specific geographic location might limit its recruiting for a staff accountant to graduates from universities in the area. This recruiting method would result in a different group of applicants from those who might apply if the employer were to advertise the opening for a staff accountant on an Internet jobs board, or encourage current employee referrals and applications.

Figure 6-1 illustrates some common considerations for determining applicant populations. At least four recruiting decisions affect the nature of the applicant population:

- *Recruiting Method*—Advertising media chosen
- *Recruiting Message*—What is said about the job and how it is said
- *Applicant Qualifications Required*—Education level and amount of experience necessary
- *Administrative Procedures*—Time of year recruiting is done, follow-ups with applicants, and use of previous applicant files

The **applicant pool** consists of all persons who are actually evaluated for selection. Many factors can affect the size of the applicant pool, including the reputation of the organization as a place to work, the screening efforts of the

FIGURE 6-1 Considerations for Determining Applicant Populations

CONSIDERATIONS FOR DETERMINING HEALTHCARE APPLICANT POPULATIONS

- Number and type of recruits needed to fill jobs
- Timing of recruiting to ensure effective placement in organization
- External and internal messages on the details of jobs to be filled
- Qualifications of applicants to be considered by recruiters
- Sources for obtaining qualified applicants for jobs to be filled
- Outside and inside recruiting means to be used by recruiters
- Administrative recruiting and application review activities
- Consideration of organization's strategies to determine recruiting goals

© 2016 Cengage Learning®

organization, the job specifications, and the information available to the application population. Assuming a suitable candidate is present, the final selection is made from the applicant pool.

It is useful to develop an *applicant tracking system* when considering the applicant pool. Using such a system can make the recruiting process more effective.[2] For example, when the size of the applicant pool increases, healthcare recruiters can identify the most effective future employees for several jobs, and not just fill current jobs because of a larger supply.[3]

Unemployment Rates and Labor Markets   When the unemployment rate is high in a given market, many people are looking for jobs. When the unemployment rate is low, there are fewer applicants. Unemployment rates vary with business cycles and present very different challenges for recruiting at different times.

Educational and Technical Labor Markets   Another way to look at labor markets is by considering the educational and technical qualifications that define the people being recruited. Many healthcare employers need individuals with specific licenses, certifications, or educational backgrounds. For instance, at a large medical center, recruiting physician leaders led to the establishment of a special search committee to set goals for the organization. Then, as part of recruiting and selection, the top candidates were asked to develop departmental vision statements and three-year goals. That information made the recruiting and selection process more effective.[4]

A prominent labor market for healthcare employers that is expected to be in high demand over the next decade is bilingual/multilingual employees, particularly those individuals who can speak Spanish. With some research showing a lack of motivation among workers to learn these languages, this educational/technical area should be in high demand with good work opportunities. Similarly, third-culture children, or individuals who have spent considerable time in geographic/cultural regions different from those of their parents, will also be in demand because of their knowledge of diverse cultural environments and flexibility.[5]

Geographic Labor Markets   One common way to classify healthcare labor markets is based on geographic location. Markets can be local, area or regional, national, or international. Local and area/regional labor markets vary significantly in terms of workforce availability and quality, and changes in a geographic labor market may force changes in recruiting efforts.

HR professionals in the healthcare industry have been especially aware of the supply and demand of workers in the labor force population and the substantial impact supply issues have had on the staffing strategies of organizations in the industry. Internal labor markets also influence recruiting. A discussion of these and other strategic recruiting decisions follows.

HEALTHCARE REFORM AND HR PRACTICES

When thinking about applicant pools, one does not normally think about physicians as applicants. But for healthcare organizations, physicians are applicants and must be considered in their applicant populations. With the passage of the Affordable Care Act (ACA), more people will enter the healthcare system in coming years and more doctors will be needed to treat them. A physician shortage was already expected before ACA was signed into law in March 2010, and now that gap will worsen. According to projections released by the Association of American Medical Colleges (AAMC) Center for Workforce Studies, 2015 will experience a shortage of about 63,000 doctors, with greater shortages on the horizon—91,500 and 130,600 for 2020 and 2025, respectively. Earlier projections had placed the shortage at about 39,600 doctors for 2015. Since 2008, AAMC projections have incorporated later utilization data and changing specialization patterns among new physicians, and have shown shortages across those specialties, as well as in primary care. With fewer physicians, it is usually the most vulnerable patients who have access problems.

Several factors are contributing to the growing demand. On top of the 32 million Americans who will get insurance cards once the ACA is fully implemented, 15 million more will become eligible for Medicare in the coming years. Meanwhile, physician supply is projected to drop because of baby boomer retirement and other factors.

Several specialties in particular could experience shortages of 62,400 doctors by 2020, according to 2008 data from the federal Health Resources and Services Administration (HRSA). General surgery is predicted to be one of the hardest-hit specialties, with a shortage of 21,400 surgeons. Ophthalmology and orthopedic surgery are each expected to need more than 6,000 physicians over current levels. Urology, psychiatry, and radiology all are expected to see shortfalls of more than 4,000 physicians, according to the HRSA figures. In addition, a recent study from the American Academy of Dermatology found that there are only 3.5 dermatologists for every 100,000 Americans, with patient wait times running as long as three months in some areas.[6]

Healthcare leaders and healthcare HR professionals will be challenged to recruit and retain physicians for their organizations against the backdrop of increasing patient needs and a shrinking physician labor pool. The development of effective physician recruitment and selection processes will be critical for hospitals, medical centers, physician groups, and other healthcare organizations as more patients access the U.S. healthcare system with the passage of the ACA.

PLANNING AND STRATEGIC DECISIONS REGARDING RECRUITING

The decisions that are made about recruiting help dictate not only the types and numbers of applicants but also how difficult or successful recruiting efforts may be. Figure 6-2 shows an overview of these recruiting decisions. **Recruiting**

FIGURE 6-2   Strategic Recruiting Decisions

involves identifying where to recruit, who to recruit, and what the job requirements will be. Another key consideration is deciding to what extent internal and external searches are to be made.

Employment Branding and Image   The **employment brand** or image of a healthcare organization is the view both employees and outsiders have of it. Healthcare organizations that are seen as desirable employers are better able to attract qualified applicants than are those with poor reputations. For example, a high-profile urban hospital might offer excellent opportunities for advancement to employees, which can greatly enhance its brand image. However, if the workplace is consistently stressful, and employees must work long hours to be considered for these advancement opportunities, the resulting employer brand can cause high turnover and fewer applicants interested in working for the hospital.

In addition, in healthcare the brand or reputation of a particular facility relative to the care it provides can also impact employment brand. Healthcare organizations that provide well-documented quality care, such as the Cleveland Clinic,[7] often use branding to improve the perceptions people have about their organizations. Besides influencing what people think, positive branding can enhance an organization's ability to recruit and retain outstanding employees by increasing the number of candidates who apply for jobs and decreasing the possibility that existing employees quit. According to research, much of this employment branding revolves around creating good rewards for employees, such as good pay, providing desirable workplace opportunities, and creating positive job characteristics.

The positive perceptions generated by these brands should also be based on a positive employee value proposition, which is developed by highlighting an organization's commitment to employee excellence and development.[8] The brand can help generate more recruits through applicant self-selection because it affects whether individuals ever consider a firm and submit applications. Recruiting and employer branding should be seen as part of organizational marketing efforts and linked to the overall image and reputation of the organization and its industry.

In the healthcare industry, one of the most successful employer branding approaches focused on nursing recruitment and retention is a concept referred to as a "magnet hospital." In 1990, the American Nurses Credentialing Center (ANCC) was incorporated as a subsidiary nonprofit organization through which the American Nurses Association (ANA) offers credentialing programs and services. At that time the ANCC instituted the Magnet Hospital Recognition Program for Excellence in Nursing Services (ANCC Magnet Recognition®). Hospitals, medical centers, and long-term care facilities are eligible to apply for magnet status if they can demonstrate the following in nursing excellence through a formal review process:

- *Transformational Leadership*—This is leadership that leads people where they need to be to meet the demands of the future.

- *Structural Empowerment*—Leadership provides an innovative environment where strong professional practice flourishes.

- *Exemplary Professional Practice*—This entails a comprehensive understanding of the role of nursing; the application of that role with patients, families, communities, and the interdisciplinary team; and the application of new knowledge and evidence.

- *New Knowledge, Innovations, and Improvements*—Magnet organizations have an ethical and professional responsibility to contribute to patient care, the organization, and the profession in terms of new knowledge, innovations, and improvements.

- *Empirical Outcomes*—Magnet-recognized organizations are in a unique position to become pioneers of the future and to demonstrate solutions to numerous problems inherent in our healthcare systems today.

Approximately 6.61 percent of all registered hospitals have achieved ANCC Magnet Recognition status, according to the American Hospital Association's *Fast Facts on US Hospitals, 2011.*[9]

Achieving this status establishes brand recognition for a healthcare employer as an outstanding place for an RN to work.[10]

Internal versus External Recruiting

Both advantages and disadvantages are associated with promoting from within the organization (internal recruitment) and hiring from outside the organization (external recruitment) to fill openings. Most healthcare organizations combine the use of internal and external methods. Historically, larger healthcare organizations, such as hospitals, medical centers, and long-term care facilities, have followed a policy of promotion from within. However, operating in rapidly changing environments and competitive conditions, healthcare organizations are placing a heavier emphasis on external sources in addition to their internal sources. Figure 6-3 lists the various recruiting methods, both internal and external, that healthcare organizations utilize. It also notes which method is the most effective for each type of worker.

Flexible Staffing

Decisions as to who should be recruited hinge on whether to seek traditional full-time employees or use more flexible approaches. Healthcare organizations are finding a need to turn to creative staffing approaches to attract and retain workers. Part-time workers are the most traditional flexible approach used in healthcare because a significant percentage of healthcare workers work part-time. In fact, the nursing profession is seen by many individuals as a part-time profession.

Healthcare employers that use **temporary employees** can hire their own temporary staff or use agencies supplying temporary workers on a rate-per-day or per-week basis. The use of more traditional temporary workers makes sense for healthcare organizations if their work is subject to fluctuations or as an opportunity to evaluate employees before placing them on the regular payroll. For example, HR departments in many large healthcare organizations have developed internal temporary staffing departments to reduce the handling costs of external temporary agency use for temporary employees.

Some healthcare organizations employ **independent contractors** to perform specific services on a contract basis, such as information technology workers helping to prepare for a major new software conversion. However, those contractors must be truly independent, as determined by the U.S. Internal Revenue Service and the U.S. Department of Labor. (See Chapter 12 for details.)

Float Pools

Nursing departments in hospitals and long-term care facilities typically use RN **resource or float pools**, where RNs are specifically hired to be available to "float" to various units when patient census or acuity needs are higher than core staffing needs can meet. Staffing shortages in healthcare organizations can compromise patient care and place extraordinary stress on healthcare workers that must work in a situation with too many patients and not enough workers.[11] Consequently, the ability of healthcare employers to supplement their staff when needed is crucial.

FIGURE 6-3 Choosing a Recruiting Method: Possible Approaches

	SERVICE WORKER	OFFICE/CLERK	PROFESSIONAL/TECHNICAL	EXECUTIVE/MANAGERIAL
1. Promotion from within	*	*	*	*
2. Job posting and bidding	*	*	*	*
3. Employee referrals	*	*	*	—
4. Executive search firms			—	*
5. Internet recruiting sites	*	*	*	*
6. Media advertisements	*	*	*	
7. Public employment agency	*	*	—	
8. Private employment agency	*	*	*	*
9. Schools and colleges		*	*	*
10. Clinical rotations, preceptorships, and internships				
11. Fellowships		*	*	*
12. Volunteers	*	*		
13. Professional associations			*	*
14. Military	—	—	*	*
15. Former employees		—	*	*
16. Special events/job fairs		*	*	*
17. Temporary help/interim staffing	*	*	*	*

*A good recruiting method
—A possible recruiting method

Resource pools (or *float pools*) are an especially good way to allow new nurses the opportunity to work in a variety of settings before deciding which unit, department, or even type of nursing is the most desirable. However, due to the ever-increasing specialization within nursing, such as oncology or cardiac care, float nurses cannot be expected to safely work in all areas of a hospital, clinic, or treatment center.

Employee Leasing

In dental practices and some physician practices and clinics, **employee leasing** is a concept that has generated some interest in recent years. An example of an employee leasing process is a clinic that signs an agreement with an employee leasing company, after which the existing staff is hired by the leasing firm. For a fee, the clinic "leases" its employees from the leasing company, which then writes the paychecks, pays the taxes, provides benefits, prepares and implements HR policies, and keeps all the required personnel records.[12]

INTERNAL RECRUITING

Internal recruiting means focusing on current employees and others with previous contact with an employing organization. Promotions, demotions, and transfers also can provide additional people for an organizational unit, if not for the entire organization. Friends of current employees, former employees, and previous applicants may also be sources. One advantage of internal recruiting sources over external sources is that management can observe the candidate for promotion (or transfer) over a period of time and can evaluate that person's potential and specific job performance. Healthcare organizations have also found that another advantage of promoting from within to fill job openings is that it gives current employees added motivation to stay with their organization and prepare for advancement through additional education and training.

Job Posting and Bidding

The major means for recruiting employees for other jobs internally within healthcare organizations is through **job posting and bidding**, whereby the employer provides notices of job openings, and employees respond by applying for specific openings. The organization can notify employees of job vacancies by posting notices in cafeterias and break rooms, and on an organizational intranet website.

Internal Recruiting Database

Computerized internal talent banks, or applicant tracking systems, can be used to identify the inventory of employees' KSAs. Employers that must deal with a large number of applications and job openings have found it beneficial to use such software as part of a human resource information system. With the growth of e-mail and intranets, more healthcare organizations are using this approach to internally post their positions.

Job posting and bidding systems can be ineffective if handled improperly. Jobs generally are posted before any external recruiting is done. The organization must allow a reasonable period of time for current employees to check on available jobs before it considers external applicants.

Promotion and Transfer

Many healthcare organizations choose to fill vacancies through promotions or transfers from within whenever possible. Although most often successful, promotions from within have some drawbacks as well. The person's performance on one job might not be a good predictor of performance on another, because different skills may be required on the new job. For instance, healthcare organizations have certainly promoted the best nurse or the best respiratory therapist to supervisory positions based on their technical competence. Because of the different capabilities required for supervisory success, these promotion decisions may not be the most effective for the organization. Also, if an organization does not have a diverse workforce, promotions may not be an effective way to speed up the movement of protected-class individuals through the organization.

Current Employee Referrals

One of the most reliable sources of people to fill vacancies involves personal acquaintances or professional associates of current employees. To potential applicants, employees can describe the advantages of a job with the organization, furnish letters of introduction, and encourage them to apply. These are external applicants recruited using an internal information source. Many healthcare employers pay employees incentives for referring individuals with specialized skills that are difficult to recruit through normal means. As an example, in a large West Coast radiology practice, employees are encouraged to refer qualified applicants for open positions. There is the enticement of a $500 bonus for the referral if it leads to a hire.

Former employees and former applicants are also good internal sources for recruitment. In both cases, there is a time-saving advantage, because more information already exists about the potential employee.[13]

EXTERNAL RECRUITING

If internal sources do not produce enough acceptable candidates for jobs, many external sources are available. These sources include schools, colleges, and universities; media sources; trade and competitive sources; employment agencies; executive search firms; and the Internet.

Schools, Colleges, and Universities

High schools or vocational/technical schools are typically good sources of new employees for many healthcare organizations. These include such positions as medical assistants, emergency medical technicians, and lab aides. A successful recruiting program with these institutions is the result of careful analysis and continual contact with individual schools. There are a number of positions within healthcare organizations where a high school degree or GED is an appropriate educational requirement; these jobs include a wide variety of service worker, clerical, and clinical support positions.

At the college or university level, the recruitment of graduating students is a large-scale operation for many healthcare organizations. Most colleges and universities maintain placement offices in which employers and applicants can meet.[14]

Media Sources

Media sources such as newspapers, magazines, television, radio, and billboards are widely used. Whatever one is used, it should be tied to the relevant labor market and provide sufficient information on the company and the job. When using recruitment advertisements in the media, employers should ask five key questions:

1. What is the ad supposed to accomplish?
2. How should the message be presented?
3. Who are the people we want to reach?
4. Where should it be placed?
5. What should the advertising message convey?

Professional Associations

Many healthcare professional societies and associations publish newsletters or magazines containing job ads. Such publications may be a good source of applicants for specialized professionals.

Employment Agencies

Every state in the United States has its own state-sponsored employment agency. These agencies operate branch offices in many cities throughout the state and do not charge fees to applicants or employers. Private employment agencies are also found in most cities. For a fee collected from the employee or the employer (usually the employer), these agencies do some preliminary screening and refer applicants for open positions.

Executive Search Firms

Some employment agencies focus their efforts on executive, managerial, and professional positions. These executive search firms are split into two groups: (1) contingency firms that charge a fee only after a candidate has been hired by a client company, and (2) retainer firms that charge a client a set fee whether or not the contracted search is successful. Both types of firms are widely used by healthcare organizations to staff specialized clinical, management, and executive positions.

INTERNET RECRUITING

Healthcare organizations first started using computers as a recruiting tool by advertising jobs on a *bulletin board service* from which prospective applicants would contact the employer. Then some organizations began to take e-mail applications. Today, the Internet has become a primary means for many healthcare employers to search for job candidates and for applicants to look for jobs.

E-recruiting Media or Methods

The growth in the Internet has led both healthcare employers and employees looking for jobs in healthcare to use Internet recruiting tools. Internet links, Web 2.0 sites, blogs, tweets, and other types of Internet/web-based applications have become viable parts of recruiting. One survey of e-recruiting software providers identified numerous firms as e-recruiting clients, and some of them serve more than 1,000 employers.[15] Of the many recruiting sites using special software, the most common ones are Internet job boards, professional/career websites, and employer websites.

Internet Job Boards   Many Internet job boards, such as Monster, Yahoo!, and HotJobs, provide places for employers to post jobs or search for candidates. Job boards offer access to numerous candidates. Healthcare recruiters can use a single website, such as MyJobHunter.com, to obtain search links to many other major job sites. Applicants can also use these websites to do one match and then send résumés to all jobs in which they are interested.[16] However, many of the individuals accessing these sites are "job lookers" who are not serious about changing jobs but are checking out compensation levels and job availability in their areas of interest.[17] Despite such concerns, HR recruiters find general job boards useful for generating applicant responses.

Professional/Career Websites   Many professional associations have employment links on their websites. As an example, for health administration jobs in clinics and physician practices in Minnesota, see the job board on the Minnesota Medical Group Management Association website.[18]

Employer Websites   Despite the popularity of job boards and association job sites, many healthcare employers have learned that their own organizational websites can be very effective and efficient when recruiting candidates and reinforcing their employer brand. Healthcare employers, regardless of their size, include employment and career information on their websites under headings such as "Employment" or "Careers." This is the place where recruiting (both internal and external) is often conducted. On many of these sites, job seekers are encouraged to e-mail résumés or complete online applications.

A healthcare organization's website should present a favorable image of themselves as an employer by outlining information on the organization, including its care focus, organizational growth potential, and some aspects of organizational operations. In addition, a recent study determined that including positive employee testimonials on recruiting websites made the employer more desirable and credible to job candidates; so HR departments and other hiring managers should consider incorporating such statements into the online-recruiting process.[19]

Recruiting and Internet Social Networking

The Internet has led to social networking of individuals on blogs, tweets, and a range of websites. HR professionals in a variety of organizations, such as UnitedHealth Group, are utilizing some form of social networking to enhance the recruitment of employees. In addition, some organizations are using Web 2.0 and other technology to better communicate with potential hires by posting employment announcements and video messages about work in the organization.

The informal use of the web and mobile devices presents some interesting recruiting advantages and disadvantages for both employers and employees. Social networking sites allow job seekers to connect with employees of potential employers. An example is LinkedIn, which has a job-search engine that allows people to search for contacts who work for employers with posted job openings.

Some healthcare employers are now engaging in social collaboration by joining and accessing social technology networks such as Facebook and others. Posting job openings on these sites means that millions of website users can see the openings and can make contact online. Often those doing recruiting can send individuals to the organization's website and then process candidates using electronic résumés or completed online applications.[20]

Job Applicants and Social Network Sites   Many healthcare workers see social media and networking websites as a key part of online recruiting. A study of 200 users of one such website indicated that the individuals who were job seeking were doing so for proactive reasons such as career opportunities, job inquiries, and others. Relatively few of them were passive job seekers who were just looking at website information.[21]

Almost half of surveyed employers indicated that instead of using general job boards, they were changing to social networking and niche job sites for recruiting workers with specific skills. However, employers who use social networking sites for recruiting must have plans and well-defined recruiting tools to take full advantage of these sites.[22]

Recruiting Using Special Technology Means

For many years, the Internet has been used by people globally. Several special Internet tools that can be used as part of recruiting efforts are blogs, e-videos, and tweets.

Blogs and Recruiting Both employers and individuals have used blogs as part of recruiting to fill jobs. For instance, describing job openings and recruiting needs on a hospital's blog could result in individuals responding to job ads in areas such as nursing, administration, HR, and other specialties.

E-videos and Recruiting With video capabilities of all types available, healthcare employers are using videos in several ways. Some firms use videos to describe their organizational characteristics, job opportunities, and recruiting means. Suppliers such as Monster.com, CareerTV, and others have worked with employer clients to produce online recruitment videos.[23]

Recruiting through Twitter Twitter can be used for many purposes, including personal, social, legal, and employment-related messages. More than 8 million people have joined Twitter.com to become "tweeters."

The Twitter system limits messages to 140 specific characters; but even so, tweeting has rapidly become a social network recruiting method. Recruiters send tweet messages to both active and passive job candidates, and then follow up with longer e-mails to computers, personal contacts, and other actions to facilitate recruiting. As could be expected, the youngest adults—those between the ages of 18 and 24—are the most avid Twitter users. Nearly a third of Internet users in this age group (31 percent) have adopted Twitter. Moreover, one in five, or 20 percent of 18- to 24-year-olds, now use Twitter on a typical day. Consequently, this can be a very effective recruiting source for individuals in that age range.[24]

Legal Issues in Internet Recruiting

With Internet recruiting expanding, new and different concerns have arisen. Several of these issues have ethical and moral, as well as legal implications. The following examples illustrate some of these concerns:

- When companies use screening software to avoid looking at the thousands of résumés they receive, are rejections really based on the qualifications needed for the job?
- How can data about an individual's protected characteristics be collected and analyzed for reports?
- Are too many individuals being excluded from the later phases of the Internet-recruiting process based on unlawful information?
- Which applicants really want jobs? If someone has accessed a job board and sent an e-mail asking an employer about a job opening, does the person actually want to be an applicant?
- What are the implications of Internet recruiting in terms of confidentiality and privacy?

Loss of privacy is a potential disadvantage with Internet recruiting. Sharing information gleaned from people who apply to job boards or even organizational websites has become common. As a healthcare organization receives résumés from applicants, it is required to track those applicants and file its EEO report. But the personal information that can be seen by employers on websites such as Facebook, LinkedIn, and others may be inappropriate and can possibly violate legal provisions.

Employment lawyers are issuing warnings to employers about using remarks posted on LinkedIn, Facebook, and Twitter in the hiring process. According to one survey of employers, about three-fourths of hiring managers in various-sized companies checked persons' credentials on LinkedIn, about half used Facebook, and approximately one-fourth used Twitter.[25] Some of the concerns raised have included postings of confidential details about an employee's termination, racial/ethnic background or gender, and the making of discriminatory comments. All of these actions could lead to wrongful termination or discrimination lawsuits. Since Internet usage has legal implications for recruiting, HR employment-related policies, training, and enforcement should be based on legal advice.

Advantages of Internet Recruiting

Healthcare employers have found many advantages to using Internet recruiting. Compared to other recruiting methods such as newspaper advertising, employment agencies, and search firms, Internet recruiting can save the company money. Another major advantage is that by reaching out to so many people potentially representing diverse backgrounds and regions, a very large pool of applicants can be generated using Internet recruiting.

Internet recruiting can also save time. Applicants can respond quickly to job postings by sending electronic responses, rather than using snail mail. Recruiters can respond more rapidly to qualified candidates to obtain additional applicant information, request additional candidate details, and establish times for further communication, including interviews.[26]

Disadvantages of Internet Recruiting

The positive things associated with Internet recruiting should be balanced against disadvantages, some of which have already been suggested. Because of broader exposure, Internet recruiting often creates additional work for HR professionals and others internally. More online job postings must be sent; many more résumés must be reviewed; more e-mails, blogs, and tweets need to be dealt with; and expensive specialized software may be needed to track the increased number of applicants resulting from Internet-recruiting efforts. Further, while different social networking websites such as LinkedIn and Twitter can be viable sources of leads, there is reason to believe that some individuals do not like to be bothered with work-related information on their Facebook accounts, and that a sufficient return on investment is not generated.[27]

Another issue with Internet recruiting is that some applicants may have limited Internet access, especially individuals from lower socioeconomic groups and from certain racial/ethnic groups, raising issues of fairness in hiring. Indeed, a recent study determined that individuals perceived greater fairness in more traditional (offline) application approaches compared to online approaches.[28] In addition, it is easy to access Internet-recruiting sources, but not all who do so are actively looking for new jobs. However, they require much employer time to process.

Internet recruiting is only one approach to recruiting, but its use has been expanding. Also, how well the Internet-recruiting resources perform must be compared to the effectiveness of other external and internal recruiting sources.

Other Sources for Healthcare Recruitment

Thanks in part to the unique aspects of the educational preparation, as depicted in Figure 6-4 for most clinical degrees and some administrative degrees, many healthcare employers have a ready-made source of applicant flow. Clinical rotations, preceptorships, and internships are part of the education and clinical development for such fields as nursing, pharmacy, medical technology, and other therapies. Fellowships are a part of the education development for healthcare administration degrees. The individuals in these educational areas pursue their on-the-job training in hospitals, clinics, nursing homes, and other healthcare provider environments, so they are easily accessed to discuss current or future openings and career opportunities.

Clinical Rotations

In clinical-preparation degree programs, a clinical rotation is required to facilitate the students' learning of the "hands-on" nature of their professions. These rotations are typically hosted by clinics, hospitals, nursing homes, or other care provision facilities. Many organizations that host clinical rotations take full advantage of the opportunity to recruit the students while they are on-site.[29]

Preceptorships and Internships

Similar to clinical rotations, preceptorships and internships may be part of the educational experience but usually occur at the later stages or end of a health

FIGURE 6-4   Unique Sources of Healthcare Applicants

© 2016 Cengage Learning®

professional's training. Many healthcare organizations have incorporated the preceptorships and internships into their normal recruitment cycle—in some instances, exclusively relying on the individuals who complete their preceptorships or internships at their facilities to fill open positions. Advanced-practice healthcare professionals, such as nurse practitioners and pharmacists, are especially recruited in this manner.

Fellowships

Many undergraduate and graduate degree programs in healthcare administration, public health, and health planning include postgraduation fellowship programs. These fellowships place the new graduates in high-level support positions to administrators, CEOs, or other healthcare executives. The "fellows," as they are called, receive on-the-job training, typically by doing special projects or studies such as preparing for a JCAHO site visit. Some of the fellowships result in opportunities for the fellows to move into middle-management positions at the completion of their program.

Summer Employment, Shadowing, and Volunteer Pools

Many healthcare employers have relied on college students as summer replacement workers. These summer replacements may be an excellent source of recruits once they graduate.

In order to encourage health-related careers, healthcare employers have established *shadowing programs*. These programs provide an individual who is considering a healthcare occupation or educational program the opportunity to accompany a healthcare professional during a typical workday. The shadowing experience allows the potential employee or student to gain a unique, up-close glimpse of the healthcare environment and position responsibilities.

Volunteer pools have also been used to attract applicants. Hospitals and extended care facilities have historically used volunteers to perform a wide array of hospitality, reception, delivery, or other services. Many healthcare facilities have well-developed programs with hundreds of volunteers that augment the paid staff. In addition to providing labor cost savings, the volunteers are an excellent source of applicants for positions if paid employment is desired.

RECRUITING EVALUATION AND METRICS

Evaluating the success of recruiting efforts is important. General areas for evaluating recruiting include the following:

- *Quantity of Applicants*—Because the goal of a good recruiting program is to generate a large pool of applicants from which to choose, quantity must be sufficient to provide choices and fill job vacancies.

- *EEO Goals Met*—The recruiting program is the key activity used to meet goals for hiring protected-class individuals. This is especially relevant when a company is engaged in affirmative action to meet such goals.
- *Quality of Applicants*—There is the issue of whether the qualifications of the applicant pool are sufficient to fill the job openings, whereby the applicants meet job specifications and perform the jobs.
- *Cost per Applicant Hired*—Cost varies, depending on the position being filled, but knowing how much it costs to fill an empty position puts turnover and salary levels in perspective.
- *Time Required to Fill Openings*—The length of time it takes to fill openings is another means of evaluating recruiting efforts. If openings are filled quickly with qualified candidates, the work and productivity of the organization are not delayed by vacancies.

In summary, the effectiveness of recruiting sources will vary, depending on the nature of the job being filled and the time available to fill it. But unless calculated, the effectiveness may not be recognized.[30]

Increasing Recruiting Effectiveness

Consideration of the following recruiting activities should be done to make recruiting more effective:

- *Résumé Mining*—A software approach to getting the best résumés for a fit from a big database
- *Applicant Tracking*—An approach that takes an applicant all the way from a job listing to performance appraisal results
- *Employer Career Website*—A convenient recruiting place on an employer's website where applicants can see what jobs are available and apply
- *Internal Mobility*—A system that tracks prospects in the organization and matches them with jobs as they come open
- *Realistic Job Previews*—A process that individuals can use to get details on the employer and the jobs
- *Responsive Recruitment*—A commitment wherein applicants receive timely responses

Recruiting effectiveness can be increased by using the evaluation data to target different applicant pools, tap broader labor markets, change recruiting methods, improve internal handling and interviewing of applicants, and train recruiters and managers.

Another key way to increase recruiting effectiveness rests with the recruiters themselves. Those involved in the recruiting process can either turn off recruits or create excitement. For instance, recruiters who emphasize positive aspects about the jobs and their employers can enhance recruiting effectiveness. Thus, it is important that recruiters communicate well with applicants and treat them fairly and professionally. Effective recruiting is crucial for every healthcare organization, as it leads to the opportunity to select individuals for employment who will enhance organizational success.

NATURE OF SELECTION

Selection is the process of choosing individuals with the correct qualifications to fill jobs in an organization. Without qualified workers, a healthcare organization is far less likely to succeed. A useful perspective on selection and placement comes from two observations that underscore the importance of effective staffing:

- *Hire hard, manage easy.* The investment of time and effort in selecting the right people for jobs will make managing them as employees much less difficult because many problems are eliminated.

- *Good training will not make up for bad selection.* When people without the appropriate aptitudes are selected, employers will have difficulty training them to do those jobs that they do not fit.[31]

Placement

The ultimate purpose of selection is **placement**, or fitting a person to the right job. Placement of people should be seen primarily as a matching process. How well an employee is matched to a job can affect the amount and quality of the employee's work, as well as the training and operating costs required to prepare the individual to do the work. Further, employee morale is an issue because good fit encourages individuals to be positive about their jobs and what they accomplish.[32]

Selection and placement activities typically focus on applicants' knowledge, skills, and abilities (KSAs), but they should also focus on the degree to which job candidates generally match the situations experienced both on the job and in the company. Psychologists label this *person–environment fit*. In HR it is usually called **person–job fit**. Fit is related not only to work satisfaction but also to company commitment and the desire to quit work.

Lack of fit between a person's KSAs and job requirements can be classified as a *mismatch*. A mismatch results from poor pairing of a person's needs, interests, abilities, personality, and expectations with characteristics of the job, rewards, and the organization in which the job is located. What makes placement difficult and complex is the need to match people and jobs on multiple dimensions.[33]

Healthcare workers already working in jobs can help identify the most important KSAs for success as part of job analysis. The fit between the individual and job characteristics is particularly important when dealing with stressful patient care jobs because employees must have the proper personalities, skills, and interpersonal abilities to be effective in those types of jobs.[34]

In addition to the match between people and jobs, employers are concerned about the congruence between people and companies, or the **person–organization fit**. Person–organization fit is important from a *values* perspective, with many organizations trying to positively link a person's principles to the values of the company. Healthcare organizations tend to favor job applicants who effectively blend into how business or patient care is conducted. If positive fit is established, healthcare organizations should have a more motivated and committed workforce that is more likely to stay and perform.[35]

Selection, Criteria, Predictors, and Job Performance

Regardless of whether a healthcare employer uses specific KSAs or a more general approach, effective selection of employees involves using selection criteria and predictors of these criteria. At the heart of an effective selection system must be the knowledge of what constitutes good job performance. Knowing what good performance looks like in a particular job helps identify what it takes for the employee to achieve successful performance. These are called selection criteria. A **selection criterion** is a characteristic that a person must possess to successfully perform work. Figure 6-5 shows that ability, motivation, intelligence,

FIGURE 6-5 Job Performance, Selection Criteria, and Predictors

What constitutes good job performance on this job?	What does it take for a person to achieve good job performance?	What can be seen or measured to predict the selection criteria?
Elements of Good Job Performance	**Characteristics Necessary to Achieve Good Job Performance (Selection Criteria)**	**Predictors of Selection Criteria**
◆ Quantity of work ◆ Quality of work ◆ Compatibility with others ◆ Presence at work ◆ Length of service ◆ Flexibility	◆ Ability ◆ Motivation ◆ Intelligence ◆ Conscientiousness ◆ Appropriate risk for employer ◆ Appropriate permanence	◆ Experience ◆ Past performance ◆ Physical skills ◆ Education ◆ Interests ◆ Salary requirements ◆ Certificates/degrees ◆ Test scores ◆ Personality measures ◆ Work references ◆ Previous jobs and tenure

conscientiousness, appropriate risk, and permanence might be selection criteria for many jobs. Selection criteria that might be more specific to managerial jobs include leading and deciding, supporting and cooperating, organizing and executing, and enterprising and performing.[36]

To determine whether candidates might possess certain selection criteria (such as ability and motivation), employers try to identify **predictors of selection criteria**, which are measurable or visible indicators of those positive characteristics (or criteria). Figure 6-5 shows how job performance, selection criteria, and predictors are interrelated. If a candidate possesses appropriate amounts of any or all of these predictors, it might be assumed that the person would stay on the job longer than someone without those predictors.[37] In addition, the information gathered about an applicant using the individual predictors included in application forms, tests, and interviews should focus on the likelihood that the person will execute the job competently once hired, so the factors need to be valid for the purposes of selection.[38]

Validity and Reliability

In selection, validity is the correlation between a predictor and job performance. In other words, validity occurs to the extent that the predictor actually predicts what it is supposed to predict. Several types of validity are used in the selection of healthcare workers. As an example, in order for a nurse to be hired as an RN in a hospital, they must be a graduate of an accredited nursing school, have passed their nursing boards to become licensed by the state in which they work, and interview with a variety of nursing professionals at the hospital who will ask them a number of questions to determine their competency to work in a particular job. All of these components of the selection process are designed to predict whether the RN candidate can safely and efficiently perform the job.

Concurrent validity is one method for establishing the validity associated with a predictor. Concurrent validity uses current employees to validate a predictor or "test." A disadvantage of the concurrent validity approach is that employees who have not performed satisfactorily at work are probably no longer with the firm and therefore cannot be tested. Also, extremely good employees may have been promoted or may have left the organization for better work situations. Any learning on the job also might confound test scores.

Another method for establishing criterion-related validity is predictive validity. To calculate **predictive validity**, test results of applicants are compared with their subsequent job performance. Job success is measured by assessing factors such as absenteeism, accidents, errors, and performance appraisal ratings. For example, if the RN noted above had one year of experience at the time of hire and demonstrated better performance than RNs without such experience, then the experience requirement can be considered a valid predictor of job performance. In addition, individual experience may be used as an important selection criterion when making future staffing decisions.

The Equal Employment Opportunity Commission (EEOC) has favored predictive validity because it includes the full range of performance and test scores. However, establishing predictive validity can be challenging for HR professionals because a large sample of individuals is needed (usually at least 30), and a significant amount of time must transpire (perhaps one year) to do the analysis.

Reliability   Reliability of a predictor or test is the extent to which it repeatedly produces the same results over time. For example, if a person took a test in December and scored 75, and then took the same test again in March and scored 76, the exam is probably a reliable instrument. Consequently, reliability involves the consistency of predictors used in selection procedures. A predictor that is not reliable is of no value in selection.

Combining Predictors

If an employer chooses to use only one predictor, such as a pencil-and-paper test, to select individuals, the decision becomes straightforward. If the test is valid, it encompasses a major dimension of a job, and an applicant does well on the test, then that person could be given a job offer. When an employer uses predictors such as three years of experience, a college degree, and acceptable aptitude test score, job applicants are evaluated on all of these requirements and the multiple predictors must be combined in some way.

Additional Legal Concerns

Sophisticated healthcare employers use a variety of preemployment steps and predictors to ensure that applicants will fit available jobs. Selection is subject to all EEO requirements.

It is increasingly important for employers to define carefully and exactly who is an applicant, given the legal issues involved. If there is no written policy defining conditions that make a person an applicant, anyone who sends unsolicited résumés might later claim that he or she was not hired because of illegal discrimination. A policy-defining *applicant* might include the following aspects:

- Applications are accepted only when there is an opening.
- Only individuals filling out application blanks are considered applicants.
- A person's application ceases to be effective after a designated date.
- Only a certain number of applications will be accepted.
- People must apply for specific jobs, not "any job."[39]

Immigration Forms   The Immigration Reform and Control Act of 1986, as amended in 1990, requires that within 72 hours of hiring, an employer must determine whether a job applicant is a U.S. citizen, registered alien, or illegal alien. Applicants who are not eligible to work in this country must not be hired. Employers use the I-9 form to identify the status of potential employees. Employers are responsible for ensuring the legitimacy of documents submitted by new employees, such as U.S. passports, birth certificates, original Social Security cards, and driver's licenses.[40] Also, employers who hire employees on special visas must maintain appropriate documentation and records.

Selection Responsibilities

Healthcare organizations vary in how they allocate selection responsibilities between HR specialists and managers. Selection activities may be centralized into a specialized organizational unit that is part of an HR department. In smaller organizations, such as clinics (especially those with fewer than 100 employees), a full-time employment specialist or unit might be impractical.

Most organizations take certain common steps to process applicants for jobs. Variations on this basic process depend on organizational size, the nature of jobs to be filled, the number of people to be selected, and the pressure of outside forces. The selection process shown in Figure 6-6 is typical in a large healthcare organization. However, all or some of the components of the process can be easily utilized in smaller organizations, such as physician or dental practices.

Reception and Job Preview/Interest Screening

In addition to matching qualified people to jobs, the selection process has an important public relations dimension. This is especially true for healthcare employees. Discriminatory hiring practices, impolite interviewers, unnecessarily long waits, inappropriate testing procedures, and lack of follow-up communications can produce unfavorable impressions of an employer, potentially having a negative impact its employment brand.

In some cases, it is appropriate to have a brief interview, called an *initial screening* or a *job preview/interest screen*, to see if the applicant is likely to match any jobs available in the organization after allowing the individual to fill out an application form. As noted in Figure 6-6, in many cases healthcare organizations conduct the preview/interest screen interview by phone.

Increasingly, the job preview/interest screen is done effectively over the Internet. Computerized processing of applicants can occur on several different levels. Computers can search résumés or application blanks for key words. Many large healthcare organizations use types of artificial-intelligence (AI) or *text-searching* software to scan, score, and track résumés of applicants.[41] Another means of computerizing screening is conducting initial screening interviews electronically. Computer-assisted interviewing techniques can use tools such as videotaped scenarios to which applicants react.

The purpose of a **realistic job preview (RJP)** is to inform job candidates of the "organizational realities" of a job so that they can more accurately evaluate their own job expectations. By presenting applicants with a clear picture of the jobs, the organization hopes to reduce unrealistic expectations, thereby reducing employee disenchantment, dissatisfaction, and turnover.

FIGURE 6-6 **Typical Selection Process for a Large Healthcare Organization**

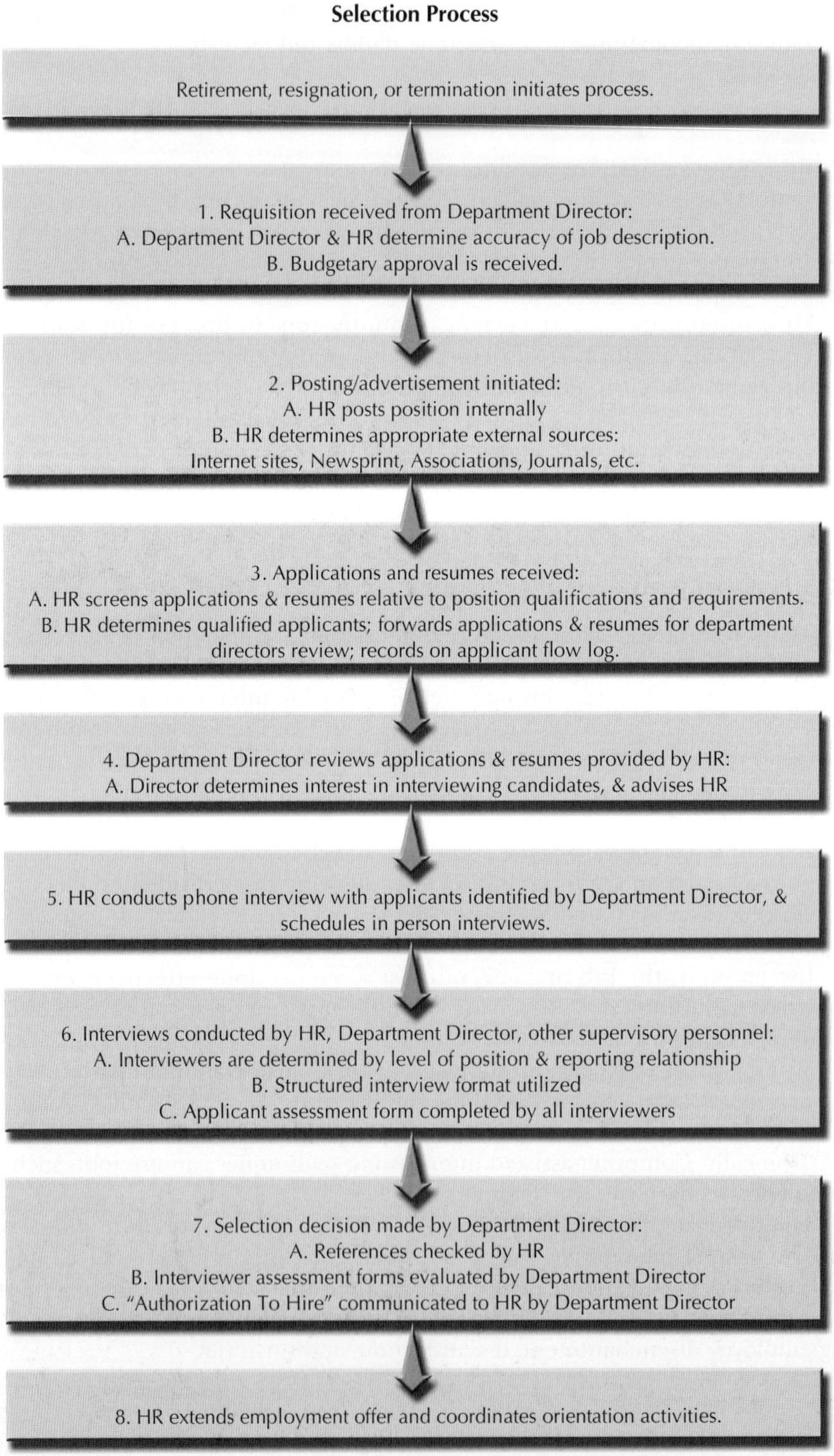

Selection Process

Retirement, resignation, or termination initiates process.

1. Requisition received from Department Director:
A. Department Director & HR determine accuracy of job description.
B. Budgetary approval is received.

2. Posting/advertisement initiated:
A. HR posts position internally
B. HR determines appropriate external sources:
Internet sites, Newsprint, Associations, Journals, etc.

3. Applications and resumes received:
A. HR screens applications & resumes relative to position qualifications and requirements.
B. HR determines qualified applicants; forwards applications & resumes for department directors review; records on applicant flow log.

4. Department Director reviews applications & resumes provided by HR:
A. Director determines interest in interviewing candidates, & advises HR

5. HR conducts phone interview with applicants identified by Department Director, & schedules in person interviews.

6. Interviews conducted by HR, Department Director, other supervisory personnel:
A. Interviewers are determined by level of position & reporting relationship
B. Structured interview format utilized
C. Applicant assessment form completed by all interviewers

7. Selection decision made by Department Director:
A. References checked by HR
B. Interviewer assessment forms evaluated by Department Director
C. "Authorization To Hire" communicated to HR by Department Director

8. HR extends employment offer and coordinates orientation activities.

Application Forms

Application forms are widely used. Properly prepared, an application form serves four purposes:

1. It is a record of the applicant's desire to obtain a position.
2. It provides the interviewer with a profile of the applicant that can be used in the interview.
3. It is a basic employee record for applicants who are hired.
4. It can be used for research on the effectiveness of the selection process.

Application Disclaimers and Notices   Application forms need disclaimers and notices so that employers state appropriate legal protections. Recommended disclosures and notices appearing on applications include:

- *Employment-at-Will*—Indicates the right of the employer or applicant to terminate the employment relationship at any time with or without notice or cause (where applicable by state law)
- *Employment Testing*—Notifies applicants of required drug tests, physical exams, or other tests
- *Reference Contacts*—Requests permission to contact references listed by applicants
- *Application Time Limit*—Indicates how long applications are active (typically six months) and that individuals must reactivate applications after that period
- *Information Falsification*—Conveys to an applicant signing the form that falsification of application information is grounds for termination

EEOC Considerations and Application Forms   Guidelines from the EEOC and court decisions require that the data requested on application forms must be job-related. Though frequently occasionally still found on application forms, questions that ask for the following information are illegal:

- Marital status
- Height/weight
- Number and ages of dependents
- Information on spouse
- Date of high school graduation
- Contact in case of emergency

Most of the litigation surrounding application forms has involved questions regarding the gender and age of a potential employee, so special consideration should be dedicated to removing any items that relate to these personal characteristics. Concerns about inappropriate questions stem from their potential to elicit information that should not be used in hiring decisions. Figure 6-7 shows a sample application form containing questions that generally are legal.

FIGURE 6-7 **Sample Employment Application**

Application for Employment
An Equal Opportunity Employer*

Today's Date _____

PERSONAL INFORMATION

Please Print or Type

Name	(Last)	(First)	(Full middle name)

Current address	City	State	Zip code	Phone number ( )

What position are you applying for?	Date available for employment?	E-mail address

Are you willing to relocate?
☐ Yes   ☐ No

Are you willing to travel if required?
☐ Yes   ☐ No

Have you ever been employed by this Company or any of its subsidiaries before?
☐ Yes   ☐ No

Indicate location and dates

Can you, after employment, submit verification of your legal right to work in the United States?
☐ Yes   ☐ No

Have you ever been convicted of a felony?
☐ Yes   ☐ No

Convictions will not automatically disqualify job candidates. The seriousness of the crime and the date of conviction will be considered.

PERFORMANCE OF JOB FUNCTIONS

Are you able to perform all the functions of the job for which you are applying, with or without accommodation?

☐ Yes, without accommodation   ☐ Yes, with accommodation   ☐ No

If you indicated you can perform all the functions with an accommodation, please explain how you would perform the tasks and with what accommodation.

EDUCATION

School level	School name and address	No. of years attended	Did you graduate?	Course of study
High school				
Vo-tech, business, or trade school				
College				
Graduate school				

PERSONAL DRIVING RECORD

This section is to be completed ONLY if the operation of a motor vehicle will be required in the course of the applicant's employment.

How long have you been a licensed driver?	Driver's license number	Expiration date	Issuing State

List any other state(s) in which you have had a driver's license(s) in the past:

Within the past five years, have you had a vehicle accident?
☐ Yes   ☐ No

Been convicted of reckless or drunken driving?
☐ Yes   ☐ No

If yes, give dates:

Been cited for moving violations? If yes, give dates:
☐ Yes   ☐ No

Has your driver's license ever been revoked or suspended?
☐ Yes   ☐ No

If yes, explain:

Is your driver's license restricted?   If yes, explain:
☐ Yes   ☐ No

*We are an Equal Opportunity Employer. We do not discriminate on the basis of race, religion, color, gender, age, national origin, or disability.

Résumés One of the most common methods applicants use to provide background information is the résumé. Technically, a résumé used in place of an application form must be treated by an employer as an application for EEO purposes. However, substituting a résumé for an application form is discouraged. The application form, if properly designed, should require the applicant's signature attesting to the accuracy and truthfulness of the information provided by the applicant. When organizations rely exclusively on résumés, they do not have those assurances to legally act if the applicants have misrepresented or falsified their information.

SELECTION TESTING

Many kinds of tests can be used to help select qualified employees. Literacy tests, skill-based tests, personality tests, and honesty tests can be used to assess various individual factors that are important for the work to be performed. These employment tests allow healthcare employers to predict which applicants will likely be the most successful before being hired.

However, selection tests must be evaluated extensively before being utilized as a recruiting tool. The development of the test items should be linked to a thorough job analysis. Also, initial testing of the items should include an evaluation by knowledge experts, and statistical and validity assessments of the items should be conducted.

Ability Tests

Tests that assess an individual's ability to perform in a specific manner are grouped as ability tests. These are sometimes further differentiated into *aptitude tests* and *achievement tests*. **Cognitive ability tests** measure an individual's thinking, memory, reasoning, verbal, and mathematical abilities. Valid tests such as the Wonderlic Personnel Test and the General Aptitude Test Battery (GATB) can be used to determine applicants' basic knowledge of terminology and concepts, word fluency, spatial orientation, comprehension and retention span, general and mental ability, and conceptual reasoning.

Physical ability tests measure an individual's abilities such as strength, endurance, and muscular movement. At a large medical center, security officers must regularly lift and carry equipment and perform other physical tasks; therefore, testing of applicants' mobility, strength, and other physical attributes is job related. Some physical ability tests measure factors like range of motion, strength and posture, and cardiovascular fitness. Care should also be taken to limit physical ability testing until after a conditional job offer is made to avoid violating provisions of the Americans with Disabilities Act (ADA).

Various skill-based tests can be used, including **psychomotor tests**, which measure a person's dexterity, hand–eye coordination, arm–hand steadiness, and other factors. Tests such as the MacQuarie Test for Mechanical Ability can measure manual dexterity for materials handling.

Many healthcare organizations use situational tests, or **work sample tests**, which require an applicant to perform a simulated task that is a specified part of the target job. Requiring an applicant for a medical secretary job to transcribe a letter that includes medical terminology quickly and accurately would be an example of a work sample test. Once again, these tests should assess criteria that are embedded in the job that is to be staffed.

Situational judgment tests are designed to measure a person's judgment in work settings. The candidate is given a situation and a list of possible solutions to the problem. The candidate then has to make judgments about how to deal with the situation. Situational judgment tests are a form of job simulation.[42]

Assessment Centers   An assessment center is not a place but an assessment exercise composed of a series of evaluative tests used for selection and development. Most often used in the selection process when filling management and executive openings, assessment centers consist of multiple exercises and are evaluated by multiple raters. In one assessment center, candidates go through a comprehensive interview, a pencil-and-paper test, individual and group simulations, and work exercises. Individual performance is then evaluated by a panel of trained raters.

The tests and exercises in an assessment center must reflect the content of the job for which individuals are being screened, and the types of problems faced on that job. For example, a large mental health agency used a series of assessment centers to hire a chief financial officer. The agency found that utilizing assessment centers improved the selection process and also provided the new executive with a good road map for individual development.

Personality Tests

Personality is a unique blend of individual characteristics that can affect how people interact with their work environment. Healthcare organizations may use various personality tests to assess the degree to which candidates' attributes match specific job criteria. For instance, a dental group with many locations offers job applicants a web-based test. The test evaluates their personal tendencies, especially relating to customer skills, and test scores are used to categorize individuals for the hiring decision. Many types of personality tests are available, including the Myers-Briggs test.

Faking Personality Tests   Faking is a major concern for healthcare employers using personality tests. Many test publishers admit that test profiles can be falsified, and they try to reduce faking by including questions that can be used to compute a social desirability or "lie" score.

Polygraphs   The polygraph, more generally and incorrectly referred to as a lie detector, is a mechanical device that measures a person's galvanic skin response, heart rate, and breathing rate. The idea behind the polygraph is that if a person answers a question deliberately incorrectly, the body's physiological responses will "reveal" the falsification through the recording mechanisms of the polygraph.

As a result of concerns about polygraph validity, Congress passed the Employee Polygraph Protection Act, which prohibits most employers from the use of polygraphs for preemployment screening purposes. Federal, state, and local government agencies are exempt from the act. Also exempt are certain private-sector employers such as security companies and pharmaceutical companies. The act does allow employers to use polygraphs as part of internal investigations of thefts or losses. But in those situations, the polygraph test should be taken voluntarily, and the employee should be allowed to end the test at any time.

In summary, many kinds of tests may be used to help select good employees. Carefully developed and properly administered employment tests allow healthcare employers to predict which applicants have the abilities to do specific jobs, who may learn better in training, and who may be more likely to stay.

SELECTION INTERVIEWING

A selection interview is designed to identify information on a candidate and clarify information from other sources. This in-depth interview is designed to integrate all the information from application forms, tests, and reference checks so that a decision can be made. Because of the integration required and the desirability of face-to-face contact, the interview is the most important phase of the selection process in many situations. Conflicting information may have emerged from tests, application forms, and references. As a result, the interviewer must obtain as much pertinent information about the applicant as possible during the limited interview time and evaluate this information against job standards. Figure 6-8 details the "do's" and "don'ts" of employment interviewing. Finally, a selection decision must be made, based on all of the information obtained in the preceding steps.

Types of Interviews

The interview is not an especially valid predictor of job performance, but it has high "face validity"—that is, it seems valid to employers, and they like it. Virtually all employers are likely to hire individuals using interviews of different types. Generally, the following types of interviews can improve the validity of the selection process.

Structured Interview   The structured interview uses a set of standardized questions that are asked of all applicants. Every applicant is asked the same basic questions, so that comparisons among applicants can more easily be made. This type of interview allows an interviewer to prepare job-related questions in advance and then complete a standardized interviewee evaluation form. Completion of such a form provides documentation if anyone, including an EEO enforcement body, should question why one applicant was selected over another.

Behavioral Event Interview   When responding to a **behavioral event interview**, applicants are asked to give specific examples of how they have performed a certain procedure or handled a problem in the past. Consistent with information

FIGURE 6-8 Employment Interviewing Do's and Don'ts

DO:

Use reminders to get back to the original line of inquiry.
Ask open-ended questions (How do you like ...?).
Use one and two-step probes (What? Why?).
Ask for laundry lists (What are the satisfactions that you look for in a job?)
Use echoes (. . . .boring work?).
Use summaries (Looking back, how did you like the place?).
Pause (15 seconds is a long time!).
Ask self-evaluation questions.
Present hypothetical situations.

DON'T:

Ask "yes" or "no" questions.
Ask leading questions.
Ask questions which reveal <u>your</u> perspective.
Ask redundant questions.
Rudely interrupt.
Talk down to an applicant.

© Cengage Learning®

detailed earlier, behavioral event interviews provide insight on how applicants will perform in the future based on how they have performed in the past. For example, a behavioral event interview question for a clinic manager applicant might be: "Describe how you have handled difficult employee relations situations in your past supervisory positions; include examples and outcomes." Applicants' responses to this question could provide important insight regarding how they would handle future employee relations situations they were confronted with, and whether their approach is compatible with the approach the organization typically would want. Like other structured selection methods, behavioral event interviews generally provide better validity than unstructured interviews.

Panel Interview

Usually, applicants are interviewed by one interviewer at a time. But when an interviewee must see several people, many of the interviews are redundant and therefore unnecessarily time-consuming. In a **panel interview**, several interviewers interview the candidate at the same time. All the interviewers hear the same responses. On the negative side, many applicants are frequently uncomfortable with the group interview format.

CRIMINAL BACKGROUND CHECKING

Due to the very nature of providing patient care and the close personal and physical contact many healthcare workers have with patients, residents, and clients, healthcare organizations have a special duty to conduct background checks.

This duty is to ensure that the patient caregivers have no previous conviction record involving crimes of violence, sexual misconduct, or criminal behavior.

Criminal background checking should take place after a conditional offer of employment has been made. It costs the organization some time and money, but it is generally well worth the effort. Unfortunately, some applicants misrepresent their qualifications and backgrounds.

Legal Constraints

Various federal and state laws have been passed to protect the rights of individuals whose backgrounds may be investigated during preemployment screening. According to the EEOC, employers may violate Title VII in the use of criminal records if they (1) intentionally discriminate against applicants with similar criminal histories by treating them differently because of a protected characteristic, or (2) maintain a criminal background check policy that has a disparate impact on a particular protected group. It is this latter form of discrimination with which employers must be particularly concerned. According to the EEOC, national data demonstrate that there is a disproportionate arrest and conviction rate for African Americans and Hispanics.[43]

States vary in what they allow employers to investigate. In some states, healthcare employers can request information directly from law enforcement agencies on applicants. In Ohio, for example, healthcare organizations and day-care centers must submit the fingerprints of applicants to determine if the applicants have disqualifying criminal histories.

Fair Credit Reporting Act   Some healthcare employers check applicants' credit histories. The logic is that individuals with poor credit histories may be irresponsible managers of money. However, this assumption may be questioned, and firms that check applicants' credit records must comply with both the Federal Fair Credit Reporting Act (FCRA) and EEO guidelines or selection. FCRA basically requires disclosing that a credit check is being made, obtaining written consent from the person being checked, and furnishing the applicant a copy of the report. Some state laws also prohibit employers from getting certain credit information.

Credit history checking should be done on applicants for jobs in which use, access, or management of money is an essential job function. Commonly, healthcare organizations check credit histories on employees who handle money or are responsible for sensitive financial information, such as accountants, business office personnel, or financial executives.

Giving References on Former Employees   In a number of court cases, individuals have sued their former employers for slander, libel, or defamation of character as a result of what the employers said to other potential employers that prevented the individuals from obtaining jobs. Because of such problems, many organizations have adopted policies restricting the release of reference information. Lawyers advise organizations who are asked about former employees to give out only name, employment date, and title.

Under the Federal Privacy Act of 1974, a governmental employer must have a signed release from a person before it can give information about that person to someone else. The recommendation is that all employers obtain a signed release from individuals during exit interviews authorizing employers to provide reference information in the future.

Clearly, employers are in a difficult position. Because of threats of lawsuits, they must obtain information on potential employees but are unwilling to give out information in return. To address these concerns, more and more states have laws that protect employers from civil liability when giving reference information in good faith that is objective and factual in nature.

Risks of Negligent Hiring   The costs of failing to check references may be high. Some organizations have become targets of lawsuits that charge them with negligence in hiring workers who have committed violent acts on the job. Lawyers say that an employer's liability hinges on how well it investigates an applicant's background. Prior convictions and frequent moves or gaps in employment should be cues for further inquiry. Details provided on the application form by the applicant should be investigated to the greatest extent possible, so the employer can show that due diligence was exercised. Also, employers should document their efforts to check background information by noting who was contacted, when, and what information was or was not provided. This documentation can aid in countering negligent hiring claims.

Medical Examinations and Inquiries

Medical information on applicants may be used to determine the individual's physical and mental capability for performing jobs. Physical standards for jobs should be realistic, justifiable, and geared to the job requirements. Workers with disabilities can perform satisfactorily in many jobs. However, in many places they are rejected because of their disabilities, rather than being screened and placed in appropriate jobs.

ADA and Medical Inquiries   The ADA prohibits the use of preemployment medical exams, except for drug tests, until a job has been conditionally offered. Also, the ADA prohibits a company from rejecting an individual because of a disability and from asking job applicants any questions relative to current or past medical history until a conditional job offer is made. Assuming a conditional offer of employment is made, some organizations ask applicants to complete a preemployment health checklist or ask for a physical examination paid for by the employer.

Drug Testing   Drug testing may be a part of a medical exam, or it may be done separately. Using drug testing as a part of the selection process has increased in the past few years, although some employers facing tight labor markets have discontinued drug testing. Employers should remember that the accuracy of drug tests varies according to the type of test used, the items tested, and the quality of the laboratory where the test samples are sent. Whether urine, blood, saliva, or hair samples are used, the process of obtaining, labeling, and transferring the samples to the testing lab should be outlined clearly, and definite policies and procedures should be established. Because of the potential impact of prescription drugs on test results, applicants should complete a detailed questionnaire on this matter before the testing. If an individual tests positive for drug use, then an independent medical laboratory should administer a second, more detailed analysis.

Genetic Testing   Another controversial area of medical testing is genetic testing. Employers that use genetic screening tests do so for several reasons. First, the tests may link workplace health hazards and individuals with certain genetic characteristics. Second, genetic testing may be used to make workers aware of genetic problems that could occur in certain work situations. The third use is the most controversial: to exclude individuals from certain jobs if they have genetic conditions that increase their health risks. Since people cannot change their genetic makeup, the potential for illegal discrimination based on genetic predisposition to future health issues is a concern that should be evaluated.

Making the Job Offer

The final step of the selection process is making a job offer. Often extended over the phone, many job offers are then formalized in letters sent to applicants. It is important that the offer document be reviewed by legal counsel and that the terms and conditions of employment be clearly identified. Care should be taken to avoid vague, general statements and promises about bonuses, work schedules, or other matters that might change later. These documents also should provide for the individuals to sign an acceptance of the offer and return it to the employer, who should place it in the individual's personnel file.

Relocation Assistance

New employees may require relocation assistance. Healthcare employers may provide relocation assistance for individuals selected who live away from the new job site. Typically, executives and physicians are the recipients of relocation assistance. Relocation assistance enables these new employees to become productive more quickly in their new locations. Such relocation assistance often includes sales of existing homes, moving expenses, house-hunting trip costs, automobile transportation, and new-home mortgage assistance. Regardless of the type of relocation assistance, the nature and extent of relocation assistance may set the tone for how new employees view their new jobs. Such assistance also aids in the adjustment of the employees' family members.

CASE

Behavioral Care Center (BCC) is a 50-bed inpatient, mental health hospital. Recently, BCC has had shortages of staff that at times have restricted the hospital's ability to admit patients. The most needed positions are RNs, LPNs, and direct patient care staff known as behavioral assistants (BAs). In order to have full coverage in the hospital, BCC needs to hire seven RNs, three LPNs, and six BAs.

The HR department posts openings on the hospital's website and encourages staff to refer friends and family to apply. Representatives from the public relations department have attended a number of job fairs to encourage applicants to apply. These strategies have normally worked for BCC. However, recently the results have not been forthcoming and the shortages are increasingly more concerning. Consequently, to deal with this crisis a task force composed of department heads has been established. The role of the task force is to evaluate the recruitment situation and make recommendations.

Questions

1. What recruitment strategies should the task force consider?
2. How should BCC strategize to avoid staffing shortages in the future?

END NOTES

1. Laura Putre, "A Clash of Ages," *H&HN* (March 2013), 40–44; Matthew W. Kreuter et al., "Lessons Learned from a Decade of Focused Recruitment and Training to Develop Minority Public Health Professionals," *American Journal of Public Health* (December 2011), Supplement, 188–195.
2. "What SMBs Should Look for in an Applicant Tracking System," September 25, 2009, *http://www.taleo.com*.
3. John Yuva, "Round Up the Recruits," *Inside Supply Management* (July 2008), 23–25; Auren Hoffman, "Why Hiring Is Paradoxically Harder in a Downturn," *HR Leaders* (July14, 2009), *http://www.hrleaders.org*.
4. Kurt Scott, "The Search for Effective Physician Leaders," *Physician Executive* (March/April 2009), 44–48.
5. Julie C. Ramirez, "Courting Chameleons," *Human Resource Executive Online* (June 16, 2009), *http://www.hreonline.com*; Joe Light, "Help Wanted: Multilingual Employees," *Wall Street Journal* (January 18, 2011), B7.
6. See *https://www.aamc.org/newsroom/reporter/april11/184178/addressing_the_physician_shortage_under_reform.html* for more information.
7. Michael E. Porter and Thomas H. Lee, "The Strategy That Will Fix Health Care," *Harvard Business Review* (October 2013), 50–70.
8. Ralf Wilden, Siegfried Gudergan, and Ian Lings, "Employer Branding: Strategic Implications for Staff Recruitment," *Journal of Marketing Management* 26 (2010),
56–73; Ron Thomas, "What to Ask as You Start 2012: Why Would Somebody Work for You?," *HR Updates* (January 3, 2012), peter.reis@me.com.
9. See *http://www.nursecredentialing.org/Magnet/ProgramOverview/New-Magnet-Model* for more information.
10. Thomas L. Powers et al., "Environmental and Organizational Influences on Magnet Hospital Recognition," *Journal of Healthcare Management* (October 2013), 353–366.
11. "Ethical Issues Related to Staff Shortages," *Healthcare Executive* (July/August 2013), 94–95.
12. David Imbrogno, "The Outsourcing of HR," *Quality* (December 2010), 34–35.
13. Judy Whitcomb, "Employee Retention," *Training* (November/December 2012), 52–54.
14. Tamara Lytle, "College Career Centers Create a Vital Link," *HR Magazine* (May 2013), 34–41.
15. "E-recruiting Software Providers," *Workforce Management* (June 22, 2009), 14.
16. "New Job Search Engine Makes Finding a Job Easier," *The Career News* (September 21, 2009), *http://www.thecareernews.com*.
17. Ann Fisher, "2014, The Year of the 'Passive' Job Hunter," Fortune.com (January 9, 2014).
18. See *http://www.mmgma.org/jobs* for more information.
19. H. Jack Walker, Hubert S. Field, William F. Giles, Achilles A. Armenakis, and Jeremy

B. Bernerth, "Displaying Employee Testimonials on Recruiting Websites: Effects of Communication Media, Employee Race, and Job Seeker Race on Organization Attraction and Information Credibility," *Journal of Applied Psychology* 94 (2009), 1354–1364.

20. Chris Tratar, "Recruiting by Relationship to Fill the Candidate Pipeline," *Workforce Management* (July 20, 2009), S5.

21. Vangie Sison, "Social Media: Attracting Talent in the Age of Web 2.0," *Workspan* (May 2009), 45–49; Sam De Kay, "Are Business-Oriented Social Networking Websites Useful Resources for Locating Passive Job Seekers?," *Business Communications Quarterly* (March 2009), 101–104.

22. Gonzalo Hernandez and Ed Frauenheim, "Logging Off of Job Boards," *Workforce Management* (June 22, 2009), 25–28.

23. Andrew R. McIlvaine, "Lights, Camera, Interview," *Human Resource Executive* (September 16, 2009), 22–25; Rita Zeidner, "Companies Tell Their Stories in Recruitment Videos," *HR Trendbook* (2008), 28.

24. A. Moscaritolo, "Twitter Usage Doubles in a Year," *PC Magazine* (June 2012), 1.

25. Tresa Baldas, "Lawyers Warn Employers Against Giving Glowing Reviews on LinkedIn," *National Law Journal* (July 6, 2009), *http://www.nlj.com.*

26. Gary Crispin, "The Future of Recruiting," *Human Resource Executive* (September 16, 2009), 32–35.

27. Joe Light, "Recruiters Rethink Online Playbook," *Wall Street Journal* (January 18, 2011), B7; Andrew R. McIlvaine, "Do Friends Let Friends Recruit via Facebook?," *Human Resource Executive Online* (July 25, 2011), *http://www.hreonline.com*; Anonymous, "The State of Social Media in the Workplace: Uses and Measurement," *T+D* (December 2011), 21.

28. Meinald T. Thielsch, Lisa Traumer, and Leoni Pytlik, "E-recruiting and Fairness: The Applicant's Point of View," *Information Technology Management* (published online April 4, 2012).

29. Paul Barr, "Ochsner's Aussie Edge," *Modern Healthcare* (March 18, 2013), 30.

30. "HR Benchmarks," *Controller's Report* (March 2010), 3–4.

31. Alan Krueger and David Schkade, "Sorting in the Labor Market," *Journal of Human Resources* 43, no. 4 (2008), 859–883.

32. Melanie Wanzek, "On Second Thought," *Sunday World Herald* (May 10, 2009), CR1.

33. Metin Celik, I. Deha Er, and Y. Ilker Topcu, "Computer-Based Systematic Executive Model of HRM in Maritime Transportation Industry: The Case of Master Selection for Embarking on Board Merchant Ships," *Expert Systems with Applications* 36 (2009), 1048–1060.

34. Michael J. Dotson, Dinesh S. Dave, and Joseph A. Cazier, "Addressing the Nursing Shortage: A Critical Health Care Issue," *Health Marketing Quarterly* 29, no. 4 (2012), 311–328.

35. Robert Grossman, "Hiring to Fit the Culture," *HR Magazine* (February 2009), 41–50.

36. Dave Bartram, "The Great Eight Competencies: A Criterion-Centric Approach to Validation," *Journal of Applied Psychology* 90 (2005), 1185–1203.

37. Murray Barrick and Ryan Zimmerman, "Hiring for Retention and Performance," *Human Resource Management* (March–April 2009), 183–206.

38. Peter Cappelli, "The Impact of a High School Diploma," *HR Executive Online* (August 18, 2008), 1–3, *http://www.hreonline.com.*

39. See *http://www.eeoc.gov/eeoc/newsroom/release/3-3-04.cfm* for more information.

40. Max Mihelich, "Form I-9 Gets an Update," *Workforce Management* (June 2013),16.

41. D. Penfold, "Top 10 Tips for Great Résumés," *Association Meetings* [serial online] (December 2010), 19.

42. Deborah L. Whetzel and Michael A. McDonald, "Situational Judgment Tests: An Overview of Current Research," 19 (2009), 188–202.

43. Linda B. Dwoskin, Melissa Bergman Squire, and Jane Patullo, "Skeletons in the Closet? Legal Developments in Screening Applicants and Employees," *Employee Relations Law Journal* [serial online] (Spring 2014), 24–48.

ORGANIZATIONAL RELATIONS AND EMPLOYEE RETENTION IN HEALTHCARE

Learning Objectives

After you have read this chapter, you should be able to:

- Explain the factors affecting the relationship between employees and healthcare organizations.

- Discuss the importance of employee retention for healthcare organizations.

- Identify the common reasons employees voluntarily leave organizations.

- Define the various organizational retention determinants.

- Describe how to compute the cost of organizational turnover.

HEALTHCARE HR INSIGHTS

Centra Inc. is a healthcare system based in Lynchburg, Virginia, that includes three hospitals: Lynchburg General, Virginia Baptist, and Southside Community Hospital. Centra Inc. employs more than 6,000 employees and 150 physicians providing care in 38 locations. It serves more than 380,000 people throughout central and southside Virginia. Centra Inc. has been designated as a "magnet hospital" by the American Nurses Credentialing Center.

Due to the high number of new nurse graduates who must work the night shift at Centra for the first time in their new career, the nurse retention coordinator and nursing leadership designed a creative program for them to help with their adjustment to night-shift work. Being a nurse graduate is difficult enough as they acquire new knowledge and skills, and night-shift work adds another layer of stress to the beginning of their professional practice.

The nurse retention coordinator recognized that disruptive sleep was not only a quality-of-life issue for the new nurse but potentially a quality-of-care issue for the patient as well. Research supports that lack of restorative sleep affects the new nurses' mental and cognitive abilities and also impacts physiologic risk, including heart disease, diabetes, and hypertension. Staff members who work the night shift are at greater risk for falling asleep at the wheel and are also more prone to make errors than staff who work day shifts.

The actual programming to help the new nurses includes information about the importance of sleep and strategies to improve their sleep environment. The overall impact of this new program is seen in the fact that 93.4 percent of the new nurse graduates report they feel as if they are getting enough sleep to perform well at work. New nurse graduates are also at high risk for leaving not only their organization within the first year but also the profession itself. Centra's data indicate a decrease in annual new graduate turnover in year-over-year comparisons. Reducing any identified level of stress for the first-year nurse positively impacts the quality of care for patients and the quality of life for the new graduate nurses.[1]

The Healthcare HR Insight demonstrates that to help workers achieve work–life balance, HR programming needs to be planned and intentional to achieve results. The organization needs to examine its:

- *HR Systems*— Recruitment, appraisal, succession planning, and access to training, making sure they support work–life balance objectives
- *Processes for Work*— How it delegates duties and responsibilities
- *Technology*— Supporting work from home and/or other technologies that reduce unnecessary time spent at work

Most important, organizations need to assess their training of top management, individual employees, and operating managers, so that these three groups are aligned in their understanding of the issues, the priorities, and how to achieve the changes necessary to truly achieve a work–life balance culture. Healthcare employers, recognizing the value of human resources, have made significant strides in their retention efforts.

Retaining competent employees of all types is a critical requirement for all healthcare providers. Given the difficulty of recruiting healthcare professionals from an aging workforce and declining new-graduate pool, it is imperative that healthcare providers focus attention on retaining their current healthcare professionals.

INDIVIDUAL–ORGANIZATION RELATIONSHIPS

The long-term economic success of healthcare organizations depends on the efforts of employees with the appropriate capabilities and motivation to perform their jobs well. Organizations that are successful over time have understood that individual relationships do matter and should be managed. At one time, loyalty and long service with one healthcare organization was considered an appropriate individual–organization relationship. The relationship between an individual and his or her employer can be affected by HR practices and can vary widely from favorable to unfavorable. Understanding the relationships between individuals and organizations is more than just academically interesting. The economic health of most organizations depends on the efforts of employees with the ability and motivation to do their jobs well. The relationship between an employee and an employer affects both of them. Important elements of these relationships include the psychological contract, job satisfaction, commitment, engagement, and loyalty (see Figure 7-1).

Psychological Contract

A concept that has been useful in understanding individuals' relationship with their employers is that of a **psychological contract**, which refers to the unwritten expectations employees and employers have about the nature of their work

FIGURE 7-1 Individual Performance and Organizational Expectations

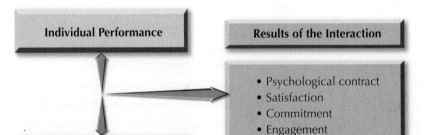

© 2016 Cengage Learning®

relationship. The psychological contract can create either a positive or a negative relationship between an employer and an individual.[2] It is based on trust and commitment that leads to meeting both the employer's and employee's expectations and needs.

Unwritten psychological contracts between employers and employees encompass expectations about both tangible items (e.g., wages, benefits, employee productivity, and attendance) and intangible items (e.g., loyalty, fair treatment, and job security).[3] Healthcare organizations detail their expectations through employee handbooks and policy manuals, but those materials are only part of the total "contractual" relationship.

The Changing Psychological Contract   Traditionally, healthcare workers expected to exchange their efforts and capabilities for secure jobs that offered competitive pay, a solid range of benefits, and career progression within an organization, among other factors.[4] But as some organizations have changed economically, they have addressed various organizational crises by downsizing and eliminating workers who had given long and loyal service. Consequently, in these organizations, a number of remaining employees question whether they should remain loyal to and stay with their employers. The psychological contract has been altered.

When individuals feel that the psychological contract provides them some control and perceived rights in the organization, they are more likely to be committed to the organization and utilize their knowledge, skills, and abilities to accomplish performance results.[5] A psychological contract usually recognizes at least the following expectations:

EMPLOYERS WILL PROVIDE	EMPLOYEES WILL CONTRIBUTE
• Competitive compensation and benefits	• Continuous skill improvement and increased productivity
• Flexibility to balance work and home life	• Reasonable length of service
• Career development opportunities	• Extra efforts and results when needed

Job Satisfaction and Commitment

In its most basic sense, **job satisfaction involves a favorable reaction to work based on positive emotional and cognitive evaluations of job experiences.** For example, if a laboratory worker in a large hospital expects clean and safe working conditions in the lab, that employee is likely to be dissatisfied if the lab is dirty, or the equipment is faulty and dangerous.

Sometimes job satisfaction is called *morale*, a term usually used to describe the job satisfaction of a group or organization. Frequently cited reasons for decline in morale include more demanding and stressful work, less contact with management, and less confidence in compensation and other rewards. Satisfied workers are less likely to leave the organization than their less-satisfied counterparts.[6]

Organizational Redesign and Morale

In today's healthcare environment, hospitals, long-term care facilities, and clinics are continually engaged in redesign. Major redesign initiatives in healthcare have been required by conversions to electronic medical records, the introduction of new technologies, and the need to do more with fewer staff.[7]

The more successful redesigns focus on individual issues, including changing mind-sets, providing clear communications, and making certain the support systems reflected the changes. Generally, good healthcare organizational redesigns are more likely to be described as improving morale or job satisfaction than the less successful redesign efforts. In fact, successful efforts can overcome employee distraction and demoralization—two of the most common challenges to successful redesign.

The degree to which an individual feels a strong connection to a firm, believes in and accepts corporate goals, and wants to stay employed with a company is called **organizational commitment**. Job satisfaction influences organizational commitment, which in turn affects employee retention and turnover. Thus, it is the interaction of the individual and job that determines levels of job satisfaction and organizational commitment.

Many organizations and researchers study job satisfaction. At any one time, the number of people dissatisfied with their jobs nationally varies from 15 to 40 percent. Higher unemployment rates usually mean more dissatisfied workers in the workforce, since it is more difficult to change jobs, and people stay longer with jobs they do not like. Individual managers have an impact on job satisfaction, and younger employees tend to have lower job satisfaction than older employees.[8] Currently, younger employees are affected by older employees delaying retirement for financial reasons; this affects their advancement opportunities, which in turn affects their job satisfaction.[9]

Figure 7-2 shows some of the most commonly recognized components of job satisfaction.

FIGURE 7-2   Components of Job Satisfaction

Nature of the Work

Adequacy of the Pay

Job Satisfaction

Coworkers

Opportunity for Advancement

Supervision

FIGURE 7-3   Descriptions of Engaged and Disengaged Employees

Engaged Employees	Disengaged Employees
• Put in extra effort • Are highly involved in their jobs • Employ both effort and thought • Are active/busy • Are fully invested in their jobs	• Simply put in time • Do not do best work • Are "checked out"/apathetic • Do only their basic jobs • React only to pay

© 2016 Cengage Learning®

Employee Engagement and Loyalty

Employee engagement can include satisfaction, support from management, using effort beyond a minimum, intention to stay, and other concepts.[10] It is a combination of several ideas often measured separately. Descriptions of "engaged employees" and "disengaged employees" are shown in Figure 7-3.

Although the concept of engagement is still evolving, a working definition might be the extent to which an employee's thoughts and behaviors are focused on the employer's success. Surveys suggest that perhaps 30 percent of workers are engaged in their jobs, half are not engaged, and about 20 percent are actively disengaged.[11]

Generational Differences   Much has been written about the differing expectations of individuals in different generations. It should be recognized that many of these observations are anecdotal and give generalizations about individuals in the various age groups. Some of the common generational labels are:

- The Silent Generation, also known as traditionalists (1925–1945);
- Baby boomers, also known as matures (1946–1964)
- Generation X or Gen X (1965–1981)
- Millennials, also known as Net Gen, Gen Y, GenerationMe, Gen Net, and digital natives (1982–1999)

Rather than identifying the characteristics cited for each of these groups, it is most important here to emphasize that people's expectations differ between generations as well as within these generation labels.[12] For healthcare employers, the differing expectations present challenges. For instance, many of the baby boomers are concerned about security and experience, whereas the younger Generation Ys often are seen as the "why?" generation who expect to be rewarded quickly, are very adaptable, and tend to be more questioning about why managers and organizations make the decisions they do.

Also, consider the dynamics of a mature manager directing Generation X and Y individuals, or Generation X managers supervising older, more experienced baby boomers. These generational differences are likely to continue to create challenges and conflicts in organizations because of the differing expectations that various individuals have. One of the most common areas of difference is seen in loyalty to organizations.

Loyalty Many employees still want security, stability, a supervisor they respect, competitive pay and benefits, and the opportunity to advance. But competition and increasing costs of doing business have led healthcare organizations to trim payrolls and to no longer offer those employment opportunities. As a result, the era of organizational loyalty is thought to have passed, and people are more inclined to move between employers.[13]

Loyalty can be defined as being faithful to an institution or employer. Loyalty is a reciprocal exchange—employees' loyalty to a company depends on their perceptions of the company's loyalty to them. The trend toward having employees bear more of the risk in their pensions, health insurance, and career development has sent a clear message that the employee must control his or her own future as the employer is not loyal.[14]

A logical extension of organizational engagement focuses specifically on *continuance commitment* factors. These are the factors that influence decisions to remain with or leave an organization, and ultimately they are reflected in employee retention and turnover statistics. Individuals who are not as satisfied with their jobs or who are not as committed to the organization are more likely to withdraw from the organization.

One kind of "withdrawal" is to leave the organization—that is, turnover. Another kind of withdrawal is absenteeism, which is simply not reporting to work on time on a regular basis. Absenteeism is covered in the next section.

EMPLOYEE ABSENTEEISM

A major issue in the relationship between employee and employer relates to employees who are absent from their work and job responsibilities. **Absenteeism** is any failure by an employee to report for work as scheduled or to stay at work when scheduled. Being absent from work may seem like an insignificant matter to an employee. But if a clinic manager needs 12 medical assistants to room patients and take vitals to maintain an appropriate schedule for the clinic doctors, and 4 of the 12 are frequently absent, either the patient satisfaction will suffer or additional workers will have to be hired to meet needs. Productivity losses due to absenteeism for some employers can be very expensive. The average daily cost is 1.3 times the wages of the absent worker.[15]

Concern over uncontrolled absenteeism must be weighed against the problem of "presenteeism," which occurs when people are sick and should stay home to avoid spreading illness but come to work anyway. This may occur for many reasons including the belief that no one else can do the job, role models who come to work sick, or overly stringent absenteeism controls.[16] Effective absence management involves striking a balance between supporting employees who are legitimately unable to work and meeting operational needs.

Types of Absenteeism

Employees can be absent from work or tardy for several reasons. Clearly, some absenteeism is inevitable because of illness, death in the family, and other personal reasons. Though absences such as those that are health related are unavoidable and understandable, they are still very costly. Many employers have sick leave policies that allow employees a certain number of paid days each year for *involuntary* absences. However, much absenteeism is avoidable, or *voluntary*. Absence can also be planned (the least disruptive), unplanned, incidental (less than a week), or extended (lasting beyond a week).

Many employees see no real concern about being absent or late to work because they feel that they are "entitled" to some absenteeism. In many healthcare organizations, a relatively small number of individuals are responsible for a large share of the total absenteeism in the organization. Regardless of the reason, employers need to know if someone is going to be absent so they can make adjustments. Due to the critical nature of many healthcare positions to support the safe delivery of patient care, healthcare employers have developed different ways for employees to report their absences.

Controlling Absenteeism

Voluntary absenteeism is best controlled if managers understand its causes and costs, and believe absenteeism *can be* controlled.[17] Once it is understood, they can use a variety of approaches to reduce it. Organizational policies on absenteeism should be stated clearly in an employee handbook and consistently enforced by supervisors and managers. Employers use methods such as the following to address absenteeism:

- *Disciplinary Approach*—Many healthcare employers use this approach. Workers who are absent the first time receive a verbal warning, and subsequent absences result in written warnings, suspension, and finally dismissal.

- *Positive Reinforcement*—Positive reinforcement includes actions such as giving employees cash, recognition, time off, and other rewards for meeting attendance standards. Offering rewards for consistent attendance, giving bonuses for missing fewer than a certain number of days, and "buying back" unused sick leave are all positive-reinforcement methods of reducing absenteeism.

- *Combination Approach*—A combination approach ideally rewards desired behaviors and punishes undesired behaviors. This carrot-and-stick approach uses policies and discipline to punish offenders, and various programs and rewards to recognize employees with outstanding attendance. For instance, employees with perfect attendance may receive incentives of gift cards and other rewards. Those with excessive absenteeism would be terminated.

- *No-Fault Policy*: A popular approach with healthcare employers that employ a large RN workforce is a no-fault policy: the reasons for absences do not matter, and the employees must manage their own attendance unless they abuse that freedom. Once absenteeism exceeds normal limits, then disciplinary action up to and including termination of employment can occur. The advantages of the no-fault approach are that there is uniformity in the ways absence is handled, and supervisors and HR staff do not have to judge whether absences count as excused or unexcused.
- *Paid-Time-Off (PTO) Programs*—Many healthcare employers have paid-time-off programs, in which vacation time, holidays, and sick leave for each employee are combined into a paid-time-off (PTO) account. Employees use days from their accounts at their discretion for illness, personal time, or vacation. If employees run out of days in their accounts, they are not paid for any additional days missed. PTO programs generally reduce absenteeism, particularly one-day absences, but they often increase overall time away from work because employees use all of "their" time off by taking unused days as vacation days.[18]

EMPLOYEE TURNOVER

Turnover occurs when employees leave an organization and have to be replaced. Healthcare organizations have found that turnover is a very costly problem. For instance, healthcare organizations in one state experienced over 30 percent turnover annually. The turnover cost in the state for nursing jobs alone was more than $125 million per year, with individual nurse turnover costs being $32,000 per person who left.[19]

The extents to which employers face high turnover rates and costs vary by organization and industry. For example, the Society for Human Resource Management (SHRM) calculates that the average for all industries is 15 percent annual turnover. Healthcare and social assistance are at 20 percent annual turnover.[20]

High turnover rates have a negative impact on several dimensions of organizational performance, especially safety, productivity, and financial performance.[21] Research shows that morale (or job satisfaction), the labor market (opportunity to leave), and intention to quit or stay have major impacts on turnover.[22] Further, a history of poor attempts at organizational change leads to higher turnover intentions.[23] However, human resources systems designed to reduce turnover can indeed succeed.[24]

Types of Employee Turnover

Turnover is classified in many ways. One classification uses the following categories, although the two types are not mutually exclusive:

- *Involuntary Turnover*—Employees are terminated for poor performance, for work rule violations, or through layoffs.
- *Voluntary Turnover*— Employees leave by choice.

Involuntary turnover is triggered at all levels by employers terminating workers because of organizational policies and work rule violations, excessive absenteeism, performance standards that are not met by employees, and other issues. Voluntary turnover can be caused by many factors, some of which are not employer controlled. Common voluntary turnover causes include job dissatisfaction, pay and benefits levels, poor supervision, geography, and personal/family reasons.

Another view of turnover classifies it on the basis of whether it is good or bad for the organization:

- *Functional Turnover*— Lower-performing or disruptive employees leave.
- *Dysfunctional Turnover*— Key individuals and high performers leave.

Not all turnover in healthcare organizations is negative. On the contrary, functional turnover represents a positive change. Some workforce losses are desirable, especially if those who leave are lower-performing, less reliable, and/or disruptive individuals. Of course, dysfunctional turnover also occurs. That happens when key individuals leave, often at crucial times. For example, a pharmacist serving a number of small rural hospitals leaves to work at a larger health system. Her departure could cause a serious gap in pharmacy coverage for these hospitals because of the difficulty of replacing her. Further, her departure may impact other healthcare professionals, causing them to seek out and accept jobs at larger organizations because she left. This is truly dysfunctional turnover.

Employees quit for many reasons, only some of which can be controlled by the organization. Another classification uses the following terms to differentiate types of turnover:

- *Uncontrollable Turnover*— Employees leave for reasons outside the control of the employer.
- *Controllable Turnover*— Employees leave for reasons that could be influenced by the employer.

Some examples of reasons for turnover the employer cannot control include: (1) the employee moves out of the geographic area; (2) the employee decides to stay home with young children or an elder relative; (3) the employee's spouse is transferred; or (4) the employee is a student worker who graduates from college. In healthcare settings this type of turnover is inevitable. Many healthcare organizations utilize college students in part-time positions as they pursue education that will advance their careers in healthcare-related fields such as nursing and physical therapy. Once these students graduate, there may or may not be opportunities for them to continue to work at the facility that gave them part-time work.

Employers recognize that reducing turnover saves money, so they must effectively address controllable turnover. Healthcare organizations are better able to retain employees if they can realistically address the concerns of their employees, thus providing a better mechanism for managing controllable turnover.

As healthcare organizations confront economic and financial problems that result in layoffs in certain departments but not others, they also face a difficult issue in that employees that are unaffected by the layoffs are more likely to consider jobs at other facilities. In this situation, turnover is more likely to occur, and efforts are needed to keep existing employees. HR actions such as information sharing, opportunities for more training/learning, and emphasis on job significance can be helpful in lowering turnover intentions of individuals.

Measuring Employee Turnover

The U.S. Department of Labor estimates that the cost of replacing an employee ranges from one-half to five times the person's annual salary depending on the position.[25] The turnover rate for an organization can be computed on a monthly or yearly basis. The following formula, in which *separations* means "departures from the organization," is widely used:

$$\frac{\text{Number of employee separations during the year}}{\text{Total number of employees at mid-year}} \times 100$$

Common turnover rates range from almost 0 percent to more than 100 percent a year and vary among industries. As a part of HR management information, turnover data can be gathered and analyzed in many ways, including the following categories:

- Job and job level
- Department, unit, and location
- Reason for leaving
- Length of service
- Demographic characteristics
- Education and training
- Knowledge, skills, and abilities
- Performance ratings/levels

Several examples illustrate why detailed analyses of turnover are important. A long-term care organization had an organization-wide turnover rate that was not severe—but 75 percent of the turnover occurred in one unit. This imbalance indicated that some action was needed to resolve problems in that unit.

At a family practice clinic, there was 20 percent annual turnover, with 60 percent of that turnover occurring in the first 60 days of employment. By analyzing turnover rates by length of service, the HR manager of the clinic learned that the recruiting, selection, and training processes needed to be changed. By reducing the number of individuals hired who could not successfully complete training and perform satisfactorily after training, the clinic reduced turnover significantly.

Likewise, a medical center found that its greatest turnover in RNs occurred 24 to 36 months after hire, so the organization instituted a two-year employee recognition program and expanded the career development and training activities for employees with at least two years of service. In all of these examples, the turnover rates declined as a result of the actions taken based on the turnover analyses done.

HR METRICS: DETERMINING TURNOVER COSTS

A major step in reducing the expense of turnover is to decide how the organization is going to record employee departures and what calculations are necessary to maintain and benchmark the turnover rates. Determining turnover costs can be relatively simple or very complex, depending on the nature of the efforts made and the data used.

Figure 7-4 shows a model for calculating the cost of productivity lost to turnover. Of course, this is only one cost associated with turnover. But it is one that is more difficult to conceptualize. If a job pays (A) $20,000 and benefits cost (B) 40 percent, then the total annual cost for one employee (C) is $28,000. Assuming that 20 employees have quit in the previous year (D) and that it takes three months for one employee to be fully productive (E), the calculation results in a per person turnover cost (F) of $3,500. Overall, the annual lost productivity (G) would be $70,000 for the 20 individuals who have left. In spite of the conservative and simple nature of this model, it easily makes the point that productivity lost to turnover is costly. As another example, if 25 RNs in a large hospital leave in a year, calculations done according to this model produce turnover costs of more than $500,000 a year.

Detailing Turnover Cost

Other areas in addition to lost productivity to be included in calculating detailed turnover costs include the following:

* *Separation Costs*—HR staff and supervisory time, pay rates to prevent separations, exit interview time, unemployment expenses, legal fees for separations challenged, accrued vacation expenditures, continued health benefits, and others

* *Vacancy Costs*—Temporary help, contract and consulting firm usage, existing employee overtime, and other costs until the person is replaced

FIGURE 7-4   Simplified Turnover Costing Model

Job Title: _____

A. Typical annual pay for this job
B. Percentage of pay for benefits multiplied by annual pay
C. Total employee annual cost (A + B)
D. Number of employees who voluntarily quit the job in the past
   12 months
E. Number of months it takes for one employee to become fully productive
F. Per person turnover cost ([E ÷ 12] × C × 50%)*
G. Annual turnover cost for this job (F × D)

*Assumes 50% productivity throughout the learning period (E).

© 2016 Cengage Learning®

- *Replacement Costs*—Recruiting and advertising expenses, search fees, HR interviewer and staff time and salaries, employee referral fees, relocation and moving costs, supervisor and managerial time and salaries, employment testing costs, reference checking fees, preemployment medical expenses, relocation costs, and others
- *Training Costs for the New Person*—Paid orientation time, training staff time and pay, costs of training materials, supervisor and manager time and salaries, coworker "coaching" time and pay, and others
- *Hidden/Indirect Costs*—Costs that are less obvious, such as reduced productivity (calculated above), decreased customer service, lower quality, additional unexpected employee turnover, missed project deadlines, and others

Turnover is an expensive HR and managerial issue that must be constantly evaluated and addressed. Metrics allowed that to be done. As noted, however, not all turnover of employees is negative. Losing low performers should be considered positive. There may be an "optimal" amount of useful turnover necessary to replace low performers and add part-time or contract workers with special capabilities to improve workforce performance.

Optimal Turnover

Turnover costs and benefits can be calculated separately for various organizational segments. HR frequently strives to minimize all turnover, but in some cases more turnover may be better. For example, reducing turnover makes sense when it is very expensive, when those leaving are more valuable than their replacements, or when there may not be suitable replacements. However, more turnover in certain segments of the organization may make sense if it costs very little, those leaving are less valuable than their replacements, or there is certainty that good replacements are available.[26] Sometimes turnover is good; other times it clearly is not. A more sophisticated view tries to optimize the impact of turnover for the organization.[27] The solution is to calculate the financial impact of different types of turnover and attach a dollar cost to it to determine the optimum level.[28]

RETENTION OF HUMAN RESOURCES

In one sense retention is the opposite of turnover. However, the reasons key people choose to stay with an employer may not be the opposite of those that compel others to quit. Retaining top talent is a concern for many healthcare employers, and understanding retention is the key to keeping more of those top performers.

Myths and Realities about Retention

Keeping good employees is a challenge for all organizations and becomes even more difficult as labor markets change. Even during down economic cycles, healthcare employers still must focus on retaining top talent.[29] Unfortunately, some myths have arisen about what it takes to retain employees. Some of the most prevalent myths and realities that exist are as follows:

1. *Money is the main reason people leave.* Money is certainly a powerful recruiting tool, and if people feel they are being paid inadequately, they may be more likely to leave. But if they are paid close to the competitive level they expect, other parts of the job become more important than the pay they receive.

2. *Hiring has little to do with retention.* This is not true. Recruiting and selecting the people who fit the jobs and who are less likely to leave in the first place, and then orienting them to the company, can greatly increase retention. It is important to select for retention. Do not hire people with a history of high turnover.

3. *If you train people, you are only training them for another employer.* Developing skills in employees may indeed make them more marketable, but it also tends to improve retention. When an employer provides employees with training and development assistance, job satisfaction may increase and employees may be more likely to stay, particularly if they see more future opportunities internally.

4. *Do not be concerned about retention during organizational change.* The time when organizational change takes place is exactly when employees worry about leaving. Although some people's jobs may have to be cut because of organizational factors, the remaining employees that the company *would like to keep* may have the most opportunity and reason to leave voluntarily. For example, during a merger or acquisition, most workers are concerned about job security and their employer's future. If they are not made to feel a part of the new organization early on, many may leave or evaluate other alternatives.

5. *If high performers want to leave, the organization cannot hold them.* Employees are "free agents," who can indeed leave when they choose. The key to keeping high-performing employees is to create an environment in which they want to stay and grow.

Drivers of Retention

Reviewing a wide range of studies and situations faced by healthcare employers and employees, it appears that there are some common areas that affect employee retention.[30] As Figure 7-5 depicts, there are some broad organizational retention components that are important. Assuming those organizational components are being delivered appropriately to individuals, then there are other factors that also affect retention. Surveys of employees consistently show that career opportunities and a comprehensive compensation program are the two most important determinants of retention.[31] Finally, the job design/work factors and fair and supportive employee relationships with others inside the organization contribute to retention as well. If all of these components are present to meet individual employee expectations, then there is a greater likelihood that voluntary and controllable turnover will be lower, thus increasing employee retention.

FIGURE 7-5 **Retention Determinants**

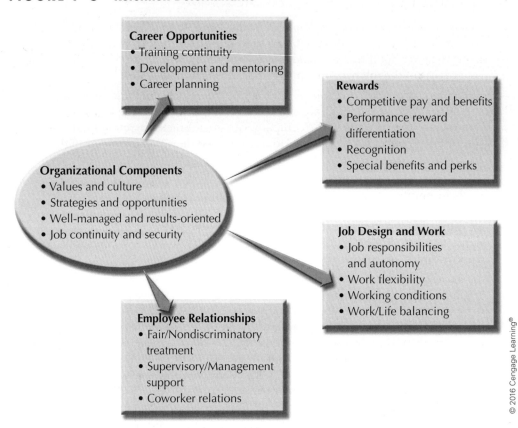

© 2016 Cengage Learning®

Organizational Culture and Values Organizational culture is a pattern of shared values and beliefs giving members of an organization meaning and providing them with rules for behavior. These values are inherent in the ways organizations and their members view themselves, define opportunities, and plan strategies. Much as personality shapes an individual, organizational culture shapes its members' responses and defines what an organization can or is willing to do.[32]

One health system well known for its culture and values is the Mayo Clinic. Mayo focuses considerable effort on instilling its values of high-quality patient care and employee excellence in customer service and employee involvement through its HR efforts. These efforts have paid off in Mayo's performance in retaining employees and being widely seen as an "employer of choice" in the healthcare industry.[33]

Job Continuity and Security Many healthcare employees have seen a decline in job security over the past decade. Downsizings, layoffs, mergers and acquisitions, and organizational restructuring have affected employee loyalty and retention. Also, as coworkers have been affected by layoffs and job reductions, the anxiety levels of the employees that are still employed rises. Consequently, employees start thinking about leaving before they also get cut. However, employees who work in organizations where job continuity and security is high tend to have higher retention rates.

ORGANIZATIONAL CAREER OPPORTUNITIES

Workers in all types of jobs consistently seek career opportunities and development efforts as affecting employee retention. This is even more true for technical professionals and those workers under age 30, where opportunities to develop skills and promotions rank above compensation as a retention concern.

Career Development   Career opportunities and development are dealt with by organizations in a number of ways. Tuition aid programs, typically offered as benefits by many healthcare employers, allow employees to pursue additional educational and training opportunities. Employees who participate in tuition assistance programs have been found to have higher retention rates than individuals who do not do so. However, just offering such a program is not sufficient. Organizations must also identify ways to use the employees' new knowledge and capabilities inside the organization. Otherwise, employees are more likely to take their new capabilities to another employer because they feel their increased "value" is not being recognized. Overall, the thrust of organizational career development efforts is designed to meet many employees' expectations that their employer is committed to keeping their knowledge, skills, and abilities current.

An example of an effective career development program is seen at Bon Secours Richmond Health System. The health system's mission to be "good help to those in need" is one that has made it more than just a place to work for many of its more than 12,000 employees. Unlike many other companies that offer employees tuition reimbursement, Bon Secours also provides up to $5,000 a year in prepayment tuition assistance for those making less than $11 an hour. This HR program and others have contributed to low annual turnover rates, and of the more than 2,000 open positions filled at Bon Secours during 2012, 41 percent were filled internally.[34]

Career Planning   Healthcare organizations also increase employee retention by having formal career-planning efforts. Employees and their managers mutually discuss career opportunities within the organization and what career development activities will enhance employees' future growth. Job-posting programs have proven to be an especially effective HR program for healthcare organizations for facilitating both inter- and intradepartmental transfers and promotions. These programs encourage employees to pursue new opportunities without leaving their current organizations.

Rewards and Retention

Rewards   The tangible rewards that people receive for working come in the form of pay, incentives, and benefits. Healthcare employees often cite better pay or benefits as the reason for leaving one employer for another. Healthcare employers do best with retention if they offer *competitive pay and benefits*, which means they must be close to what other employers are providing and what individuals believe to be consistent with their capabilities, experience, and performance. If compensation is not close to market, often defined as within 10 to 15 percent of the "market" rate, turnover is likely to be higher.

However, the reality of compensation is a bit more complex than it seems at first glance. Studies typically show a modest positive relationship between pay level and satisfaction with a job. However, there is a great deal of variance across employees—some value money more than others and for different reasons. Employee preferences are outside the control of employers.[35]

Another part of reward is that individuals need to be satisfied with both the actual levels of pay and the processes used to determine pay. That is why the performance management and performance appraisal processes must be designed so they are linked to compensation increases. To strengthen links between organizational and individual performance, healthcare and other private-sector organizations are increasingly using variable pay and incentive programs.[36]

Competitive Benefits   Another compensation issue affecting employee retention is having competitive benefits programs. Offering health insurance, retirement, tuition assistance, and many other benefits commonly offered by competing employers is vital. Employers also are learning that having some *benefits flexibility* aids retention. When employees choose how much and what benefits they will have from a "cafeteria" of choices, given a set sum of money available from the employer, the employees can tailor the benefits to what they want. For instance, a married worker who has health insurance coverage under a spouse's health plan at another organization may instead prefer to contribute more to a 401(k) or 403(b) plan or purchase additional life insurance.

Special Benefits and Perks   A number of healthcare employers have used a wide range of special benefits and perks to attract and retain employees. The more creative perks that large health system employers can offer include providing access to a day-care center, hair salon, post office, and dry cleaners to make their employees' lives easier. However, even small employers like an individual dentist practice can provide perks like flexible work schedules and paid lunches. By offering these special benefits and perks, healthcare employers hope to be seen as more desirable employers where individuals will remain for longer stays. Flextime, signing bonuses, and relocation cost reimbursement are frequently offered to employees in areas of critical shortage, especially RNs, therapists, and pharmacists.

Differentiation of Compensation   Many individuals expect their rewards to be differentiated from others based on performance. For instance, if a mental health case worker receives about the same pay increase and overall pay as others who have lower productivity, are absent more, and work fewer hours, then the lack of differences in compensation may create a feeling of "unfairness." This inequity may lead to the individual deciding to look for another job that pays more money and where differences lead to differential compensation amounts.

When healthcare organizations have surveyed their employees, many have found that individuals are more satisfied with the levels of their pay than the processes used to determine pay. That is why the performance management system and performance appraisal processes in healthcare organizations must be linked to compensation increases. If some individuals receive high performance ratings but their compensation changes only the same as for others, then their desire to stay with the organization may diminish.

To achieve greater links between individual performance and compensation, a growing number of healthcare organizations are using variable pay and incentive programs. These programs provide bonuses or lump-sum payments to reward extra performance.

The introduction of variable pay programs has been viewed in a controversial light for nonprofit healthcare organizations. Critics argue that extreme levels of variable pay for executives or employed physicians are inappropriate and contribute to the rising cost of healthcare. However, healthcare organizations frequently compete for the same talent with private-sector firms who can offer a wide range of variable pay options, including stock options.

Recognition   As depicted in Figure 7-6, *employee recognition* as a form of reward can be both tangible and intangible. The tangible recognition comes in many forms, such as employee-of-the-month plaques, perfect-attendance certificates, or other special awards. Recognition also can be intangible and psychological in nature. Feedback from managers and supervisors that acknowledges extra effort

FIGURE 7-6   Employee Recognition

Tangible Recognition	Intangible Recognition

• Movie Tickets
• Extra Days Off
• Bonuses
• Gift Certificates
• Special Merit Awards
	• Thank You Notes
	• Public Acknowledgement
	• Personal Compliments about a Job Well Done by Managers
	• Certificates of Recognition For:
	  - Perfect Attendance
	  - Perfect Safety Record

© 2016 Cengage Learning®

and performance of individuals provides recognition, even if monetary rewards are not given. Examples of this type of recognition include:

- At Beach Cities Health District in Redondo Beach, California, employees are eligible to receive the "The Quarterly Core Value Award," which honors the worker who best represents one of the Health District's core values: compassion, integrity, accountability, and excellence. The honored employee receives a personalized plaque and spotlight in the newsletter.

- At Woman's Hospital, Baton Rouge, Louisiana, managers award a "Pink Token" program to recognize employees on the spot for exceptional work or service to patients. The tokens can be cashed in for merchandise at the hospital.[37]

Retention and Selection

Retention is affected by the *selection process*, which tries to achieve a *person–job match* whereby individuals' knowledge, skills, and abilities are matched to the demands of the jobs they could be hired to perform. A number of organizations have found that high employee turnover rates in employees' first few months of employment often are linked to inadequate selection screening efforts. Once individuals have been placed into jobs, several job/work factors affect retention. Since individuals spend significant time at work, they expect *working conditions* to be good, given the nature of what is being done. Such factors as space, lighting, temperature, noise, layout, and other physical and environmental factors affect retention of employees. Also, employees expect to work with modern equipment and technology.

Additionally, there should be a *safe work environment*, wherein risks of accidents and injuries have been addressed. This is especially true for healthcare employers where safety risks can include exposure to disease, harmful chemicals, and radiation.

WORK–LIFE BALANCE

The changing demographics of the U.S. workforce have led to many individuals having to balance work responsibilities, family needs, and personal life demands. With more single-parent families, dual-career couples with children, and workers responsible for aging elderly relatives, balancing work and family roles may sometimes be very difficult. Such factors as work and family time demands and resources all must be considered.

Work–life programs offered by employers can include a wide range of items. Some include work/job options, such as flexible work scheduling, job sharing, or telecommuting. Others include benefits program components, such as flexible benefits, on-site fitness centers, child-care or elder-care assistance, veterinarian care for pets, flexible time off, and sick leave policies. Perhaps the greatest benefit of work flexibility is that it meshes well with work–family efforts by employers. The purpose of all these offerings is to communicate to individuals that the employer cares about the employees and recognizes the challenges of balancing work–life demands.

Balancing Patient Care Needs with Work Schedule Flexibility   The ability to have flexibility in work schedules and in how work is completed is more

---

HEALTHCARE REFORM AND HR PRACTICES

Although the details of the Affordable Care Act (ACA) may be complex, a simple but critical issue incorporated in healthcare reform for providers that receive Medicare reimbursement is the need to provide not just exceptional care but also superior customer service. Healthcare providers that fail to earn high patient satisfaction scores may face reduced Medicare reimbursement, as patient feedback accounts for nearly one-third of a healthcare provider's Medicare reimbursement score. Patient satisfaction, as measured by the Hospital Consumer Assessment of Healthcare Providers and Systems (HCAHPS) survey, is tied to Medicare reimbursement. The HCAHPS survey asks patients to score providers on a variety of care quality issues. With low scores, providers such as hospitals could lose hundreds of thousands of dollars in annual Medicare reimbursement.

The need to provide superior customer service is not new to healthcare, especially as patients have gained a greater voice and choice in where they seek medical services. And since few patients are medical experts, achieving high patient satisfaction scores in nonclinical areas becomes critical, as every patient has expectations about customer service. Reform requirements serve to make the need to provide superior service an imperative.

For hospitals, mental health providers, physician groups, and others to earn high patient satisfaction scores, it is critical that employees in all capacities deliver high-quality service. For employees to deliver the type of high-quality service that generates high patient satisfaction scores, employees must have a high level of job satisfaction, as patient satisfaction is linked to the level of genuine employee satisfaction. In other words, satisfied employees are more inclined to provide superior service to the customers (patients) they serve.[38]

---

important for retention. Healthcare professionals frequently cite this issue as the reason for leaving the healthcare workplace (especially in hospitals), leading them to find positions in workplaces with less scheduling variability.

Healthcare managers are very aware of the need to balance patient care delivery, staffing requirements, and work schedule flexibility. Patient care must come first, but the lack of predictability of patient census in environments such as in-patient nursing units or emergency rooms requires scheduling that can frustrate even the most flexible workers.

One way hospitals, clinics, physician and dental offices, and nursing homes have creatively provided work flexibility is through the use of different *work scheduling alternatives*. Examples of these alternatives include:

- *Staffing with Part-Time and Casual Workers*— This involves replacing one or two full-time employees with multiple part-time and casual employees who can be scheduled for up to 16 or more hours per week, but with the opportunity to pick up additional hours if patient care needs require additional staff.

- *Developing Patient Census Prediction and Staffing Models*—Although it is difficult to predict with 100 percent accuracy, some healthcare providers have become proficient at predicting the *core* staffing needs of their units, clinics, or departments. Based on such variables as time of year, surgery demands, or seasonal infectious disease patterns, higher levels of *variable* staffing can be used. Based on good historical data, these staffing models can be surprisingly accurate.
- *Weekend Shifts*—Many healthcare organizations rely on employees that work only weekend shifts.
- *Parent Shifts*—In an effort to provide shifts that allow employees to achieve work–life balance, some healthcare organizations have established parent shifts. These shifts are designed to provide employees with the time to be with their children at critical child-care times during the workday.
- *Internal Staffing Pools*—Many healthcare organizations have developed internal staffing or float pools in lieu of utilizing external temporary employment agencies. These pools allow the organization to tap into the necessary staffing as patient care needs require and also offer a significant amount of flexibility for the staff on the pool.

Employee Relationships with Supervisors and Coworkers

A final set of factors found to affect retention is based on the relationships that employees have in organizations. Healthcare organizations have long been aware of how poor supervisory skills and attitudes have affected employee retention. A poor supervisor can outweigh all the other positive efforts extended by the organization. Figure 7-7 depicts what the supervisor can do to contribute to employee retention.

FIGURE 7-7 Supervisory Retention Efforts

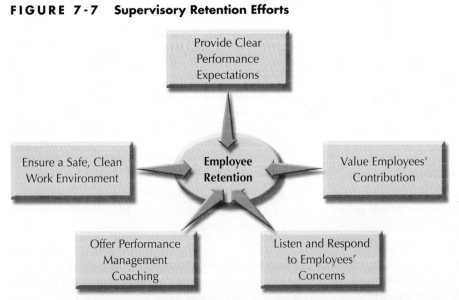

© 2016 Cengage Learning®

One expectation that employees have is that they will be treated fairly at work. Such areas as the reasonableness of HR policies, the fairness of disciplinary actions, and the means used to decide work assignments and opportunities all affect employee retention. If individuals feel that policies are unreasonably restrictive or applied inconsistently, then they might be more likely to look at jobs offered by other employers.

Particularly important with the increasing demographic diversity of U.S. workplaces is that all employees, regardless of their gender, age, and other factors, have *nondiscriminatory treatment*. Organizational commitment and job satisfaction of ethnically diverse individuals may be affected by perceived discriminatory treatment.

Other concerns that affect employee retention are supervisory/management support and coworker relations. Many individuals build close relationships with those with whom they work. Coupled with coworker relationships is having supportive supervisory and management relationships. A supervisor builds positive relationships and aids retention by giving clear performance expectations, ensuring a safe, clean work environment, valuing the employee's contribution, and providing coaching. As defined by individual employees, having a "good" boss means that communication is likely to be more open and the supervisor listens and responds to the employees' concerns.

RETENTION MANAGEMENT PROCESS

The previous sections have summarized the results of many studies and popular HR practices to identify factors that can affect retention. Retention is important because turnover can cause poor performance in otherwise productive units. The focus now turns toward the keys to managing retention as part of effective HR management. Figure 7-8 shows the retention management process.

Employee Surveys Employee surveys can be used to diagnose specific problem areas, identify employee needs or preferences, and reveal areas in which HR activities are well received or viewed negatively. Whether the surveys cover general employee attitudes, job satisfaction, or specific issues, the survey results must be examined as part of retention measurement efforts. For example, a growing number of "mini-surveys" on specific topics are being sent via e-mail questionnaires, blogs, and other means.

Examples of the categories and questions used in surveys are:

Communication

- I know what the business objectives of the company are.
- I could speak to anyone here, regardless of level.

Customer and Quality Orientation

- Customer satisfaction is one of our priorities.
- My work group's day-to-day activities demonstrate that quality is a top priority.

FIGURE 7-8   **The Retention Management Process**

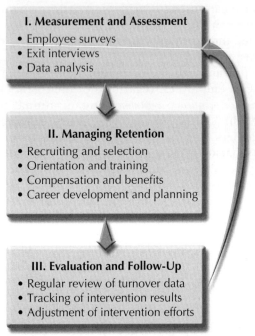

© 2016 Cengage Learning®

Empowerment

- My job allows me the freedom I need to use my own judgment.
- Management encourages me to be innovative and creative in my work.

Management

- There is an atmosphere of trust between employees and management.
- Management believes employees are a valuable asset.[39]

Regardless of the topics in a survey, employee input provides data on the "retention climate" in an organization. By obtaining data on how employees view their jobs, their coworkers, their supervisors, and organizational policies and practices, these surveys can be starting points for reducing turnover and increasing the length of time that employees are retained. Some employers conduct attitude surveys yearly, while others do so intermittently.

By asking employees to respond candidly to an attitude survey, management is building employees' expectations that actions will be taken on the concerns identified. Therefore, an important part of conducting an attitude survey is providing feedback to those who participated in it. It is especially important that even negative survey results be communicated to avoid fostering the appearance of hiding the results or placing blame.

Exit Interviews One widely used means for assisting retention assessment efforts is the **exit interview,** in which individuals who are leaving the organization are asked to give their reasons. HR must regularly summarize and analyze the data by category (e.g., reasons for leaving, department, length of service, etc.) to provide managers and supervisors with information for improving company efforts.[40]

Many HR departments regularly contact former employees who were valuable contributors, as they may be willing to provide more information on e-mail questionnaires or in telephone conversations conducted sometime after they have left the organization. For instance, one healthcare firm contacts former employees within 60 days after they have exited. Many times these follow-up conversations reveal the "real" reasons for departures, other than what was said in the exit interviews.[41] This healthcare firm also has a program in which ex-employees are invited to return as "alumni" and have lunch with former coworkers. This has led to many departed individuals indicating they would like to return to the organization because the jobs they took elsewhere did not turn out to be as "promising" as they had anticipated. Thus, rehiring can be aided by ongoing efforts such as e-mails, exit interview follow-ups, and continuing contacts with good former employees.[42]

Conducting Exit Interviews

Departing employees may be reluctant to divulge their real reasons for leaving. A skilled HR interviewer may be able to gain useful information that departing employees do not wish to share with managers and supervisors. The following suggestions may be useful when conducting exit interviews:

- Decide who will conduct the exit interview and when the discussion will occur. Often these interviews occur on the last day or so of a departing individual's employment.

- Emphasize that the information provided by the departing employee will be treated confidentially and used to make improvements.

- Utilize a checklist or a set of standard questions so that the information can be summarized. Typical areas covered include reasons for leaving, supervision, pay, training, liked and disliked aspects of the job, and details on the organization to which the employee is moving.

When doing the actual exit interview, numerous questions can be asked. Those typically asked include the following:

[Q]: Why are you leaving?

[Q]: What have you liked and disliked about your job and managers?

[Q]: What company actions have made you and other employees more or less positive?

[Q]: What would or would not lead you to recommend the employer to future possible hires?

[Q]: Did you receive adequate training and support?

[Q]: Did the job match your expectations when you were hired?

[Q]: What was frustrating about working here?

[Q]: What suggestions do you have to improve working conditions?

Retention Interventions

Based on what the measurement and assessment data reveal, a variety of HR interventions can be undertaken to improve retention. Turnover can be controlled and reduced in several ways. During the *recruiting process,* the job should be outlined and a realistic preview presented, so that the reality of the job matches the expectations of the new employee. By ensuring that the expectations of potential employees match what the organization is likely to offer, this may reduce voluntary turnover.

Another way to eliminate turnover is to improve the *selection process* in order to better match applicants to jobs. By fine-tuning the selection process and hiring people who will not have disciplinary or performance problems or whose work histories suggest higher turnover potential, employers can reduce turnover. Once selected, individuals who receive effective orientation and training are less likely to leave.

Other HR factors are important as well. *Compensation* is important because a competitive, fair, and equitable pay system can help reduce turnover. Inadequate benefits also may lead to voluntary turnover, especially if other employers are offering significantly higher compensation levels for similar jobs. *Career development* and *planning* can help an organization keep employees. If individuals believe they have few opportunities for career development and advancement, they are more likely to leave the organization. *Employee relations,* including fair/nondiscriminatory treatment and enforcement of HR policies, also can enhance retention.

Healthcare HR professionals should use the information on retention determinants and the assessment information to identify what changes are needed to improve retention. Usually, a multifaceted approach is needed, rather than just focusing on one area. For example, just changing benefits without considering the recruitment and selection processes may not result in attracting and hiring individuals more likely to stay longer. That is why it is important to evaluate and follow up to see if retention intervention efforts have produced lower turnover rates and extended the stays of existing employees.

Evaluation and Follow-Up

Management can take numerous actions to deal with retention issues. The choice of a particular action depends on the analysis of the turnover and retention problems in a particular organization and should be tailored for that organization. Once retention intervention efforts have been implemented, it is important that they be evaluated and that appropriate follow-up and adjustments be made. Regular *review of turnover data* can identify when turnover increases or decreases among different employees classified by length of service, education, department, gender, or other factors.

Tracking intervention results also should be part of evaluation efforts. Some healthcare organizations may use pilot programs to see how turnover is affected before extending the changes to the entire organization. For instance, to test the effect of flextime scheduling on employee turnover, a clinic might allow flexible scheduling in one department on a pilot basis. If the turnover rate of the employees in that department drops in comparison with the turnover in other departments still working set schedules, then the experimental pilot project may indicate that flexible scheduling can reduce turnover. Next, the clinic might extend the use of flexible scheduling to other departments.

Retention of employees can be increased through use of a coordinated process. Numerous examples of healthcare organizations that have focused on retention management illustrate that attracting and retaining human resources can contribute significantly to organizational success.

CASE

Hanson Rehabilitation Hospital is a 40-bed short-stay, residential treatment center specially designed and staffed to provide care for individuals rehabbing from hip replacement surgery. A hospital of this nature must have a caring, engaged staff dedicated to providing excellent care and high levels of customer service. Management, recognizing the correlation between satisfied employees and satisfied patients, routinely conducts employee satisfaction surveys.

At a recent management team meeting, the hospital's CEO discussed the upcoming employee survey and asked each team member what they had done in their respective departments to improve the satisfaction scores of their employees since the last survey. The director of physical therapy indicated that he had instituted a recognition program that entailed

surveying the patients on a weekly basis and asking them about the therapists that provided therapy for them. The therapists that received the most compliments received a thank-you note and coffee shop gift card, plus were acknowledged at the departmental staff meetings. The director felt that the employees were really motivated by this program; and those that had received the recognition were very proud of the accomplishment.

Questions

1. What is the value of routinely conducting employee engagement surveys?
2. Why would the director of physical therapy's recognition program potentially improve the departmental employee engagement survey scores?

END NOTES

1. Cheryl Burnette, "Smart Sleep for New Grads," *Nursing Management* (May 2010), 10–13.
2. T. H. Ng et al., "Psychological Contract Breaches, Organizational Commitment, and Innovation-related Behaviors," *Journal of Applied Psychology* 94 (2010), 744–751.
3. S. D. Montes and D. Zeig, "Do Promises Matter? An Exploration of the Role of Promises in Psychological Contract Breach," *Journal of Applied Psychology* 95 (2009), 1243–1260.
4. S. Tietze and S. Nardin, "The Psychological Contract and the Transition from

Office-Based to Home-Based Work," *Human Resource Management Journal* 21 (2011), 318–334.

5. S. Svensson and Lars-Erik Wolven, "Temporary Agency Workers and Their Psychological Contracts," *Employee Relations* 32 (2010), 184–199.

6. Edel Conway and Kathy Monks, "Unraveling the Complexity of High Commitment: An Employee-Level Analysis," *Human Resource Management Journal* 19 (2009), 140–148.

7. R. De Filippi, "Changing Environment Requires New Thinking Strategies on Addressing Workforce Shortages," *AHA News* (February 8, 2010), 4–5.

8. Paola Spagnoli et al., "Satisfaction with Job Aspects: Do Patterns Change Over Time?" *Journal of Business Research* 65 (2012), 609–616.

9. Lin Grensing-Pophal, "Holding Pattern," *HR Magazine* (March 2009), 64–68.

10. Brad Shuck and Karen Wollard, "Employee Engagement and HRD: A Seminal Review of the Foundations," *Human Resource Development Review* 9 (2010), 89–110.

11. N. Schullery, "Workplace Engagement and Generational Differences in Values," *Business Communication Quarterly* (June 2013), 252–265.

12. Adrienne Fox, "Raising Engagement," *HR Magazine* (May 2010), 35–40.

13. Bob Pike, "Who Else Values Loyalty?," *Training* (November/December 2011), 69.

14. The Wharton School, "Declining Employee Loyalty: A Casualty of the New Workplace," *Human Resource Executive Online* (July 16, 2012), 1–5

15. Michael Klachefsky, "Health-Related Lost Productivity: The Full Cost of Absence," *Productivity Insight #2*, Standard Insurance Company (August 2012), 1.

16. Denise Baker-McClearn et al., "Absence Management and Presenteeism: The Pressures on Employees to Attend Work and the Impact of Attendance on Performance," *Human Resource Management Journal* 20 (2010), 311–328.

17. "2012 Wellness & Benefits Administration Benchmarking Study," *Medical Benefits* (November 15, 2012), 10–11.

18. Vivienne Walker and David Barnford, "An Empirical Investigation into Health Sector Absenteeism," *Health Services Management Research* 24 (August 2011), 142–150.

19. "Estimating Turnover Costs," *http://www. workforce.com.*

20. Eric Krell, "5 Ways to Manage High Turnover," *HR Magazine* (April 2012), 63–65.

21. Jason D. Shaw, "Turnover Rates and Organizational Performance," *Organizational Psychology Review* 1 (August 2011), 187–213.

22. Robert P. Steel and John W. Lounsbury, "Turnover Process Models: Review and Synthesis of a Conceptual Literature," *Human Resource Management Review* 19 (2009), 271–282.

23. Prashant Bordia, "Haunted by the Past: Effects of Poor Change Management History on Employee Attitudes and Turnover," *Group and Organization Management* 36 (April 2011), 191–222.

24. Rosemary Batt and Alexander J. S. Colvin, "An Employment Systems Approach to Turnover: HR Practices, Quits, Dismissals, and Performance," *The Academy of Management Journal* 54 (August 2011), 695–718; I. Y. Haines et al., "The Influence of HR Management Practices on Employee Voluntary Turnover Rates in the Canadian Non-Government Sector," *Industrial and Labor Relation Review* 63 (2010), 228–246.

25. For details on industries, types of jobs, and other components, go to *http://www .dol.gov.*

26. Wayne F. Cascio, "Be a Ringmaster of Risk," *HR Magazine* (April 2012), 38–43.

27. W. Stanley Siebert and Nikolay Zubanov, "Searching for the Optimal Level for Employee Turnover," *Academy of Management Journal* 52 (2009), 294–313.

28. Gary Kranz, "Keeping the Keepers," *Workforce Management* (April 2012), 34–37.

29. "Companies Must Develop Retention Plans for Critical Talent," *BNA: Report on Salary Surveys* (September 2013), 10–12.

30. David G. Allen et al., "Retaining Talent: Replacing Misconceptions with Evidence-Based Strategies," *Academy of Management Perspectives* 24 (May 2010), 48–64.

31. Audrey Tillman, "Improving Worker Satisfaction Yields Improved Worker-Retention Rates," *Employment Relations Today* (Winter 2013), 27–31.

32. David A. Garvin, "Can a Strong Culture Be Too Strong?," *Harvard Business Review* (January–February 2014), 113–117.

33. See *http://mayoclinichealthsystem.org/about-us/mission-and-values* for more information.

34. S. Johnson, "A Holistic Approach to Employee Engagement," *Modern Healthcare* (October 28, 2013), S4.

35. David C. Wyld, "Does Money Buy More Happiness on the Job?," *Academy of Management Perspectives* 25 (February 2011), 101–102.

36. Caroline Yang, "Maximize Employee Retention through Total Rewards Programs," *Workspan* (June 2011), 25–28; Lani P. Barovick, "Sharing the Rain," *HR Magazine* (November 2010), 51–54.

37. "Innovative Ways Some Best Places Are Using Formal Employee Recognition and Appreciation Programs, "*Modern Healthcare* (October 28, 2013), S6.

38. "Health Care Reform and Patient Access," *Health Care Registration: The Newsletter for Health Care Registration Professionals* (July 2013), 1–9.

39. Used with permission from Stanard and Associates, Chicago, Illinois.

40. Robert A. Giacalone, "Researching Exit Interviews," *Human Resource Executive Online* (March 1, 2012), 1–3.

41. M. Sureesh Baabu et al., "Exit Interviews and Their Empanelment," *SRM Management Digest* (2011), 315–319.

42. Joyce L. Gioia, "Meaningful Exit Interviews Help One Bank Cut Turnover and Save," *Global Business and Organizational Excellence* (January/February 2011), 36–43.

Training and Development in Healthcare Organizations

Learning Objectives

After you have read this chapter, you should be able to:

- Discuss how job performance and training can be integrated.

- Identify how organizational and training strategies are linked.

- Define various learning styles.

- Describe the orientation, training, and staff development requirements of the Joint Commission.

- Explain the unique aspects of healthcare employee development.

HEALTHCARE HR INSIGHTS

Healthcare organizations, regardless of size, nature, or type of care provided, must dedicate time and resources to the training and development of employees. Even though many healthcare jobs require specific educational background and degrees along with certifications and registrations—such as MDs, RNs, and occupational therapists—these workers must still receive training and development on specific aspects of the care they deliver and the facilities in which they work. For noncredentialed healthcare workers such as clerical and service support staff, the training challenges can be even greater. As such, healthcare organizations are constantly working to improve the training provided and ensuring that the worker receiving the training is retaining as much of the training information as possible. An example of a training success story is detailed below.

At one food services department in a large hospital system, a new training program was designed to help increase patient satisfaction. What was new was that the training was not conducted in a classroom setting because the trainers questioned if that was the most effective environment for learning for their trainees and the information being taught. Through research, application, and evaluation, the trainers designed a new training model. Key ingredients of the new training methodology focused on:

- Shadowing the workers before the training to get to know them and observe them as they worked
- Meeting with management to identify the training goals
- Building a trust relationship with the staff before initiating training
- Engaging with the staff to educate them on the concepts and skills specific to their situations
- Designing training specific to each situation

Through this thoughtfully planned and executed initiative, the success of the training was well-documented by improvement in patient satisfaction scores directly related to key elements of the training that focused on the courtesy and helpfulness of the food workers.[1] The new realities of today's healthcare environment require healthcare HR and training professionals to be innovative and resourceful in developing effective training for healthcare workers.

Both training and development are critical in healthcare organizations to ensure the ongoing delivery of safe, competent care. **Training** is a process whereby people acquire capabilities to aid in the achievement of organizational goals. Since this process is tied to a variety of organizational purposes, training can be viewed either narrowly or broadly. In a limited sense, training provides employees with specific, identifiable knowledge and skills for use on their current jobs. **Employee development** is broader in scope and focuses on individuals gaining new capabilities useful for both current and future jobs.

NATURE OF TRAINING IN HEALTHCARE ORGANIZATIONS

Contemporary training in healthcare organizations has evolved significantly over the past decade. Overall, more employers are recognizing that training is vital. Organizations must change if they are to survive because the environment in which they must compete changes. This is especially true in healthcare organizations today. For this reason, employee training is an ongoing process for most organizations. In the United States, more than $126 billion is spent on training annually, or more than $1,000 per employee on average.[2] Historically, healthcare organizations have lagged behind in training expenditures in comparison to organizations in other industries.

As part of strategic competitiveness, employees whose capabilities stay current and who receive regular training are better able to cope with the challenges and changes occurring in healthcare. Compare the healthcare environment of today—with all of the new technologies, the explosion of web technology, and the increasing cost pressures—to the industry five years ago. Without continual training, healthcare organizations may not have staff members with the KSAs needed to provide care and manage organizational. Training in healthcare organizations is offered in many different areas and in different ways, as noted in Figure 8-1.

Training also assists organizational competitiveness by aiding in the retention of employees. A primary reason why many individuals stay or leave organizations is career training and development opportunities. Healthcare employers that invest in training and developing their employees do so in part to enhance their retention efforts.

Although training expenditures may decline as organizational cost cutting occurs, more progressive healthcare organizations seldom reduce training efforts significantly. In fact, some healthcare organizations have invested in training as a way to increase revenues. As an example, Children's Medical Center of Dallas, one of the largest pediatric hospitals in the United States, has created a consolidated education infrastructure designed to help its employees develop and gain better efficiencies and effectiveness to drive performance change.[3]

Legal Issues and Training

Some legal issues must be considered when designing and delivering training. One concern centers on the criteria and practices used to select individuals for inclusion in training programs. Healthcare organizations need to ensure these

---

FIGURE 8-1   *Common Types of Nonclinical Healthcare Training*

- Sexual Harassment Prevention
- Fire Safety (OSHA Requirements)
- Personal Computer Courses
- Team Building Skills
- Interpersonal Communication Skills
- JCAHO (Joint Commission on Accreditation of Healthcare Organizations) Standards
- Patient Safety
- Quality Improvement Techniques
- Customer Service Skills
- Cultural Competence

factors are job-related and do not result in disparate impact because training can prompt advancement in the organization. Failure to accommodate the participation of individuals with disabilities in training can also expose organizations to EEO lawsuits. Further, using psychological assessments to identify soft skills like emotional intelligence falls under the uniform guidelines and must be validated.[4]

Another legal issue involves requiring employees to sign *training contracts* to protect the costs and time invested in specialized employee training. For instance, a mental health therapy organization paid $5,000 each to train four therapists and certify them in a specialized type of therapy. The organization required that each therapist sign a training contract whereby one-fourth of the cost would be forgiven each year the employee stayed following the training. A therapist who left sooner would be liable to the organization for the unforgiven balance. Healthcare organizations and other employers often use training contracts, especially for expensive external training.

Finally, the Department of Labor has ruled that nonexempt employees who are receiving training outside normal working hours (e.g., at home by completing web-based classes) must be compensated for their time. In one situation, a company required employees to spend about 10 hours at home completing a web-based class. In this case, the company had to pay the employees for their 10 hours of training under the Fair Labor Standards Act.[5]

Integration of Job Performance, Training, and Learning

Job performance, training, and employee learning must be integrated to be effective. First, since training interventions are best when moved closer to the job in order to achieve real-time learning, the linkage between training and job performance is vital. Consider the following example. As a new respiratory therapist receives orientation to the intensive care unit (ICU), the trainee works closely with an experienced respiratory therapist. The experienced therapist serves in the role of preceptor, providing the new therapist with guidance and hands-on training. Trainees can watch the trainer (preceptor) perform procedures in the proper manner, attempt to safely replicate the actions, and receive real-time feedback in the actual work setting.

Second, organizations prefer more authentic (and hence more effective) training experiences for their trainees, using real organizational problems to advance employee learning. Rather than separating the training experience from actual job performance context, trainers who incorporate everyday operations as learning examples increase the realism of training exercises and scenarios. Many healthcare organizations, such as Cincinnati Children's Hospital, have initiated diversity and cultural competence awareness and skills training. The objective of Cincinnati Children's Hospital's training is to present actual employee, patient/parent, and visitor situations that include cultural competence and diversity-related issues to the trainees and to teach them how to react and respond appropriately. During the training, real incidents of diversity conflict are discussed, along with what actions were effective and ineffective in dealing with the various situations. Effective responses are presented as best practice approaches to dealing with various diversity issues. This is an example of another way that training, learning, and job performance have become more integrated.[6] As a result, training becomes more performance focused. More information is provided about providing culturally competent care in the Healthcare Reform and HR Practices feature.

HEALTHCARE REFORM AND HR PRACTICES

At the core of healthcare reform is the concept of expanding healthcare access to more people living in the United States. In addition to dealing with the affordability issues that many potential consumers of healthcare face, another major issue is that of access to cultural competent care.[7]

Cultural competency is one of the main ingredients in closing the disparities gap in health care. It is the way patients and doctors can come together and talk about health concerns without cultural differences hindering the conversation, but rather enhancing it. Quite simply, healthcare services that are respectful of and responsive to the health beliefs, practices, and cultural and linguistic needs of diverse patients can help bring about positive health outcomes.

Culture and language may influence:

- Health, healing, and wellness belief systems
- How illness, disease, and their causes are perceived, by both by the patient/consumer and healthcare providers
- The behaviors of patients/consumers who are seeking health care and their attitudes toward health care providers
- The delivery of services by the provider who looks at the world through his or her own limited set of values, which can compromise access for patients from other cultures.

The increasing population growth of racial and ethnic communities and linguistic groups, each with its own cultural traits and health profiles, presents a challenge to the healthcare delivery service industry in this country. The provider and the patient each bring their individual learned patterns of language and culture to the health care experience which must be transcended to achieve equal access and quality health care.[8]

Effective health communication is as important to healthcare as clinical skill. To improve individual health, healthcare providers need to recognize and address the unique culture, language, and health literacy of diverse consumers and communities. This requires training to build both awareness and skills. Healthcare organizations, like Cincinnati Children's Hospital, have developed and implemented both clinical and nonclinical culturally competent training to ensure that their patients regardless of culture are receiving high-quality patient care.

Training as Performance Consulting

Performance consulting is a process by which a training facilitator (either internal or external to the organization) and the organizational client work together to boost workplace performance. As depicted in Figure 8-2, performance consulting is based on desired and actual organizational results being compared to desired and actual employee performance. Once these comparisons are made, then performance consulting considers all the factors in dealing with performance issues:[9]

- Focusing on identifying and addressing *root causes* of performance problems
- Recognizing the *interaction of individual and organizational factors* that work together to influence employee performance
- Comparing the *actions and accomplishments of high performers* with actions of more typical performers

Regardless of whether the trainer is internal to the organization or is an outside training consultant, training cannot automatically solve every employee performance problem. Instead, training must be viewed as one piece of a larger, *bundled* solution. For instance, some employee performance issues might be resolved by creating a training program for employees, while other situations might call for job design changes.

The following example illustrates the performance consulting approach. Assume you are the HR training specialist in a large medical center, and the director of patient care contacts you about creating a training program for

FIGURE 8-2   Performance Consulting

© 2016 Cengage Learning®

the nurses on the patient care units. Over the last six months, the director has received various complaints about the nurses' interactions and communications with staff from other medical center departments that support the units. The director asks you to develop a customized training program on effective communications and collaborative working relationships.

Instead of just developing a training program, users of performance consulting gather more information to identify: (1) the root causes of the communication problems, (2) the various individual RNs and organizational factors that are contributing to this issue, and (3) the primary reasons for the gap between effective RNs and lower-performing RNs on the units. Obtaining all of this information helps in determining whether *any* form of training will play a role in an integrated performance improvement solution. Perhaps recent changes in patient volumes have resulted in higher work demands on the RNs and have contributed to their need to demand more responsiveness from support department personnel. Whatever the causes, a tailored and comprehensive approach is needed to address the communications and interaction issues.

ORGANIZATIONAL STRATEGY AND TRAINING

Training represents a significant expenditure for most healthcare employers. However, it is too often viewed tactically rather than strategically, which means that training is seen as a short-term activity rather than one that has longer-term effects on organizational success. However, this may be changing. For example, during the last recession, many healthcare organizations chose to maintain training that was necessary for long-term strategic goals. Training is frequently supported by words from management but is among the first expenses to be cut when times get difficult.[10]

Strategic Training

Training can indeed help the organization accomplish its goals. As in the earlier situation where the director of patient care was convinced that her employees needed communications skills training, it is not uncommon for operating managers, HR professionals, and trainers to react to problems by saying, "I need a training program on X." With a strategic training focus, it is more likely that there will be an assessment of such requests to determine what training or non-training solutions should be used to address the performance issues. Such a focus also encourages performance and training expectations to be set so that results of the training are measurable.

For maximum impact, HR and training professionals should get involved with the business and partner with operating managers to help solve their problems. Additionally, strategic training can help reduce the mind-set that training alone can solve most employee or organizational problems. With a strategic focus, the organization is more likely to assess whether training can actually address these issues and what else might be done.

Not *all* training is effective. Only one-quarter of respondents to a McKinsey survey said their training programs measurably improved business performance, and most companies do not measure training effectiveness. Most simply ask whether participants liked the training or not.[11] To be a strategic investment training must align with the organization's goals and provide something of value.

THE TRAINING PROCESS

Effective training requires the use of a systematic training process. Figure 8-3 depicts the training process as having four phases: *assessment, design, delivery,* and *evaluation.* Using such a process reduces the likelihood of unplanned, uncoordinated, and haphazard training efforts that may significantly reduce the learning that should happen from occurring. A discussion of each phase of the training process follows.

Assessment of Training Needs

Since training should be designed to help a healthcare organization accomplish its objectives, assessing organizational training needs is the diagnostic phase of setting training objectives. **Assessment** considers employee and organizational

FIGURE 8-3   Systematic Training Process

Training Needs Assessment
- Analyze training needs
- Identify training objectives and criteria

Training Design
- Pretest trainees
- Select training methods
- Plan training content

Training Delivery
- Schedule training
- Conduct training
- Monitor training

Evaluation of Training
- Measure training outcomes
- Compare outcomes to objectives and criteria

© 2016 Cengage Learning®

performance issues to determine if training can help. Using the performance consulting approach mentioned earlier, managers must consider nontraining factors as well, such as compensation, organization structure, job design, physical work settings, and others. But if training is necessary, then the assessment efforts lead to analyzing the need for training and specifying the objectives of the training effort. For example, looking at the performance of clerks in a patient accounting department, a manager might believe that their data entry and keyboard abilities are weak and that they would profit by having instruction in these areas. As part of assessment, the clerks might be given a keyboard data entry test to measure their current skills. An objective of increasing the clerks' keyboard entry speed to 60 words per minute without errors might be established. The number of words per minute without errors is the criterion against which training success can be measured, and it represents the way in which the objective is made specific.

Establishing Training Objectives and Priorities   Once the training needs have been identified using the various analyses, then training objectives and priorities should be established. All of the gathered data are used to compile a **gap analysis**, which identifies the distance between where an organization is with its employee capabilities and where it needs to be. Training objectives and priorities are set to close the gap. Three types of training objectives can be set:

> *Knowledge:* Impart cognitive information and details to trainees.
>
> *Skill:* Develop behavior changes in how jobs and various task requirements are performed.
>
> *Attitude:* Create interest in and awareness of the importance of training.

The success of training should be measured in terms of the objectives set. Useful objectives are measurable. For example, an objective for a new Medicare biller might be to "demonstrate the ability to explain the various billing processes in the department within two weeks." This objective serves as a check on internalization, or whether the person really learned and is able to use the training.

Since training seldom is an unlimited budget item and there are multiple training needs in an organization, it is necessary to prioritize needs. Ideally, training needs are ranked in importance on the basis of organizational objectives. The training most needed to improve the performance of the organization should be done first in order to produce visible results more quickly.[12]

TRAINING DESIGN

Once training objectives have been determined, training design can start. Whether job-specific or broader in nature, training must be designed to address the specific objectives. Effective training design considers the learners and instructional strategies, as well as how to maximize the transfer of training from class to the job site.

Working in healthcare organizations should be a continual learning process. Different approaches are possible because learning is a complex psychological

FIGURE 8-4   Training Design Elements

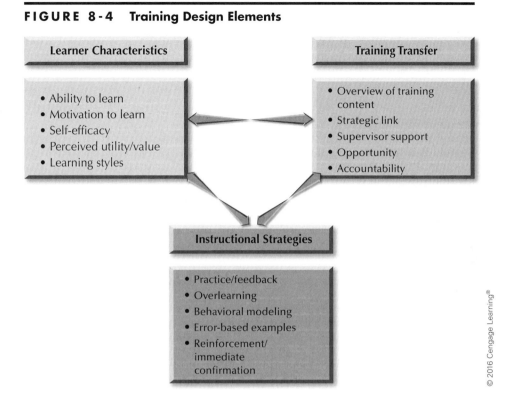

process. Each of the elements shown in Figure 8-4 must be considered for the training design to be effective and produce learning.

Learner Characteristics

For training to be successful, learners must be ready and able to learn. Learner readiness means that individuals have the ability to learn. However, individuals also must have the motivation to learn, have high confidence, see value in learning, and have a learning style that fits the training.

Ability to Learn   Learners must possess basic skills, such as fundamental reading or math proficiency, and sufficient cognitive abilities. This has posed a problem for some healthcare organizations, resulting in the need to provide remedial education for employees. Hospitals or long-term care facilities may discover that some workers lack the cognitive ability to comprehend their training. Some have found that a significant number of job applicants and current employees lack the reading, writing, and math skills needed to learn the jobs. Healthcare employers deal with the lack of basic employee skills in several ways:

- Offer remedial training to existing employees who need it.
- Test and hire workers who already have the necessary skills.
- Work with local schools to help better educate potential hires for jobs.

Motivation   A person's desire to learn training content, referred to as *motivation to learn,* is influenced by multiple factors. For example, differences in gender and ethnicity and the resulting experiences may affect the motivation of adult learners. The student's motivational level may also be influenced by the instructor's motivation and ability, friends' encouragement to do well, classmates' motivational levels, the classroom's physical environment, and the training methods used. Regardless of what motivates, without that motivation the student will not learn the material.

Self-Efficacy   Learners must possess **self-efficacy**, which refers to a person's belief that he or she can successfully learn the training program content. For learners to be ready for and receptive to the training content, they must believe that it is possible for them to learn the material. As an example, some college students' levels of self-efficacy diminish in math or statistics courses when they do not feel adequately able to grasp the material. These perceptions may have nothing to do with their actual ability to learn but rather reflect the way they see themselves and their abilities.[13] Instructors and trainers must find appropriate ways to boost the confidence of trainees who are unsure of their learning abilities because people who believe strongly that they can learn perform better and are more satisfied with the training they receive.

Perceived Utility/Value   Training that is viewed as useful is more likely to be tried on the job. Perceived utility or value of training is affected by a need to improve, the likelihood that training will lead to improvement, and the practicality of the training for use on the job. Learners must perceive a close relationship between the training and skill sets they need in order for training to be used on the job. Based on the requirements of most jobs in healthcare organizations, the perceived utility/value is relatively easy to demonstrate. As an example, an RN receiving training in the appropriate handling of biohazards should easily see the value to her own safety relative to the training.

Learning Styles   People learn in different ways. For example, *auditory* learners learn best by listening to someone else tell them about the training content. *Tactile* learners must "get their hands on" the training resources and use them. *Visual* learners think in pictures and figures and need to see the purpose and process of the training. Trainers who address all these styles by using multiple training methods can design more effective training.

   Training design must also sometimes address special issues presented by **adult learning**. Certainly, the training design must consider that all the trainees are adults, but adults come with widely varying learning styles, experiences, and personal goals. For example, training older adults in technology may require greater attention to explaining the need for changes and enhancing the older trainees' confidence and abilities when learning new technologies. In contrast, younger adults are more likely to be familiar with new technology because of their earlier exposure to computers and technology, but less able to work alone to learn skills.

Malcolm Knowles's classic work on adult learning suggests five principles for designing training for adults.[14] According to that work and subsequent work by others, adults:

- Have the need to know why they are learning something
- Have a need to be self-directed
- Bring more work-related experiences into the learning process
- Enter into a learning experience with a problem-centered approach to learning
- Are motivated to learn by *both* extrinsic and intrinsic factors

Instructional Strategies

An important part of designing training is to select the right mix of teaching strategies to fit learner characteristics. Practice/feedback, overlearning, behavioral modeling, error-based examples, and reinforcement/immediate confirmation are some of the prominent strategies available in designing the training experience.

Practice/Feedback   For some training, it is important that learners practice what they have learned and get feedback on how they have done so they can improve. **Active practice** occurs when trainees perform job-related tasks and duties during training. It is more effective than simply reading or passively listening. For instance, assume a person is being trained as a surgery scheduler. After being given some basic instructions and scheduling details, the trainee calls a patient and uses the knowledge received to schedule the patient for surgery.

Behavioral Modeling   The most elementary way in which people learn and one of the best is through **behavioral modeling**, which involves copying someone else's behavior. The use of behavioral modeling is particularly appropriate for skill training in which the trainees must use both knowledge and practice. It can aid in the transfer of skills and the usage of those skills by those who are trained. For example, a new supervisor can receive training and mentoring on how to handle disciplinary discussions with employees by observing as the HR director or department manager deals with such problems.

Behavioral modeling is used extensively as the primary means for training supervisors and managers in interpersonal skills.[15] Fortunately or unfortunately, many supervisors and managers end up modeling behaviors they see their bosses exhibit. For that reason, supervisor training should include good role models to show learners how to properly handle interpersonal interactions with employees.

Error-Based Examples   The error-based examples method involves sharing with learners what can go wrong when they do not use the training properly. A good example is sharing with a new medical assistant what can happen when they are not aware of a situation when asking a patient about their medical history. Situational awareness training that includes error-based examples improves situational awareness. Error-based examples have been incorporated in physician, nursing, paramedic, and first responder training and have wide potential uses in other situations.[16] Case studies showing the negative consequences of errors are a good tool for communicating error-based examples.[17]

Reinforcement and Immediate Confirmation   The concept of **reinforcement** is based on the *law of effect*, which states that people tend to repeat responses that give them a positive reward and to avoid actions associated with negative consequences. Positively reinforcing correct learned responses while providing negative consequences at some point for wrong responses can change behavior.[18] Closely related is an instructional strategy called **immediate confirmation**, which is based on the idea that people learn best if reinforcement and feedback are given as soon as possible after exhibiting a response. Immediate confirmation corrects errors that, if made and not corrected throughout the training, might establish an undesirable pattern that would need to be unlearned. It also aids with the transfer of training to the job.

Training Transfer

Finally, trainers in healthcare settings should design training for the best possible transfer from the classroom to the job. Transfer occurs when trainees actually use on the job what knowledge and information they learned in training. The amount of training that effectively gets transferred to the job is estimated to be relatively low, especially given all the time and money spent on training. Not all employees apply training to their jobs immediately after training. Among those who do not use the training immediately, the likelihood of it being used decreases over time.[19]

Effective transfer of training meets two conditions. First, the trainees can take the material learned in training and apply it to the job context in which they work. Second, employees maintain their use of the learned material over time. Many things can increase the transfer of training.[20] Offering trainees an *overview of the training content* and *how it links to the strategy* of the organization seems to help with both short-term and longer-term training transfer. Another helpful approach is to ensure that the *training mirrors the job* context as much as possible. For example, training managers to be better selection interviewers could include role-playing with "applicants" who answer in the same manner that "real" applicants would respond.

One of the most consistent factors in training transfer is the *support* new trainees receive *from their supervisors* to use their new skills when they return to the job.[21] Supervisor support of the training, feedback from the supervisor, and supervisor involvement in training are powerful influences in transfer. *Opportunity to use the training* is also important. To be trained on something but never to have the opportunity to use it obviously limits transfer. Learners need the opportunity to use new skills on the job if the skills are to remain.

Finally, *accountability* helps transfer training from class to job. Accountability is the extent to which someone expects the learner to use the new skills on the job and holds them responsible for doing so.[22] It may require supervisory praise for doing the task correctly and sanctions for not showing proper trained behavior, but making people accountable for their own trained behavior is effective.

Types of Training

Training can be designed to meet a number of different objectives. One useful classification tool is to view training as being of several types based on these objectives:

- *Required and Regular Training*—Done to comply with various mandated or legal requirements (e.g., JCAHO, Equal Employment Opportunity or EEO), and as training for all employees (new employee orientation)
- *Job/Technical Training*—Done so that employees can perform their jobs, tasks, and responsibilities well (e.g., customer service, computer and machine operations)
- *Interpersonal and Problem-Solving Training*—Conducted to address both operational and interpersonal problems and improving organizational working relationships (e.g., team building, conflict resolution)
- *Developmental and Innovation Training*—Focused to enhance individual and organizational capabilities for the long-term future (e.g., organizational change, creative thinking)

Orientation/Onboarding: Training for New Employees

As required by the Occupational Safety and Health Administration (OSHA) and for those healthcare organizations that subscribe to JCAHO or CARF, all newly employed healthcare employees must attend orientation. All employees who routinely rotate to different areas of the health facility should also receive orientations to each of the areas. Examples of employees who rotate include RNs, respiratory therapists, agency nurses, and other contingency staff employees. Additionally, orientation is required for employees who have been reemployed, transferred, or promoted to new duties and for employees who have been impacted by departmental or organizational redesigns.

Orientation requires cooperation between individuals in the HR unit and operating managers and supervisors.[23] In small healthcare organizations without an HR department, the new employee's supervisor or manager usually assumes most of the responsibility for orientation.[24] In larger healthcare organizations, managers and supervisors, as well as the HR department, often work as a team to orient new employees. There are several key purposes of orientation. The most important ones are to:

- Establish a favorable employee impression of the organization and the job.
- Provide organization and job information.
- Enhance interpersonal acceptance by coworkers.
- Accelerate new employees' socialization and integration into the organization.
- Ensure quicker employee performance, productivity, and safety.

Effective orientation efforts contribute to both short-term and longer-term employment success. One way that orientations are being made more effective is through the use of electronic orientation. Employers place general employee orientation information on organizational intranets or on employee self-serve

HR systems. New employees can log on and go through much of the general material on organizational history, structure, products and services, mission statements, and other background information instead of having to sit in a classroom where the information is delivered in person or by videotape. The more specific questions and areas can be addressed by HR staff and others after the web-based information has been reviewed by the new employees. Figure 8-5 shows the typical components of organizational and departmental orientations. As noted, many of the topics would lend themselves to web-based presentation complemented by group meetings.

Unfortunately, many new employee orientation sessions are seen as boring, irrelevant, and a waste of time by both new employees and their department supervisors and managers. Many healthcare organizations are reconsidering their approach to new employee orientations in an effort to make the event more interesting and relevant. As an example, a large home health agency conducts its new employee orientation at a breakfast meeting, with extensive use of videos and presenters that incorporate humor and real-situation information in the presentations.

FIGURE 8-5 Typical Components of Healthcare Orientations

ORGANIZATIONAL ORIENTATION	DEPARTMENTAL ORIENTATION
• Mission vision and values	• Departmental structure
• Organizational ethics	• Patient/work flow
• Organizational structure	• Tour of area
• Customer service requirements	• Job responsibilities
• Patient safety	• Performance standards
• OSHA and general safety	• Departmental relationships
• Maintaining confidentiality	• Unit/Department-specific safety information
• Infection control practices	• Department policies
• Patient rights	
• Benefits, compensation, and HR policies	
• Security and fire safety	

© Cengage Learning®

Encourage Self-Development

Not all of the training and education needs of healthcare employees can be met through organizational, departmental, or supervisory-guided training. Employee training needs are often individualized and require employees to take the initiative to meet their own needs. However, the organization must encourage and provide employees with the resources and encouragement to pursue self-development.[25] Encouraging and facilitating self-development can take many forms, including the following:

- Resource libraries or learning labs where employees can research information or develop procedural skills in a self-paced manner
- Computer-based training (CBT) that employees can access either at the health facility or from their home computers

- Opportunities to attend professional society meetings that offer a variety of workshops and educational forums
- Tuition reimbursement or stipends to pursue technical or college-level course work

Beyond the importance of encouraging self-development for purposes of ensuring staff competency, a healthcare organization's investment in the self-development efforts described above can contribute to staff retention. Retention of competent staff further contributes to safe, high-quality patient care.

Ongoing Training and Development

Training and development take many forms in the healthcare setting. These include, among others: (1) on-the-job preceptorship by the supervisor or another proficient employee, (2) in-service education on new procedures, policies, or processes, (3) continuing education classes, and (4) professional development workshops or seminars. The general objectives of these training and development efforts are to continually ensure employee competence and to enhance employees' overall knowledge of their job duties, department, and organization.[26] The specific objectives include the following:

- Correct performance or competence deficiencies.
- Provide training on new technology, techniques, or processes.
- Meet safety or regulatory compliance requirements in such areas as blood-borne pathogens or fire safety standards.
- Prepare employees for new job duties or promotional opportunities.

Ensuring ongoing training and development of healthcare employees is typically the responsibility of the employees' supervisors or department heads. However, HR plays a significant role in helping supervisors monitor attendance at organizational-level training (such as safety training) and providing processes for documenting attendance at these programs.

Delivery of Training

The amount of each type of training done varies by organization, depending on the strategic plans, resources, and needs identified in various organizations. Once training has been designed, the actual delivery of training can begin. It is generally recommended that the training be piloted or conducted on a trial basis in order to ensure that the training meets the needs identified and that the design is appropriate. However, regardless of the type of training done, there are a number of different approaches and methods of training that can be used. The growth of training technology has expanded the choices available.

Regardless of the approaches used, there are a variety of considerations that must be balanced when selecting training approaches and methods. The common variables considered are:

- Nature of training
- Subject matter
- Number of trainees
- Individual versus team
- Self-paced versus guided
- Training resources
- Costs
- Geographic locations
- Time allotted
- Completion timeline

To illustrate, supervisory training for a large clinic with three locations in different, nearby geographic areas may bring supervisors together for a two-day workshop, once every quarter. However, a large, multistate nursing home system may use web-based courses to reach supervisors throughout the country.

Internal Training

Training internally tends to be viewed as being very applicable to the job. It is also popular because it saves the cost of sending employees away for training, and it often avoids the cost of outside trainers. Often, skills-based technical training is conducted inside organizations. Technical training is usually skills based (e.g., training to run laboratory equipment). Due to rapid changes in healthcare technology, the building and updating of technical skills have become crucial training needs. Basic technical skills training are also being mandated by federal regulations in areas where OSHA, the Environmental Protection Agency (EPA), and other agencies have regulations.[27] Web-based training and intranets also are growing as internal means of training.

- *Informal Training*—One internal source of training is **informal training**, which occurs through interactions and feedback among employees. Much of what employees know about their jobs is learned informally from asking questions and getting advice from other employees and their supervisors, not from formal training programs.
- *On-the-Job Training*—The most common type of training at all levels in an organization is **on-the-job training (OJT)**. Different from informal training, which often occurs spontaneously, OJT should be planned. The supervisor or manager doing the training must be able to teach as well as to show the employee what to do. On-the-job training is by far the most commonly used form of training in healthcare organizations because it is flexible and relevant to what the employee is doing.

External Training

External training, or training that takes place outside the employing organization, is used extensively by healthcare organizations of all sizes. Organizations use external training if they lack the capability to train people internally or when many people need to be trained quickly. External training may be the best option for training in smaller organizations because of limitations in the size of their training staffs and in the number of employees who need various types of specialized training. Whatever the size of the organization, external training provides these advantages:

- It may be less expensive for a healthcare employer to have an outside trainer conduct training in areas where internal training resources are limited, especially if the training is of a specialized nature, such as electronic health record data entry.

- The organization may not have sufficient time to develop internal training materials.

- The staff may not have the necessary level of expertise for the subject matter in which training is needed.

- There are advantages to having employees interact with managers and peers in other organizations during external training programs.

Outsourcing of Training   Many employers of all sizes outsource training to external training firms, consultants, and other entities. Perhaps one-third of training expenditures go to outside training sources. The reasons more outside training is not used may be cost concerns and a greater emphasis on internal linking of training to organizational strategies.

A popular route for healthcare employers is to use vendors and suppliers to train employees.[28] Benefits brokers, such as Lochton or Willis, routinely provide HR workshops and seminars for their clients. In addition, several computer software vendors offer employees technical certifications on their software.

Government-Supported Job Training   Federal, state, and local governments provide a wide range of external training assistance and funding.[29] The Workforce Investment Act (WIA) provides states with block grant programs that target adult education, disadvantaged youth, and training employees. Employers hiring and training individuals who meet the WIA criteria receive tax credits and other assistance for six months or more, depending on the program regulations.

At state and local levels, employers who add to their workforces can take advantage of programs that provide funding assistance to offset training costs. As an example, many states offer workforce-training assistance for employers. Quick Start (Georgia), Smart Jobs (Texas), and Partnership (Alabama) are three well-known training support efforts. Such programs are often linked to two-year and four-year colleges throughout the state.[30]

Educational Assistance Programs   Many healthcare employers provide additional education for their employees through tuition reimbursement programs. Typically, the employee pays for a course that applies to a college degree and is reimbursed upon successful completion of the course. The amounts paid by the employer are considered nontaxable income for the employee up to amounts set by federal laws.

One concern about traditional forms of employee educational programs is that they may pose risks for the employer. Upon completion of the degree, the employee may choose to take the new skills and go elsewhere. Employers must plan to use the new skills immediately following employee graduation to improve retention.[31]

E-learning: Online Training

E-learning is use of a web-based technology to conduct training online. E-learning is popular with healthcare employers, especially rural and military healthcare due to the lack of training resources in the immediate vicinity of their facility or deployment. The major reasons are cost savings and access to more employees. Training conducted with some kind of learning technology is likely to continue to increase. Almost 30 percent of learning hours today are totally technology based, according to an American Society for Training and Development (ASTD) report, and e-learning is preferred by workers under the age of 30.[32]

Distance Training/Learning   Many college and university classes use some form of Internet-based course support. Hundreds of college professors use various packages to make their lecture content available to students. These packages enable virtual chat and electronic file exchange among course participants and enhance instructor–student contact.

Many large healthcare employers similarly use interactive two-way television to present classes. The medium allows an instructor in one place to see and respond to a "class" in any number of other locations. With a fully configured system, employees can take courses from anywhere in the world. Webinars are a type of web-based training that has reached a level of popularity both as company training and as a source of profit for the organization.[33]

Simulations   Computer-based training involves a wide array of multimedia technologies—including sound, motion (video and animation), graphics, and hypertext—to tap multiple learner senses. Computer-supported simulations within e-learning can replicate the psychological and behavioral requirements of a task, often in addition to providing some physical resemblance to the trainee's work environment. An example of a training simulation that is very prevalent in healthcare is the use of mannequins that are really "computerized patients" that allow physicians and other care providers to learn skills without practicing on a live patient.[34]

Mobile Learning   Predictions have been that training will incorporate more use of mobile devices such as smartphones, tablets, or netbooks; the potential uses seem endless.[35] However, barriers to mobile learning include budget restrictions, integrating this technology with existing training, and security concerns.[36] But while the physical classroom, webinars, and formal e-learning courses are not going away, mobile learning is on the rise.[37] Some current ways mobile devices can be used in training include the following: Healthcare professionals such as pharmacists can access a PDR* on a tablet.[38] Employees can use mobile devices to access instruction manuals for hardware and software. In class, courses can be augmented with five-minute videos accessible from mobile devices, turning classrooms into blended learning environments.[39]

Blended Learning   Generally, technology is moving from center stage to becoming embedded in the learning and training processes. As learning and work merge even more closely in the future, technology is likely to integrate seamlessly into the work environment of more employees.

However, e-learning does not work well as the sole method of training, according to employers. A solution seems to be **blended learning**, which might combine short, fast-paced, interactive computer-based lessons and teleconferencing with traditional classroom instruction and simulation. Deciding which training is best handled by which medium is important.

A blended learning approach can use e-learning for building knowledge of certain basics, a web-based virtual classroom for building skills, and significant in-person, traditional, instructor-led training sessions and courses. Use of blended learning provides greater flexibility in the use of multiple training means and enhances the appeal of training activities to different types of employees.[40] Healthcare organizations have successfully utilized blended learning in providing safety training. Figure 8-6 describes the advantages and disadvantages of e-Learning.

Evaluation of Training

Evaluation of training compares the posttraining results to the objectives expected by managers, trainers, and trainees. Too often, training is done without any thought of measuring and evaluating it later to see how well it worked. Because training is both time-consuming and costly, evaluation should be done.

Cost–Benefit Analyses   One way to evaluate training results is to examine the costs associated with the training and the benefits received through a cost–benefit analysis. Figure 8-7 shows some costs and benefits that may result from training. Although some benefits (such as attitude changes) are hard to quantify, comparison of costs and benefits associated with training remains a way to determine if training is cost effective. For example, one nursing home evaluated a traditional safety training program and found that the program did not lead to a reduction in accidents. Therefore, the training was redesigned so that better safety practices did result.

---

* The *Physicians' Desk Reference* (**PDR**) is a commercially published compilation of manufacturers' prescribing information on prescription drugs updated annually. It is designed to provide healthcare professionals with the full legally mandated information relevant to writing prescriptions (just as its name suggests).

FIGURE 8-6   Advantages and Disadvantages of E-Learning

Advantages	Disadvantages
• Is self-paced; trainees can proceed on their own time • Is interactive, tapping multiple trainee senses • Enables scoring of exercises/assessments and the appropriate feedback • Incorporates built-in guidance and help for trainees to use when needed • Allows trainers to update content relatively easily • Can enhance instructor-led training • Is good for presenting simple facts and concepts • Can be paired with simulation	• May cause trainee anxiety • Some trainees may not be interested in how it is used • Requires easy and uninterrupted access to computers • Is not appropriate for some training (leadership, cultural change, etc.) • Requires significant upfront investment both in time and costs • Requires significant support from top management to be successful • Some choose not to do it even if it is available

© 2016 Cengage Learning®

FIGURE 8-7   Balancing Costs and Benefits of Training

Typical Costs	Typical Benefits
• Trainer's salary and time • Trainees' salaries and time • Materials for training • Expenses for trainer and trainees • Cost of facilities and equipment • Lost productivity (opportunity cost)	• Increase in production • Reduction in errors and accidents • Reduction in turnover • Less necessary supervision • Ability to use new capabilities • Attitude changes

© 2016 Cengage Learning®

Return-on-Investment Analysis and Benchmarking   In healthcare organizations, executive leadership expects training to produce a return on investment (ROI). Still, too often training is justified because someone liked it, rather than on the basis of resource accountability.[41] ROI simply divides the return produced because of the training by the cost (or investment) of the training.

In addition to evaluating training internally, many healthcare organizations use benchmark measures to compare it with training done in other organizations. To do benchmarking, HR professionals gather data on training in their organization and compare them with data on training at other organizations in the same industry and in companies of a similar size. Comparison data are available through the ASTD and its Benchmarking Service. This service has training-related data from more than 1,000 participating employers who complete detailed questionnaires annually. Training can also be benchmarked against data from the American Productivity and Quality Center and the Saratoga Institute.

Joint Commission Standards and Orientation, Training, and Development

JCAHO standards have a significant focus on staff orientation, training, and development. As depicted in Figure 8-8, the standards require a process for the ongoing and continuous effort of assuring staff competency through orientation, training, and development, and through encouraging self-development. In addition, the standards require that data on competence patterns be monitored to identify trends and respond to employees' learning needs. These factors work together to ensure staff competency.

FIGURE 8-8   Ensuring Staff Competence

© 2016 Cengage Learning®

Competence Trends and Employees' Learning Needs In addition to the training described above, the Joint Commission also requires organizations to monitor patient care and safety incidents to determine employee-learning needs. As an example, a medical center evaluates the number of incidents of inadvertent needle sticks on each of the patient care units. This evaluation determines if any special training would be required on a particular unit based on an exceptionally high number of sticks in comparison to other units. Training focusing on remedying competence issues is extremely important in meeting Joint Commission HR standards. Monitoring trends and initiating training efforts designed to deal with issues should be well documented and presented to the reviewers during a Joint Commission on-site inspection.

DEVELOPING HUMAN RESOURCES

Development represents efforts to improve employees' abilities to handle a variety of assignments and to cultivate employees' capabilities beyond those required by their current job. Development should benefit both organizations and employees. Employees and managers with appropriate experiences and abilities may enhance organizational competitiveness and the ability to adapt to a changing environment. In the development process, individuals' careers may also evolve and shift to new or different focuses. For instance, Atlantic Health, a two-hospital care system in New Jersey, has implemented a leadership development program intended to prepare their staff for current and future leadership challenges.[42]

Development differs from training. It is possible to train people to administer medications, enter data in the electronic medical record, set up an operating room, or prep a dental patient for a tooth extraction. However, development in areas such as judgment, responsibility, decision making, and communication presents a bigger challenge. These areas may or may not develop through ordinary life experiences of individuals. A planned system of development experiences for all employees, not just managers, can help expand the overall level of capabilities in an organization. Figure 8-9 profiles development and compares it with training.

Possible Development Focuses

Some important and common management capabilities that may require development include an action orientation, quality decision-making skills, ethical values, and technical skills. Abilities to build teams, develop subordinates, direct others, and deal with uncertainty are equally important but much less commonly developed capabilities for successful managers.

One point about development is clear: in numerous studies that asked employees what they want out of their jobs, training and development ranked at or near the top. The primary assets that individuals have are their knowledge, skills, and abilities (KSAs), and many people view the development of their KSAs as an important part of their jobs.

Lifelong or Continuous Learning Learning and development are closely linked. For most people, lifelong learning and development are necessary and desirable.[43] For many healthcare professionals, lifelong learning may mean

FIGURE 8-9 **Development vs. Training**

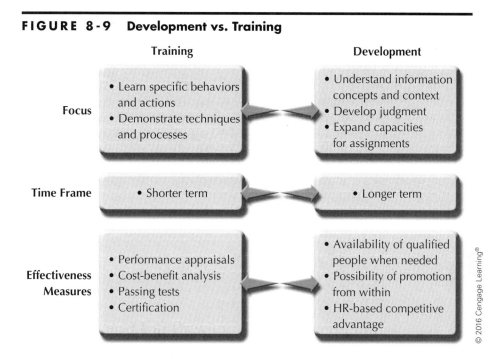

meeting continuing education requirements to retain certifications or licenses. For example, dentists and nurses must complete continuing education requirements in most states to keep their licenses to practice. For other employees, learning and development may involve training to expand existing skills and to prepare for different jobs, for promotions, or even for new jobs after retirement.

Assistance from employers needed for lifelong development typically comes through programs at work, including tuition reimbursement programs. However, much of lifelong learning is voluntary, takes place outside work hours, and is not always formal. Although it may have no immediate relevance to a person's current job, learning often enhances an individual's confidence, ideas, and enthusiasm.

Redevelopment   Whether due to a desire for career change or because the employer needs different capabilities, people may shift jobs in midlife or mid-career. Redeveloping people in the capabilities they need is logical and important. In the last decade, the number of college enrollees over the age of 35 has increased dramatically. But helping employees go back to college is only one way of redeveloping them. Some healthcare organizations offer redevelopment programs to recruit experienced workers from other fields. For example, rural hospitals needing RNs have sponsored second-career programs.

Development Needs Analyses

Like employee training, employee development begins with analyses of the needs of both the organization and the individuals. Either the employer or the individual can analyze what KSAs a given person needs to develop. The goal, of course, is to identify strengths and weaknesses. Methods that organizations use to assess development needs include assessment centers, psychological testing, and performance appraisals. Development metrics are used to determine effectiveness.

Assessment Centers   Collections of test instruments and exercises designed to diagnose individuals' development needs are referred to as **assessment centers**. In a typical assessment center experience, an individual spends two or three days away from the job performing many assessment activities. These activities might include role-playing, tests, cases, leaderless-group discussions, computer-based simulations, and peer evaluations. Assessment centers provide an excellent means for determining individual potential.[44]

Psychological Testing   Psychological tests have been used for years to determine employees' developmental potential and needs. Intelligence tests, verbal and mathematical reasoning tests, and personality tests are often given. Psychological testing can furnish useful information on individuals about such factors as motivation, reasoning abilities, leadership style, interpersonal response traits, and job preferences. The biggest problem with psychological testing lies in interpretation, because untrained managers, supervisors, and workers usually cannot accurately interpret test results. After a professional scores the tests and reports the values to others in the organization, untrained managers may attach their own meanings to the findings. Also, some psychological tests are of limited validity, and test takers may fake desirable responses. Thus, psychological testing is appropriate only when the testing and feedback processes are closely handled by a qualified professional.

Performance Appraisals   Well-done performance appraisals can be a source of development information. Performance data on productivity, employee relations, job knowledge, and other relevant dimensions can be gathered in such assessments.

Development Metrics   Organizations can use metrics to determine employees' developmental needs as well as measure development success. For example, assessments that target the proper skills needed to perform work can be used to identify the content that should be included in development programs.[45]

Succession Planning

Succession planning is an important part of HR development. **Succession planning** is a process of identifying a longer-term plan for orderly replacement of key employees. The need to replace key employees results from promotions, transfers, retirements, deaths, disability, departures, or other reasons. Succession planning often focuses on top management, such as ensuring a CEO successor. However, succession planning should not be limited to top executive positions. For example, a large children's mental health therapy agency whose clinical director is planning retirement must consider the implications for maintaining continuity in delivering competent patient care and clinical leadership. The need to plan for and eventually replace this key manager is a *strategic HR issue*.

Two coordinated activities begin the actual succession planning process. First, the development of preliminary replacement charts ensures that the right individuals with sufficient capabilities and experience to perform the targeted jobs are available at the right time. These charts both show the backup "players" for each position and identify positions without a current qualified backup. The charts identify who could immediately take over key jobs if someone leaves, retires, dies unexpectedly, or otherwise creates a vacancy, and the development necessary to ready some of the other individuals to do so.

Benefits of Formal Succession Planning

Succession planning can be done formally and informally. As healthcare organizations become larger, the benefits of formal succession planning become greater, and for these larger organizations, formal planning is recommended. Key benefits include the following:

- Having a supply of highly qualified individuals ready for future job openings
- Providing career opportunities and plans for individuals, which helps retention and performance motivation
- Providing a basis for the continual review of staffing requirements as organizational changes occur over time

Common Succession Planning Mistakes   CEO succession should be a focus of the boards of directors, not solely HR. But focusing only on CEO and top management succession is one of the most common mistakes made. Other mistakes include the following:

- Starting too late, when openings are already occurring
- Not linking well to strategic plans
- Allowing the CEO to direct the planning and make all succession decisions
- Looking only internally for succession candidates

All of these mistakes are indicative of poor succession planning.[46] Longer-term succession planning should include mid-level and lower-level managers, as well as other key nonmanagement employees.

According to a recent study conducted for the American College of Healthcare Executives, only 21 percent of the freestanding hospitals participating in the study reported that leadership succession planning is routinely done in their organization. Approximately one in six indicated that as part of their succession plan they had identified a successor to their chief executive officer. Respondents were associated with hospitals with a median of 70 staffed beds; 64 percent indicated they were in rural settings.[47]

Choosing a Development Approach

Common development approaches can be categorized under three major headings. Investing in human intellectual capital can occur on or off the job and in "learning organizations." Development becomes imperative as "knowledge work," such as research skills and specialized technology expertise, increases for almost all employers. But identifying the right mix of approaches for development needs requires analyses and planning.

Job-Site Development Approaches

All too often, unplanned and perhaps useless activities pass as development on the job. To ensure that the desired development actually occurs, managers must plan and coordinate their development efforts. Managers can choose from various job-site development methods.[48]

Coaching The oldest on-the-job development technique is **coaching**, which involves observation and feedback given to employees by immediate supervisors. Coaching is the continual process of learning by doing. For coaching to be effective, employees and their managers must have a healthy and open relationship.

Unfortunately, organizations may be tempted to implement coaching without sufficient planning. Even someone who is good at a job will not necessarily be able to coach someone else to do it well. "Coaches" can easily fall short in guiding learners systematically, even if they know which experiences are best.[49] The coach's job responsibilities may take priority over learning and coaching of subordinates. Also, the intellectual component of many capabilities might be better learned from a book or a course before coaching occurs. Outside consultants may be used as coaches at the executive level.

Committee Assignments A very popular and well-used development approach in healthcare, especially in large hospitals, medical centers, and long-term care facilities, is committee assignments. Assigning promising employees to important committees may broaden their experiences and help them understand the personalities, issues, and processes governing the organization. For instance, employees on a safety committee can gain a greater understanding of safety problems and management, which would help them to become supervisors. They may also experience the problems involved in maintaining employee safety awareness. However, managers need to guard against committee assignments that turn into time-wasting activities.

Job Rotation The process of moving a person from job to job is called **job rotation**, and it is widely used as a development technique. For example, a promising young manager may spend three months in a plant, three months in finance, and three months in HR. When properly handled, such job rotation fosters a greater understanding of the organization and aids with employee retention by making individuals more versatile, strengthening their skills, and reducing boredom. A disadvantage of job rotation is that it can be expensive because a substantial amount of time is required to acquaint trainees with the different people and techniques in each new unit.

Assistant to Positions Some healthcare organizations create "assistant to" positions, which are staff positions immediately under a manager (e.g., assistant to HR director). Through such jobs, trainees can work with outstanding managers they might not otherwise have met. These assignments provide useful experiences if they present challenging or interesting tasks to trainees.

Off-Site Development Approaches

Off-the-job development techniques give individuals opportunities to get away from their jobs and concentrate solely on what is to be learned. Contact with others who are concerned with slightly different problems and come from different organizations may provide employees with new and different perspectives. Various off-site methods can be used.

Classroom Courses and Seminars   Most off-the-job development programs include some classroom instruction. People are familiar with classroom training, which gives it the advantage of being widely accepted. But the lecture system sometimes used in classroom instruction encourages passive listening and reduced learner participation, which is a distinct disadvantage. Sometimes trainees have little opportunity to question, clarify, and discuss the lecture material. The effectiveness of classroom instruction depends on multiple factors: group size, trainees' abilities, instructors' capabilities and styles, and subject matter.

Organizations often send employees to externally sponsored seminars or professional courses, such as those offered by numerous professional and consulting entities. Examples would include annual conferences conducted by the American Hospital Association for hospital administrators or Medical Group Management Association for clinic administrators.[50] Organizations also encourage continuing education by reimbursing employees for the costs of college courses. Tuition reimbursement programs provide incentives for employees to study for advanced degrees through evening and weekend classes that are given outside of their regular workdays and hours.

Outdoor Development Experiences   Some organizations send executives and managers to experiences held outdoors, called *outdoor training* or outdoor development. The rationale for using these wilderness excursions, which can last one day or a week (or longer), is that such experiences can increase self-confidence and help individuals reevaluate personal goals and efforts. For individuals in work groups or teams, shared risks and challenges outside the office environment can create a sense of teamwork. The challenges may include rock climbing in the California desert, whitewater rafting on a river, backpacking in the Rocky Mountains, or handling a longboat off the coast of Maine.

Survival-type management development courses may have more impact than many other management seminars. But companies must consider the inherent perils. Some participants have been unable to handle the physical and emotional challenges associated with rappelling down a cliff or climbing a 40-foot tower. The decision to sponsor such programs should depend on the capabilities of the employees involved and the learning objectives.

Sabbaticals and Leaves of Absence   A **sabbatical** is an opportunity provided by some companies for employees to take time off the job to develop and rejuvenate, as well as to participate in activities that help others. Some employers provide paid sabbaticals, while others allow employees to take unpaid sabbaticals. The length of time taken off from work varies greatly.

Academic healthcare organizations that offer sabbaticals speak well of the results. Positive reasons for sabbaticals are to help prevent employee burnout, offer advantages in recruiting and retention, and boost individual employee morale. Some organizations give employees three to six months off to work on socially desirable projects. Such projects have included leading training programs in underserved neighborhoods or participating in corporate volunteer programs to aid nonprofit organizations. As an example, United Way and Community Chest organizations have "Executive-on-Loan" programs that are excellent opportunities for both healthcare executives and the healthcare organization. The executive gets to learn and do new and different activities, and the organization gets to contribute in a high-value and unique way to the community.

Leaves of absence for educational purposes may or may not be provided with pay. Some healthcare organizations allow employees the opportunity to access vacation time or continue benefits while on leaves of this nature. An educational leave of absence is typically granted to allow employees the time to commit full attention and effort to their education in order to enhance their job performance when they return.

Management Development

Although development is important for all employees, it is essential for managers. Effective management development imparts the knowledge and judgment needed by managers. Without appropriate development, managers may lack the capabilities to best deploy and manage resources (including employees) throughout the organization. Necessary capabilities are often a focus of management development and include leadership, dealing with change, coaching and advising subordinates, controlling operations, and providing performance feedback.

Experience plays a central role in management development. Indeed, experience often contributes more to the development of senior managers than classroom training does, because much of their experience occurs in varying circumstances on the job over time. Yet, despite a need for effective managers, finding such managers for middle-level jobs is often difficult. At the middle-management level, some individuals refuse to take management jobs. Many very talented healthcare professionals such as RNs, respiratory therapists, or pharmacists who could potentially make excellent managers refuse to do so because it would remove them from day-to-day patient care responsibilities. Sometimes the increase in pay is not enough to compensate for the increased workload and responsibilities. Many are also disenchanted with the "thanklessness" of the job, commenting that they would be caught between unhappy employees and nonsupportive senior management.

Managerial Modeling A common adage in management development says that managers tend to manage as they were managed. In other words, managers learn behavior by modeling or copying someone else's behavior. This tendency is not surprising, because a great deal of human behavior is learned by modeling. Children learn by modeling the behaviors of their parents and older children. Management development efforts can take advantage of natural human behavior by matching young or developing managers with appropriate models and then reinforcing the desirable behaviors exhibited.[51] Note that the modeling process involves more than straightforward imitation or copying; it is considerably more complex. For example, one can learn what not to do by observing a model who does something wrong. Thus, exposure to both positive and negative models can benefit a new manager.

Management Coaching   Coaching combines observation with suggestions. In the context of healthcare management development, coaching involves a relationship between two managers for a period of time as they perform their jobs. Effective coaching requires patience and good communication skills. Like modeling, it complements the natural way humans learn. Effective coaching often includes the following:

- Explaining appropriate behavior
- Making clear why actions were taken
- Accurately stating observations
- Providing possible alternatives/suggestions
- Following up/reinforcing

Mentoring

Mentoring is a relationship in which experienced managers aid individuals in the earlier stages of their careers. Such a relationship provides an environment for conveying technical, interpersonal, and organizational skills from the more-experienced to the less-experienced person.[52] Not only does the inexperienced employee benefit, but also the mentor may enjoy the challenge of sharing his or her wisdom.

However, mentoring is not without its problems. Young minority managers frequently report difficulty finding mentors. Also, men generally show less willingness than women to be mentors. Further, mentors who are dissatisfied with their jobs and those who teach a narrow or distorted view of events may not help in the development of new managers. Fortunately, many managers have a series of advisors or mentors during their careers and may find advantages in learning from the different mentors.

SPECIAL ISSUES IN HEALTHCARE EMPLOYEE DEVELOPMENT

The healthcare industry is a diverse collection of various types and sizes of organizations. From an employment perspective, the jobs and careers within the industry are even more diverse. From physician to medical assistant, CEO to line supervisor, architect to repair technician, many types of positions and professions are represented in the healthcare industry. There are a number of important considerations in healthcare employee development, including the size and sophistication of the organization, academic and credential requirements, and organizational strategies.

Depending on the type of facility or entity within the healthcare industry, employee development can be either nonexistent or unplanned/haphazard or very well developed and thoroughly planned. In small facilities, such as clinics or rural nursing homes, the organizational structures are often flat with minimal opportunities for promotion or even lateral transfers; consequently, employee development is typically not a priority. Conversely, large, integrated health systems carefully craft employee development plans aimed at identifying and developing the best and the brightest for future clinical management and executive positives within their organizations.

Academic and Credential Requirements

For many healthcare environments, advancement is entirely dependent on academic attainment and credentials. As an example, medical laboratory technicians cannot be promoted to physicians because they lack the appropriate educational background. Although this example seems obvious, this reality and others like it are important considerations in healthcare employee development. Although physicians are rarely provided with management or leadership skills development, they often find themselves in positions of leadership. Since they provide medical direction and leadership and own the practice, clinic, or hospital, it follows that they would also provide leadership in nonmedical areas.

The key criterion for their leadership role is their academic preparation as an MD, without which they could not be in their position. In many of the clinical and administrative management roles, similar situations occur. Figure 8-10 provides examples of other healthcare management positions that normally require specific academic preparation or credentials.

FIGURE 8-10 Samples of Healthcare Positions and Academic Preparation/Credentials

POSITION	ACADEMIC PREPARATION/CREDENTIALS
Clinical	
Director of Pharmacy	Pharm D.
Director of Nursing	RN, MSN
Director or Respiratory Care	BS Respiratory Care, Registered Respiratory Therapist (RRT)
Administrative	
Nursing Home Administration	Certification in Nursing Home Administration
Facilities Director	Professional Engineer (PE)
Director of Finance	Certified Public Accountant (CPA)
Director of Health Information	Registered Health Information Administrator (RHIA)

© Cengage Learning®

HR Development and Organizational Restructuring

When healthcare organizational strategies involve restructurings and downsizing, it is difficult to know what a career is, much less how to develop one. Further, some employers wonder why they should worry about career "development" for employees when the future likely holds fewer internal promotion opportunities and more movement in and out of organizations by individuals. Even though these views may seem extreme, employee development has changed recently in three significant ways:

- The middle management "ladder" in healthcare organizations now includes more horizontal than upward moves.

- Many organizations target their efforts to ensure that their focus is on core competencies.

- The growth of project-based work makes careers a series of projects, not just steps upward in a given organization.

Traditionally, career development efforts targeted managerial personnel to look beyond their current jobs and to prepare them for a variety of future jobs in the organization. But development for all employees, not just managers, is necessary for organizations to have the needed human resource capabilities for future growth and change.

Mergers, acquisitions, restructurings, and layoffs all have influenced the way healthcare employees and organizations look at careers and development. In the "new career world," individuals—not the organization—manage their own development. Such self-development consists of personal educational experiences, training, organizational experiences, projects, and even changes in occupational fields. Under this system, the individual defines career success, which may or may not coincide with the organizational view of success.

CASE

Associated Community Health Center (ACHC), a family practice with 250 employees and nine locations servicing the suburbs of a large city, is facing a variety of HR issues. The HR manager conducted an HR audit to evaluate the problems and make recommendations for improvement. Her findings fell into four categories:

- *Retention Issues*—Focusing specifically on RN staffing, one of the most critical positions for ACHC, the current RN turnover rate is 26 percent. The RN vacancy rate or the percentage of open positions for RNs is 20 percent.
- *Staff Complaints*—The HR manager, through staff interviews, learned that ACHC's employees were concerned about a variety of issues, including

late performance reviews, a lack of promotional opportunities, and poor communications between supervisors and staff.
- *Patient Concerns*—The HR manager evaluated patient feedback forms to gain insight into the HR issues. From the patients' feedback, a number of related HR issues were identified. These included: rude behavior on the part of patient schedulers, inattentiveness to patients by reception staff, and long patient waits without explanation.
- *Clinical Incidents*—In order to evaluate the effect of the HR issues on the quality of patient care being provided by the ACHC, the HR manger reviewed data on clinical incidents. Two

important categories of clinical incidents were noted:

- 20 percent of X-rays taken had to be retaken due to poor quality.
- 15 percent of laboratory test results were lost or misfiled, requiring either retests or a delay in reporting.

The HR manager was very concerned about the findings. However, she was confident that with effective HR programming, the issues detailed above could be addressed.

Questions

1. Which of ACHC's issues could be improved through orientation, training, or staff development programming?
2. Based on your answer to Question 1, detail the types of activities that could be effective in dealing with the issues you identified.

END NOTES

1. Adapted from Patty Thurgood and Fran Klene, "EMBED. A Recipe for Transformational Learning," *T&D* (August 2012), 28–29.
2. Herman Aguinis and Kurt Kraiger, "Benefits of Training and Development for Individuals and Teams, Organizations and Society," *Annual Review of Psychology* 60 (2009), 451–474.
3. Deanna Hartley, "The Cure for Conventional Learning," *Chief Learning Officer* (September 2012), 22–25.
4. Gabrielle Wirth and Gary Gansle, "Jump toward Emotional Intelligence," *HR Magazine* (October 2012), 87–90.
5. James Hall and Marty Denis, "Compensability of Job-Related Training," *Workplace Management* (April 6, 2009), 10.
6. See *http://www.cincinnatichildrens.org/careers/working/diversity/diversity/* for more information.
7. Joseph R. Swedish, "Practitioner Application," *Journal of Healthcare Management* (September/October 2010), 351–352.
8. See *http://minorityhealth.hhs.gov/templates/browse.aspx?lvl=2&lvlID=11* for more information.
9. Wendy Axelrod and Jeannine Coyle, "5 Development Myths," *Leadership Excellence* (August 2013), 9.
10. Jennifer Schramm, "Undereducated," *HR Magazine* (September 2011), 136.
11. Aaron DeSmet et al., "Getting More from Your Training Programs," *McKinsey Quarterly* (October 2010), 1–6.
12. A. Chatzimouratidis, I. Theotokas, and I. Lagoudis, "Decision Support Systems for Human Resource Training and Development," *International Journal of Human Resource Management* (February 2012), 662–693.
13. Yaping Gong et al., "Employee Learning Orientation, Transformational Leadership, and Employee Creativity: The Mediating Role of Employee Creative Self-Efficacy," *The Academy of Management Journal* 52 (August 2009), 765–778.
14. Malcolm S. Knowles, Elwood F. Holton III, and Richard A. Swanson, *The Adult Learner*, 6th ed. (New York: Elsevier, 2005).
15. "Best Practices and Outstanding Initiatives," *Training* (January/February 2011), 96.
16. D. Jackson, "Immersion Training," *Fire Chief* (April 2013), 44–48.
17. Tal Katz-Navon et al., "Active Learning: When Is More Better? The Case of Resident Physician's Medical Errors," *Journal of Applied Psychology* 94 (2009), 1200–1209.
18. Kendra Lee, "Reinforce Training," *Training* (May/June 2011), 24.
19. Harry J. Martin, "Improving Training Impact through Effective Follow-Up," *Journal of Management Development* 29 (2010), 520–534.

20. Brian D. Blume et al., "Transfer of Training: A Meta-Analytic Review," *Journal of Management* 36 (2010), 1065–1102.

21. Harry J. Martin, "Workplace Climate and Peer Support as Determinants of Training Transfer," *Human Resource Development Quarterly* 21 (Spring 2010), 87–104.

22. Lisa M. Burke and Alan M. Saks, "Accountability in Training Transfer," *Human Resource Development Review* 8 (2009) 382–402.

23. "Benefits of Onboarding," *Training* (July/August 2011), 7.

24. Donald L. Caruth et al., "Getting Off to a Good Start," *Industrial Management* (March/April 2010), 1–4.

25. Karen Voloshin and Julie Winkle Giulioni, " 'Less Is More' Leadership Development," *T+D* (September 2013), 26–29.

26. Paul Harris, "Instilling Competencies from Top to Bottom," *T+D* (October 2011), 65–66.

27. E. Boehm Jr., "OSHA Targets Long-Term Care with Injury-Reduction Program: Enforcing Policies and Procedures with Training Will Diminish Risk," *Long-Term Living: For the Continuing Care Professional* (Summer 2012), 16–18.

28. "Tips to Outsource Training," *Training* (September/October 2010), 7.

29. Kathryn Tyler, "Mining for Training Treasure," *HR Magazine* (September 2009), 99–102.

30. Patricia Claghorn, "Certainly Not Half Baked: A True Community College and Business Partnership," *T + D* 65 (July 2011), 20.

31. M. Weinstein, "Please Don't Go," *Training* (May 2011), 28–34.

32. American Society of Training and Development, *http://www.astd.org*.

33. Kendra Lee, "Ensure Webinar-Based Training Success," *Training* (November/December 2010), 14.

34. Matt Bolch, "Focus on Games and Simulations," *Training* (October/November 2009), 53–56.

35. Kristie Donnelly, "Learning on the Move," *Development and Learning in Organizations* 23 (2009), 8–11.

36. Lorrie Lykins, "Creating a Viable Mobile Learning Strategy Remains a Challenge," *T+D* (June 2012), 26.

37. Bill Roberts, "From E-learning to Mobile Learning," *HR Magazine* (August 2012), 61–65.

38. Ibid., 62.

39. Jennifer Hofmann, "Top 10 Challenges of Blended Learning," *Training* (March/April 2011), 12–13.

40. P. J. Elkeles, "A Flexible Approach to Developing Leadership," *Workforce Management* (May 2010), 28.

41. Kendra Lee, "Create a Simple Plan for ROI," *Training* (July/August 2011), 14; Phaedra Brotherton, "Organizations Lag Behind in Measuring Learning's Value," *T+D* 65 (February 2011), 16–17.

42. Joseph Trunfio, "Developing Prospects," *Modern Healthcare* (May 17, 2010), 18.

43. Joelle K. Jay, "Become a Better Leader: Commit to Continuous Learning," *Supervision* (May 2012), 16–17.

44. Jayson Saba et al., "Assessments in Talent Management," *Aberdeen Group* (2009), 1–23, *http://www.aberdeen.com*.

45. Kendra Lee, "Use Diagnostic Skills Assessments," *Training* (February 2010), 22, *http://www.trainingmag.com*.

46. Paula Ketter, "Sounding Succession Alarms," *T+D* (January 2009), 20.

47. "Most Freestanding Hospitals Do Not Conduct Leadership Succession Planning," *Hospitals & Health Networks* (January 2005), 65–66.

48. Alina Dizik, "Training without a Campus," *Wall Street Journal* (April 15, 2009), D4.

49. "What Is a Coaching Culture?," *Coaching Conundrum 2009 Global Executive Summary* Blessing White, 2009, 5–23.

50. See *http://www.AHA.org and http://www.MGMA.com* for more information.

51. I. Chang, "Smart Talk," *NAFE Magazine* (Spring 2010), 40.

52. K. Reding and D. O'Bryan, "10 Best Practices for Business Student Internships," *Strategic Finance* (October 2013), 43–48.

9

PERFORMANCE MANAGEMENT IN HEALTHCARE ORGANIZATIONS

Learning Objectives

After you have read this chapter, you should be able to:

- Discuss the importance of performance management.
- Compare and contrast the administrative and development uses of performance appraisals.
- Review the informal versus systematic appraisal processes.
- Describe the various methods of appraising performance.
- Identify the various rater errors that occur during the appraisal process.

HEALTHCARE HR INSIGHTS

One of the new realities of the U.S. healthcare system is that healthcare organizations will be evaluated not only by patients, payers (insurance companies and government payers), and accreditation organizations on the quality of care they provide, but also by the quality of the patient experience. Hospitals, clinics, and physician groups are being required to survey their patients on various dimensions of their experiences including doctor–patient communication, nurse–patient communication, and responsiveness of the staff. Failing to achieve satisfactory levels of patient satisfaction could jeopardize the level of reimbursement the provider receives[1] and could even result in negative comments about the provider on Angie's List.[2] As an example, an urgent care center received poor ratings on a healthcare consumer satisfaction blog for long waiting times. Those poor ratings negatively impacted the urgent care center's patient volumes until they added more doctors, resulting in reduced wait times and fewer patient complaints.

Healthcare HR professionals are challenged to develop effective performance evaluation processes that include clear customer service expectations (among other performance requirements), accurate patient experience measurement methods, and positive feedback and/or remediation efforts based on reliable performance assessments. The employee performance evaluation process for healthcare organizations should be strategically linked to key organizational initiatives—chief among which in today's healthcare setting is driving high levels of patient satisfaction.

PERFORMANCE MANAGEMENT

Regardless of the size or type of an organization, it is important to utilize an evaluation process that is designed to meet both the organizational objectives and the performance evaluation needs of managers and employees. Healthcare organizations develop performance management systems to define expectations for employees and to manage their performance. These systems (1) identify job expectations, (2) measure, evaluate, and reward performance, and (3) provide for improvement where needed.[3]

As depicted in Figure 9-1, performance management is a vital link between organizational strategy and its outcomes. For example, if a nurse manager at a rehabilitation hospital has the ability to perform her duties but the organization does not support her with the appropriate equipment and staff, she will not succeed in her position. In many cases, some performance factors are present, but if any of the factors are missing, individuals will not be able to perform according to their job standards.

Performance management is often confused with one of its key components—performance appraisal. **Performance management** is a series of activities designed

FIGURE 9-1 **Performance Management Linkage**

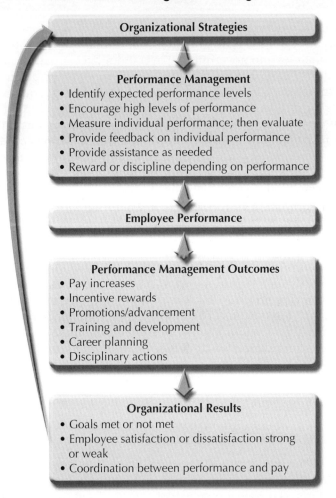

Organizational Strategies

Performance Management
- Identify expected performance levels
- Encourage high levels of performance
- Measure individual performance; then evaluate
- Provide feedback on individual performance
- Provide assistance as needed
- Reward or discipline depending on performance

Employee Performance

Performance Management Outcomes
- Pay increases
- Incentive rewards
- Promotions/advancement
- Training and development
- Career planning
- Disciplinary actions

Organizational Results
- Goals met or not met
- Employee satisfaction or dissatisfaction strong or weak
- Coordination between performance and pay

© 2016 Cengage Learning®

to ensure that the organization gets the performance it needs from its employees. **Performance appraisal** is the process of determining how well employees do their jobs relative to a standard and communicating that information to them. Performance appraisal is a part of performance management rather than its entirety.[4]

At a minimum, a performance management system should do the following:

- Make clear what the organization expects.
- Document performance for personnel records.
- Identify areas of success and needed development.
- Provide performance information to employees.

A successful performance management system allows managers to better prepare employees for their work responsibilities by focusing on the most important components of these activities.[5] For example, in one clinic employees are rated on standardized job criteria by their supervisor, but they also complete self-evaluations. They are given the supervisor's completed evaluation forms several days ahead of appraisal meetings to consider the ratings. "Performance agreements" that follow explicitly connect the individual actions to the clinic's goals, and the communication involved in forging those agreements ensures that managers and employees understand important performance issues.

Based on organizational goals, healthcare managers organize their employees' jobs to provide care and service that patients, residents, or clients value. Employee performance is monitored to ensure that each job is performed successfully in a manner that supports the accomplishment of organizational objectives. Employee performance is then measured by job standards defined by job criteria.

Job Criteria

Job criteria identify factors employees must meet for satisfactory job performance. Criteria in most jobs are weighted for importance. As an example, a laboratory technician's job may have several criteria, but those that require the technician to do quality-control checks on lab results may receive greater weight.

Criteria may be classified as trait based, behavior based, or results based. **Trait-based criteria** identify subjective personal traits, such as having a positive attitude that may contribute to job success. **Behavior-based criteria** identify behaviors, such as persuasion skills, that may lead to successful completion of job expectations. In some cases, both trait-based and behavior-based qualities are difficult to identify and evaluate objectively. **Results-based criteria**, such as completing projects on time, are easier to identify and evaluate.

Criteria Relevance   When developing systems to measure performance, managers should include criteria that are relevant to the job. Job criteria relevance is determined by job description accuracy and its translation into performance standards. For example, measuring the performance of a nurse anesthetist for presentation skills would not be relevant, but measuring his or her anesthesia management abilities would be relevant because they are tied to a primary job responsibility. Reviewing the job description and the criteria before doing a performance appraisal helps to eliminate criteria that are not vital for use.

Potential for Criteria Problems   All jobs are a compilation of duties and tasks. Most healthcare organizations formally or informally develop job descriptions and performance appraisals. When the measurement process omits significant criteria, the measures are **deficient**. For example, if an appointment scheduler was not measured for the ability to meet patient, physician, and staff needs when scheduling appointments, the criteria for evaluation would be considered deficient. If irrelevant criteria are included in the measurement process, it is **contaminated**. The same scheduler should be measured for scheduling accuracy, but measuring the scheduler's ability to program a computer would be an illustration of contaminated criteria. It is advisable for HR professionals and line managers to review job descriptions and performance appraisals regularly to prevent using deficient or contaminated criteria.

Performance Standards

Each job is assigned a set of standards with which to compare employees' performance levels. Managers, with the assistance of HR professionals, determine performance standards for each job before employees begin work. Employees should be given performance standards when they are first employed because they will be evaluated during performance appraisals on how they meet those standards.

Performance-Focused Organizational Cultures

Organizational cultures can vary on many dimensions, and one of these differences involves the degree to which performance is emphasized. The organizational cultures of some healthcare organizations are based on an *entitlement* approach, meaning that *adequate* performance and stability dominate the organization. Employee rewards vary little from person to person and have little to do with individual performance differences. As a result, performance appraisal activities are viewed as having few ties to performance and being primarily a "bureaucratic exercise."

At the other end of the spectrum is a *performance-driven* organizational culture focused on results and contributions. In this context, performance evaluations link results to employee compensation and development.[6] This approach is particularly important when evaluating leadership performance because healthcare organizations should hold top leaders accountable for organizational outcomes and motivate them to improve quality of care, the patient experience, and financial performance. As an example, Baptist Health Care,[7] a community-owned, not-for-profit health care system serving patients in northwest Florida and south Alabama with four hospitals, multiple outpatient settings, and more than 6,400 employees and employed physicians, strives to be a performance-driven health system. In evidence of its performance-driven culture, it has significantly reduced operating expenses and improved revenue by aligning leaders' goals with financial performance and engaging staff in steps toward improvement. The key components of its performance management strategy are the consistent use of a balanced framework for goal setting and alignment and a focus on commitment and accountability.[8]

There are benefits to developing a performance-focused culture throughout the organization. Organizations with performance-focused cultures have more positive performance than do those with a maintenance-orientation culture.[9] Figure 9-2 shows the components of a successful performance-focused culture, which usually means pay depends on performance. However, a pay-for-performance approach can present several challenges to organizations. For example, many urban-based health systems with large unionized workforces usually have an entitlement philosophy, and pay-for-performance plans are seen as creating inequity, if some employees were to receive bonuses and others receive no extra compensation. Tying bonuses to criteria such as productivity and professional growth has been met with harsh criticism under those conditions.

FIGURE 9-2   Components of a Performance-Focused Culture

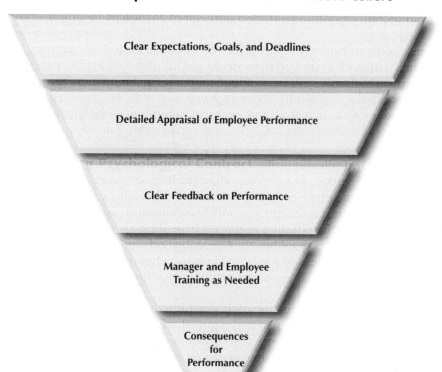

Clear Expectations, Goals, and Deadlines

Detailed Appraisal of Employee Performance

Clear Feedback on Performance

Manager and Employee Training as Needed

Consequences for Performance

© 2016 Cengage Learning®

Despite these issues, it appears that a performance-based pay culture is desirable. It is sometimes argued that healthcare organizations are not doing enough about poor performers, and that failure to deal with poor performance is unfair to those who work hard. But as the pressure continues to mount on healthcare organizations to reduce costs and improve efficiencies, healthcare managers and HR professionals will have to focus more attention on dealing with poor-performing employees and physicians.[10]

PERFORMANCE APPRAISAL

One of the most important managerial duties in healthcare organizations is to evaluate employees' performance.[11] During performance reviews, managers should discuss how well employees are meeting their job standards. The process of evaluating an employee's performance is called the **performance appraisal**.

For healthcare organizations that subscribe to the Joint Commission on Accreditation of Healthcare Organizations (JCAHO) process, an important consideration in the development and implementation of a healthcare organizational performance appraisal process is compliance with JCAHO standards.

Joint Commission Standards and Performance Appraisal

Acknowledging the linkage between the provision of safe patient care and effective performance evaluation, a number of the JCAHO's human resources, leadership, and organizational performance improvement standards are related to performance appraisals. The components of a JCAHO-acceptable performance appraisal system include the following characteristics:

- Job descriptions identifying duties and required competencies
- A performance evaluation process and supporting documents
- Competency assessment checklists

Performance evaluation and competency assessment are two different, but much related, processes. Some healthcare organizations conduct performance evaluations and competency assessments simultaneously, and others treat them as separate processes. Performance evaluations are used to determine how well employees are performing the duties and responsibilities of their positions as described in the job descriptions. Competency assessments are used to determine whether the employees have the knowledge, skills, ability, training, education, and licensure to meet the requirements of their position.

Conflicting Roles of Performance Appraisals

Organizations generally use performance appraisals in two potentially conflicting ways. One use is to provide a measure of performance for consideration in making pay or other administrative decisions about employees. This *administrative* role often creates stress for healthcare managers doing the appraisals and the employees being evaluated because the rater is placed in the role of judge. The other use focuses on the *development* of individuals.[12] In this role, the manager acts more as a counselor and coach than as a judge. The developmental performance appraisal emphasizes current training and development needs, as well as planning employees' future opportunities and career directions. Whether a performance appraisal is to be used in an administrative capacity or as a developmental tool affects several aspects of the process.[13] Figure 9-3 shows both uses for performance appraisals.

Administrative Uses of Appraisals Three administrative uses of appraisal impact managers and employees the most: (1) determining pay adjustments; (2) making job placement decisions on promotions, transfers, and demotions; and (3) choosing employee disciplinary actions up to and including termination of employment.

FIGURE 9-3   Conflicting Roles of Performance Appraisal

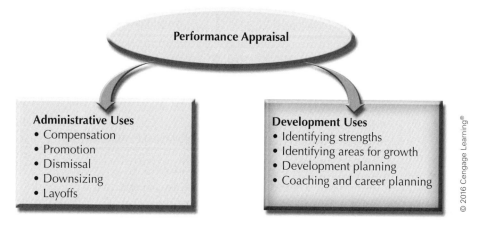

© 2016 Cengage Learning®

A performance appraisal system is often the link between employee job performance and the additional pay and rewards that they can receive. Performance-based compensation affirms the idea that pay raises are given for performance accomplishments rather than for length of service (seniority), or granted automatically to all employees at the same percentage levels. In pay-for-performance compensation systems, managers have evaluated the performance of individuals and have made compensation recommendations. If any part of the appraisal process fails, better-performing employees may not receive larger pay increases, and the result is perceived inequity in compensation.

Many U.S. workers, in both the healthcare industry and other industries, indicate that they see little connection between their performance and the size of their pay increases due to flaws in performance appraisals. Consequently, people argue that performance appraisals and pay discussions should be done separately. Two realities support this view. One is that employees often focus more on the pay received than on the developmental appraisal feedback. The other is that managers sometimes manipulate ratings to justify the pay they wish to give individuals. As a result, many employees view the appraisal process as a game because compensation increases have been predetermined before the appraisal is completed.

To address these issues, some healthcare organizations first conduct performance appraisals and discuss the results with employees, and then several weeks later hold a shorter meeting to discuss pay issues. By adopting such an approach, the results of the performance appraisal can be considered before the amount of the pay adjustment is determined. Also, the performance appraisal discussions between managers and employees can focus on issues for improvement—not just pay raises.

Employers are obviously interested in the administrative uses of performance appraisals such as decisions about promotions, terminations, layoffs, and transfer assignments. Promotions and demotions based on performance must be documented through performance appraisals; otherwise, legal problems can occur.[14]

Developmental Uses of Appraisals   For healthcare workers, a performance appraisal can be a primary source of information and feedback. By identifying strengths, weaknesses, potentials, and training needs through performance appraisal feedback, supervisors can inform employees about their progress, discuss areas in which additional training may be beneficial, and outline future developmental plans.[15] Given the nature of many healthcare jobs, providing accurate and timely feedback to healthcare workers is critical to ensuring safe patient care.[16]

The purpose of giving feedback on performance is both to reinforce satisfactory employee performance and to address performance deficiencies. The developmental function of performance appraisal can also identify areas in which the employee might wish to grow. For example, in a performance appraisal interview targeted exclusively to development, an employee found out that the only factor keeping her from being considered for a management job in her dental practice was the lack of a working knowledge of the dental coding. The director of the practice suggested that she consider taking some online courses in that area.

The use of teams provides a different set of circumstances for developmental appraisals. The manager may not see all of an employee's work, but the employee's team members do. Team members can provide important feedback. However, whether teams can handle administrative appraisals is still subject to debate; clearly some cannot. When teams are allowed to design appraisal systems, they tend to "get rid of judgment" and avoid differential rewards. Thus, group appraisal may be best suited for developmental rather than administrative purposes. Given the 24/7 nature of many healthcare organizations, it is not unusual for the manager of a unit or even an entire facility to rarely have direct contact with many of his or her employees on different shifts or the weekend. However, the manager must still evaluate those employees regardless of shift. The use of team evaluations can be used in these situations to help the manager get evaluation information.

Decisions about the Performance Appraisal Process

A number of decisions must be made when designing performance appraisal systems. Some important ones involve identifying the appraisal responsibilities of the HR unit and of the operating managers, selecting the type of appraisal system to use, and establishing the timing of appraisals.

Appraisal Responsibilities   If done properly, the appraisal process can benefit both the organization and the employees. As Figure 9-4 shows, the HR unit typically designs a performance appraisal system. Managers then appraise employees using the appraisal system. During development of the formal appraisal system, managers usually offer input about how the final system will work.

It is important for managers to understand that appraisals are *their* responsibility. Through the appraisal process, good employee performance can be made

FIGURE 9-4 **Typical Division of HR Responsibilities: Performance Appraisal**

HR Unit	Managers
• Design and maintains appraisal system • Train raters • Track timely receipt of appraisals • Review completed appraisals for consistency	• Typically rate performance of employees • Prepare formal appraisal documents • Review appraisals with employees • Identify development areas

© Cengage Learning®

even better, poor employee performance can be improved, and poor performers can be removed from the organization. Performance appraisal must not be simply an HR requirement but should also be an important management process because guiding employees' performance is among the most important responsibilities a manager has.

Type of Appraisals: Informal Versus Systematic   Performance appraisals can occur in two ways: informally and/or systematically. A supervisor conducts an *informal appraisal* whenever necessary. The day-to-day working relationship between a manager and an employee offers an opportunity for the evaluation of individual performance. A manager communicates this evaluation through various conversations on or off the job, or by on-the-spot discussion of a specific occurrence. Although such informal feedback is useful and necessary, it should not replace formal appraisal. Frequent informal feedback to employees can prevent surprises during a formal performance review. However, informal appraisal can become *too* informal.

A *systematic appraisal* is used when the contact between a manager and employee is more formal, and a system is in place to report managerial impressions and observations on employee performance. This approach to appraisals is quite common. Systematic appraisals feature a regular time interval, which distinguishes them from informal appraisals. Both employees and managers know that performance will be reviewed on a regular basis, and they can plan for performance discussions.

Timing of Appraisals   Healthcare organizations that utilize a formal or systematic appraisal process typically require managers to conduct appraisals once or twice a year, most often annually. Appraisals can also occur in 60 to 90 days after hiring, again at six months, and annually thereafter. *Probationary* or *introductory employees*, who are new and in a trial period, should be informally evaluated often—perhaps weekly for the first month, and monthly thereafter until the end of the introductory period. After that, annual reviews are typical. For healthcare workers in hard-to-fill positions, some healthcare employers use accelerated appraisals—every six months instead of every year. This is done to retain those employees since more feedback can be given and pay raises may occur more often.

Legal Concerns Regarding Performance Appraisals

Since appraisals are supposed to measure how well employees are doing their jobs, it may seem unnecessary to emphasize that performance appraisals must be job-related. However, it is important for evaluations to adequately reflect the nature of work performed. Healthcare organizations need to have appraisal systems that satisfy the courts. Therefore, as well as meeting performance management needs, the elements of a legal performance appraisal system typically include the following:

- Performance appraisal criteria based on job analysis
- Absence of disparate impact
- Formal evaluation criteria that limit managerial discretion
- A rating instrument linked to job duties and responsibilities
- Documentation of the appraisal activities
- Personal knowledge of and contact with each appraised individual
- Training of supervisors in conducting appraisals
- A review process that prevents one manager, acting alone, from controlling an employee's career
- Counseling to help poor performers improve

Of course, having all these components is no guarantee against lawsuits. However, including them does improve the chance of winning lawsuits that might be filed.[17]

WHO CONDUCTS APPRAISALS?

Performance appraisals can be conducted by anyone familiar with the performance of individual employees. Possible rating situations are depicted in Figure 9-5.

Supervisory Rating of Subordinates

The most widely used means of rating healthcare workers is based on the assumption that the immediate supervisor is the person most qualified to evaluate an employee's performance realistically and fairly. To help provide accurate evaluations, some supervisors keep records of their employees' performance so that they can reference these notes when rating performance. For instance, the manager of the memory care unit at a long-term care facility might periodically observe a nurse aide's interactions with patients and make notes so that constructive performance feedback can be provided at a later date. Training supervisors to do observation and evaluation well improves the process.[18]

FIGURE 9-5 Who Conducts Performance Appraisal

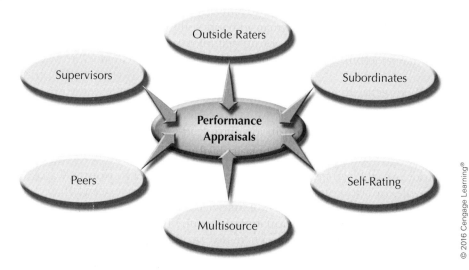

© 2016 Cengage Learning®

Employee Rating of Managers

Many healthcare organizations ask employees to rate the performance of their immediate managers. These performance appraisal ratings are generally used for management development purposes.

Having employees rate managers provides three primary advantages. First, in critical manager–employee relationships, employee ratings can be quite useful for identifying competent managers. Second, this type of rating program can help make a manager more responsive to employees. This advantage can quickly become a disadvantage if the manager focuses on being "nice" rather than on managing; people who are pleasant but have no other qualifications may not be good managers in many situations. Finally, employee appraisals can contribute to career development efforts for managers by identifying areas for growth.

A major disadvantage of having employees rate managers is the negative reaction many have to being evaluated by employees. Also, the fear of reprisals may be too great for employees to give honest ratings. This may prompt workers to rate their managers based solely on the way they are treated rather than on critical job requirements. The problems associated with this appraisal approach limit its usefulness to certain situations, including managerial development and improvement efforts.[19]

Team/Peer Rating

Having employees and team members rate each other is another type of appraisal in healthcare organizations with the potential to both help and hurt. Peer and team ratings are especially useful when supervisors do not have the opportunity to observe each employee's performance, but work group members do.

For instance, some of the advanced training programs in the U.S. military use peer ratings to provide candidates extensive feedback about their leadership qualities and accomplishments. Peer evaluations are also common in medical residency programs where professors commonly require students to conduct peer evaluations after the completion of group-based projects.

It is possible that any performance appraisal, including team/peer ratings, can negatively affect teamwork and participative management efforts. Although team members have good information on one another's performance, they may not choose to share it in the interest of sparing feelings; alternatively, they may unfairly attack other group members. Many healthcare organizations attempt to overcome such problems by using anonymous appraisals and/or having a consultant or HR manager interpret team/peer ratings.

Self-Rating

Self-appraisal works in certain situations.[20] As a self-development tool, it requires employees to think about their strengths/weaknesses and set goals for improvement.[21] Overall, the use of self-appraisals in healthcare organizations has increased. For instance, one organization successfully incorporated self-ratings into a traditional rating approach that did not generate enough dialogue and direction for individual development; reactions from both workers and supervisors were favorable.

However, employees may use quite different standards and not rate themselves in the same manner as supervisors. Research exploring whether people might be more lenient or more demanding when rating themselves is mixed, with self-ratings being frequently higher than supervisory ratings. Still, employee self-ratings can be a useful source of performance information for development.[22]

Outsider Rating

People outside the immediate work group may be asked to participate in performance reviews. This "field review" approach can include someone from the HR department as a reviewer, or completely independent reviewers from outside the organization. Examples include a review team evaluating a hospital president, or a panel of doctors from various medical centers evaluating a colleague at another medical center on their performance and the quality of their research. The effectiveness of the use of outside evaluators depends a great deal on the situation, as noted above.

The patients and clients of healthcare organizations are excellent sources for outside appraisals. As noted in the HR Healthcare Insights for this chapter, the importance of a positive patient experience is critical to the success of healthcare organizations. Consequently, factoring patient or client satisfaction data in elements of a healthcare workers appraisal is routinely used in many healthcare organizations.

Multisource/360-Degree Rating

Multisource rating, or 360-degree feedback, has grown in popularity in health-care organizations. Multisource feedback recognizes that for many healthcare jobs, employee performance is multidimensional and crosses departmental and organizational boundaries. Therefore, information needs to be collected from many sources to adequately and fairly evaluate an incumbent's performance in one of these jobs.

The major purpose of 360-degree feedback is *not* to increase uniformity by soliciting like-minded views. Instead, it is designed to capture evaluations of the employee's different roles to provide richer feedback during an evaluation.

Significant administrative time and paperwork are required to request, obtain, and summarize feedback from multiple raters. Using electronic systems for the information can greatly reduce the administrative demands of multisource ratings and increase the effectiveness (i.e., privacy and expediency) of the process.

As originally designed and used, multisource feedback focuses on the use of appraisals for the development of individuals. Conflict resolution skills, decision-making abilities, team effectiveness, communication skills, managerial styles, and technical capabilities are just some of the developmental areas that can be evaluated. It is widely believed that 360-degree feedback is more useful in a personal growth system than in an administrative system, although its use is growing in administrative systems.[23]

The popularity of 360-degree feedback systems has led to the results being used for compensation, promotion, termination, and other administrative decisions. When using 360-degree feedback for administrative purposes, managers must anticipate the potential problems.[24] Differences among raters can present a challenge, especially when using 360-degree ratings for discipline or pay decisions. Bias can just as easily be rooted in customers, subordinates, and peers as in a boss, and the lack of accountability of those sources can affect the ratings. "Inflation" of ratings is common when the sources know that their input will affect someone's pay or career.

Research on multisource/360-degree feedback has revealed both positives and negatives. More variability than expected may be seen in the ratings given by the different sources. Thus, supervisor ratings may need to carry more weight than peer or subordinate input to resolve the differences. One concern is that those peers who rate poor-performing coworkers tend to inflate the ratings so that the peers themselves can get higher overall evaluation results in return.

Another concern is whether 360-degree appraisals improve the process or simply multiply the number of problems by the number of raters.[25] Also, some wonder whether multisource appraisals really create sufficiently better decisions to offset the additional time and investment required. These issues appear to be less threatening when the 360-degree feedback is used *only for development*, so healthcare organizations should consider using multisource feedback primarily as a developmental tool to enhance future job performance while minimizing the use of multisource appraisals as an administrative tool.[26]

HEALTHCARE REFORM AND HR PRACTICES

At California's MemorialCare Health System, a six-hospital nonprofit based in Fountain Valley, California, evaluating physician performance shows how it is complying with the various requirements of healthcare reform. MemorialCare is part of a movement by hospitals around the United States to change how doctors practice by monitoring their progress toward goals, such as giving recommended mammograms. Technology is making it easier to monitor doctors' work as patients' details are compiled electronically instead of on paper charts.

The federal health law is speeding these trends. Under the law, hospital payments and penalties from the federal Medicare program will be linked to their performance on quality gauges, particularly rehospitalizations, which are costly.

To succeed under the new healthcare economics, hospital executives say, they must lean on doctors, who make nearly all the key decisions on what treatments, tests, and drugs patients get. Concerned about alienating their doctors, hospitals are delivering the feedback in sessions led by fellow physicians, not outsiders. Executives refer to their efforts as "aligning" with physicians, not telling them what to do.

MemorialCare is keeping detailed data on how the doctors perform on many measures—including adolescent immunizations, mammograms, and keeping down the blood-sugar levels of diabetes patients. The results are compiled, number-crunched, and eventually used to help determine how much money doctors will earn.[27]

TOOLS FOR APPRAISING PERFORMANCE

Performance can be appraised by a number of methods. Some organizations use one method for all jobs and employees, some use different methods for different groups of employees, and others use a combination of methods.[28] The following discussion highlights different tools that can be used, as well as some of the advantages and disadvantages of each approach.

Category-Scaling Methods

The simplest methods for appraising performance are category-scaling methods, which require a manager to mark an employee's level of performance on a specific form divided into categories of performance. A *checklist* uses a list of statements or words from which raters check statements that are most representative of the characteristics and performance of employees. Often, a scale indicating perceived level of accomplishment on each statement is included with the checklist, which then becomes a type of graphic rating scale.

One form of a category-scaling method is the **graphic rating scale**, which allows the rater to mark an employee's performance on a continuum indicating low to high levels of a particular characteristic. Because of the straightforwardness

FIGURE 9-6   Clinical Employee Performance Evaluation

Employee: _____   **Date of Evaluation:** _____

The rating categories are:
1. Does not meet minimum requirements; clearly below the acceptable level.
2. Improvement needed for performance to meet expected standards.
3. Performance meets expected standards.
4. Performance frequently exceeds expected standards.
5. Outstanding performance; consistently exceeds expected standards.

PERFORMANCE FACTORS

KNOWLEDGE OF WORK: Degree of familiarity with accepted job procedures and equipment use, extent of information possessed and knowledge of relevant sources.   1   2   3   4   5

Comments:

TECHNICAL KNOWLEDGE: Consider effective utilization of available technology to maximize productivity. Remains current on new technology through formal or self-training.   1   2   3   4   5

Comments:

PATIENT CARE SKILLS: Establishes good rapport with patients; ability to effectively assist patients through procedures; educates patients on procedures performed; reacts to patient needs and concerns in a timely manner; provides timely follow-up when necessary.   1   2   3   4   5

© 2016 Cengage Learning®

of the process, graphic rating scales are common in performance evaluations. Figure 9-6 shows a sample appraisal form that uses a graphic rating scale with essays. Three aspects of performance can be appraised using graphic rating scales: *descriptive categories* (such as quantity of work, attendance, and dependability), *job duties* (taken from the job description), and *behavioral dimensions* (such as decision making, employee development, and communication effectiveness).

Each of these types can be used for different jobs. How well employees meet established standards is often expressed either numerically (e.g., 1, 2, 3, 4, 5) or verbally (e.g., "outstanding," "meets standards," "below standards"). If two or more people are involved in the rating, they may find it difficult to agree on the exact level of performance achieved relative to the standard in evaluating employee performance. Notice that each level specifies performance standards or expectations to reduce variation in interpretations of the standards by different supervisors and employees.

Concerns with Graphic Rating Scales   Graphic rating scales in many forms are widely used because they are easy to develop and provide a uniform set of criteria to evaluate the job performance of different employees. However, the use of scales can cause rater error because the form might not accurately reflect the relative importance of certain job characteristics, and some factors might need to be added to the ratings for one employee, while others might need to be dropped. If they fit the person and the job, the scales work well. However, if they fit poorly, managers and employees who must use them might complain about "the rating form."

Behavioral Rating Scales In an attempt to overcome some of the concerns with graphic rating scales, employers may use behavioral rating scales designed to assess individual actions instead of personal attributes and characteristics. Different approaches are used, but all describe specific examples of employee job behaviors. In a **behaviorally anchored rating scale (BARS)**, these examples are "anchored" or measured against a scale of performance levels.

When creating a BARS system, identifying important *job dimensions*, which are the most important performance factors in a job description, is done first. Short statements describe both desirable and undesirable behaviors (anchors). These are then "translated," or assigned, to one of the job dimensions. Anchor statements are usually developed by a group of people familiar with the job. The group then assigns each anchor a number that represents how effective or ineffective the behavior is, and the anchors are fitted to a scale.

Several problems are associated with the behavioral approach. First, creating and maintaining behaviorally anchored rating scales requires extensive time and effort. In addition, many appraisal forms are needed to accommodate different types of jobs in an organization. For instance, because nurses, dietitians, and admissions clerks in a hospital all have distinct job descriptions, a separate BARS form needs to be developed for each position.

Comparative Methods

Comparative methods require that managers directly compare the performance levels of their employees against one another, and these comparisons can provide useful information for performance management. An example of this process would be an information systems supervisor comparing the performance of one programmer with that of other programmers. Comparative techniques include ranking and forced distribution.

Ranking The **ranking** method lists the individuals being rated from highest to lowest based on their performance levels and relative contributions. One disadvantage of this process is that the sizes of the performance differences between employees are often not clearly indicated. For example, the job performance of individuals ranked second and third may differ little, while the performance of those ranked third and fourth differ a great deal. This limitation can be mitigated to some extent by assigning points to indicate performance differences. Ranking also means someone must be last, which ignores the possibility that the last-ranked individual in one group might be equal to the top-ranked employee in a different group. Further, the ranking task becomes unwieldy if the group of employees to be ranked is large.

Forced Distribution Forced distribution is a technique for distributing ratings that are generated with any of the other appraisal methods and comparing the ratings of people in a work group. With the **forced distribution** method, the ratings of employees' performance may be distributed along a bell-shaped curve.[29] For example, a medical clinic administrator ranking employees on a five-point scale would have to rate 10 percent of the employees as a 1 ("unsatisfactory"), 20 percent as a 2 ("below expectations"), 40 percent as a 3 ("meets expectations"), 20 percent as a 4 ("above expectations"), and 10 percent as a 5 ("outstanding").

Forced distribution has been used in some form by an estimated 30 percent of all firms with performance appraisal systems. A classic example of the use of forced distribution is at General Electric where managers are required to identify the top 20 percent of their employees, who as a result are rewarded richly so that few would leave. Conversely, the managers are also required to identify the bottom 10 percent, who then are given a chance to improve or leave.

Advantages and Disadvantages of Forced Distribution One reason why some healthcare organizations have mandated the use of forced distributions for appraisal ratings is to deal with "rater inflation." If employers do not require a forced distribution, performance appraisal ratings often do not match the normal distribution of a bell-shaped curve.

The use of a forced distribution system forces managers to identify high, average, and low performers. Thus, high performers can be rewarded and developed, while low performers can be encouraged to improve or leave. Advocates of forced ranking argue that forced distribution ensures that compensation increases truly are differentiated by performance rather than being spread equally among all employees.

But the forced distribution method suffers from several drawbacks.[30] Perhaps in a truly exceptional group of employees there is not 10 percent who are unsatisfactory. Another problem is that a supervisor may resist placing any individual in the lowest (or the highest) group. Difficulties also arise when the rater must explain to an employee why he or she was placed in one group while others were placed in higher groups. In some cases, the manager may make false distinctions between employees. By comparing people against each other, rather than against a standard of job performance, supervisors trying to fill the percentages may end up giving employees very subjective ratings. Finally, forced ranking structures can increase anxiety in employees, promote conformity, and encourage manipulation of the system.

Narrative Methods

Managers may be required to provide written appraisal narratives. Some appraisal methods are entirely written, rather than using predetermined rating scales or ranking structures. Documentation and descriptive text are the basic components of the critical-incident and essay methods.

Critical Incident In the critical-incident method, the manager keeps a written record of both favorable and unfavorable actions performed by an employee during the entire rating period. When a critical incident involving an employee occurs, the manager writes it down. For instance, when a social worker at a community clinic spends considerable time with a patient helping him access financial assistance for his medical care, the clinic manager might document this exceptional patient support for later review during an annual evaluation. The critical-incident method can be used with other approaches to document the reasons why an employee was given a certain rating.

Essay The essay method requires a manager to write a short essay describing each employee's performance during the rating period. Some free-form essays are without guidelines; others are more structured, using prepared questions that must be answered. The rater usually categorizes comments under a few general headings. The essay method allows the rater more flexibility than other methods do—sometimes too much. As a result, appraisers often combine the essay with other methods.

The effectiveness of the essay approach depends both on a supervisor's writing and observation skills. Some supervisors do not express themselves well in writing and as a result produce poor descriptions of employee performance, whereas others have excellent writing skills and can create highly positive impressions of their employees. If well composed, essays can provide highly detailed and useful information about an employees' job performance.[31]

Management by objectives (MBO) specifies the performance goals that an individual and manager identify together. Goal setting has been extensively researched.[32] Each manager sets objectives derived from the overall goals and objectives of the organization; however, MBO should not be a disguised means for a superior to dictate the objectives of individual managers or employees. Other names for MBO include *appraisal by results, target coaching, work planning and review, performance objective setting,* and *mutual goal setting.*

MBO Process Implementing a guided self-appraisal system using MBO is a four-stage process. The stages are as follows:

1. *Job review and agreement:* The employee and the supervisor review the job description and the key activities that constitute the employee's job. The idea is to agree on the exact makeup of the job.

2. *Development of performance standards:* Together, the employee and the supervisor develop specific standards of performance and determine a satisfactory level of performance that is specific and measurable—for example, a physician assistant seeing at least five patients per hour.

3. *Setting of objectives:* Together, the employee and the supervisor establish objectives that are realistically attainable.

4. *Continuing performance discussions:* The employee and the supervisor use the objectives as a basis for continuing discussions about the employee's performance. Although a formal review session may be scheduled, the employee and the supervisor do not necessarily wait until the appointed time to discuss performance. Objectives can be mutually modified as warranted.

The MBO process seems to be most useful with managerial personnel and clinical employees who have a fairly wide range of flexibility and control over their jobs.

Combinations of Methods

No single appraisal method is best for all situations, so a performance measurement system that uses a combination of methods may be sensible. Using combinations may offset some of the advantages and disadvantages of individual methods. Category-scaling methods are easy to develop, but they usually do little to measure strategic accomplishments. Further, they may make inter-rater reliability problems worse. Comparative approaches help reduce leniency and other errors, which makes them useful for administrative decisions such as determining pay raises. But comparative approaches do a poor job of linking performance to organizational goals, and by themselves do not provide feedback for improvement as well as other methods do.

Narrative methods work well for development because they potentially generate more feedback information. However, without good definitions of performance criteria or standards, they can be so unstructured as to be of little value for administrative uses. The MBO approach works well to link performance to organizational goals, but it can require much effort and time for defining objectives and explaining the process to employees. Narrative and MBO approaches may not work as well for lower-level jobs as for positions with more varied duties and responsibilities.

When managers can articulate what they want a performance appraisal system to accomplish, they can choose and mix methods to realize advantages of each approach. For example, one combination might include a graphic rating scale of performance on major job criteria, a narrative for developmental needs, and an overall ranking of employees in a department. Different categories of employees (e.g., salaried exempt, salaried nonexempt, maintenance) might require different combinations of methods.

RATER ERRORS

For employees to benefit from feedback during the appraisal process, managers should be trained to avoid evaluation errors. Figure 9-7 illustrates some of the common types of errors that occur in appraisals. A discussion of each follows.

Recency

One of the most common errors managers make when conducting appraisals is to use only recent events to judge employees' performance. To avoid this error, managers need to keep information about employees' performance throughout the year and use that information during the annual review. Reviewers should keep both negative and positive information from the entire evaluation period.

Central Tendency, Leniency, and Strictness Errors

Managers who tend to rate all of their employees within a narrow range are referred to as **central-tendency raters**. In this error, managers would not distinguish among poor, average, and above-average performers.

FIGURE 9-7 Common Rater Errors

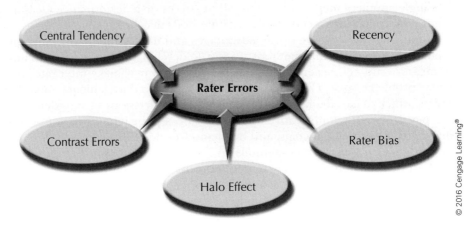

© 2016 Cengage Learning®

Managers who give all of their employees high ratings are described as **lenient raters**. Conversely, managers who give their employees low ratings make the mistake of being overly **strict raters**. In all of these situations, managers undermine the performance appraisal process, leaving employees without ideas about where they really stand. Also, not evaluating each employee objectively against performance standards is more likely to result in frustration on the part of the evaluated employee.

Rater Bias

Rater bias occurs when a manager reflects a bias against a certain employee or employee group based on the manager's own values or prejudices. Biased appraisals may be associated with age, gender, or religion, among others. In these cases, the manager's supervisor should also be involved in the process before the manager meets with the employee.

Halo Effect

The **halo effect** occurs when a manager rates an employee high or low on all job standards based on one characteristic. For example, if a hospital house-keeping employee is always willing to assume extra shifts, the manager may rate that employee highly on all aspects of his or her performance, based entirely on that one characteristic. Another example of the halo effect would be if an employee who admits patients provides excellent customer service but is consistently disagreeable with coworkers. The manager, in this example of the halo effect, would give a favorable overall rating based only on the employee's excellent customer skills, ignoring the divisive behaviors that lead to departmental problems.

Contrast Errors

Contrast errors in the performance review process occur when a manager compares employees to each other rather than to job performance standards. The more effective approach is to rate employees against job requirements, not other employees.

APPRAISAL FEEDBACK

It is important to communicate appraisal information to employees to provide them with a clear understanding about how they are performing. At an appraisal meeting, any misunderstanding about an employee's performance can be clarified. Effective healthcare managers typically coach employees about their performance and provide development opportunities, which can also enhance employee retention efforts.[33] The performance feedback meeting is most effective when it is interactive and mutually beneficial to managers and employees. While the formal performance appraisal process provides information in longer-term time intervals, generally annually, the use of informal appraisal feedback is effective when used more frequently and summarized at the formal feedback session.

Feedback Systems

Feedback systems have three components: collecting data, evaluating the data, and taking action based on the data. As shown in Figure 9-8, collecting data is how a manager gathers information about an employee's performance. Evaluating the data is the critical second step, which includes objectively determining how the employee performed relative to job standards. For example, if a ward clerk in a hospital can process significantly higher numbers of doctors' orders for lab tests, that data might lead the manager to give high marks for performance. But if the employee accomplishes this task at the expense of not responding to questions from other staff members or from patients and their families, the performance rating might be different.

The final step in the feedback system is taking action based on the results of the appraisal. In some cases, the action is processing a pay increase. In other cases, the action is a development plan. For many employees, the action is recognition of performance and encouragement to continue to perform well.

After completing appraisals, managers need to communicate results to give employees a clear understanding of how they compare to performance standards and organizations expectations. Organizations commonly require managers to discuss appraisals with employees. The appraisal feedback interview

---

FIGURE 9-8   Feedback Process

Collect Data → Evaluate Data → Take Action

© 2016 Cengage Learning®

provides an opportunity to clear up any misunderstandings on both sides. In this interview, the manager should focus on coaching and development as well, and not just tell the employee, "Here is how you rate and why."[34]

The Appraisal Interview

The appraisal interview presents both an opportunity and a challenge. It can be an emotional experience for the manager and the employee because the manager must communicate both praise and constructive criticism. A major concern for managers is how to emphasize the positive aspects of the employee's performance while still discussing ways to make needed improvements. If the interview is handled poorly, the employee may feel resentment, which could lead to future performance problems. Consequently, a manager should identify how employees add value to the organization and show appreciation when employees make valuable contributions.[35]

Employees usually approach an appraisal interview with some concern. They may feel that discussions about performance are both personal and important to their continued job success. At the same time, they want to know how their managers view their performance.

Reactions of Managers and Employees

Healthcare managers who must complete evaluations of their employees often resist the appraisal process.[36] Many feel that their role requires them to assist, encourage, coach, and counsel employees to improve their performance. Many healthcare managers also perform the same functions as their employees working alongside them every day. This is very typical in small clinics, mental health agencies, and physical and occupational therapy organizations. Consequently, being a performance "judge" on the one hand and a coach and colleague on the other hand may cause internal conflict.

Knowing that appraisals may affect employees' future careers may also cause altered or biased ratings. This problem is even more likely when managers know that they will have to communicate and defend their ratings to the employees, their bosses, or HR specialists. Managers can simply make the employee's ratings positive and avoid unpleasantness. But avoidance helps no one. A manager owes an employee a well-done appraisal, no matter how difficult an employee is or how difficult the conversation about performance might be.

Employees may well see the appraisal process as a threat and feel that the only way for them to get a higher rating is for someone else to receive a low rating. This win–lose perception is encouraged by comparative methods of rating. Emphasis on the self-improvement and developmental aspects of appraisal appears to be the most effective way to reduce this reaction.[37]

Another common employee reaction resembles students' response to tests. A professor may prepare a test that she perceives to be fair, but students may see it differently. Likewise, employees being appraised may not necessarily agree with the manager doing the appraising. However, in most cases, employees will view appraisals done well as what they are meant to be—constructive feedback. Many employees want appraisals, but some may find it difficult to get honest feedback.[38]

EFFECTIVE PERFORMANCE MANAGEMENT

Regardless of the approach used, healthcare managers must understand the intended outcome of performance management.[39] When performance management is genuinely used to develop employees as resources, it usually works. When a key part of performance management, the performance appraisal, is used to punish employees, performance management is less effective. In its simplest form, performance appraisal is the observation: "Here are your strengths and weaknesses, and here is a way to develop for the future."

Done well, performance management can lead to higher employee motivation and satisfaction. To be effective, a performance management system, including the performance appraisal processes, should be:

- Beneficial as a development tool
- Useful as an administrative tool
- Legal and job related
- Viewed as generally fair by employees
- Effective in documenting employee performance
- Clear about who are high, average, and low performers

CASE

The performance review program at Valley Urgent Care was developed some years ago and has generally served the organization well. The supervisors took the responsibility to conduct timely, meaningful reviews very seriously. The review process consisted of ratings on the following skills and competencies:

- Customer service
- Clinical abilities
- Communications with patients and fellow employees
- Attendance
- Work attitude

However, the employees and supervisors have commented that the review process lacked relevance and was in need of updating. They indicated that there were not enough evaluation categories to adequately evaluate the complexity and variety of jobs at Valley Urgent Care. Additional categories that were suggested included computer skills, compliance with HIPAA, willingness to take on additional duties, and leadership.

Valley Urgent Care's administrator agreed that it was time to review the evaluation process and criteria has asked the HR manager to pull together a work team of managers to develop a new process that would be more relevant and meaningful to the organization and employees.

Questions

1. Why would the employees see the current review process as irrelevant?
2. What types of changes should the work team consider in order to improve the process and criteria?

END NOTES

1. David O. Weber, "The Patient Experience," *Trustee Magazine* (November 2013), 1–5; W. M. Jennings, "Even in Healthcare, Quality Is Free," *Modern Healthcare* (2013), 18.

2. See *http://www.angieslist.com/articles/angies-list-top-doctors-dentists.htm* for more information.

3. Andrew R. McIlvaine, "There's Got to Be a Better Way," *Human Resource Executive* (July/August 2012), 13–15; Samuel A. Culbert, "The Case for Killing Performance Reviews," *Human Resource Executive Online* (July 16, 2012), 1–2.

4. Jamie A. Gruman and Alan M. Saks, "Performance Management and Employee Engagement," *Human Resource Management Review* 21 (2011), 123–136.

5. Michael Cohn, "6 Steps to Manager Performance," *Employee Benefit News* (October 2011), 12–13.

6. Jake C. Messersmith et al., "Unlocking the Black Box: Exploring the Link between High Performance Work Systems and Performance," *Journal of Applied Psychology* 96 (2011), 1105–1118.

7. See *http://www.ebaptisthealthcare.org/BHC/AboutUs.aspx* for more information.

8. Kerry Vermillion et al, "Innovations in Performance Management," *Healthcare Financial Management* (May 2010), 98–104.

9. Y. Gong et al., "Human Resource Management and Firm Performance," *Journal of Applied Psychology* 94 (2009), 263–275.

10. Chapin White et al., "Understanding Differences between High-and Low-Price Hospitals: Implications for Efforts to Rein In Costs," *Health Affairs* (February 2014), 324–331.

11. L. Piper, "Generation Y in Healthcare: Leading Millennial in an Era of Reform," *Frontiers of Health Services Management* (Fall 2012), 16–28.

12. Marie-Helene Budworth and Sara Mann, "Performance Management Where Do We Go from Here?," *Human Resource Management Review* 21 (2011), 81–84.

13. Jochen Reb and Gary J. Greguras, "Understanding Performance Ratings: Dynamic Performance, Attributions, and Rating Purpose," *Journal of Applied Psychology* 95 (2010), 213–220.

14. Dana Mattioli et al., "Bad Call: How Not to Fire a Worker," *Wall Street Journal* (September 9, 2011), B1; Jathan Janove, "Reviews—Good for Anything?," *HR Magazine* (June 2011), 121–126.

15. Ann Pace, "A New Era in Performance Management," *T+D* 65 (October 2011), 10.

16. L. Butcher, "Progress, but Still a Long Way to Go," *Modern Healthcare* (October 14, 2013), 30–31.

17. "Employee Claims She Was Fired in Retaliation for Coworker's Complaint," *Legal Alert for Supervisors* (February 14, 2014), 1–2.

18. Stephanie C. Payne et al., "Comparison of Online and Traditional Performance Appraisal Systems," *Journal of Management Psychology* 24 (2009), 526–544.

19. Paul Rowson and Kip Kipley, "Tips to Help Managers Optimize Performance Appraisals," *Workspan* (October 2010), 28–33.

20. Barbara M. Moskal, "Self-Assessments: What Are Their Valid Uses?," *Academy of Management Learning and Education* 9 (June 2010), 314–320.

21. Lawrence C. Bassett, "No Such Things as Perfect Performance Management," *Human Resource Executive* 26 (September 16, 2012), 6.

22. John W. Fleenor et al., "Self–Other Ratings Agreement in Leadership: A Review," *The Leadership Quarterly* 21 (2010), 1005–1034.

23. Rainer Hensel et al., "360° Feedback: How Many Raters Are Needed for Reliable Ratings?," *The International Journal of Human Resource Management* 21 (2010), 2813–2830.

24. Tracy Maylett, "360 Degree Feedback Revisited: The Transition from Development to Appraisal," *Compensation and Benefits Review* (2009), 1–8.

25. B. J. Hoffman and D. J. Woehr, "Disentangling the Meaning of Multisource Performance Ratings Source and Dimension Factors," *Personnel Psychology* 62 (2009), 735–765.

26. J. Zenger and J. Folkman, "Develop Strengths," *Leadership Excellence* (January 2013),12.

27. Mathews A. Wilde, "Hospitals Prescribe Big Data to Track Doctors at Work," *Wall Street Journal*, eastern ed. (July 12, 2013), A10.

28. James Smither and Manuel London, eds., *Performance Management: Putting Research into Action* (San Francisco: Jossey-Bass, 2009), 297–328.

29. Dori Meinert, "A Crack in the Bell Curve," *HR Magazine* (April 2012), 22.

30. Deidra J. Schleicher et al., "Rater Reactions to Forced Distribution Rating Systems," *Journal of Management* 35 (August 2009), 899–927.

31. Stéphane Brutus, "Words versus Numbers: A Theoretical Exploration of Giving and Receiving Narrative Comments in Performance Appraisal," *Human Resource Management Review* 20 (2010), 144–157.

32. Lisa D. Ordóñez et al., "Goals Gone Wild: The Systematic Side Effects of Overprescribing Goal Setting," *Academy of Management Perspectives* 23 (February 2009), 6–16; E. A. Locke and Gary P. Latham, "Has Goal Setting Gone Wild or Have Its Attackers Abandoned Good Scholarship?," *Academy of Management Perspectives* 23 (February 2009), 17–23; Osnat Bouskila-Yam and Avraham N. Kluger, "Strength-Based Performance Appraisal and Goal Setting," *Human Resource Management Review* 21 (2011), 137–147; and A. Kleingeld et al., "The Effect of Goal Setting on Group Performance: A Meta-Analysis," *Journal of Applied Psychology* 96 (2011), 1289–1304.

33. Rick Contel, "Performance-Based Coaching," *Chief Learning Officer* (December 2012), 18–22.

34. Michael E. Gordon and Lea P. Stewart, "Conversing about Performance," *Management Communication Quarterly* 22 (February 2009), 473–501.

35. Adrienne Fox, "Curing What Ails Performance Reviews," *HR Magazine* (January 2009), 52–56.

36. Michael Rosenthal, "Performance Review 201," *Training* (July/August 2010), 44.

37. E. M. Mone and Manuel London, *Employee Engagement through Effective Performance Management* (New York: Taylor and Francis, 2009).

38. Robert S. Kaplan, "Top Executives Need Feedback: Here's How They Can Get It," *McKinsey Quarterly* (September 2011), 1–8.

39. Steve Browne, "HR Roundtable: Should Performance Reviews Live or Die?," TLNT (November 17, 2011), *Sbrowne@larosas.com.*

10 EMPLOYEE RELATIONS IN THE HEALTHCARE INDUSTRY

Learning Objectives

After you have read this chapter you should be able to:

- Review the common components of an employment agreement.
- Define *employment-at-will* and identify exceptions to this concept.
- Describe *due process* and explain alternative dispute resolution processes.
- Discuss issues associated with drug testing for healthcare employees.
- Identify elements common to employee handbooks.
- Outline the progressive discipline process.

HEALTHCARE HR INSIGHTS

A female physical therapist (PT) who worked for an adult rehabilitation center mistakenly was given the pay stub of a male colleague. Before she discovered that the pay stub was for one of her male colleagues, she observed his gross-pay figure, which was significantly higher than her normal gross pay. Once she realized that this was not her pay stub, she returned it immediately to the payroll department, who in turn delivered it to the right employee.

After much thought and concern about what she had seen, she decided to talk to her manager. She had tried to objectively evaluate the situation, but she was unable to reconcile the significant difference between her pay and that of her fellow male therapist. They had both graduated from very highly regarded PT schools; they both started their employment with the rehabilitation center about the same time; and as far as she knew, they were comparable in their skills and abilities.

When she finally met with her manager to discuss the situation, he reacted very negatively and initially accused her of inappropriately acquiring her fellow employee's gross-pay information. She was eventually able to explain the mistake to the manager's satisfaction, however, the conversation then became very confrontational. The manager refused to discuss the wage difference and threatened to discipline her if she discussed this situation with other employees or brought it to the attention of the human resources department.

Now even more concerned about the situation, she contacted the local office of the Equal Employment Opportunity Commission (EEOC) to discuss her concerns. Upon hearing her side of the story, the commission's representative advised her of her right to file a discrimination charge on the basis of her gender under the Lilly Ledbetter Fair Pay Act of 2009.[1] In addition, since her manager had threatened her with discipline if she took her concerns further, she was also advised that she could file a retaliation charge.

The EEOC, upon objective analysis, determined that all of the male therapists were paid on average 25 percent higher than their female counterparts without any significant documented differences in tenure, ability, or performance. As a result of the investigation, a sizable back-pay settlement was reached between the EEOC on behalf of the female PTs and the rehabilitation center.

Healthcare organizations typically manage their relationships with employees through HR policies, procedures, and practices. Employers also base their relationships with employees upon a series of rights that are defined and mandated by various federal, state, and local laws and statutes and through important court decisions, referred to as case law. In addition, employers and employees may define their rights and obligations with contractual agreements. Regardless, organizations either purposefully or by inference develop philosophies and practices that define the nature of their employment relationships with employees.

NATURE OF EMPLOYER–EMPLOYEE RELATIONS

An **employee relations philosophy** includes all aspects of how an organization guides, responds to, and communicates with its employees.[2] How this philosophy is used strategically serves as an important differentiation that may cause an employee to select one organization over another. Employee satisfaction is a retention issue as well. Managers, employees, and candidates for employment might consider the following questions as they evaluate whether to remain employed or take a job at an organization:

- Is the work environment governed by too many policies and procedures?
- Is the organization willing to manage the relationship with realistic and appropriate rules and requirements?

An organization may elect to develop an employee relations philosophy statement that outlines the employment relationship. In healthcare organizations, HR can provide strategic leadership when it encourages and facilitates the development of an employee relations statement and the policies and procedures that support the philosophy. In today's healthcare workplace, employee relations philosophies are more important than ever because of the shortage of skilled healthcare personnel. It is important for healthcare organizational leadership to carefully articulate its philosophy and adopt policies that provide a positive work environment, which can contribute to higher levels of employee satisfaction and productivity.[3]

RIGHTS AND RESPONSIBILITIES

There are two types of employee rights: those guaranteed by law and those governed by contracts. Figure 10-1 depicts the key laws, regulations, and agreements that affect the rights and responsibilities of both employees and employers.

FIGURE 10-1   Rights and Responsibility of Employees and Employers

STATUTORY RIGHTS	CONTRACTUAL RIGHTS
• Federal and state regulations	• Employment contracts/agreements
• Equal employment opportunity (EEO)	• Separation agreements
• Health and safety regulations (OSHA)	• Retention agreements
• Employee benefits laws (ERISA)	• Training contracts
• Wage and hour law (FLSA)	• Drug testing permissions
• Professional association guidelines	
• Workers' compensation	
• Unemployment compensation	

© Cengage Learning®

Statutory Rights

Existing laws, legislation, and evolving case law identify and protect healthcare employees' rights. In addition to general **statutory rights**, other regulations apply specifically to healthcare workers. An example of a law specific to healthcare employees is the Health Insurance Portability and Accountability Act of 1996 (HIPAA). Certain aspects of this act require healthcare organizations and healthcare workers to protect the access to and confidentiality of healthcare consumers', including employees', medical information as revealed through medical records, employee benefits information, or processes that facilitate the payment of medical bills. Failure to do so can result in significant liability and penalties for organizations and individual workers, especially if they willfully violate the law.[4] Although aspects of HIPAA are healthcare-specific, most statutory rights apply to workers in all industries.

Many of the general rights guaranteed for employees in all industries have been created to allow employees to assert their rights and be heard by external agencies, such as the Equal Employment Opportunity Commission, the National Labor Relations Board, and OSHA (Occupational Safety and Health Administration). These rights are a matter of law and employers must recognize them, but employers and employees sometimes disagree with the intent of regulations and negotiate clarifications as they resolve their differences.

In addition, professional regulatory bodies for healthcare workers generate regulations that define and govern the conduct of their members. In some professions, such as physician assistants, states have implemented practice standards and professional behavior requirements.[5] These standards usually define clinical competency and professional behavior. In addition, as an obligation of a practice standard, healthcare professionals, in a given state, may be required to report staffing issues that could lead to unsafe patient care.

Contractual Rights

Rights of employees may be extended by a contract based on terms and conditions agreed to by employers and employees. These contracts specifically define and formalize working relationships.

A formal agreement between an employer and an employee about their working relationship is called an **employment contract**. The contract, in most cases, is a written document prepared by an attorney who represents the organization.[6] In most organizations, employment contracts are reserved for executives and key managers. Employment contract provisions for executives may include compensation, general benefits, performance-based incentive and bonus provisions, executive benefits such as additional retirement benefits, severance pay, benefit continuation, outplacement services, and others. However, in the healthcare industry, employment agreements have also been used to attract and retain employees for hard-to-fill positions such as physical therapists or ICU nurses.

FIGURE 10-2 **Employment Contract Contents**

Employment Contract Contents

- Terms of the contract—Duration
- Provisions for renewing the contract—Automatic or mutually agreed
- Duties and responsibilities—Job description
- Compensation—Salary and variable pay
- Benefits—Group and individual
- Severance benefit—Continuation of salary and benefits after job ends
- Noncompete clauses—Restriction on choice of future employers
- Nonsolicitation clauses—Raiding clients and staff after job ends
- Dispute-resolution clauses—Settling contract disputes
- Change-in-control clauses—Change of ownership, board, management
- Termination and resignation clauses—Immunity from state and federal laws

© Cengage Learning®

Employment agreements often include provisions identifying job expectations, length of employment, termination rights, and protection from claims based on federal and state laws. In some contracts, provisions prohibit the employees from competing with the organization when they leave voluntarily. These **noncompete provisions** are usually offered in exchange for substantial benefits and economic security for the employees agreeing to be bound by the noncompete restrictions.[7] Figure 10-2 describes common elements in an employment contract.

Retention Agreements   Another type of agreement is a **retention agreement**, designed to retain key employees during mergers, consolidations, or changes in organizational leadership.[8] In healthcare organizations, retention agreements help to provide stable leadership and management during times of change. Retention agreements usually provide for cash bonuses and special benefits to the recipients for staying with the employer for a specified period during times of change or instability.

Implied Contracts

Employees without agreements are subject to the employer's policies and procedures, including employee handbooks, which have been held to be implied contracts defining the employment relationship. Unwritten agreements between employers and employees are called **implied contracts**.[9] These contracts are often the focus of disputes between employers and employees. For instance, if an employer hires an employee for an undefined period or promises job security but no document is written and signed, a court may decide whether an implied contract exists. If an employee believes that the terms of the employment agreement were implied in conversations or through an oral job offer, the employee may sue to achieve the implied terms that were denied.

Employment Practices Liability Insurance

A type of liability insurance protects organizations against costly lawsuits initiated by their employees. This insurance is known as **employment practices liability insurance (EPLI)**. The key goal of EPLI is to offer legal and risk-management advice to organizations to minimize their legal exposure and negotiate settlements to employee claims. In organizations, general liability insurance policies do not include coverage for suits filed by employees based on employment-related claims[10].The types of claims typically filed include discrimination, sexual harassment, wrongful termination, and breach of contract. To obtain EPLI coverage, the insurance company usually requires an organization to undergo an audit of its HR policies and practices, including policy manuals, employee handbooks, employment forms, and other HR practices and processes.

EMPLOYEE RELATIONS AND RIGHTS OF EMPLOYEES

Employees' rights and organizational employee relations philosophies may clash when employees think their contractual or implied contractual rights have been violated. Several doctrines—employment-at-will, just cause, and due process—affect both employees and employers when settling disputes.

Employment-at-Will

Hiring and firing an employee has historically been the employer's right. However, several employment law cases have challenged that right, and employers and their attorneys have responded by establishing and communicating **employment-at-will provisions**. The employment-at-will statements are usually contained in the employee handbook or in HR policy and procedure manuals. The statement says that employers have the right to hire, fire, and promote whomever they choose. In exchange for the employer's right to employment-at-will, employees receive the right to terminate their employment at any time for any reason. Typical employment-at-will verbiage is shown in Figure 10-3.

Exceptions to the At-Will Doctrine   The legal system has identified three exceptions to the at-will doctrine: *public-policy decisions, implied contractual disputes,* and *good faith and fair dealing*. These arguments are raised to assert employees'

FIGURE 10-3 Employment-at-Will Language

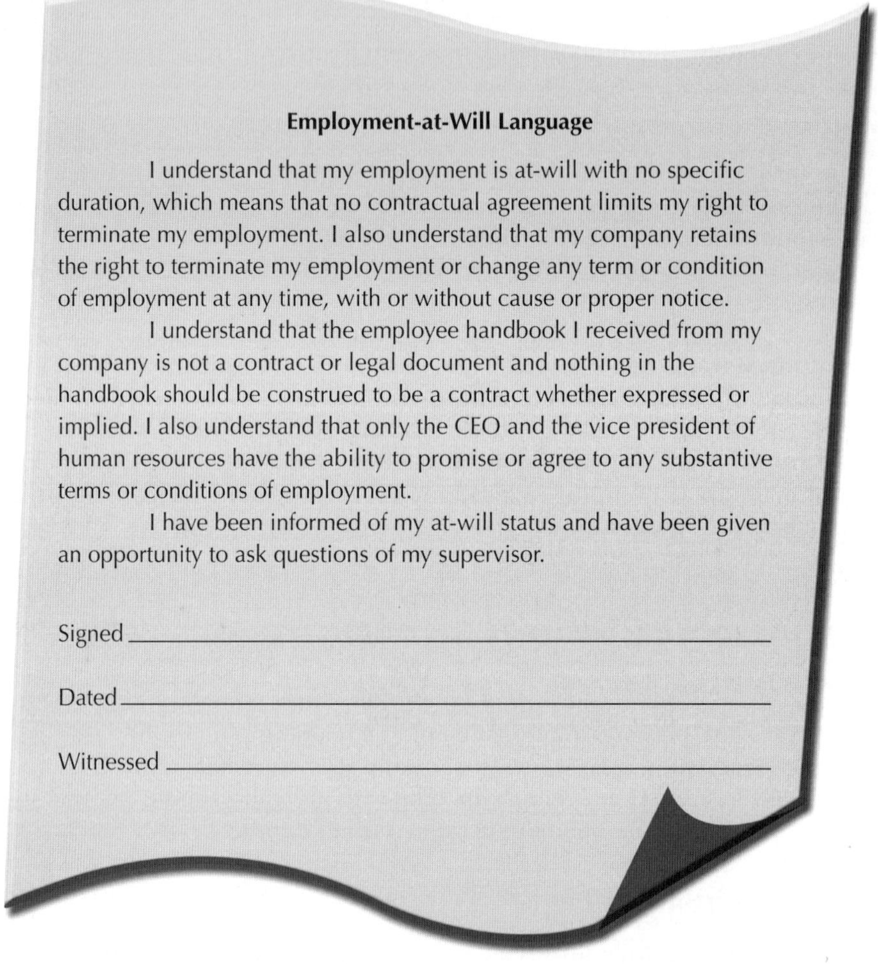

Employment-at-Will Language

I understand that my employment is at-will with no specific duration, which means that no contractual agreement limits my right to terminate my employment. I also understand that my company retains the right to terminate my employment or change any term or condition of employment at any time, with or without cause or proper notice.

I understand that the employee handbook I received from my company is not a contract or legal document and nothing in the handbook should be construed to be a contract whether expressed or implied. I also understand that only the CEO and the vice president of human resources have the ability to promise or agree to any substantive terms or conditions of employment.

I have been informed of my at-will status and have been given an opportunity to ask questions of my supervisor.

Signed _____

Dated _____

Witnessed _____

© Cengage Learning®

rights when they believe their rights have been violated, and many legal jurisdictions have recognized these exceptions to the employment-at-will doctrine.

- A **public-policy violation** occurs when an employee is fired for reporting illegal activities by the employer as required by federal or state law.
- An **implied contract** might promise that an employee will be employed indefinitely or might seem to suggest continued employment as long as an employee performs the job satisfactorily.
- A **good faith** and **fair dealing** exception provides that the employer and the employee have entered into a relationship whose objective is treating each other fairly. If the employer is treating the employee unfairly by being unreasonable, such as assigning difficult work or inconvenient shifts, the employee can assert that the employer is not acting in good faith.[11]

Wrongful Discharge and the Importance of Documentation

One of the most prevalent claims against employers by disgruntled former employees is that of *wrongful discharge*. Wrongful discharge occurs when employers discharge their employees for reasons that are illegal, improper, or inconsistent with organizational policies, procedures, or rules. To avoid wrongful discharge claims, organizations must ensure that discharged employees are dealt with properly by following applicable policies and procedures that relate to discharge.[12] For example, if a clinic has a process for discipline, the employee should be discharged only after that process has been followed. If the process is not followed, the clinic could be accused of not providing the employee with due process.

Wrongful-discharge suits have become a major issue for many healthcare organizations. The items listed in Figure 10-4 are commonly used to defend healthcare organizations against wrongful-discharge lawsuits, including some of the key preventions discussed next.

New Employee Orientation Materials   Employees receive a wide variety of orientation information as they begin their employment. Included in that information should be a thorough review of key policies, such as: sexual harassment prevention policies, appropriate use of the Internet and e-mail policies, employee code of conduct, and related policies that provide new employees with clear expectations for their behavior while on the job. Many healthcare employers also include a review of their employee handbook, requiring employees to sign a form acknowledging that the employee has a responsibility to read the handbook and agree to follow the employer's policies and procedures, contained therein.

In the healthcare industry, a review of *patient confidentiality policies* is part of the orientation materials. Confidentiality of patient information is a highly held value by healthcare organizations and, as noted earlier, a significant compliance issue due to the requirements of HIPAA and HITECH.[13] Many healthcare employers have included a special sign-off for employees attesting to their understanding and commitment to protecting patient confidentiality. This type of documentation can be used in discharge decisions by the employer and used to defend against wrongful discharge claims.

FIGURE 10-4   Documentation for Defense in Wrongful Discharge Lawsuits

- New employee orientation materials
- Employee handbook
- At-will employment statement—Signed
- Departmental orientation documents
- Documentation of employee meetings

- Discharge letter with reason for termination
- Performance appraisals
- Job descriptions
- Performance management activities (counseling statements, warnings, and suspensions)

© 2016 Cengage Learning®

Employee Handbooks The employee handbook in most organizations acts as a guideline for employees about the policies and work rules that need to be followed. Job expectations and behaviors are also explained in the handbook, and employees are required to acknowledge that they will, as a condition of employment, follow the handbook.

Discharge Letters Discharge letters document the reason and conditions of the discharges. Some states require the disclosure of the reasons for discharges to employees within a set time period.[14]

Discipline Processes and Performance Appraisals The majority of information that is used to defend an employer against wrongful-discharge suits is generated through discipline and performance management policies and programs. Documentation of discipline decisions and the performance management process helps employers explain the reasons for discharge decisions.

Job Descriptions Job descriptions contain vital information about the job duties and responsibilities for employees. In many cases, employees are given their job descriptions and sign a document acknowledging that they have received a copy.

Just Cause

Just cause is reasonable justification for taking employment-related action. The need for a "good reason" for disciplinary actions such as dismissal usually can be found in union contracts but not in all at-will situations. Even though definitions of *just cause* vary, the overall concern is fairness. To be viewed by others as *just*, any disciplinary action must be based on facts in the individual case. Violations of these requirements can result in legal action. For instance, a court could easily rule that a high-performing worker was not fired for just cause if he had been terminated for poor performance after taking unpaid time off associated with the Family and Medical Leave Act to help a sick relative. Figure 10-5 contains points that determine just cause.

Due Process

Healthcare employees may contest disciplinary actions if they feel they have not been afforded **due process**, which is the opportunity to explain and defend their actions against charges of misconduct or other reasons relating to the disciplinary process. Like just cause, it is about fairness. Due process is the requirement that the employer use a fair process to determine if there has been employee wrongdoing and that the employee has an opportunity to explain and defend his or her actions. Oftentimes, this requires a company to properly investigate the reasons for HR decisions and to give individuals an opportunity to express their concerns to unbiased reviewers of the situations in question.

FIGURE 10-5   Just Cause Determinants

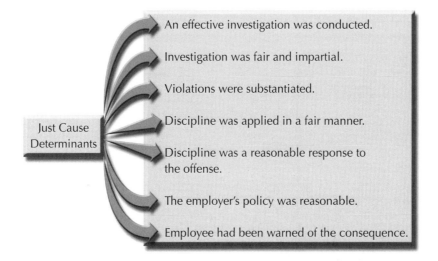

Just Cause Determinants

- An effective investigation was conducted.
- Investigation was fair and impartial.
- Violations were substantiated.
- Discipline was applied in a fair manner.
- Discipline was a reasonable response to the offense.
- The employer's policy was reasonable.
- Employee had been warned of the consequence.

© 2016 Cengage Learning®

Figure 10-6 shows some factors to be considered when combining an evaluation of just cause and due process. How HR managers address these factors determines whether the courts perceive employers' actions as fair.

Constructive Discharge

When an employer creates adverse working conditions that force an employee to resign, **constructive discharge** has occurred.[15] Sometimes a supervisor or manager will wage a purposeful campaign against an employee to get the employee to quit. Work schedules are changed or work assignments are unfavorable or supervisors just make the job difficult. When courts have ruled that constructive discharge has occurred, an employee may be awarded compensation, including back pay and punitive damages. Constructive-discharge claims are becoming more frequent, and healthcare employers should be aware of this issue when "encouraging" employees to resign.

Numerous healthcare employers use an **open-door policy**, which means that workers who have a complaint can talk directly to someone in charge. However, this policy can be mishandled, so nonunion firms benefit from having formal complaint procedures that are well defined because they provide more systematic due process for employees than do open-door policies.

Work-Related Alternative Dispute Resolution

Disputes between management and employees over work issues are normal and inevitable, but how the parties resolve their disputes is important. Open-door policies, formal grievance procedures, and lawsuits provide several resolution methods. However, companies are looking to alternative means of settlement.

FIGURE 10-6   Criteria for Evaluating Just Cause and Due Process

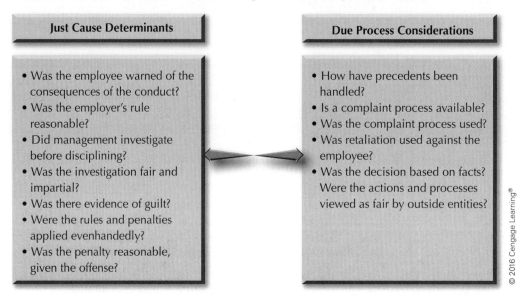

Just Cause Determinants	Due Process Considerations
• Was the employee warned of the consequences of the conduct? • Was the employer's rule reasonable? • Did management investigate before disciplining? • Was the investigation fair and impartial? • Was there evidence of guilt? • Were the rules and penalties applied evenhandedly? • Was the penalty reasonable, given the offense?	• How have precedents been handled? • Is a complaint process available? • Was the complaint process used? • Was retaliation used against the employee? • Was the decision based on facts? Were the actions and processes viewed as fair by outside entities?

© 2016 Cengage Learning®

Dissatisfaction with expenses, delays in the court system when lawsuits are filed, and damages to employer–employee relationships have prompted growth in alternative dispute resolution (ADR) methods such as arbitration, peer review panels, ombuds, and mediation.[16] However, these methods must be considered fair by employees if disputes are to be effectively handled. Research determined that appropriate communication of decisions, giving employees a chance to provide input, and the membership composition of the panel strongly influenced individual perceptions of overall fairness.[17]

Arbitration   Disagreements between employers and employees can result in lawsuits and large legal bills for settlements. Most employees who believe they have experienced unfair treatment do not get legal counsel, but their discontent and complaints are likely to continue. Consequently, to settle disputes employers can use arbitration in nonunion situations.

Arbitration is a process that uses a neutral third party to make a binding decision, thereby eliminating the necessity of using the court system. Arbitration has been a common feature in union contracts. However, it must be set up carefully if employers want to use it in nonunion situations. Since employers often select the arbitrators, and because arbitrators may not be required to issue written decisions and opinions, some see the use of arbitration in employment-related situations as unfair.[18]

The arbitration process is well known to the healthcare industry for settling medical malpractice claims. Doctors and healthcare facilities involved in medical claims frequently find the use of arbitration a more effective and faster means of settling small-dollar claims.

Some organizations use *compulsory arbitration,* which requires employees to sign a preemployment agreement stating that all disputes will be submitted to arbitration; employees waive their rights to pursue legal action until the completion of the arbitration process. Requiring arbitration as a condition of employment is legal, but employers must follow it rather than try to waive it in some cases. However, a legal check of compulsory arbitration as part of ADR should be done before adopting the practice. In addition, organizations should ensure that arbitrators function in an equitable manner, arbitration decisions and awards are reflective of the law, and proper attempts are made by organizations to communicate arbitration agreements to employees.

Peer Review Panels   Some employers allow their employees to appeal disciplinary actions to an internal committee of employees, also known as conflict resolution committees. This panel reviews the actions and makes recommendations or decisions. Peer review panels use fellow employees and perhaps a few managers to resolve employment disputes. Panel members are specially trained volunteers who sign confidentiality agreements, after which the company assigns them to hear appeals.

These panels have several advantages including reduced lawsuits, provision of due process, decreased costs, and management and employee development. Also, peer review panels can complement a formal complaint process for nonunion employees because solutions can be identified and made binding without court action. If an employee does file a lawsuit, the employer presents a stronger case when a group of the employee's peers previously reviewed the employer's decision and found it to be appropriate.

Ombuds   Some healthcare organizations ensure process fairness through **ombuds**—employees outside the normal chain of command who act as independent problem solvers for both management and employees. At many large and medium-sized firms, ombuds have effectively addressed complaints about unfair treatment, employee–supervisor conflicts, and other workplace behavior issues. Ombuds address employees' complaints and operate with a high degree of confidentiality. Any follow-up to resolve problems is often handled informally, except when situations include unusual or significant illegal actions.

Mediation   Ombuds, as well as other individuals and groups who oversee dispute cases, will sometimes use *mediation* as a tool for developing appropriate and fair outcomes for all parties involved. Facilitative and directive forms of mediation rely on an approach that ultimately helps identify resolutions to the problems collectively explored. Transformative mediation is more exploratory in nature, with participants identifying their own problems, fixing damaged relationships, and developing realistic solutions. The focus of transformative mediation is to settle disputes and figure out how employees can more effectively interact with each other on the job.[19]

BALANCING EMPLOYER SECURITY AND EMPLOYEE RIGHTS

Many employees have exercised their rights to privacy in the workplace, and employers have been forced to agree that some employee information is private and confidential and cannot be used for or against employees. Balancing employer security with employee rights requires managers to review HR policies and practices regularly.

Employee Records

The **Privacy Act of 1974** issued regulations that affect HR record-keeping systems, policies, and procedures for governmental employers. In some states, laws have been passed regarding employee records issues. As an example, a California law *covering all* employers subject to wage-and-hour laws allows employees to inspect at reasonable intervals any personnel records relating to performance or to a grievance proceeding.[20]

Many healthcare organizations have responded to federal and state laws by developing policies regarding access to personnel records. The purpose of these policies is to protect employee information. Often, such policy statements include who has access to the employee record and how employees can dispute information in their personnel file. Figure 10-7 lists the documents that should and should not be included in personnel files.

Employee Medical Records   Record-keeping and retention practices have been affected by the following provision in the Americans with Disabilities Act (ADA):

> Information from all medical examinations and inquiries must be kept apart from general personnel files as a separate confidential medical record available only under limited conditions specified in the ADA.

FIGURE 10-7   **Personnel File Contents**

Include:

- Application for employment
- New employee orientation information—Checklist
- Letter offering the job
- Compensation records
- Performance appraisals
- Performance management documentation
- Training records

Do Not Include:

- Employee health files
- Performance comments by co-workers

© 2016 Cengage Learning®

As interpreted by attorneys and healthcare HR professionals, this provision requires that all medical-related information be maintained separately from all other confidential files. The Health Insurance Portability and Accountability Act (HIPAA) also contains regulations designed to protect the privacy of employee medical records. Both regular and confidential electronic files must be considered. As a result of all the legal restrictions, healthcare employers have routinely established several separate personnel records files from the employee's health record files.

Electronic Records   Other policies that govern personnel files deal with information available through a human resources information system (HRIS). An HRIS is an electronic record system.[21]

Security of Employee Records   It is important to establish access restrictions and security procedures for employee records, whether in the form of electronic data or hard-copy files. These restrictions and procedures are designed to protect the privacy of employees and protect employers from potential liability for improper disclosure of personal information. Individuals' Social Security numbers, personal addresses, and other contact information should be protected.

A legal regulation called the Data Protection Act requires employers to keep personnel records up-to-date and keep only the details that are needed.[22] The following guidelines are offered regarding employer access and storage of employee records:

- Restrict access to records to a limited number of individuals.
- Use confidential passwords for accessing employee records in various HR databases.
- Set up separate files and restricted databases for especially sensitive employee information.
- Inform employees about which types of data are retained.
- Purge employee records of outdated data.
- Release employee information only with employee consent.

Personnel files and records are usually maintained for three years. However, different types of records should be maintained for shorter or longer periods of time based on various legal and regulatory standards.

Employees' Right to Free Speech

Employees have challenged employers' right to enforce policies that limit free speech. Several areas of conflict between employers and employees are discussed next.

Employee Advocacy of Controversial Views   Questions of free speech arise over the right of employees to advocate controversial viewpoints at work. Numerous examples can be cited. For instance, can an employee of a hospital that performs abortions openly discuss his or her concerns with other employees about that procedure? Can a disgruntled employee at a nonunion employer wear a union badge on a cap at work? In situations such as these, healthcare organizations must follow due process procedures and demonstrate that any disciplinary actions taken against employees can be justified by job-related reasons.

The best way to handle these concerns is to (1) attempt informal resolution first, (2) clearly outline the boundaries and standards for appropriate behavior in a formalized policy that addresses work expectations, and (3) have a signed nondisclosure privacy agreement.

Whistleblowing   An employee's free speech is protected when reporting employer public-policy violations. Employees who report such activity are called *whistleblowers,* and statutes that allow employees to report illegal activities by their employers protect them. A common area for healthcare whistleblowers is Medicare fraud and abuse. Legislation has been developed to protect whistleblowing healthcare workers from retaliation, such as discipline and termination. Under current federal legislation, employees may receive payment for reporting fraud and abuse that is verified by federal agencies. The award to the employee can be up to 10 percent of the penalty assessed against the organization.[23]

Most large healthcare organizations provide some process, such as a confidential telephone hotline number to call and bring the alleged impropriety forward within the organization before the whistleblower identifies potential issues to federal or state agencies. Employees in healthcare organizations that have internal processes are not required to use them, but they are encouraged by their employers to do so.

Technology and Employer–Employee Issues

The extensive use of technology by employers and employees is constantly creating new issues to be addressed. For example, terminating workers for openly complaining about an employer on social media has come under scrutiny based on recent court rulings. As a result of a lawsuit brought by the National Labor Relations Board, American Medical Response of Connecticut Inc. agreed to pay a settlement and modify its online communications policies for terminating an employee after she posted negative comments about her manager on Facebook. However, interpretation of the ruling suggests that it does not condone excessive disloyalty or communication of highly sensitive content.[24]

Monitoring Electronic Communications   The use of e-mail has become a major issue regarding employee and workplace privacy. Employers have good reason to monitor what is said and transmitted through their Internet and voice-mail systems, despite employees' concerns about free speech. Organizations want to reduce employee misconduct, protect organizational resources, make sure that employees are working, and follow federal guidelines.[25] Many employers have specialized software that can retrieve deleted electronic communications and e-mail, and some even record each keystroke made on their computers. Many healthcare organizations have even developed statements on computer screen savers to remind employees about appropriate and inappropriate computer use.

Employees have varying opinions about electronic monitoring based on different situational factors, which can present many challenges. For example, a recent study found that individuals were more accepting of electronic monitoring in companies than in universities.[26] Another study determined that increased e-mail monitoring resulted in privacy concerns among employees, which could harm relationships in the workplace.[27] Organizations need to consider such issues when developing policies regarding the monitoring of electronic communications.

HR Policies on Electronic Communications   Given all the time and effort healthcare workers spend with technology through both work and personal activities, it is important for HR professionals to provide guidance to executives, managers, and employees. Many employers have developed and disseminated electronic communications policies. Figure 10-8 depicts recommended employer actions for such policies including monitoring. These policies should describe to employees why monitoring is needed, the methods used, and the amount of monitoring planned. Employees should also sign off indicating that they understand their purpose and scope. Inappropriate communication and material should be clearly discussed, and individuals should receive guidance about the company's standards for using communication systems to send and receive private messages. With regard to the implementation of procedures, employers should monitor just enough to be prudent, and audits can be conducted to determine if policies are being enforced.[28]

FIGURE 10-8   Recommended Employer Actions Regarding Electronic Communications

1. Develop an Electronic Communications Policy

2. Communicate the Policy to Employees

3. Obtain Signed Permission from Employees

4. Monitor for Business Purposes Only

5. Enforce the Policy through Disciplinary Procedures

Employers' efforts can also guard against employees' accessing pornographic or other websites that could create problems for the employer. If law enforcement investigations find evidence of such access, the employer could be accused of aiding and abetting illegal behavior. Many employers have purchased software that tracks the websites accessed by employees, and some employers use software programs to block certain websites that are inappropriate for business use.

Honesty in the Workplace

One of the most significant problems facing employers is theft by employees. All theft is serious, but in healthcare organizations drug theft is particularly disconcerting. Drug theft can occur when drugs are taken from the drug inventory; however, a more serious violation occurs when staff divert drugs from patients for their own use.

Most healthcare employers use background checks to screen new employees and deny employment to individuals convicted of drug-related crimes. In addition, managers, security personnel, and pharmacy staff should cooperatively develop a plan to prevent the theft of drugs, especially narcotics. Elaborate systems, including inventory checks after each shift, have reduced theft of drugs from supply cabinets, but diverting patients' medications is more difficult to discover.[29]

Surveillance An employer is allowed to search an employee's work area if a manager has legitimate business reasons for doing so, such as suspicion of theft or illegal activities. Employees are not protected from monitoring and searches if there is reason to believe they are engaged in activities that violate the employer's work rules.

Employer Investigations Healthcare employers have typically conducted investigations when employees were suspected of theft; however, healthcare employers are now concerned about a variety of issues including illegal drug use, workplace violence, and workers' compensation fraud. Investigations are conducted by security personnel when the organization is large enough to have a security department. In other cases, managers or HR professionals investigate employees' activities. It is important to conduct thorough inquiries to avoid concerns about improper or incomplete investigations, which could result in misleading information about a particular incident or issue.

An organization can develop rules that facilitate investigations. Some examples of these rules follow: Have at least one witness present when confronting an employee. Do not touch or restrain the employee. Inform the employee that he or she is free to leave the meeting at any time. Have at least one witness of the same gender present to avoid harassment claims. If the employee refuses to respond or participate, make clear that such behavior is insubordination and that disciplinary action will be taken if the incident warrants it. Figure 10-9 illustrates various forms of investigations.

FIGURE 10-9   Various Forms of Workplace Investigations

Since some of the more common reasons for investigations in healthcare settings include the illegal use of or theft of drugs, patient mistreatment, or other behavior that reflects on professional competency, some of the issues investigated by healthcare managers need to be reported to law enforcement and agencies that license healthcare professionals.[30]

Off-the-Job Behavior

Employers are reluctant to monitor employees' off-the-job behaviors unless the activities have definite job-related consequences. For example, a healthcare employer would want to know if an employee will miss work because he or she is incarcerated, particularly if the employee is in the final stages of progressive discipline for attendance problems. However, the situation becomes more complex if the employee is jailed for public intoxication during chemical dependency rehabilitation.

Healthcare employers are typically not concerned about their employees' off-the-job behaviors unless the behaviors disrupt the work environment and jeopardize patient care—the employer must then take action. Some organizations establish employee assistance programs to help employees with on- and off-the-job behaviors that threaten their jobs. Employee assistance programs provide counseling and other help to employees who have emotional, physical, or personal problems.

Employer Drug Testing

Healthcare organizations have shown leadership in designing policies and practices to provide a drug-free workplace. These policies are consistent with the **Drug-Free Workplace Act of 1988**, whose purpose is to make workplaces safe, healthy, and efficient for employees, patients, and visitors.[31] Policy violations in healthcare organizations may include unlawful possession, use, distribution, or manufacture of a controlled substance at the facility or on facility grounds. Policy statements prohibit employees from arriving at work under the influence of drugs, including alcohol. Many healthcare organizations have adopted drug-testing policies that help to ensure that the workplace is free from drug use, including conducting testing for drugs during preemployment screening. Most healthcare organizations will withdraw conditional job offers to candidates who fail the test. Other drug testing may occur "for cause," randomly, or after an injury or incident.

HR Policies, Procedures, and Rules

All organizations have policies, procedures, and rules that govern their employee relationships program. In many organizations these documents are recorded and organized into an employee handbook or HR policy and procedure manual. The employee handbook could be a stand-alone source of policies and procedures for smaller healthcare organizations, or a condensed version of the HR policy and procedure manual for larger employers. See Figure 10-10 for an example of an employee handbook table of contents. There are differences between policies, procedures, and rules, which can be described as follows:

- Policies are general statements about the organization's position on an issue and are used to guide management decision making.
- Procedures define the customary way an organization deals with an issue.
- Rules define expected behaviors of employees at work.

Coordinating Policies and Procedures

Coordinating, implementing, and using policies regarding employees in healthcare organizations is an important HR responsibility. Effective policies, when interpreted consistently and applied uniformly, may protect

FIGURE 10-10 Employee Handbook Table of Contents

SURGICAL ASSOCIATES
EMPLOYEE HANDBOOK
TABLE OF CONTENTS

© 2016 Cengage Learning®

organizations from lawsuits and complaints. Agencies and review bodies that monitor and periodically review policies in the healthcare industry include state departments of health, the federal Health Care Financing Administration, and the Joint Commission on Accreditation of Healthcare Organizations (JCAHO).

Several steps assure successful development and implementation of policies and procedures. The process includes identifying the need for a policy, developing a draft, formally reviewing the draft with the organizational leadership team, outside legal counsel/HR consultant's review, distributing the policy, training the management group to use the policy for its intended purpose, and implementing the policy.

Policies are usually drafted in a standard format and contain a policy statement with procedures and definitions. Cross-referencing policies helps managers who want additional or related information. HR practitioners usually provide consultative resources to managers regarding interpretation and implementation.

Communicating HR Information

Keeping the lines of communication open between management and employees is very important, especially when the organization has made important decisions, such as adding new services or building new facilities. Communicating HR information is equally important to employees. Healthcare employers want workers to know about HR changes, such as training and development opportunities, benefit enrollment information, and new rules, among many others.

HR communication focuses on the receipt and dissemination of HR data and information throughout the organization. *Downward communication* flows from senior management to the rest of the organization, informing employees about what is and will be happening in the organization and what are the expectations and goals of top management.[32] *Upward communication* enables managers to know about the ideas, concerns, and information needs of employees. Various methods are used to facilitate both types of communication.

Organizations communicate with employees through internal publications and media, including company newspapers and magazines, organizational newsletters, videotapes, Internet and intranet postings, and e-mail announcements. Whatever the means used, managers should continually make efforts to communicate information employees need to know. The spread of electronic communications allows for more timely and widespread dissemination of HR information.

One form of upward communication is a *suggestion system.* This program encourages employees to offer ideas that might improve the organization and its operations. Suggestion systems often include recognition and financial rewards to employees who provide cost-saving or process-improvement ideas.

EMPLOYEE DISCIPLINE

Following established HR policies, procedures, and regulations, and maintaining high-quality job performance are required for organizations to deliver excellent products and services.[33] Healthcare organizations develop discipline systems to help employees meet their job responsibilities, improve their performance, and establish successful employee–employer working relationships.

Although they usually represent a small number, problem employees can be disruptive to the work environment, and their performance must be dealt with in a timely manner. In these cases, management provides training and feedback to employees, with the expectation that their behaviors and performance will improve. Typical discipline issues include absenteeism, tardiness, interpersonal issues, insubordination, inability to meet job standards, and low productivity.

Nonproductive Reasons for Not Using Discipline

Managers may be reluctant to use discipline for a variety of reasons. The most common reasons for not using discipline include fear of lawsuits, lack of support from the organization, fear of retaliation from employees, fear of not being liked by employees, guilt, loss of friendship, and the loss of time and energy to manage the discipline process. To counter these reasons, healthcare organizations should train supervisors and managers about the effective and fair use of discipline.

Productive Reasons for Not Using Discipline

A recent trend in healthcare relative to employee discipline, especially relating to clinical settings, is the concept of establishing a nonpunitive approach to managing clinical mistakes to ensure that staff can identify and understand errors in practice. Historically, when clinical mistakes have been made a typical response would have been to discipline the employee responsible for the error. However, by learning from these errors, practitioners can improve their skills, thereby improving the quality of the care they provide. Consequently, many healthcare employers carefully analyze the nature of the mistake made by a clinical employee and consider alternatives to discipline such as retraining, reassignment, or nondiscipline coaching if the situation warrants it.[34]

Training Managers

Management training and coaching should be designed to include the importance of discipline, including treating employees with respect and dignity. Building supervisory skills to facilitate discussions and to counsel employees is

HEALTHCARE REFORM AND HR PRACTICES

The management of employed and contracted physicians by hospitals and large medical systems is a relatively new phenomenon in the U.S. healthcare system. Historically, the great percentage of physicians were and are partners or salaried employees under contractual agreements—working in group practices, freestanding ambulatory care clinics, diagnostic centers, or managed care organizations.[35] However, with the advent of healthcare reform, there are many more integrated hospital–physician arrangements designed to create a more seamless and aligned delivery of care with the goals of improving quality and reducing costs.[36]

Throughout the United States, new hospital–physician structures are being established, including the acquisition by hospitals of private physician practices, and the employment of primary care and specialist physicians under various compensated (employed) relationships. For many healthcare organizations, this is new ground because establishing an employed relationship with physicians is different from the employed relationship with other healthcare workers, such as RNs or social workers. Physicians, by the nature of their practice, have a unique influence on the healthcare workplace. As an example, even though they may not have a supervisory title they still direct others in providing care, and often some part of their compensation is based on "clinical" management responsibilities.

To be effective healthcare HR professionals must approach the development and implementation of a physician employee relations program very differently than the employee relations program for nonphysician employees. Although such elements of the organizational employee relations program such as HR policies and codes of conduct must be the same, other elements are different. Chief among them would be how to effectively communicate with employed physicians and how to manage, evaluate, and discipline programs for physicians. As more physicians become employed by larger healthcare providers, the physician relationship challenges and opportunities will continue to increase.

especially important. Performance discussions should provide positive assistance so that employees can improve their job performance.[37]

To determine when to use the discipline process, managers must evaluate each issue on a case-by-case basis to determine which type of discipline to administer. When the issue is easily resolved, no disciplinary action may be necessary.

FIGURE 10-11 **Progressive Discipline Process**

Counseling

First Offense — Verbal Warning

Second Offense — Written Warning

Third Offense — Suspension

Fourth Offense — Discharge

© Cengage Learning®

A common employee discipline process is called **progressive discipline**, which utilizes a series of identifiable steps to communicate concerns to employees. Each step is separate and distinct and is designed to warn the employee to change his or her work performance or behavior or further discipline will occur. Figure 10-11 depicts a typical progressive discipline system.

Counseling   The goal of this step is to tell the employee what job expectations are not being met and talk about how to make improvements in performance. The employee may be unaware of a problem; therefore, counseling by the manager should be positive and encouraging. As an example, if a laboratory technician fails to follow appropriate safety guidelines in the laboratory, counseling from the manager may be needed.

Verbal Caution   The second step is a verbal caution, which represents an escalation in the process. If the employee has not improved work performance, the manager then issues a verbal warning. The goal of this step is to point out behavior or performance deficiencies and explain the importance of improvement in these areas. In this step, the manager decides whether to require any additional training to help the employee meet expectations. In the laboratory technician example, the manager might initiate a verbal caution and require the technician to review and discuss the safety guidelines for the laboratory.

Written Reprimand   If the employee does not improve performance or behavior, the manager can conduct another conference in which job expectations are outlined and documented in writing. Additional resources including training may be offered to help the employee achieve the expected performance results. This step is a warning that performance or behavior needs to improve to avoid the next step in the disciplinary process. If, as noted in the previous example, the technician continues to disregard safety guidelines, the manager would give a written warning, clearly stating the reason for discipline, the steps that must be taken to improve, and the consequences if disregard for safety procedures continues. Specifically, if disregard for safety procedure continues, the technician could be suspended and then ultimately discharged.

Suspension   An employee will be suspended if performance or behavior still has not improved. The length of the suspension depends on the severity of the performance deficiency. This step is critical for the employee because the next step is final—discharge.

Discharge   When an employee cannot or will not perform satisfactorily, termination may be necessary. The final stage in the discipline process must be managed very carefully. This stage is used when an employee's performance is so below standard or behavior is so egregious that termination is appropriate and consistent with the progressive discipline process. Except in certain situations, employees have received warnings so the discharge should not be a surprise. The manager should clearly define why the employee is being discharged. The discharge meeting should be carefully planned and is often attended by an HR representative. All wage and benefit information should be communicated in writing in the event the employee does not remember all of the discussion. It is important to end the meeting and help the employee exit the workplace in a dignified way.

Separation Agreements   In some termination situations, formal contracts may be used. One type is a **separation agreement**, in which an employee who is being terminated agrees not to sue the employer in exchange for specified benefits, such as additional severance pay or other "considerations."

For such agreements to be legally enforceable, the financial considerations should usually be additional items, not part of normal termination benefits. When using separation agreements, care must be taken to avoid the appearance of constructive discharge of employees. Use of such agreements should be reviewed by a legal counsel.

EMPLOYEE RELATIONS PROGRAMS

In addition to all of the policies, procedures, rights and responsibilities, and discipline procedures, most organizations strive to affect their employees positively by using innovative strategies. Some of the more common programs follow.

Employee Assistance Programs

Organizations provide employee assistance programs (EAPs) to help their employees cope with personal life management issues that affect their work. Initially, the most common use of EAPs was to deal with drug and alcohol abuse, but EAPs have been extended to include legal, financial, marital, and interpersonal issues. The services may be offered two ways: through internal programs staffed by company employees, or by an outside service. EAP programs, whether offered internally or externally, are designed to help employees with problems that may affect their productivity. EAP counselors must be qualified to treat a wide variety of employee issues and problems.

Employer of Choice Programs

Organizations interested in becoming an "employer of choice" (EOC) must redefine their HR practices to clearly demonstrate their commitment to their employees.[38] A successful employer of choice philosophy requires a plan with the following components:

- Long-term top management commitment to becoming an EOC
- Defined organizational purpose
- Innovative and competitive compensation and benefit programs
- Staff development opportunities
- Rewards for innovation and creativity
- Rewards aligned with performance
- Culture that respects diversity encourages staff participation, and rewards employee and organizational success.[39]

Standards of Behavior

Another popular method to improve organization–employee relationships is to develop a series of expectations the organization has for all employees. Standards of behavior, especially revolving around patient satisfaction initiatives, have become popular as a means to clearly identify behavioral expectations. The standards may include the following expectations:

- Respect
- Excellence
- Cooperation
- Compassion
- Communication
- Fairness and equity
- Self-care
- Personal accountability

Standards are usually developed and aligned to organizational values that are communicated continuously. The standards should define how the expectations affect employees on a daily basis.[40]

CASE

Carol County Hospital (CCH) is a private, not-for-profit acute-care hospital located in a medium-sized market. It is a 75-year-old corporation, offering full-service care, including general medical, emergency, and general surgical, with special emphasis on oncology, cardiac, obstetrical, and rehabilitation treatment and care. The following table summarizes CCH's employee relations indicators, which can be used to assess how well the organization manages its interactions with staff members.

	2012	2013	2014	COMPARATIVE DATA
EMPLOYEE RELATIONS INDICATORS				
Turnover rate	14%	22%	26%	12%
Absence rate	5%	7%	12%	10%
Vacancy rate	8%	18%	20%	10%
Discrimination charges	2	8	12	n/a
OSHA complaints	2	12	14	n/a
EMPLOYEE ASSISTANCE REFERRALS				
Drug/alcohol	60	75	100	70
Career stress	30	35	50	30
Other	20	30	20	50
Totals	110	140	170	150

Questions

1. Assess CCH's employee relations program. What statistics have you considered in your assessment?

2. What HR metrics are important to consider in assessing any (potential) employee relations issues?

END NOTES

1. See *http://www.eeoc.gov/laws/statutes/epa_ledbetter.cfm* for more information.

2. C. Sahoo and S. Mishra, "A Framework towards Employee Engagement: The PSU Experience," *ASCI Journal of Management* (September 2012), 94–112.

3. C. Comaford, "The Value of Valuing Employees," *Health Care Registration: The Newsletter for Health Care Registration Professionals* (August 2013), 7–9.

4. See *http://www.hhs.gov/ocr/privacy/* for more information.

5. See *https://www.aapa.org/the_pa_profession/federal_and_state_affairs/resources/item.aspx?id=755* for more information.

6. G. Chambers, "Get It All in Writing Contract," *Employers Law* (November 2013),18–19.

7. J. Koen and J. Reinhardt, "Employment Contracts: Preventative Medicine for Post-Termination Suits, *Supervision* (April 2013), 10–14.

8. "Proactive Strategies Play Big Role in Keeping Top Talent in Mergers," *Public Accounting Report* (March 2013), 1–7.

9. J. Elegido, " Does It Make Sense to Be a Loyal Employee?," *Journal of Business Ethics* (September 2013), 495–511.

10. C. Meyer III, "The Case for Employment Practices Liability Insurance," *Employee Relations Law Journal* (Fall 2012), 54–58.

11. M. Zachary, "Employment at Will and Public Policy," *Supervision* (November 2012), 21–25.

12. M. Harcourt et al., "Employment at Will versus Just Cause Dismissal: Applying the Due Process Model of Procedural Justice," *Labor Law Journal* (Summer, 2013), 67–85.

13. See *http://www.healthit.gov/buzz-blog/privacy-and-security-of-ehrs/privacy-security-electronic-health-records/* for more information.

14. As an example, the state of Minnesota requires employers to provide a letter disclosing the reason for discharge within five days of the written request of a terminated employee—"Notice of Termination Statute," M.S.A. 181.932.

15. J. Plumstead, "Dodging a Disagreement," *Employers Law* (March 2011), 18–19.

16. Donna Maria Blancero, Robert G. DelCampo, and George F. Marron, "Just Tell Me! Making Alternative Dispute Resolution Systems Fair," *Industrial Relations* 49 (2010), 524–542.

17. Ibid.

18. Michael Delikat, "Arbitrating Workplace Disputes," *Human Resource Executive Online* (June 16, 2010), *http://www.hreonline.com.*

19. Jim Hanley, "Transformative Mediation," *HR Magazine* (April 2010), 64–65.

20. *See https://www.dir.ca.gov/dlse/FAQ_RightToInspectPersonnelFiles.htm* for more information.

21. D. Zielinski, "HRIS Features Get More Strategic," *HR Magazine* (December 2011), 15.

22. For details on the retention of employee records and documents, go to *http://www.hrcompliance.ceridian.com.*

23. See *http://www.medicare.gov/forms-help-and-resources/report-fraud-and-abuse/report-fraud/reporting-fraud.html* for more information.

24. Sam Hananel, "Facebook: Protected Speech," *Denver Post* (February 8, 2011), 7B.

25. William P. Smith and Filiz Tabak, "Monitoring Employee E-mails: Is There Any Room for Privacy?," *Academy of Management Perspectives* 23 (2009), 33–48.

26. Frances S. Grodzinsky, Andra Gumbus, and Stephen Lilley, "Ethical Implications of Internet Monitoring: A Comparative Study," *Information Systems Frontiers* 12 (2010), 433–441.

27. Jason L. Snyder, "E-mail Privacy in the Workplace," *Journal of Business Communication* 47 (2010), 266–294.

28. Ibid.

29. R. Vrabel, "Identifying and Dealing with Drug Diversion," *Health Management Technology* (December 2010), 1–5.

30. See *https://www.ncsbn.org/Nursing_Licensure.pdf* for more information about RN license issues.

31. See *http://www.dol.gov/elaws/asp/drugfree/require.htm for more information.*

32. C. Galunic and I. Hermreck, "How to Help Employees 'Get' Strategy," *Harvard Business Review* (December 2012), 24.

33. D. Sofranec, "Prevent Toxic Employees from Poisoning Your Practice," *Medical Economics* (December 25, 2012), 28–33.

34. M. Brady, "How to Improve Patient Care by Learning from Mistakes," *Emergency Nurse* (February 2013), 32–35.

35. Leiyu Shi and Douglas A. Singh, *Essentials of the U.S. Health Care System*, 3rd ed. (Jones and Bartlett Learning: Burlington, MA: 2013), 82.

36. James J. Pizzo and Mark E. Grube, "Keys to Lasting Partnerships," *Trustee* (July/August 2011), 23–26.

37. Rick Contel, "Performance-Based Coaching," *Chief Learning Officer* (December 2012), 18–22.

38. R. Hosking, "Making Your Company an Employer of Choice," *Officepro* (October 2011), 3.

39. Adapted from Henry Jackson, "Becoming Employers of Choice," *HR Magazine* (March 2014), 10 and "Becoming an Employer of Choice from the Inside Out," *Public Relations Tactics* (May 2013), 13.

40. K. Baird and A. Kirby, "Engaging Leaders in the Patient Experience," *Healthcare Executive* (January 2014), 62–65.

Chapter

11

LABOR RELATIONS AND HEALTHCARE ORGANIZATIONS

Learning Objectives

After you have read this chapter, you should be able to:

- Explain the labor relations challenges facing the healthcare industry.
- Describe the National Labor Relations Act, including the unique healthcare provisions.
- Outline the stages of the unionization process.
- Discuss the collective bargaining process.
- Identify the contract negotiations process in the healthcare industry.

HEALTHCARE HR INSIGHTS

In 1967 the National Labor Relations Board (NLRB) first recognized the right of healthcare workers to organize and participate in collective bargaining with their employers.[1] In 1974, Congress amended the National Labor Relations Act (NLRA) to cover both for-profit and nonprofit healthcare organizations under the provisions and restrictions of the act.[2] Since the amendment to the NLRA, unions and healthcare employers have had an interesting history, ranging from significant animosity between them to collaborative partnerships.

An example of a confrontational relationship between a healthcare organization and a union is one that exists between Beth Israel Deaconess Medical Center located in Boston, Massachusetts, and 1199 Service Employees International Union (SEIU). 1199SEIU established a website called Eye on B.I., the expressed purpose of which is to conduct a very public information campaign designed to embarrass and discredit the hospital in the eyes of the community it serves. The topics discussed on the Eye on B.I. website include patient problems, financial discrepancies, and board member conflicts of interest.[3]

An area where unions and healthcare employers have worked well together is in that of workplace safety. Both sides typically share common objectives in protecting workers from injury, exposure to infectious disease, or death due to unsafe working conditions. An example of a partnering relationship involved the workplace death of a psychiatric technician at Napa State Hospital in California at the hands of a patient. Shortly after the tragedy occurred, six separate unions representing hospital workers worked closely with management to form an alliance around the issue of safety, calling it the Safety Now Coalition. The Coalition is focused on securing an alarm system for the facility. Thanks to their efforts, a personal-distress alarm system was designed, and the hospital's 2,000-plus staff members now wear the device. If they experience a crisis with a patient or a personal health emergency, they can pull a switch and immediately alert others at the facility to their identity and exact location.[4] According to the unions, other safety issues continue to exist, but the personal-distress alarm system is seen as a positive step to improving worker safety.

A union is a formal association of workers that promotes its members' interests through collective bargaining. It is the official employee representative, and it executes its responsibilities by negotiating labor contracts and administering the contracts until they expire.

According to the Bureau of Labor Statistics, during the most recent reporting period the **union membership rate**—the percentage of wage and salary workers who were members of unions—was 11.3 percent. The number of wage and salary workers belonging to unions is 14.5 million. In 1983, the first year for which comparable union data are available, the union membership rate was 20.1 percent, and there were 17.7 million union workers.

Public-sector workers had a union membership rate more than five times higher than that of private-sector workers. Workers in education, training, and library occupations and in protective service occupations have the highest unionization rate for each occupation group. Men have a higher union membership rate than women. Black workers are more likely to be union members than white, Asian, or Hispanic workers.[5]

UNIONS IN THE HEALTHCARE INDUSTRY

As indicated above, union membership has been on the decline in the United States. However, union membership is on the increase in healthcare. Specifically, registered nurses and other nonphysician occupations are fueling the growth trend.[6] Union activity in healthcare has been heavily concentrated in metropolitan areas and on the east and west coasts of the United States. Also, unions tend to be more successful in northern states—in part, because these areas have a long history of unionism.

Increased unionism in the future of healthcare seems likely. Service workers in healthcare organizations are seeking union protection, and local nurses' unions are merging with larger national unions to enhance their protection. Unions that typically have not represented healthcare workers are making organizing attempts as they see opportunities in healthcare. Even physicians are forming unions to negotiate their compensation through collective bargaining agreements.

Why Employees Unionize

Generally, healthcare employees seek union assistance because they believe that their employers have not treated them respectfully, and they believe a union can negotiate better financial benefits, job security, and working conditions. Financial concerns may cause employers to find ways to deliver care more cost effectively, but some of the new systems result in lower staffing ratios, which may affect quality of patient care. Employees involved in patient care professions have worried about changes in staff-to-patient ratios and have asked unions to represent them and negotiate staffing ratios with their employers.[7]

The process of unionizing a healthcare employee group can be initiated by either employees or union organizers. The union assesses the potential for success before it commits union resources to a costly organizing campaign. Once the union decides there is potential interest by a group of employees, representatives begin the campaign.

In large part, unions continued relevance in the healthcare industry is due to the financial pressures on healthcare organizations. Declining reimbursements and the increase of uninsured patients have led to financial cutbacks in programs and staff. Healthcare jobs are continually at risk due to these pressures. Healthcare workers frequently feel powerless to protect their jobs and do not believe that management values them. Consequently, they may seek union representation to give a more powerful voice to their concerns. Figure 11-1 depicts why healthcare workers may consider union representation.[8]

FIGURE 11-1   **Healthcare Workers' Reasons for Seeking Union Representation**

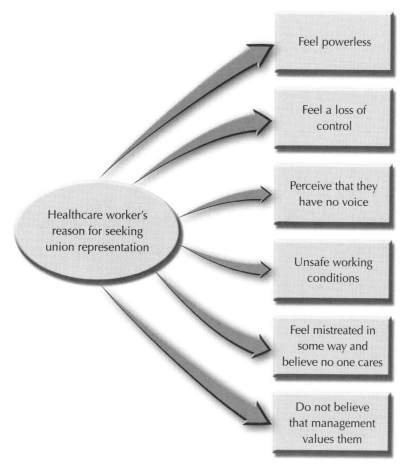

The risk of unionization decreases significantly when a healthcare organization is transparent in its employee communication program and adopts positive policies and supportive HR practices.[9] Healthcare workers want to be informed, respected, and included in decision making. Also, they want to participate in care decisions for patients.

Why Employers Resist Unions

Most nonunion healthcare organizations would rather not have to negotiate with unions because they affect how employees and workplaces are managed. Unions are criticized for creating inefficiencies at work that cause waste and poor performance.[10]

Union workers frequently get compensated better than do nonunion workers, but on the flip side, higher pay and benefits might be related to higher job performance. Despite this higher productivity, managers still try to identify labor-saving ways of doing work to offset increased expenses.

Regardless of how leaders of nonunion healthcare organizations view unions, they should be careful in how they handle their employees when a union initiates a union campaign. Treating employees who are interested in organizing in an aggressive or hostile manner can result in significant negative consequences for the organization.

Human Resource Professionals and Unionization   To prevent unionization, as well as to work effectively with unions already representing employees, both HR professionals and operating managers must be attentive and responsive to employees. The pattern of dealing with unionization varies among organizations. In some firms, management handles labor relations and HR has limited involvement. In other organizations, the HR unit takes primary responsibility for resisting unionization or dealing with unionized employees.[12]

Labor-Relations Philosophy

Once established, some employers pursue a strategy of good relations with unions, while others choose an aggressive, adversarial approach.[13] A healthcare organization's philosophy of labor relations reflects a strategic decision whether to have a relationship that is adversarial, collaborative, or somewhere between the two. Upper management must support the philosophy, middle management must agree to implement the intent of the philosophy, and supervisors should be trained to deal effectively with employees and unions, whether the philosophy is adversarial, collaborative, or somewhere in between.

Adversarial Relationships

Traditionally, the relationships between healthcare organizations and unions have been adversarial, an atmosphere in which both parties try to control the process and relationship by winning beneficial contracts for the organization or the workers. Decisions made in adversarial relationships are usually not favorable for long-term relationships, especially when one party perceives that it is continually compromising to maintain the relationship. Both parties are suspicious and may use information and communication selectively to gain a negotiating advantage. The organization controls the economics, while the union has the power to call a strike when a satisfactory agreement is not reached.

Collaborative Relationships

In some unionized healthcare organizations, a philosophy emerges that supports collaborative relationships. The goal of these nonadversarial relationships of shared responsibility is to address the mutual interests and issues of both sides. They openly share information and make decisions in a collaborative manner.

A fundamental belief is that decisions made by consensus are more robust than decisions resulting from compromise.

LEGAL FRAMEWORK FOR UNION–MANAGEMENT RELATIONS

Three acts, passed over a period of years, constitute the framework for union–management relations: (1) the Wagner Act, (2) the Taft-Hartley Act, and (3) the Landrum-Griffin Act. Each act was passed to focus on some facet of the relations between unions and management. Figure 11-2 indicates the primary focus of each act.

Wagner Act (National Labor Relations Act)

The National Labor Relations Act, more commonly referred to as the Wagner Act, has been called the Magna Carta of labor and was, by anyone's standards, prounion. Passed in 1935, the Wagner Act was an outgrowth of the Great Depression. With employers having to close or cut back their operations, workers were left with little job security. Unions stepped in to provide a feeling of solidarity and strength for many workers. The Wagner Act declared, in effect, that the official policy of the U.S. government was to encourage collective bargaining. Specifically, it established the right of workers to organize, unhampered by management interference, through unfair labor practices.

National Labor Relations Board The Wagner Act established the National Labor Relations Board as an independent entity to enforce the provisions of the act. The NLRB administers all provisions of the Wagner Act and of subsequent labor relations acts. The primary functions of the NLRB include conducting unionization elections, investigating complaints by employers or unions through its fact-finding process, issuing opinions on its findings, and prosecuting violations in court. The five members of the NLRB are appointed by the president of the United States and confirmed by the U.S. Senate.

FIGURE 11-2 Legal Framework for Union–Management Relations

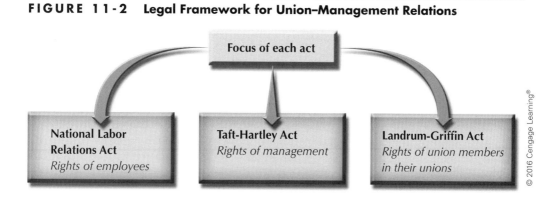

© 2016 Cengage Learning®

Taft-Hartley Act (Labor Management Relations Act)

The passage in 1947 of the Labor Management Relations Act, better known as the Taft-Hartley Act, was accomplished as a means to offset the prounion Wagner Act by limiting union actions. It was considered to be promanagement and became the second of the major labor laws.

The new law amended or qualified in some respect all the major provisions of the Wagner Act and established an entirely new code of conduct for unions. The Taft-Hartley Act forbade unions from engaging in a series of unfair labor practices, much like those prohibitions on management behavior. Coercion, discrimination against nonmembers, refusing to bargain, excessive membership fees, and other practices were not allowed by unions. A 1974 amendment extended coverage of the Taft-Hartley Act to private, nonprofit hospitals and nursing homes.

The Taft-Hartley Act also established the Federal Mediation and Conciliation Service (FMCS) as an agency to help management and labor settle labor contract disputes. The act required that the FMCS be notified of disputes over contract renewals or modifications if they were not settled within 30 days after the designated date.

National Emergency Strikes   The Taft-Hartley Act allows the president of the United States to declare that a strike presents a national emergency. A national emergency strike is one that would impact an industry or a major part of it in such a way that the national economy would be significantly affected. The act allows the U.S. president to declare an 80-day cooling-off period during which union and management continue negotiations. Only after that period can a strike occur if settlements have not been reached.

Right-to-Work Provision   One provision of the Taft-Hartley Act, section 14(b), deserves special explanation. This section allows states to pass laws that restrict compulsory union membership. Accordingly, several states have passed **right-to-work laws**, which prohibit requiring employees to join unions as a condition of obtaining or continuing employment. The laws were so named because they allow a person the right to work without having to join a union.

In states with right-to-work laws, employers may have an **open shop**, which indicates workers cannot be required to join or pay dues to a union. Thus, even though a union may represent a group of employees at an organization, individual workers cannot be required or coerced to join the union or pay dues. Consequently, in many of the right-to-work states, individual membership in union groups is significantly lower.

The nature of union–management relations is affected by the right-to-work provisions of the Taft-Hartley Act. Right to work generally prohibits the **closed shop**, which requires individuals to join a union before they can be hired. Because of concerns that a closed shop allows a union to control who may be considered for employment and who must be hired by an employer, section 14(b) prohibits the closed shop except in construction-related occupations.

In states that do not have right-to-work laws, different types of arrangements exist. Three different types of "shops" are as follows:

- *Union Shop*—Arrangement requires that individuals join the union, usually 30 to 60 days after being hired.
- *Agency Shop*—Arrangement requires workers who do not join the union to make payments equal to union dues and fees to get union representation services.
- *Maintenance-of-Membership Shop*—Arrangement requires workers to remain members of the union for the period of the labor contract.

The nature of the shop is negotiated between the union and the employer. Employees who fail to meet the requirements are often terminated from their jobs.

Landrum-Griffin Act (Labor Management Reporting and Disclosure Act)

The third of the major labor laws in the United States, the Landrum-Griffin Act, was passed in 1959. Since a union is supposed to be a democratic institution in which union members freely vote, elect officers, and approve labor contracts, the Landrum-Griffin Act was passed in part to ensure that the federal government protects the democratic rights of the members. Under the Landrum-Griffin Act, unions are required to establish bylaws, make financial reports, and provide union members with a bill of rights. The law appointed the U.S. secretary of labor to act as a watchdog of union conduct.

There is a need for such legislative oversight to protect individual union members. For instance, in some situations union officers have been known to physically harass individuals who did not like them. In other cases, officials have seized union resources and used them for their own personal gain.

Civil Service Reform and Postal Reorganization Acts

Passed as part of the Civil Service Reform Act of 1978, the Federal Service Labor Management Relations statute made major changes in how the federal government deals with unions. The act also identified areas subject to bargaining and established the Federal Labor Relations Authority (FLRA) as an independent agency similar to the NLRB. The FLRA, a three-member body, was given the authority to oversee and administer union–management relations in the federal government and investigate unfair practices in union organizing efforts.

In a somewhat related area, the Postal Reorganization Act of 1970 established the U.S. Postal Service as an independent entity. Part of the 1970 act prohibited postal workers from striking and established a dispute resolution process for them to follow.

Proposed Employee Free Choice Act

The proposed Employee Free Choice Act would allow unions to sign up workers on cards (referred to as "card check") and become recognized without an election by secret ballot.[14] As a result, the "campaigns" to organize, which unions dislike, would be eliminated because simply getting 50 percent of the workers in a unit to sign a card would be sufficient to bring in the union.[15] Further, the proposed law would require a contract to be negotiated within a certain time period or one could be imposed by an arbitrator.[16] Employers take issue with this approach because it goes against the U.S. tradition in which negotiated contracts must be agreed to by both parties.

NLRA and the Healthcare Industry

As noted in the Healthcare HR Insights, prior to 1974 the healthcare industry was not covered by the NLRA. In Congress, lawmakers were concerned that if healthcare workers were allowed to organize, there could be a disruption in vital healthcare services.

During the 1960s and early 1970s, the healthcare industry was growing rapidly, and union leaders saw an opportunity to recruit a large number of members, many of whom believed their wage and benefits programs were not competitive. In 1974 Congress repealed the clause that had exempted the healthcare industry from employee unionization. However, lawmakers added several provisions to the NLRA that would protect communities in case of union strikes during contract negotiations. Important provisions in the law include a 10-day strike notice and a requirement to use federal and state mediation services.

10-Day Strike Notice   One of the provisions passed in 1974 required unions to give a notice of 10 days of their intent to strike. In most cases, the 10-day notice coincides with the contract expiration. If a union fails to give the 10-day notice to the employer, the NLRB is not required to protect striking workers, leaving healthcare employers the option of hiring permanent replacement workers and terminating the illegally striking employees.

Although this provision was created to provide healthcare organizations with some warning about an impending strike, most healthcare organizations begin planning well in advance. The 10-day notice is built into negotiation work plans and is usually coordinated with the contract ratification vote. If the members reject the contract and vote to strike, the 10-day notice is issued. However, the 10-day strike notice requirement is frequently a disputed issue as a strike looms for a healthcare organization. As an example, a clinic terminated some of its striking nurses in the belief that the union did not act in accordance with the 10-day strike notice requirement. However, the nurses were subsequently reinstated when the union appealed the decision.[17]

Negotiation Notification   The act also requires healthcare employers and unions to inform the FMCS of the parties' intent to begin negotiations 90 days before the contract expires. The notification process allows the mediation service to assign a mediator to the negotiations and offer any training the negotiating parties might need.

Impasse   Another provision in the act helps to expedite the negotiating process when an **impasse** occurs. If the negotiating parties have a dispute they cannot resolve, they must report the situation to the FMCS. A mediator is assigned to facilitate a resolution. In healthcare organizations that use collaborative labor relations, a mediator is usually included in the negotiations from the initial meeting.

Strikes and the Board of Inquiry When negotiations have failed and a strike is possible, the FMCS director may appoint a **board of inquiry** to investigate, report, and recommend to the director solutions to resolve the contractual disputes. In this case, the current labor contract must be extended for 30 days while the board of inquiry completes its work. The use of a board of inquiry is a last step in the process to settle a contract dispute.

THE UNIONIZATION PROCESS IN HEALTHCARE

The process of unionizing healthcare employees has been relatively unchanged since 1974, when healthcare employees gained the right to bargain collectively. Unions typically conduct campaigns in organizations if the relationship between employees and managers has been negative. The most common way to measure the potential of a union campaign is to assess those relationships. Unionizing is frequently a vote against management rather than a vote for the union. The role of the manager in creating a positive work environment is essential for the organization that is interested in a nonunion work environment. Managers interact with employees on a daily basis and have the opportunity to build positive working relationships that negate the need for union representation. If the organization and management fail to develop proactive policies and practices and fail to practice preventive labor relations, the employees may seek representation by the union.[18]

To unionize, it must be shown that a majority of employees who are eligible to vote want union representation. A number of steps comprise the unionization process, and they are shown in Figure 11-3.

FIGURE 11-3 Union Campaign Process

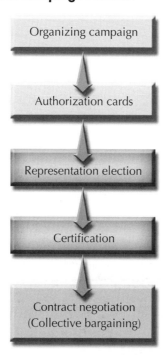

Organizing campaign

Authorization cards

Representation election

Certification

Contract negotiation
(Collective bargaining)

Organizing Campaign

Although there has been significant pressure to revise the campaign process with the passage of the Employee Free Choice Act, as well as the efforts by the National Labor Relations Board to implement the so-called quickie election rule, the campaign process is well defined.[19] The campaign to form a union usually begins when a group of employees who are dissatisfied with their employer approaches a union to seek its expertise in organizing workers into a union. Alternatively, a union may target an organization or a group of employees about their potential interest in being represented. Unions make an early determination of whether there is sufficient interest in representation before they agree to invest resources in an organizing campaign.

If a union decides interest is sufficient, it conducts informational meetings with the employees at an off-site location to share information about the union and its capabilities. The meetings, often unknown to managers, provide opportunities for employees to air concerns about their working conditions, which helps the union to assess the likelihood of a successful campaign. Union representatives also present data about wage and benefit contracts in the industry and other organizations to help convince workers that union representation will be financially beneficial for them. Typically, the union organizer will identify one to two informal leaders who are employees who have issues with or are generally unhappy with the organization to host the initial meetings. As an example, in a recent nursing home organizing attempt, the union organizer and a dietary aide who worked at the nursing home coincidentally met at their sons' Little League game. The dietary aide was complaining about her job and the nursing home, and the organizer offered the assistance of the union. The dietary aide subsequently became the access point for the union to meet with other employees and discuss their concerns and how the union could represent them.

Authorization Cards

To prove that a sufficient number of employees are interested in union representation, the NLRB requires the union to get signatures from employees on **authorization cards**. Employees who sign the authorization cards have authorized the union to seek a representation election that could formalize the union's role in negotiating labor contracts on behalf of the employee group.

When the union has signatures from at least 30 percent of the employees, it can make a formal request to the NLRB to authorize a representation election. Some unions prefer at least a 50 percent signature rate or they will not file with the NLRB. An organization will often challenge a number of the signed cards, arguing that they are not valid for a variety of reasons. If the union has more than the 30 percent of required signed cards, the invalidation of some of the cards will not halt the process from going forward. If the NLRB agrees that the union has met the 30 percent requirement, it orders an election.

Official notification to the organization occurs when the union requests an election. Management is given an opportunity to review and perhaps contest the union's request. The NLRB will hold a hearing, if necessary, to hear arguments from both sides.

Healthcare and Bargaining Units

Management often argues that the union is trying to organize a group that has not been determined to be an appropriate bargaining unit according rules developed by the NLRB in 1991. If the organization can prove that the union is not following the NLRB rules, the request for the representation election will be denied.

As the healthcare industry began to unionize, disputes occurred about the composition and number of unions. The NLRB, at the request of Congress, determined that hospitals have eight distinct employee groups that could be considered bargaining units, as depicted in Figure 11-4.[20] In all other healthcare facilities, the NLRB considers the "community of interest" and determines the bargaining unit on a case-by-case basis.[21] Employees who constitute a bargaining unit generally have mutual (community of) interests in the following areas:

- Wages, hours, and working conditions
- Physical location as well as amount of interaction and number of working relationships between employee groups
- Supervision by similar levels of management

Usually, healthcare organizations prefer fewer groups with larger numbers of employees. Unions usually are interested in smaller groups, which often lead to more successful organizing campaigns.

FIGURE 11-4   Appropriate Bargaining Units in Hospitals

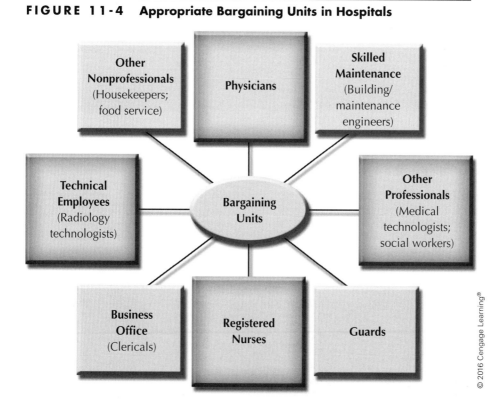

© 2016 Cengage Learning®

When management challenges a union's formation, the NLRB determines whether an employee group is part of the appropriate bargaining group. If management and the union do not agree on who is and who is not included in the unit, the regional office of the NLRB must make the determination. A major criterion in deciding the composition of a bargaining unit is what the NLRB calls a "community of interest." At a medical center where nursing assistants and orderlies work closely together and may even have interchangeable job duties, there would be every likelihood that the employees in those two jobs would be in the same bargaining unit, probably in an "other nonprofessionals" unit.

Supervisors and Bargaining Units   Provisions of the NLRA exclude supervisors from coverage when attempting to vote for or join unions. As a result, supervisors and managers in healthcare organizations cannot be included in bargaining units for unionization purposes.

But who qualifies as a supervisor is not always clear. The NLRB uses a detailed definition that identifies a supervisor as any individual with authority to hire, transfer, discharge, discipline, and use independent judgment with employees. Numerous NLRB and court decisions have been rendered on specific situations. A major case decided by the U.S. Supreme Court found that charge nurses with RN degrees were supervisors because they exercised independent judgment. This case and others have provided employers and unions with some guidance about who should be considered as a supervisor and thus excluded from bargaining units.

Unfair Labor Practices   One of the major roles of the NLRB is resolving unfair labor practices. Figure 11-5 illustrates the unfair labor practices for both management and unions that are defined in section 8(a) and 8(b) of the NLRA. Most charges of unfair labor practices are filed by unions.

It is important for organizations to avoid unfair labor practices. Accordingly, managers should receive training about unfair labor practices. A good general rule is to avoid making any promises or threats to employees during an organizing campaign.

FIGURE 11-5   Unfair Labor Practices

MANAGEMENT	UNIONS
• Interfering with, restraining, or coercing employees in the exercise of their right to organize or bargain collectively	• Interfering with, restraining, or coercing employees in the exercise of their right to organize or to bargain collectively
• Dominating or interfering with the formation or administration of any labor organization	• Causing an employer to discriminate or discourage union membership
• Encouraging or discouraging membership in any labor organization by discriminating with regard to hiring, tenure, or conditions of employment	• Refusal to bargain in good faith
	• Conducting secondary boycotts
• Discharging or otherwise discriminating against an employee because he or she filed charges or gave testimony under the Act	• Organization or recognition picketing by a union where the employer has recognized another union as the official bargaining agent
• Refusing to bargain in good faith	

© Cengage Learning®

Representation Elections

If the NLRB is satisfied that the union has received enough authorization cards and that the employees who seek representation are an appropriate bargaining unit, it orders an election, supervised by an NLRB official and representatives from both the union and management. A union election is determined by a **simple majority**—50 percent plus one—of the employees who voted on the election day.

Management and the union encourage employees to vote because the employees who vote on election day determine whether the union will be sanctioned as the official bargaining agent for all of the employees in that group. Generally, research and surveys have revealed that a higher turnout of voters usually is beneficial for management because employees with neutral feelings about the organization or the union are more likely to vote against the union. Figure 11-6 discusses the "do's" and "don'ts" for management actions during campaigns.

If the union or management thinks the election was handled improperly or unfair labor practices occurred during the election, either entity may challenge the election results. If the NLRB determines no violations occurred, it rules on the election results. If the union does not win the election, it is prohibited from conducting another organizing campaign for 12 months.

FIGURE 11-6 Do's and Don't's

DO (LEGAL)	DON'T (ILLEGAL)
• Tell employees about current wages and benefits and how they compare with those in other firms • Tell employees that the employer opposes unionization • Tell employees the disadvantages of having a union (especially cost of dues, assessments, and requirements of membership) • Show employees articles about unions and relate negative experiences elsewhere • Explain the unionization process to employees accurately • Forbid distribution of union literature during work hours in work areas • Enforce disciplinary policies and rules consistently and appropriately	• Promise employees pay increases or promotions if they vote against the union • Threaten employees with termination or discriminate when disciplining employees • Threaten to close down or move the company if a union is voted in • Spy on or have someone spy on union meetings • Make a speech to employees or groups at work within 24 hours of the election (before that, it is allowed) • Ask employees how they plan to vote or if they have signed authorization cards • Encourage employees to persuade others to vote against the union (such a vote must be initiated solely by the employee)

© 2016 Cengage Learning®

Certification–Decertification

If the union receives the necessary votes and is **certified** by the NLRB, it then becomes the exclusive bargaining representative of the employee group, and the employer is required to negotiate in good faith with the union. As the certified employee representative, the union is then ready to negotiate the initial contract. Throughout union negotiations and contract administration, the union must be involved in discussions with employees about any items considered a subject of bargaining.

Decertification   When an employee group decides that the union no longer meets its needs, it can **decertify** the union. Only employees can initiate a decertification process, and management must stay out of the process altogether or risk an unfair labor practice charge. Decertification is rare in the healthcare industry because employees believe their unions will continue to protect them against employers who are unwilling to make significant workplace improvements.

The process for decertifying a current union is much like the certification process. Employees, without help from their employer, must obtain signatures from at least 30 percent of the employees who are union members. The NLRB conducts an election and decertifies the union when it determines that a **simple majority**—50 percent plus one—of employees want decertification. Six months must pass after certification before employees can decertify their union.

Contract Negotiation (Collective Bargaining)

The collective bargaining process begins when the NLRB notifies the management and union that the union has the official right to represent the employees. Both sides are required to bargain in good faith; that is, they must meet and exchange information about contractual issues, including economic and workplace policies and procedures. Since the labor contract finally agreed to by both parties is a legal document, supervisors and managers, as agents of the organization, must follow the contract provisions to avoid grievances or unfair labor practice charges. Negotiating the initial contract can be difficult and time-consuming because both parties must start without any contract language about working conditions, wages, and benefits, among other issues. Developing an effective initial contract requires significant attention to detail because it will be the foundation for union–management relationships.

Collective bargaining is the process whereby representatives of management and workers negotiate over wages, hours, and other terms and conditions of employment. This give-and-take process between representatives of the two organizations attempts to establish conditions beneficial to both. It is also a relationship based on relative power.

Collective Bargaining Issues

A number of issues can be addressed during collective bargaining. Although not often listed as such in the contract, management rights and union security are two important issues subject to collective bargaining. These and other issues, common to collective bargaining, are discussed next.

Management Rights   Virtually all labor contracts include **management rights,** which are rights reserved so that the employer can manage, direct, and control its business. By including such a provision, management attempts to preserve its unilateral right to make changes in areas not identified in a labor contract. A typical provision might read as follows:

> The employer retains all rights to manage, direct, and control its business in all particulars, except as such rights are expressly and specifically modified by the terms of this or any subsequent agreement.

Union Security A major concern of union representatives when bargaining is the negotiation of **union security provisions**, which are contract clauses to help the union obtain and retain members. One type of union security clause in labor contracts is the *no-layoff policy*, or *job security guarantee*. Such a provision is especially important to many union workers because of all the mergers, downsizings, and job reductions taking place in many healthcare organizations. However, for these very reasons, management is often unwilling to consider this type of provision.

Union Dues Issues A common union security provision is the *dues checkoff* clause, which provides for the automatic deduction of union dues from the payroll checks of union members. The dues checkoff provision makes it much easier for the union to collect its funds, and without it, the union must collect dues by billing each member separately.

However, unions' ability to use such checkoff clauses for contributions to political and congressional candidates has been challenged in federal court. A U.S. Supreme Court case supported the constitutionality of state laws that require labor unions to get written consent before using nonmember fees for political purposes. The Court noted that agency shop agreements were acceptable, and that public-sector unions could levy fees on nonmember employees. However, it also noted that unions need to obtain authorization from nonmembers when agency fees are being used to support political campaigns.

Classification of Bargaining Issues

The NLRB has defined collective bargaining issues in three ways. The categories it has used are mandatory, permissive, and illegal.

Mandatory Issues Issues identified specifically by labor laws or court decisions as subject to bargaining are **mandatory issues**. If either party demands that issues in this category be subject to bargaining, then that must occur. Generally, mandatory issues relate to wages, benefits, nature of jobs, and other work-related subjects. Mandatory subjects for bargaining include the following:

- Discharge of employees
- Grievances
- Work schedules
- Union security and dues checkoff
- Retirement and pension coverage
- Vacations and time off
- Rest and lunch break rules
- Safety rules
- Profit-sharing plans
- Required physical exam

Permissive Issues Issues that are not mandatory and that relate to certain jobs are **permissive issues**. For example, benefits for retired employees can be bargained over if both parties agree.

Illegal Issues   A final category, **illegal issues**, includes those issues that would require either party to take illegal action. Examples would be giving preference to union members when hiring employees. If one side wants to bargain over an illegal issue, the other side can refuse.

COLLECTIVE BARGAINING PROCESS

The collective bargaining process involved in negotiating a contract consists of four typical stages: preparation and initial demands, negotiations, settlement or impasse, and strikes and lockouts. Throughout the process, management and labor deal with the terms of their relationship.

Preparation and Initial Demands

Both labor and management representatives spend considerable time preparing for negotiations.[22] Employer and industry data concerning wages, benefits, working conditions, management and union rights, productivity, and absenteeism are gathered. If the organization argues that it cannot afford to pay what the union is asking, the employer's financial situation and accompanying data become relevant to the process. However, the union must request such information before the employer is obligated to provide it. Typical bargaining includes initial proposals of expectations by both sides. The amount of rancor or calmness exhibited may set the tone for future negotiations between the parties.

Core Bargaining Issues   The primary focus of bargaining for both union and management is on the core areas of wages, benefits, and working hours and conditions. Unions for healthcare workers frequently focus on specific aspects of working conditions, such as staffing ratios, mandatory overtime, and safety issues.[23]

Continuing Negotiations

After taking initial positions, each side attempts to determine what the other side values highly so that the best bargain can be struck. For example, the union may be asking the employer to pay for dental benefits as part of a package that also includes wage increases and retirement benefits. However, the union may be most interested in the retirement benefits and may be willing to trade the dental payments for better retirement benefits. Management must determine what the union has as a priority and decide exactly what to give up.

Good Faith   Provisions in federal law require that both employers and union bargaining representatives negotiate in good faith. In good faith negotiations, the parties agree to send negotiators who can bargain and make decisions, rather than people who do not have the authority to commit either group to a decision. To be more effective, meetings between the parties should be conducted professionally and address issues, rather than being confrontational. Refusing to bargain, scheduling meetings at absurdly inconvenient hours, and using other conflicting tactics may lead to employers or unions filing complaints with the NLRB.

Interest-Based Bargaining   A new technique that has been used effectively in the negotiating process is **interest-based bargaining**, which emphasizes problem solving and consensus building.[24] Employers and unions may receive training from the Federal Mediation and Conciliation Service (FMCS) regarding how to discuss issues, interests, options, and solutions. Interest-based bargaining has been successful in some situations, but it requires both sides to be open to collaborative relations.

The typical steps in interest-based bargaining are as follows:

- Select an issue
- Clarify the issue
- Discuss each party's interests (not positions or demands)
- Generate options through brainstorming
- Evaluate options
- Select options that meet mutual needs
- Document agreed solutions

Settlement and Contract Agreement

After reaching an initial agreement, the bargaining parties usually return to their respective constituencies to determine if the informal agreement is acceptable. A particularly crucial stage is **ratification** of the labor agreement, which occurs when union members vote to accept the terms of a negotiated labor agreement. Before ratification, the union negotiating team explains the agreement to the union members and presents it for a vote. If the members approve the agreement, it is then formalized into a contract. Figure 11-7 lists the typical items in a labor agreement.

FIGURE 11-7   Typical Items in a Labor Agreement

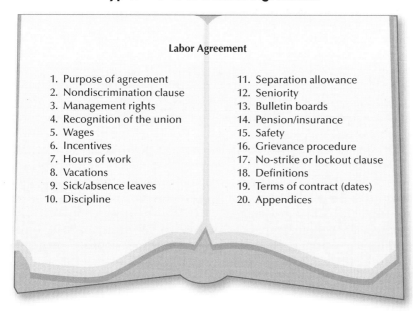

Labor Agreement

1. Purpose of agreement
2. Nondiscrimination clause
3. Management rights
4. Recognition of the union
5. Wages
6. Incentives
7. Hours of work
8. Vacations
9. Sick/absence leaves
10. Discipline
11. Separation allowance
12. Seniority
13. Bulletin boards
14. Pension/insurance
15. Safety
16. Grievance procedure
17. No-strike or lockout clause
18. Definitions
19. Terms of contract (dates)
20. Appendices

© 2016 Cengage Learning®

Bargaining Impasse

Regardless of the structure of the bargaining process, labor and management do not always reach agreement on the issues. If they reach an impasse, then the disputes can be taken to conciliation, mediation, or arbitration.

Conciliation and Mediation   When an impasse occurs, an outside party such as the FMCS may help the two deadlocked parties to continue negotiations and arrive at a solution. In **conciliation**, the third party assists union and management negotiators to reach a voluntary settlement, but makes no proposals for solutions. In **mediation**, the third party may suggest ideas for solutions to help the negotiators reach a settlement.

In conciliation and mediation, the third party does not attempt to impose a solution. Sometimes fact finding helps to clarify the issues of disagreement as an intermediate step between mediation and arbitration.

Arbitration   In **arbitration**, a neutral third party makes a decision. Arbitration can be conducted by an individual or a panel of individuals. "Interest" arbitration attempts to solve bargaining impasses, primarily in the public sector. This type of arbitration is not frequently used in the private sector because companies generally do not want an outside party making decisions about their rights, wages, benefits, and other issues. However, grievance or "rights" arbitration is used extensively in the private sector. Fortunately, in many situations, agreements are reached through negotiations without the need for arbitration. When disagreements continue, strikes or lockouts may occur.

Planning for Strikes

Although it might seem contrary to the mission of contract negotiations, planning for a strike begins at about the same time negotiations start. Crucial concerns are listed in the Figure 11-8.

Unions prepare members for the economic and emotional realities of a work stoppage while managers prepare to care for patients during the strike. Managers and union officials have a variety of challenges and concerns to deal with when a strike is imminent. Managers are concerned about patient care, covering work schedules, diverting patients and services during the strike, the economic impact of the strike on the organization, the conflict between striking and non-striking employees, and public image.

In the event of a strike, union officials are also faced with critical challenges that require time and thought. Common issues include: lost wages of striking members, solidarity of striking workers, emotional conflicts of caregiving union members, replacement workers, quality of patient care, relationships with non-striking employees, and public image.

Professional healthcare employees face several dilemmas in a strike situation. Among these is a reluctance about participating in a work stoppage when it means stopping patient care. But when a strike is called, each union member must decide whether to honor the strike or cross the picket line. Management's challenges include finding a balance in how managers treat striking workers, who will eventually return to work, and in negotiating a contract that is fair and equitable.

FIGURE 11-8   Strike Concerns

MANAGEMENT	UNION
• Communicating to the community, physicians, and non-striking employees about the contingency plan • Training managers and supervisors to provide patient care • Determining how many patients the reduced staff can cover • Contacting temporary staffing agencies to provide temporary workers during the strike • Deciding where patients will be referred to other nonstriking providers • Determining how to treat staff members who cross the picket line • Securing the facility and grounds to avoid disruptions • Arranging for supplies and equipment deliveries across the picket line • Contracting vendors with union contracts to assure no sympathy strike by other unions	• Communicating to the NLRB and management of intent to strike • Communicating strike authorization to members • Planning logistics of maintaining the picket line • Scheduling pickets • Providing information hotline to update striking members • Planning public relations to influence public opinion

© Cengage Learning®

If the number of patients remains the same during the strike, other, nonstriking caregivers will likely have to fill in where striking staff members are absent. Assigning substitutes to care for patients is complex because managers must consider quality issues, including credentialed staff replacements, levels of authority for substitute caregivers, and appropriate staff-to-patient ratios. Conflict and resentment build in these situations. Long strikes cause even greater conflict. Because healthcare is labor intensive and specialized, the likelihood that managers and supervisors can continue to carry the workload alone is unrealistic during a long strike.

The emotional impact of a strike or difficult negotiations must not be minimized when an organization finally negotiates a contract. When the issues are resolved and the workforce returns to work, rebuilding relationships with the employees who were on strike will be vital to meeting organization objectives. In most cases, the objective of both parties is to come to a satisfactory settlement and return to work as soon as possible.

Strikes, Lockouts, and Other Tactics

If a deadlock cannot be resolved, an employer may revert to a lockout—or a union may revert to a strike. During a **strike**, union members refuse to work to put pressure on an employer. Often, the striking union members picket or demonstrate against the employer outside the place of business by carrying placards and signs. Despite current trends, evidence suggests some employees are using the strike because they believe their interests are not being adequately considered by politicians, organizations, and managers. Healthcare is so important that a threat of a strike, let alone the actual strike, is very disconcerting to consumers of healthcare who fear a strike could impact their access to care. As an example, when thousands of nurses walked off the job for a one-day strike against 14 hospitals in

Minneapolis and St. Paul, the outcry both for and against the strike was significant and quickly polarized the community. Both sides were deluged by pleas from community leaders, politicians, and government officials to quickly resume bargaining and end the strike. Within days, negotiations concluded with a new contract.[25]

In a **lockout**, management shuts down operations to prevent union members from working. This action may avert possible damage or sabotage to the facility or injury to employees who continue to work. It also gives management leverage in negotiations. This is a rare occurrence in a traditional healthcare facility such as a hospital or long-term care facility.

Types of Strikes   Five types of strikes can occur:

- *Economic strikes* happen when the parties fail to reach agreement during collective bargaining.
- *Unfair labor practices strikes* occur when union members leave their jobs over what they feel are illegal employer actions, such as refusal to bargain.
- *Wildcat strikes* occur during the life of the collective bargaining agreement without approval of union leadership and violate a no-strike clause in a labor contract. Strikers can be discharged or disciplined.
- *Jurisdictional strikes* exist when members of one union walk out to force the employer to assign work to them instead of to members of another union.
- *Sympathy strikes* take place when one union chooses to express support for another union involved in a dispute, even though the first union has no disagreement with the employer.

As a result of the decline in union power, work stoppages due to strikes and lockouts are relatively rare. In a recent year, all national strikes were settled quickly. Many unions are reluctant to go on strike because of the financial losses their members would incur or the fear that a strike would cause the employer to go bankrupt. In addition, management has shown its willingness to hire replacements, and some strikes have ended with union workers losing their jobs.

Replacement of Workers on Strike   Management retains and sometimes uses its ability to simply replace workers who strike. These replacements are called "scabs." Workers' rights vary depending on the type of strike that occurs. For example, in an economic strike, an employer is free to replace the striking workers. But with an unfair labor practices strike, the workers who want their jobs back at the end of the strike must be reinstated.

Other Tactics   Besides picketing and strikes, unions and their members might resort to unorthodox or even aggressive practices to express their discontent about employer practices and advance their prolabor agenda.

Contract Administration

Implementing the labor contract on a daily basis is the next critical issue that labor and management face. The contract is a legal agreement that must be followed during its term, and it must be implementable by managers who might not have been involved in the negotiations. During bargaining, negotiators must keep contract administration issues in mind and anticipate conflicts and contract interpretation issues to avoid administration problems.

Labor–Management Committees

Labor–management committees comprise management representatives, union members, and bargaining agents and they meet regularly. Union members are elected by their colleagues; management representatives are assigned by organization leaders. Managers and union members communicate issues to the committee as a result of their daily interactions.

GRIEVANCE MANAGEMENT

Employee dissatisfaction is a potential source of trouble for employers, whether it is expressed or not. Hidden dissatisfaction grows and creates reactions that may be completely out of proportion to the original concerns. Therefore, it is important that dissatisfaction be given an outlet. A **complaint**, which is merely an indication of employee dissatisfaction, is one outlet. If an employee is represented by a union, and the employee says, "I should have received the job transfer because I have more seniority, which is what the union contract states," and he or she submits it in writing, then that complaint becomes a grievance. A **grievance** is a complaint formally stated in writing whether or not a union is involved.

Management should be concerned with both complaints and grievances because both indicate potential problems within the workforce.[26] Without a grievance procedure, management may be unable to respond to employee concerns because managers are unaware of them. Therefore, a formal grievance procedure provides a valuable communication tool for organizations, whether a union is present or not. In North America, a wide variety of grievance procedures and dispute resolution approaches are used to address employee dissatisfaction, particularly in workplaces that do not deal with a union presence. For instance, alternative dispute resolution techniques such as mediation, panel assessments, open-door policies, and peer reviews can be effective. But when employees are organized, companies often use some form of arbitration to tackle grievances.[27]

Grievance Responsibilities

The typical division of responsibilities between the HR unit and operating managers for handling grievances is shown in Figure 11-9. These responsibilities vary considerably from one organization to another, even among unionized firms. But the HR unit usually has more general responsibilities. Managers must accept the grievance procedure as a possible constraint on some of their decisions.

Grievance Procedures

Grievance procedures are specific communication channels that are used to resolve grievances between employees and employers. Many times, first-line supervisors are usually closest to a problem and should be one of the primary

FIGURE 11-9 Typical Division of HR Responsibilities: Grievance Management

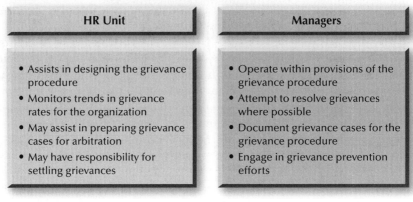

HR Unit	Managers
• Assists in designing the grievance procedure • Monitors trends in grievance rates for the organization • May assist in preparing grievance cases for arbitration • May have responsibility for settling grievances	• Operate within provisions of the grievance procedure • Attempt to resolve grievances where possible • Document grievance cases for the grievance procedure • Engage in grievance prevention efforts

© 2016 Cengage Learning®

problem solvers in employee grievance cases. However, supervisors can be distracted by other work matters and may even be the subject of an employee's grievance. Consequently, grievances need to be handled with a specified resolution approach so that problems are appropriately resolved.

Union Representation in Grievance Procedures An employee who is a member of the union generally has a right to union representation if the employee is being questioned by management and if discipline may result. If these so-called Weingarten rights (named after the court case that established them) are violated and the employee is dismissed, the employee usually will be reinstated with back pay. Employers are not required to allow nonunion workers to have coworkers present in grievance procedure meetings.

Steps in a Grievance Procedure

Grievance procedures can vary in the steps included. Figure 11-10 shows a typical grievance procedure, which consists of the following steps:

1. The employee discusses the grievance with the union steward (the representative of the union on the job) and the supervisor.
2. The union steward discusses the grievance with the supervisor's manager and/or the HR manager.
3. A committee of union officers discusses the grievance with appropriate company managers.
4. The representative of the national union discusses the grievance with designated company executives or the corporate industrial relations officer.
5. If the grievance is not solved at this stage, it goes to arbitration. An impartial third party may ultimately dispose of the grievance.

Grievance arbitration is a means by which a third party settles disputes arising from different interpretations of a labor contract.[28] This process should not be confused with contract or issues arbitration, discussed earlier, in which

FIGURE 11-10   Employee Grievance Process

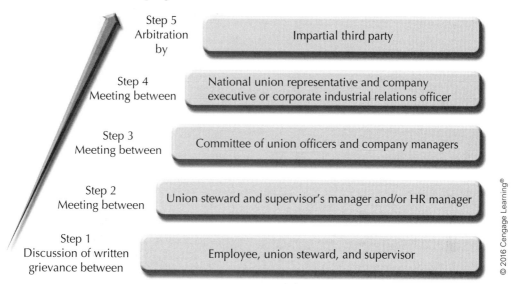

Step 5 Arbitration by	Impartial third party
Step 4 Meeting between	National union representative and company executive or corporate industrial relations officer
Step 3 Meeting between	Committee of union officers and company managers
Step 2 Meeting between	Union steward and supervisor's manager and/or HR manager
Step 1 Discussion of written grievance between	Employee, union steward, and supervisor

© 2016 Cengage Learning®

arbitration is used to determine how a contract will be written. The U.S. Supreme Court has ruled that grievance arbitration decisions issued under labor contract provisions are enforceable and generally may not go to court to be changed. Grievance arbitration includes many topic areas, with discipline and discharge, safety and health, and security being common concerns.

HEALTHCARE REFORM AND HR PRACTICES

Throughout the history of unions in the United States, they have always played an important role in the political landscape of the country. Union leaders have routinely been outspoken on political issues at the national, state, and local levels that affect their members, such as labor law and economic policy. As healthcare union leaders strategize about the future of the healthcare industry and increasing union membership, various aspects of healthcare reform will play a significant role.

Unions have been overwhelming supportive of the passage and implementation of the Affordable Care Act (ACA). In exchange for union (labor) support of the ACA, the Obama administration made concessions to labor that are seen as laying the groundwork for more unionization of healthcare workers. With the passage of the ACA, more healthcare workers, including physicians, will leave small, independent healthcare practices, where they are not an accessible or desirable target for unions, and become employed by large healthcare systems. Once employed by the private hospitals, medical centers, and government-operated facilities, these workers can be unionized—the result of which is to provide unions with greater opportunity for increasing union membership in the healthcare industry.[29]

CASE

A specialty clinic, with four unions representing 40 percent of the employees, has learned that the Teamsters Union has been contacted by an employee group to conduct a unionization campaign to represent some of the employees, including service workers, clerical workers, and all levels in the accounting department. The clinic's labor-relations philosophy would be characterized as traditional and noncollaborative. It has decided to resist the union's attempt to organize the employees.

The four groups of employees who are currently represented by unions include: technical employees, registered nurses, pharmacists, and maintenance workers. Some 70 employees are represented by the current contracts. The registered nurses constitute 40 percent of the 70 union members. The group that has been proposed in the organizing attempt includes 45 employees, and the service workers (housekeeping, food service, and nursing assistants) constitute 75 percent of the proposed members.

Management is concerned about the organizing campaign. Relationships with the current unions have not been very productive, and further unionization will lead to more distrust between management and employees. Management is concerned about the union's ability to call strikes in the future, which may require the organization to severely limit services and could greatly affect its financial stability.

Management must decide whether to mount a campaign to prevent the union from organizing. If it decides to mount a campaign, management must develop a strategy to present arguments to the employees for not having union representation.

Questions

1. What steps must the Teamsters Union follow to cause an election to occur?
2. During the union campaign, how should the managers conduct themselves to avoid being accused of committing unfair labor practices?

END NOTES

1. See Butte Medical Properties, 168 N.L.R.B. 266 (1967).
2. 29 U.S.C. 152(14).
3. See *http://www.eyeonbi.org/* for more information.
4. Kerana Todorov, "Napa State Hospital Reports Reduced Violence," *Napa Valley Register* (October 10, 2013).
5. See BLS News Release: Union Membership 2013.
6. Donna Malvey, "Unionization in Healthcare Background and Trends," *Journal of Healthcare Management* (May/June 2010), 154–157.
7. "Regional Briefs—New Agreement Focuses on Caregivers Quality Patient Care," *Managed Care Outlook* (July 1, 2011), 4–5.
8. Donna Malvey, "Unionization in Healthcare Strategies," *Journal of Healthcare Management* (July/August 2010), 236–240.
9. L.Polevoi, "Is an Open-Door Policy the Best Policy?," *Managing People at Work* (November 2013), 5.
10. Carol Gill, "Union Impact on the Effective Adoption of High Performance Work Practices," *Human Resource Management Review* 19 (2009), 39–50.
11. Erin Patton, "Union Organizing (How Can We Prevent a Union from Organizing in Our Company?)," *HR Magazine* (September 2009), 28.
12. Ibid., 28.
13. Mark Schoeff, "A Step Back," *Workforce Management* (January 19, 2009), 18–22.

14. John Hollon, "A Poor 'Choice,' " *Workforce Management* (January 19, 2009), 42 and Steve Raabe, "Unions Facing Tough Times," Denver Post (September 15, 2010), 1K, 6K.

15. John Matchulat, "The Unions Rejoice Act: An Examination of the Intent and Potential Impact of EFCA," *Employee Relations Law Journal* (Spring 2009), 16–55.

16. Douglas Seaton and Emily Ruhsam, "The Employee Free Choice Act: No Choice for Employer or Employee," *Employer Relations Law Journal* (Spring 2009), 3–15.

17. Alexandria Clinic P.A. and Minnesota Licensed Practical Nurses Association, Case 18-CA-15371 (2003).

18. *NLRB v. Kentucky River Community Care, Inc.*, 121 S.Ct. 1861 (2001).

19. "Quickie-Election Rule … It's Back," *HR Magazine* (March 2014), 15.

20. 29 C.F.R. 103.30(a).

21. "Circuit Court of Appeals Upholds the NLRB's New 'Overwhelming Community of Interest' Bargaining Unit Test," *Venulex Legal Summaries* (October 2013), 1–3.

22. Eric Krell, "The Rebirth of Labor Relations," *HR Magazine* (February 2009), 57–60.

23. A. Selvam, "Striking Out: Nurses Unions Go Up Against Hospitals as Year Ends," *Modern Healthcare* (January 2, 2012), 14–15 and Linda Briskin, "Resistance, Mobilization and Militancy: Nurses on Strike," *Nursing Inquiry* (2012), 285–296.

24. See *http://www.fmcs.gov/internet/itemDetail .asp?categoryID=140&itemID=15950* for more information.

25. "Regional News: MIDWEST," *Modern Healthcare* (September 20, 2010), 24.

26. Nancy Woodward, "New Guidelines Adopted for Workplace Grievances," *HR Magazine* (June 2009), 32.

27. Bernard Walker and Robert T. Hamilton, "Employee–Employer Grievances: A Review," *International Journal of Management Reviews* 13 (2011), 40–58.

28. Matthew Franckiewicz, "How to Win Your Arbitration Case Before It Even Starts," *Labor Law Journal* (2009), 115–120.

29. Mallory Factor, "Obamacare's Unionized 'Gotcha,'" *Forbes* (September 10, 2012), 30.

12 HEALTHCARE COMPENSATION PRACTICES

Learning Objectives

After you have read this chapter, you should be able to:

- Describe the differences between an entitlement compensation philosophy and a performance-focused compensation philosophy.

- Define the issues confronting the healthcare industry in complying with the Fair Labor Standards Act (FLSA).

- Identify the steps in the compensation administration process.

- Explain the issues associated with awarding pay increases.

- Discuss the five components of executive compensation.

Experienced nurses are a valuable human resource for healthcare organizations. Based on that experience, competent nurses can provide quick and accurate assessments of their patients' health and well-being, help orient and train less experienced staff, and have the flexibility to perform many other duties such as being in charge and providing patient education.

Registered nurses rank in the top 15 jobs held by workers aged 65 and older.[1] Yet many of these experienced workers have every desire to remain in the workforce if their employers actively attempt to retain them. A study sponsored by the Robert Wood Johnson Foundation focused on understanding why some healthcare organizations are successful at retaining experienced nurses, and the findings were compelling. First, there must be commitment by senior leadership to retain older experienced nurses. Second, the organizational culture must value aging. Third, there must be a comprehensive compensation program, including market-based pay, phased retirement benefits, and flexible work arrangements.. The study also looked at the direct cost to replace a full-time RN, which totaled in excess of $35,000. These costs included termination payouts, hiring temporary staff, increased overtime to provide coverage, and the time required to train new staff.[2]

As the healthcare industry deals with ever-increasing demands for services and care, the need for experienced and competent workers will continue to grow. Healthcare workers, especially skilled professionals, will have many choices as to where they work or even if they work. Healthcare organizations must focus on results-oriented retention strategies in order to meet their patients' needs. At the heart of those strategies are competitive pay practices.

In developing compensation strategies, healthcare organizations are confronted with a number of challenges and issues. Employers, insurance companies, and federal and state governments are demanding higher-quality care at lower or contained costs.[3] Further, the demand for healthcare in this country is accelerating at an unprecedented rate as the baby-boom generation ages, yet fewer individuals are pursuing healthcare careers. In order to attract and retain competent and motivated workers, healthcare organizations must aggressively compete with each other and with other industries for skilled workers. The net effect is that healthcare HR compensation strategies must do the impossible: balance these competing factors and priorities and deliver compensation programs that meet the needs of their organizations and their employees.

COMPENSATION RESPONSIBILITIES IN HEALTHCARE ORGANIZATIONS

In larger healthcare organizations, such as hospitals, large clinics, and long-term care facilities, healthcare HR professionals typically guide the development and administration of an organizational compensation system, including responsibilities for developing base pay programs, pay structures, and compensation administration policies. In small organizations, like dental practices and chiropractic offices, office managers or practice leaders develop these programs.

Healthcare HR professionals may or may not do actual payroll processing; payroll is often the responsibility of the accounting or finance departments. Although this labor-intensive responsibility has historically been outsourced, today many healthcare organizations are doing this in-house because of improvements in software and cloud processing.[4] Operating managers evaluate the performance of employees and consider their performance when deciding compensation increases within the policies and guidelines established by the HR unit and upper management.

Compensation systems in healthcare organizations must be closely linked to organizational objectives and strategies. An effective compensation program addresses four objectives:

- Legal compliance with all appropriate laws and regulations
- Cost-effectiveness for the organization
- Internal, external, and individual equity for employees
- Performance enhancement for the organization

Healthcare employers must balance compensation costs at a level that both ensures organizational competitiveness and provides sufficient rewards to employees for their knowledge, skills, abilities, and performance accomplishments. In order to attract, retain, and reward employees, employers provide several types of compensation.

Components of Compensation

Tangible rewards can be measured, and it is possible to calculate the monetary value of each reward. Tangible rewards include base pay and variable pay. Employees can easily compare the tangible rewards offered by various organizations. Alternatively, **intangible rewards** cannot be as easily measured or quantified. How would an employee put a dollar value on having decision-making authority or working in a supportive work environment? The perceived value of such intangible rewards can differ among employees, making the total rewards calculation complex. Recent research shows that work–life balance programs and employee well-being efforts make a significant difference to workers and in some cases can outweigh the tangible rewards offered by a company.[5]

Base Pay   The basic compensation that an employee receives, usually provided as an hourly wage or a salary, is called **base pay**. Many organizations use two base pay categories, hourly and salaried, which are identified according to the way pay is determined and the nature of the jobs. Hourly pay is most common and is based on time. Employees paid by the hour receive **wages**, which are payments calculated on the basis of the time worked. In contrast, employees paid a **salary** receive the same payment each period regardless of the number of hours worked.

Variable Pay   **Variable pay** is compensation linked directly to individual, team, or organizational performance. The most common types of variable pay in healthcare organizations are shift differentials, bonuses, incentive program payments, and seniority award. Hay Group, a compensation consulting firm, found that organizations are increasing the use of variable pay as a means of aligning compensation with changing business strategies and improving performance.[6] Variable pay, including executive compensation, is discussed in Chapter 13.

Benefits   Many organizations provide indirect rewards in the form of employee benefits. With indirect compensation, employees receive financial rewards without receiving actual cash. A **benefit** is an indirect reward given to an employee or a group of employees for organizational membership, regardless of performance. Examples of benefits are health insurance, vacation pay, and retirement pensions. Benefits are discussed in Chapter 13.

Healthcare Compensation Approaches

Healthcare organizations regard pay as an important tool for recruiting, motivating, and retaining good people. Indeed, those goals have changed little over time, but the ways in which some healthcare organizations approach them differ dramatically from previous approaches. Performance-based pay, tailored to the strategic circumstances of each organization, may consist of base pay, an annual bonus, and a choice of various other benefits. Such a "total rewards" package would have been uncommon for a worker in 1950, but it is increasingly common today. Figure 12-1 presents the typical distribution among the types of compensation paid by healthcare organizations.

Traditional Compensation Approach   For some healthcare organizations, a traditional compensation approach makes sense and offers certain advantages in specific competitive situations. It may be more legally defensible, less complex, and viewed as more "fair" for average- and below-average-performing employees. However, the total rewards approach helps retain top performers, can be more flexible when the economy goes up or down, and is favored by top-performing organizations. But it clearly will *not* work in every situation.

Traditional compensation systems have evolved over time to reflect a logical, rational approach to compensating employees. Job descriptions identify tasks and responsibilities and are then used to decide which jobs are more valuable. These systems calculate the value that each job contributes to the organization based on an evaluation of the job. That value is used to establish a pay range that reflects progression as employees grow and presumably improve their ability to perform the job.

FIGURE 12-1 **Total Rewards Components**

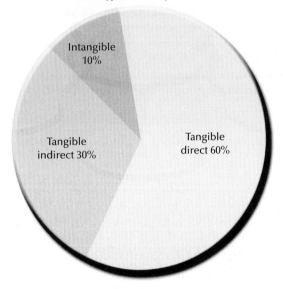

Typical Distribution Among the
Three Types of Compensation

© 2016 Cengage Learning®

TOTAL REWARDS

Compensation is an important factor affecting how and why people choose to work at one organization over others. To attract and retain high-quality talent healthcare employers must design reward packages that will appeal to a variety of people. Companies address pay and benefits with a **total rewards** philosophy. The total rewards package includes all forms of compensation, the monetary and nonmonetary rewards provided by a healthcare organization to attract, motivate, and retain employees as shown in Figure 12-2. The effectiveness of the reward system depends on linking compensation to organizational objectives and strategies so that employees are encouraged to work in a manner that benefits the organization and its stakeholders.[7] For example, a large specialty practice in the Midwest links the performance pay of its front-desk receptionists to their customer service scores as rated by the patients they check in at the front desk.

An effective total rewards approach balances the interests and costs of the organization with the needs and expectations of employees.[8] This can be a difficult process. On the one hand, compensation-related costs represent one the largest portion of total operating expenses in healthcare organizations, typically more than 50 percent.[9] On the other hand, employees want to be compensated fairly and have their individual needs met. Employees continually make choices between spending more time at work or engaging in leisure activities. If compensation for working is not valued as highly as free time to

FIGURE 12-2   Elements of Total Rewards

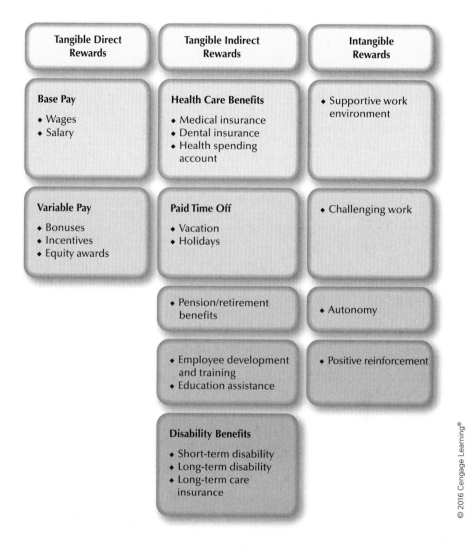

pursue enjoyable activities, people will decide to work less and play more.[10] The challenge for any healthcare organization is to achieve an optimal relationship between costs and employee impact while considering many financial and operational factors.[11]

The concept of total rewards requires a much broader understanding of pay or compensation than has traditionally been the case in healthcare organizations. A total rewards philosophy emphasizes how an organization can use *both* tangible and intangible rewards to strengthen employee motivation and commitment, especially in challenging economic times.[12] Indeed, a lagging economy will likely require employers to make difficult but necessary adjustments to total rewards to reflect new business conditions. Broadly defining compensation should also help companies develop creative policies that keep employees motivated. Examples of creative compensation include the ability to earn more paid time off for exemplary performance, on-site child care, and paid sabbaticals.

Healthcare organizations strive to maintain their costs at a level that rewards employees fairly for their knowledge, skills, abilities, and performance accomplishments, while allowing the organization to remain competitive and successful. WorldatWork is a leading professional association that focuses on compensation. The organization has developed a well-respected model of total rewards that includes tangible direct, tangible indirect, and intangible rewards.[13] Figure 12-3 identifies elements of three primary components of the total rewards package. It shows that total rewards can be broadly defined and also indicates that intangible rewards are an important aspect of the package.

FIGURE 12-3   Total Rewards Philosophy

St. Luke's Hospital endorses a compensation strategy the supports a total rewards philosophy that places it in the 50th percentile or higher when compared to similar sized organizations in our market place. Our compensation philosophy supports our strategic objective of attracting and retaining the most qualified employees available to our organization. Pay practices are reviewed on an annual basis and are approved by the Board based on business conditions and our ability to pay.

The components of our program include: Base Pay, Employee Benefits and a Pension Plan.

Base Pay - Consistent with our compensation philosophy, St. Luke's will pay competitive base hourly rates and salaries to our employees: 1) New hires will receive competitive offers of employment based on our assessment of their ability to contribute to the success of the practice. We will only recruit experienced professionals with prior physician practice or clinic background. 2) On or about the employee's anniversary date of employment they will receive a review of their performance and based upon meeting or exceeding their job standards they will be eligible for a salary increase. St. Luke's will strive to be fair and equitable in all aspects of its salary administration program. Compliance with state and federal statues on pay, pay equity and equal opportunity is a requirement of our program. The only differentiators that will be considered in both assigning a new employee a base rate and awarding existing employees an annual rate adjustment are:

1. The position for which they are employed.
2. Previous relevant experience (for new hires).
3. Current tenure (existing employees)
4. Performance (existing employees)
5. Attendance (existing employees)
6. Market sensitivity (both new hires and existing employees).

Market Awareness: St. Luke's will continue to monitor the market place to ensure that its compensation philosophy is maintained.

Employee Benefits - St. Luke's recognizes the importance of providing a comprehensive benefit package to its employee. The package is designed to meet the employee's short-term priorities for health, time-off and education, as well as their long-term needs for security and retirement.

Pension Plan - St. Luke's total compensation program includes the critical component of retirement funding in recognition of the need to provide its employees the opportunity to financially prepare for retirement as a reward for dedication and loyalty.

FIGURE 12-4   **Compensation Approaches: Traditional Versus Total Rewards**

Traditional Compensation Approach	Total Rewards Approach
Compensation is primarily base pay.	Variable pay is added to base.
Bonuses/perks are for executives only.	Annual/long-term incentives are provided to executives, managers and employees.
Fixed benefits are tied to long tenure.	Flexible and portable benefits are offered.
Pay grade progression is based on organizational promotions.	Knowledge/skill-based broadbands determine pay grades.
Organization-wide standard pay plan exists.	Multiple plans consider job family location, and business units.

© 2016 Cengage Learning®

Determining which rewards are valued by employees and applicants and finding affordable ways to provide those rewards can be challenging. Total reward programs should be evaluated on an ongoing basis to ensure that employees find them satisfying and that they are cost-effective and sustainable for the organization.[14] The organizational culture, compensation philosophy, and pay policy should all be complementary and consistent.[15] Figure 12-4 is an example of a hospital's total rewards philosophy statement.

Compensation Philosophies

The two basic compensation philosophies lie on opposite ends of a continuum. At one end of the continuum detailed in Figure 12-5 is the *entitlement* philosophy, and at the other end is the *performance-oriented* philosophy. Most compensation systems fall somewhere in between.

Entitlement Orientation   Many traditional organizations that give automatic increases to their employees every year practice the entitlement philosophy. Further, most of those employees receive the same or nearly the same percentage increase each year. Employees and managers who subscribe to the entitlement philosophy believe that individuals who have worked another year are *entitled* to a raise in base pay. They also believe all incentives and benefits programs should continue and be increased, regardless of changing industry or economic conditions. Commonly, in organizations following an entitlement philosophy, pay increases are referred to as *cost-of-living* raises, even if they are not tied specifically to economic cost-of-living indicators.

Following an entitlement philosophy ultimately means that as employees continue their employment, the employer's costs increase, regardless of employee performance or organizational competitive pressures. Market data will be monitored but will not necessarily drive compensation strategy decisions unless significant recruitment or retention issues are identified for a particular job, group, or position (e.g., RNs or nurse anesthetists).

Hospitals and medical centers have especially struggled with the entitlement orientation of their long-term employees. Today's market pressures on

FIGURE 12-5   Continuum of Compensation Philosophies

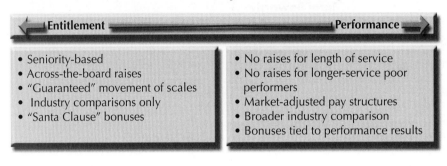

Entitlement ← ═══════════════════ → Performance

- Seniority-based
- Across-the-board raises
- "Guaranteed" movement of scales
- Industry comparisons only
- "Santa Clause" bonuses

- No raises for length of service
- No raises for longer-service poor performers
- Market-adjusted pay structures
- Broader industry comparison
- Bonuses tied to performance results

© 2016 Cengage Learning®

healthcare organizations and the declining revenues described in earlier chapters would argue for a merit- or performance-based approach to paying annual increases. However, two factors have contributed to the entitlement orientation: (1) decades of paying automatic increases and (2) collective bargaining agreements that require automatic step increases.

Performance Orientation   Where a performance-oriented philosophy is followed, organizations do not guarantee additional or increased compensation simply for completing another year of organizational service. Instead, pay and incentives reflect performance differences among employees. Employees who perform well receive larger compensation increases, while those who do not perform satisfactorily see little or no increase in compensation. Thus, employees who perform satisfactorily maintain or advance in relation to market compensation levels, whereas poor or marginal performers may fall behind. Bonus compensation may be paid on the basis of individual, team, or organizational performance.[16]

Decisions about Healthcare Compensation Levels

Even though healthcare organizations might wish to pay the top wages and salaries relative to their competition, that might not be possible because of the significant pressure healthcare organizations face to control their costs. Three basic approaches to healthcare compensation include market-based pay, competency-based pay, and team pay. An overview of each approach is presented in this section.

Market-Based Pay   Some healthcare organizations establish specific policies about where they wish to be positioned in the labor market. These policies use a *quartile strategy*, as illustrated in Figure 12-6. Data in pay surveys reveal that the actual dollar difference between quartiles is generally 15 percent to 20 percent.

Most employers choose to position themselves in the *second quartile*, in the middle of the market (median), based on pay survey data of other employers' compensation plans. Choosing this level attempts to balance employer cost pressures and the need to attract and retain employees by providing mid-level compensation levels.

FIGURE 12-6   Market Based Compensation Strategies

Third Quartile: Above-Market Strategy

(Employer positions pay scales so that
25% of firms pay above and 75% pay below

Second Quartile: Middle-Market Strategy

(Employer positions pay scales so that
50% of firms pay above and 50% pay below

First Quartile: Below-Market Strategy

(Employer positions pay scales so that
75% of firms pay above and 25% pay below

© 2016 Cengage Learning®

An employer using a *first-quartile* approach might choose to pay below-market compensation for several reasons. The employer might be experiencing a shortage of funds, and be unable to pay more and still meet objectives. Also, when an abundance of workers is available, particularly those with lower skills, a below-market approach can be used to attract sufficient workers at lesser cost. The downside of this strategy is that higher turnover of workers is more likely. If the labor market supply tightens, then attracting and retaining workers becomes more difficult.

A *third-quartile* approach uses an aggressive pay-above-market emphasis. This strategy generally enables an organization to attract and retain sufficient workers with the required capabilities and to be more selective when hiring. However, because it is a higher-cost approach, organizations often look for ways to increase the productivity of employees receiving above-market wages.

In many cases, depending on the availability of workers with certain skills (e.g., pharmacists or certified nurse anesthetists), organizations may adopt a strategy to utilize a third-quartile approach for those positions, yet pay at first- or second-quartile levels for less-hard-to-fill positions. This approach entails a "market-driven" philosophy for the hard-to-fill positions.[17]

Competency-Based Pay   The design of most compensation programs rewards employees for carrying out their tasks, duties, and responsibilities. The job requirements determine which employees have higher base rates. Employees receive more for doing jobs that require a greater variety of tasks, more knowledge and skills, greater physical effort, or more demanding working conditions.[18]

However, some healthcare organizations are emphasizing competencies rather than tasks, competencies such as the ability to perform a particular clinical procedure or the attainment of a clinical credential such as a certified emergency nurse. A number of organizations are paying employees for the competencies they demonstrate rather than just for the specific tasks performed. This type of pay program rewards employees who exhibit more versatility and continue to develop their skills and abilities.

In knowledge-based pay (KBP) or skill-based pay (SBP) systems, employees start at a base level of pay and receive increases as they learn to do other jobs or gain other skills and therefore become more valuable to the employer. For example, in an RN clinical ladder program, RNs will have the opportunity to move up two or more pay levels based on their ability to demonstrate higher levels of clinical competency. Penn State Hershey Hospital has a clinical ladder program designed to recognize and reward nurses who demonstrate clinical excellence.[19] The success of competency plans requires managerial commitment to a philosophy different from those traditionally found in organizations.

This approach places far more emphasis on training and developing employees to help them succeed in this type of program. Due to the extensive commitment to training and the need to monitor the competencies of employees that competency-based pay systems require, they are more likely to be implemented in larger healthcare organizations. Also, work flow must be adapted to allow workers to move from job to job as needed. Additionally, clinical ladder programs have been used effectively for other healthcare professions, such as medical technologists, physical therapists, and pharmacists.

When a healthcare organization moves to a competency-based system, considerable time must be spent identifying the required competencies for various jobs. Progression of employees must be possible, and they must be paid appropriately for all of their competencies. Figure 12-7 depicts the pay structure of a clinical nursing ladder program. Any *limitations* on the numbers of people who can acquire more competencies should be clearly identified. Some healthcare organizations limit, for budget reasons, the number of nurses that can attain the highest level on the clinical ladder. *Training* in the appropriate competencies is particularly critical. Also, a competency-based system needs to acknowledge

---

FIGURE 12-7 **Structure of a Clinical Nursing Ladder Program**

Clinical Nurse (CN) I
- Nurses with less than 12 months experience are hired as a CN I
- Compensation changes annually

Clinical Nurse (CN) II
- Nurses with greater than 12 months experience hired as a CN II
- Demonstrated ability to orient new staff
- Internal candidates receive a lump payment when promoted to a CN II

Clinical Nurse (CN) III
- Nurses with 3+ years of experience are eligible
- Demonstrated expertise in a nursing specialty (critical care, diabetes, etc.)
- Compensation = 5% increase

Clinical Nurse (CN) IV
- Nurses with 5+ years of experience are eligible
- Demonstrated expertise in a nursing specialty (critical care, diabetes, etc.)
- Recognized as a subject matter expert (SME), as demonstrated by presentations at national conferences, faculty appointment, etc.
- Compensation = 6% increase

© 2016 Cengage Learning®

or certify employees as they acquire certain competencies, and then to verify the maintenance of those *competencies.* In summary, use of a competency-based system requires significant investment of management time and commitment.

Individual versus Team Rewards   As healthcare organizations have shifted to using work teams, they face the logical concern of how to develop compensation programs that build on the team concept. At issue is how to compensate the individual whose performance may also be evaluated on the basis of team achievement. Paying all members of a team the same amount, even though they demonstrate differing competencies and levels of performance, obviously creates equity concerns for many employees.[20]

Many organizations use team rewards as variable pay added to base pay. For base pay, individual compensation is based on competency- or skill-based approaches. Variable pay rewards for teams are most frequently distributed annually as a specified dollar amount, not as a percentage of base pay. Rather than substituting for base pay programs, team-based rewards appear to be useful in rewarding performance of a team beyond the satisfactory level. More discussion on team-based incentives is contained in the next chapter.

Perceptions of Pay Fairness

Most people in healthcare organizations work to gain rewards for their efforts. Except in volunteer or charitable organizations, people expect to receive what they feel is fair tangible compensation for their efforts. Whether base pay, variable pay, or benefits, the extent to which employees perceive compensation to be fair often affects their performance and how they view their jobs and employers.[21]

Pay Secrecy versus Openness   Another compensation issue concerns the degree of secrecy healthcare organizations have regarding their pay systems. Pay information that may be kept secret in "closed" systems relates to information about individual pay amounts, pay raises, and incentive payouts. Some firms have policies that prohibit employees from discussing their pay with other employees, and violations of these policies can lead to disciplinary action. A recent survey shows that more than half of all employees feel that their employer discourages or forbids employees from sharing pay information with each other. However, such policies may violate the National Labor Relations Act, and the courts have supported employees' right to discuss pay and benefit issues.[22]

Beyond the legal issues, however, healthcare organizations should examine the reasons for severely restricting employee discussion of pay. If an organization has implemented competitive pay practices and has a fair and reasonable pay structure, employee concerns about inequity can be reduced by sharing this information. Explaining pay grades and pay decision rules can enhance employee perceptions of fair treatment and help them understand why different jobs are paid at different rates. Maintaining a cloak of secrecy invites curiosity and suspicion from employees, which may result in less trust about how they are being paid.

External Equity   External equity considers the rates paid by other organizations in determining a competitive position for an organization's compensation program. Maintaining external equity is extremely important for healthcare employers to effectively compete for workers, especially in consideration of the shortage of skilled healthcare workers today. If a healthcare employer does not provide compensation that employees view as equitable compared to other organizations, that employer is more likely to experience higher turnover.[23] Other drawbacks include greater difficulty in recruiting qualified and high-demand individuals. Also, by not being competitive, the employer is more likely to attract and retain individuals with less knowledge, skills, and abilities, resulting in lower overall organizational performance. Organizations track external equity by using pay surveys, which are discussed later in this chapter.

LEGAL REQUIREMENTS FOR PAY SYSTEMS

In managing compensation systems, healthcare organizations must comply with a myriad of federal, state, and local regulations and reporting requirements. Important areas addressed by the laws include minimum wage standards and hours of work. The following discussion examines the laws and regulations affecting base compensation; laws and regulations affecting incentives and benefits are examined in later chapters.

Fair Labor Standards Act (FLSA)

The primary federal law affecting compensation is the Fair Labor Standards Act (FLSA), which was passed in 1938. Compliance with FLSA provisions is enforced by the Wage and Hour Division of the U.S. Department of Labor (DOL). Penalties for wage-and-hour violations often include awards of up to two years of back pay for affected current and former employees along with a monetary penalty. Willful violations may be penalized by up to three years of back pay. For example, a large medical center had allowed the nursing supervisors to arbitrarily pay overtime wages to some regularly scheduled charge nurses, who had been classified as exempt employees. This was done to encourage these charge nurses to pick up additional shifts. Some of the charge nurses who had not been recipients of the overtime pay complained to the Wage and Hour Division. Upon investigation, the division determined that the payment of indiscriminate overtime wages to otherwise exempt employees nullified their exempt status, and the Division subsequently negotiated a large back-pay award for the charge nurses.

The DOL launched a public service campaign called We Can Help, an outreach program to encourage low-wage and immigrant workers to report pay complaints.[24] The provisions of both the original act and subsequent revisions focus on the following major areas:

- Minimum wage
- Limits on the use of child labor
- Exempt and nonexempt status (overtime provisions)

Minimum Wage   The FLSA sets a minimum wage to be paid to a broad spectrum of covered employees. Congressional action is the only way the minimum wage can be changed. A lower minimum wage is set for "tipped" employees, such as restaurant servers, but their compensation must equal or exceed the minimum wage when average tips are included. Eight states raised their minimum wage levels by an average of 32 cents per hour. If a state's minimum wage is higher than the federal minimum wage, employers must pay this higher wage. Employers that operate in multiple states must monitor legislation that might affect their operations. Some research suggests that minimum wage increases lead to a reduction in employment or working hours for entry-level workers, while other studies show that there is no impact on employment.[25]

A debate continues about the use of a living wage versus the minimum wage. A **living wage** is one that is supposed to meet the basic needs of a worker's family. In the United States, the living wage typically aligns with the amount needed for a family of four to be supported by one worker so that family income is above the officially identified "poverty" level. Although many employees working in healthcare organizations earn significantly above the federal minimum wage and the livable wage, many do not, especially front-line staff working in extended care facilities.

Without waiting for U.S. federal laws to change, many U.S. cities have passed local living-wage laws. Those favoring living-wage laws stress that even the lowest-skilled workers need to earn wages above the poverty level. Those opposed to living-wage laws point out that many of the lowest-paid workers are single, which makes the "family of four" test inappropriate. Obviously, there are ethical, economic, and employment implications on both sides of this issue.[26]

Child Labor Provisions   The child labor provisions of the FLSA set the minimum age for employment with unlimited hours at 16 years. For hazardous occupations, the minimum is 18 years of age. Individuals 14 to 15 years old may work outside school hours with certain limitations. Many employers require age certificates for employees because the FLSA makes the employer responsible for determining an individual's age. Age certificates are supplied by high schools.

Exempt and Nonexempt Statuses   Under the FLSA, employees are classified as exempt or nonexempt. **Exempt employees** hold positions for which employers are not required to pay overtime. **Nonexempt employees** must be paid overtime. The current FLSA regulations used to establish whether or not a job qualifies for exempt status classify jobs into five categories as shown in Figure 12-8. The regulations identify several factors to be considered when determining exempt status. The regulations are complex, and a thorough review of each job is recommended to ensure proper classification and prevent misclassifying employees. Job duties can change over time, and it is wise to periodically review all jobs in the organization.[27] To review the details for each exemption, go to the U.S. DOL's website at *http://www.dol.gov.*

When designing base pay, healthcare employers often categorize jobs into groupings that tie the FLSA status with the method of payment. Employers are

FIGURE 12-8 **Determining Exempt Status under the FLSA**

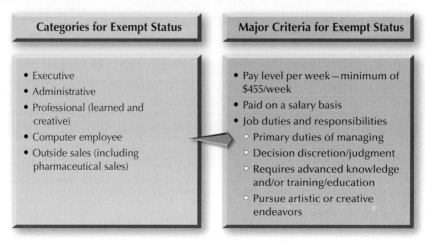

Categories for Exempt Status	Major Criteria for Exempt Status

• Executive
• Administrative
• Professional (learned and creative)
• Computer employee
• Outside sales (including pharmaceutical sales)
	• Pay level per week—minimum of $455/week
	• Paid on a salary basis
	• Job duties and responsibilities
	  ○ Primary duties of managing
	  ○ Decision discretion/judgment
	  ○ Requires advanced knowledge and/or training/education
	  ○ Pursue artistic or creative endeavors

© Cengage Learning®

required to pay overtime for *hourly* jobs to comply with the FLSA. Employees in positions classified as *salaried nonexempt* are also entitled to overtime pay. Salaried nonexempt positions sometimes include secretarial, clerical, and salaried blue-collar positions (like shift supervisor). A common mistake made by employers is to avoid paying overtime to all salaried employees, even though some may qualify for nonexempt status. Exempt status is not necessarily granted to all salaried jobs; each job must be evaluated on a case-by-case basis. The FLSA does not require employers to pay overtime for *salaried exempt* jobs.

Overtime The FLSA established overtime pay requirements at one and one-half times the regular pay rate for all hours worked over 40 in a week, except for exempt employees. There are other exceptions to the overtime requirements, such as farmworkers, but these exceptions are rare.

The workweek is defined as a consecutive period of 168 hours (24 hours × 7 days), which does not have to be a calendar week. Hospitals and nursing homes are allowed a special definition of the workweek to accommodate their 24/7 scheduling demands. This is referred to as 8 and 80. Effectively, hospitals and long-term care facilities that adopt this method pay overtime for hours worked beyond 8 in a day or 80 in a 14-day period. No daily number of hours requiring overtime is set, except for special provisions relating to hospitals and other specially designated organizations.

Common Overtime Issues For individuals who are nonexempt, employers must consider many issues. These include the following:

• *Compensatory Time Off*—"Comp" hours are earned by public-sector nonexempt employees in lieu of payment for extra time worked at the rate of one and one-half times the number of hours over 40 that are worked in a week. Comp time is prohibited in the private sector and cannot be legally offered to employees working for private organizations.

- *Incentives for Nonexempt Employees*—Employers must add the amount of direct work-related incentives to an employee's base pay and then calculate overtime pay as one and one-half times the higher (adjusted) rate of pay.

- *Training Time*—Time spent in training must be counted as time worked by nonexempt employees unless it is voluntary or not directly job related.

- *Travel Time*—Travel time must be counted as work time if it occurs during normal work hours for the benefit of the employer. Travel to and from work is not considered compensable travel time.

- *Donning and Doffing Time*—Some jobs require employees to change clothes or to spend a significant amount of time donning protective equipment before they report for duty.[28] This is clearly an issue in healthcare organizations because many healthcare jobs require employees to wear protective clothing such as scrubs to perform their duties. Regulations regarding putting on and taking off such clothing are complex. How much time is allowed and/or whether it is paid time to dress for work is frequently debated in many healthcare organizations. Questions regarding specific cases should be researched with the DOL.

The FLSA does not require employers to provide breaks or lunch periods, or to pay double-time for any hours worked. State laws vary on these topics, so employers should research compliance requirements in all states in which they operate. The complexity of overtime determination and related matters can be confusing for managers, employees, and HR professionals. The DOL has many informative publications on its website that clarify these issues.

Independent Contractor Regulations

The growing use of contingent workers by many organizations has drawn the attention of several enforcement agencies such as the Internal Revenue Service (IRS), DOL, U.S. Treasury Department, and state taxing authorities. When workers are improperly classified as independent contractors, payroll tax revenues are lost and workers are not insured for unemployment or work-related injuries.[29] According to some estimates, 3.4 million employees are misclassified as independent contractors, costing the United States $54 billion in underpaid employment taxes and $15 billion in unpaid FICA and unemployment taxes.[30]

For an employer, classifying someone as an independent contractor rather than an employee offers major advantages. Figure 12-9 provides guidance as to how to determine if an individual is an employee or independent contractor. The employer does not have to pay Social Security, unemployment, or workers' compensation costs. These additional payroll levies may add 10 percent or more to the costs of hiring the individual as an employee. A recent healthcare case that pursued by both the IRS and DOL was against an urgent care clinic that employed physicians as independent contractors. Even though the physicians worked relatively infrequently and held jobs elsewhere, the IRS determined that they were employees and not independent contractors. The clinic was required to pay a substantial penalty to resolve the case and treat the physicians as regular W-2 employees going forward.

FIGURE 12-9 IRS Guidelines for Independent Contractor Status

Behavioral Control/Instructions/Training That the Business Gives to the Worker

- When and where to do the work
- What tools and equipment to use
- What workers to hire or to assist with the work
- Where to purchase supplies and services
- What work must be performed by a specified individual
- What order or sequence to follow
- How work results are achieved

Financial Control

- Extent of the worker's investment
- Extent to which worker makes services available to a relevant market
- How the business pays the worker
- Whether or not the business reimburses travel expenses
- The extent to which the workers can realize a profit or loss

Type of Relationship

- Written contracts
- Whether the business provides employee-type benefits to the worker
- Permanency of the relationship
- Extent to which services provided by the worker are a key aspect of the regular business of the company

Source: IRS, Publication 15A, 2012

The misclassification of employees as independent contractors has become such a serious problem that the IRS launched an amnesty program to allow employers to report misclassifications and pay for past payroll tax obligations. The hope was that through the Voluntary Classification Settlement Program, employers would come forward rather than wait for an audit, which is likely to be much more costly and time-consuming.[31]

Most federal and state entities rely on the criteria for independent contractor status established by the IRS.[32] Each case is analyzed and the weight of evidence is used to make the final determination.[33] Key differences between an employee and an independent contractor are evaluated by reviewing behavioral control, financial control, and relationship-type factors.

Additional Laws Affecting Compensation

Several compensation-related laws apply to organizations that have contracts with the U.S. government. Consequently, these laws may or may not impact healthcare organizations. These laws require that federal contractors pay a **prevailing wage**, which is determined by a formula that considers the rate paid for a job by a majority of the employers in the appropriate geographic area. The Davis-Bacon Act of 1931, the Walsh-Healy Public Contracts Act, and the McNamara-O'Hara Service Contract Act include prevailing wage clauses that apply to firms engaged in federal construction projects or that work directly on federal government contracts.

Garnishment occurs when a creditor obtains a court order that directs an employer to set aside a portion of an employee's wages to pay a debt owed to the creditor. Regulations passed as a part of the Consumer Credit Protection Act limit the amount of wages that can be garnished. The act also restricts the right of employers to terminate employees whose pay is subject to a single garnishment order. All 50 states have laws applying to wage garnishments.

DEVELOPMENT OF A BASE PAY SYSTEM

As Figure 12-10 shows, the development of a base wage and salary system begins with the assumption that accurate job descriptions and job specifications are available. The job descriptions then are used for *job evaluation* and *pay surveys*. These activities are designed to ensure that the pay system is both internally equitable and externally competitive. The data compiled in these two activities are used to design *pay structures*, including *pay grades* and minimum-to-maximum *pay ranges*. After the development of pay structures, individual jobs must be placed in the appropriate pay grades and employees' pay adjusted based on length of service and performance. Finally, the pay system must be monitored and updated.

Job Evaluation

Job evaluation provides a systematic basis for determining the relative worth of jobs within an organization. It flows from the job analysis process and relies on job descriptions and job specifications. In a job evaluation, every job is examined and ultimately priced according to the following features:

- Relative importance of the job
- KSAs needed to perform the job
- Difficulty of the job

FIGURE 12-10   Compensation Administration Process

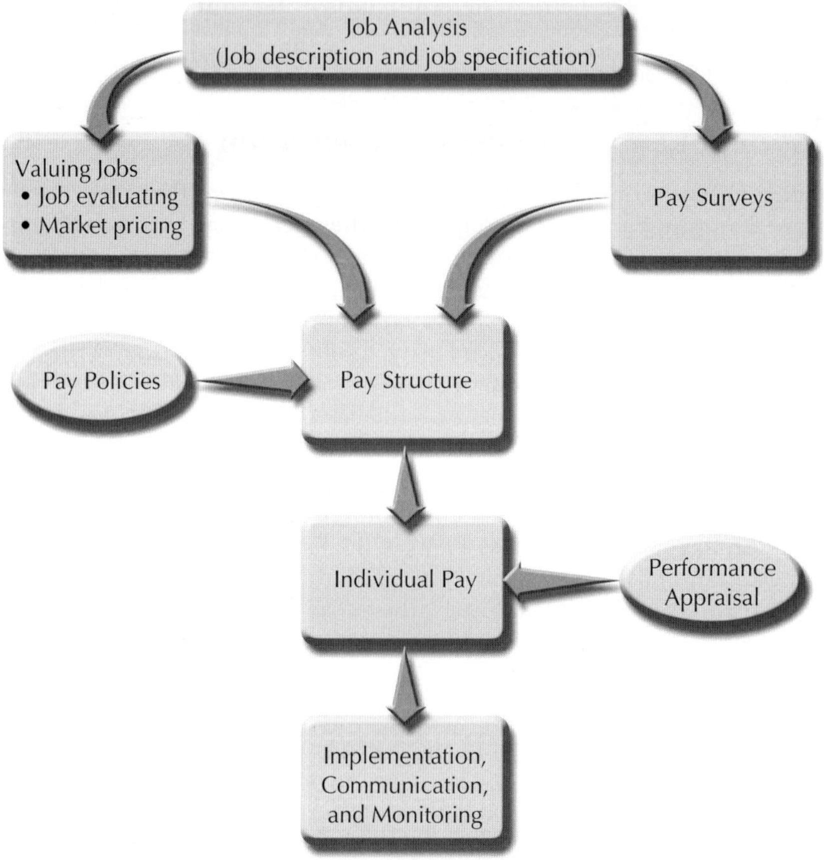

Healthcare employers want their employees to perceive their pay as appropriate in relation to pay for jobs performed by others. Because jobs vary widely in healthcare organizations, it is particularly important to identify **benchmark jobs**— jobs that are found in other healthcare organizations and performed by several individuals who have similar duties that are relatively stable and that require similar KSAs. For example, benchmark jobs commonly used in a hospital patient financial services department are biller, collector, and cash application clerk. Benchmark jobs are used with the job evaluation methods discussed here because they provide "anchors" against which unique jobs can be evaluated and then compared to benchmarked jobs.

Given the diversity of healthcare organizations, there are a variety of methods used to determine internal job worth through job evaluation. All methods have the same general objective, but they differ in complexity and means of measurement. Regardless of the method used, the intent is to develop a usable, measurable, and realistic system to determine compensation in an organization.

Job Evaluation Methods

The *ranking method* is a simple system that places jobs in order, from highest to lowest, by their value to the organization. This is a qualitative method in which the entire job is considered rather than individual components. The ranking method generally is more appropriate in a small organization that has relatively few jobs. For example, the ranking method might be used at a small family practice clinic with only two or three distinct job titles.

The *classification method* is often used in public-sector healthcare organizations like county mental health facilities. Descriptions of job classes are written and then each job is put into a grade according to the class it best matches. A major difficulty with this method is that subjective judgments are needed to develop the class descriptions and to place jobs accurately in them.

The *factor-comparison method* is a complex quantitative method that combines the ranking and point factor methods (explained below). Organizations that use this method must develop their own key jobs and factors. The factor-comparison method is time-consuming and difficult to use, which accounts for its limited popularity in organizations.

Point Factor Method   The most widely used job evaluation method, the point factor method, looks at compensable factors in a group of similar jobs and assigns weights, or *points*, to them. A **compensable factor** identifies a dimension that is part of every job and can be rated for each job. For example, all jobs require some level of education and experience for successful performance.

The point factor method is the most popular job evaluation approach because it is relatively simple to use and considers the components of a job rather than the total job. However, point factor systems have been criticized for reinforcing traditional organizational structures and job rigidity. Although not perfect, the point factor method is generally better than the ranking and classification methods because it quantifies job elements. Compensable factors are derived from job analysis and reflect the nature of different types of work performed in the organization.

Legal Issues and Job Evaluation

Employers usually view evaluating jobs to determine rates of pay as a separate issue from selecting individuals for those jobs or taking disciplinary action against individuals. Because job evaluation affects the employment relationship, specifically the pay of individuals, it involves legal issues that must be addressed. Fairness, nondiscrimination, and objectivity are critical requirements of whatever job evaluation process is utilized.

Job Evaluation and the Americans with Disabilities Act (ADA)   The Americans with Disabilities Act requires employers to identify the essential functions of a job. It is important that all facets of jobs are examined during a job evaluation. For example, a materials management job in a community hospital requires a distribution clerk to stock and distribute stock carts to the patient units. Twice per day the clerk usually delivers a cart, which might weigh up to 100 pounds, to a unit. The movement of the cart probably is not an essential function. But if job evaluation considers the physical demands associated with pushing the cart, then the points assigned may be different from the points assigned if only the essential functions are considered.

Job Evaluation and Gender Issues   Critics have charged that traditional job evaluation programs place less weight on knowledge, skills, and working conditions for many female-dominated jobs in office and clerical areas than on the same factors for male-dominated jobs in craft and manufacturing areas. As discussed earlier, advocates of pay equity view the disparity in pay between men's jobs and women's jobs as evidence of gender discrimination. These advocates also have attacked typical job evaluations as being gender biased. Employers counter that because they base their pay rates heavily on external equity comparisons in the labor market, they are simply reflecting rates the market economy sets for jobs and workers, rather than engaging in discrimination. Most court decisions have supported the employers' opinion.

Market Pricing

While the point factor method has served employers well for many years, the trend is moving to a more externally focused approach. The majority of healthcare organizations utilize **market pricing**, which uses market pay data to identify the relative value of jobs based on what other employers pay for similar jobs.

Key to market pricing is identifying relevant market pay data for jobs that are good "matches" with the employer's jobs, type of practice (acute care versus ambulatory care), and geographic considerations. Market pricing as part of strategic compensation decisions can ensure market competitiveness of compensation levels and practices. However, there will not always be a perfect match for each job in the external market.

Advantages of Market Pricing   The primary advantage cited for the use of market pricing is that it closely ties organizational pay levels to what is actually occurring in the market, without being distorted by "internal" job evaluation. An additional advantage of market pricing is that it allows an employer to communicate to employees that the compensation system is truly "market linked." Employees often see a compensation system that was developed using market pricing as having "face validity" and as being more objective than a compensation system that was developed using traditional job evaluation methods.

Disadvantages of Market Pricing   The biggest disadvantage of market pricing is that pay survey data may be limited or may not be gathered in methodologically sound ways. Additionally, tying pay levels to market data can lead to wide fluctuations on the basis of market conditions. Skills that are in great demand today can quickly become obsolete. Consider the nursing job market during the past two decade when pay levels varied significantly. The supply versus the demand of nurses seems to always be in flux. When the supply is low nursing wages are very high, but when the supply is sufficient nurses' wages tend to stabilize very quickly. The debate over the use of job evaluation versus market pricing is likely to continue because there are advantages and disadvantages to both approaches.[34]

Wage Surveys

Another part of building a pay system is surveying the pay that other healthcare organizations provide for similar jobs. A **wage survey** is a collection of data on compensation rates for workers performing similar jobs in other organizations. An employer may use surveys conducted by other organizations, or it may decide to conduct its own survey.

Whether available electronically or in printed form, national surveys on many jobs and industries come from the U.S. Department of Labor, Bureau of Labor Statistics, and through national trade associations. Many healthcare employers participate in wage surveys sponsored by various healthcare trade associations, such as the Medical Group Management Association (MGMA), which surveys physician practices, clinics, and the ambulatory departments of hospitals and medical centers.

Properly using surveys from other sources requires that certain questions be addressed:

- *Participants*— Is the survey a realistic sample of those employers with whom the organization competes for employees?

- *Broad Based*— Is the survey balanced so that organizations of varying sizes, industries, and locales are included?

- *Timeliness*— How current are the data (determined by the date when the survey was conducted)?

- *Methodology*— How established is the survey, and how qualified are those who conducted it?

- *Job Matches*— Does it contain job summaries so that appropriate matches to job descriptions can be made?

The results of the pay survey usually are made available to those participating in the survey in order to gain their cooperation. Most surveys specify confidentiality, and data are summarized to assure anonymity. Different job levels often are included, and the pay rates are presented both in overall terms and on a regional basis to reflect regional pay differences. Figure 12-11 depicts a section of a clinic wage survey.

One reason for employers to use outside consultants to conduct pay surveys is to avoid charges that the employers are attempting "price-fixing" on wages. The federal government has filed suit in the past, alleging that by sharing wage data, employers may be attempting to hold wages down artificially, in violation of the Sherman Antitrust Act.

FIGURE 12-11 **Sample Clinic Wage Survey**

| Region | Number of Incumbents | Number of FTE's | Weighted Average Hourly Rate | Reported Pay Ranges (Averages) | | |
				Minimum Hourly Rate	Midpoint Hourly Rate	Maximum Hourly Rate
Staff Accountant						

Responsible for balancing accounts, entering journal transactions, reconciling general ledger accounts, processing payables, performing calculations, posting transactions, may prepare/process payroll and works under the direction of a senior level accounting staff member, Controller or Director of Finance/CFO. Requires Bachelors Degree in Accounting with zero to five year's experience.

Region	Number of Incumbents	Number of FTE's	Weighted Average Hourly Rate	Minimum Hourly Rate	Midpoint Hourly Rate	Maximum Hourly Rate
Metro	15	14.7	$24.73	$20.02	$25.15	$30.29
All	18	17.7	$26.37	$20.55	$25.44	$30.47

Accounts Payable Clerk

Responsible for processing accounts payable invoices, automated payments, internal check requests and may handle expense reimbursement accounts. Requires Associates Degree in Accounting with two plus year's experience.

Region	Number of Incumbents	Number of FTE's	Weighted Average Hourly Rate	Minimum Hourly Rate	Midpoint Hourly Rate	Maximum Hourly Rate
Central	5	3.7	$16.97	$15.98	$19.54	$22.77
Metro	18	15.5	$20.25	$15.71	$19.63	$23.01
All	26	21.5	$20.63	$16.21	$20.00	$23.08

Source: Based on data from, W.J. Flynn and Associates, LLC 2014

Different Pay Structures

In organizations that have a number of different job families, pay survey data may reveal different levels of pay resulting from market factors. These differences may lead to the establishment of several different pay structures, rather than just one structure. Examples of some common pay structures include: (1) hourly and salaried; (2) office, technical, professional, and managerial; (3) clinical allied health and support; and (4) clerical, information technology, professional, supervisory, management, and executive. The nature and culture of the organization are considerations for determining how many and which pay structures to have.

Establishing Pay Grades   In the process of establishing a pay structure, organizations use **pay grades** to group individual jobs having approximately the same job worth. Although no set rules govern establishing pay grades, some overall suggestions can be useful. Generally, from 11 to 17 grades are used in small and medium-sized healthcare organizations with fewer than 500 employees.

Broadbanding   The practice of using fewer pay grades with much broader ranges than in traditional compensation systems is called **broadbanding**. Combining many grades into these broad bands is designed to encourage horizontal movement and therefore more skill acquisition. The main advantage of broadbanding is that it is more consistent with the flattening of organizational levels and the growing use of jobs that are multidimensional. A problem with broadbanding is that many employees expect a promotion to be accompanied by a pay raise and movement to a new pay grade. By removing this grade progression, employees may feel that there are fewer promotional opportunities. Most companies continue to rely on traditional pay grade structures with only about 10 percent adopting a broadband structure.[35]

Pay Ranges

The pay range for each pay grade also must be established. Using the market line as a starting point, the employer can determine minimum and maximum pay levels for each pay grade by making the market line the midpoint line of the new pay structure. For example, in a particular pay grade, the maximum value may be 20 percent above the midpoint located on the market line and the minimum value 20 percent below it.

As Figure 12-12 shows, a smaller minimum-to-maximum range should be used for lower-level jobs than for higher-level jobs, primarily because employees in lower-level jobs tend to stay in them for shorter periods of time and have greater promotion possibilities. For example, a clerk-typist might advance to the position of secretary or word-processing operator. In contrast, a pharmacist likely would have fewer possibilities for upward movement in an organization. However, using the same percentage range at all levels can make administration of a pay system easier in small firms. If broadbanding is used, then much wider ranges, often exceeding 100 percent, may be used.

Compensation experts recommend having an overlap between grades. This structure means that an experienced employee in a lower grade can be paid more than a less-experienced employee in a job in the next pay grade. With pay grade overlap, an individual in the higher-grade job, for example grade 4, may be paid less than someone in a grade 3 job but has more room for pay progression. Thus, over time the pay of a person in the grade 4 job may surpass the pay of a person in grade 3, who may "top out" because of the pay grade 3 maximum. Compensation experts have suggested that the same monetary amounts can appear in as many as four different pay grades.

Once pay grades and ranges have been computed, then the current pay of employees must be compared to the draft ranges. If the pay of a significant number of employees falls outside the ranges, then a revision of the pay grades and ranges may be needed. Also, once costing and budgeting scenarios are run in order to assess the financial impact of the new pay structures, then pay policy decisions about market positioning may have to be revised, by either lowering or raising the ranges.

FIGURE 12-12   Typical Pay Range Widths for Healthcare Positions

Types of Jobs	Range Above Minimum	% Around Midpoint
Executives	50%–70%	+ or – 20–25%
Mid-Management/Professionals	40%–50%	+ or –16–20%
Technicians/Skilled Craft & Clerical	30%–40%	+ or –13–16%
General Clerical/Others	25%–35%	+ or –11–15%

Individual Pay

Once organizations have determined pay ranges, they can set the pay for specific individuals. Setting a range for each pay grade gives flexibility by allowing individuals to progress within a grade instead of having to be moved to a new grade each time they receive a raise. A pay range also allows managers to reward the better-performing employees while maintaining the integrity of the pay system.

Rates Out of Range

Regardless of how well constructed a pay structure is, there usually are a few individuals whose pay is lower than the minimum or higher than the maximum. These situations occur most frequently when organizations that have had an informal pay system develop a new, more formalized one.

Red-Circled Employees   A **red-circled employee** is an incumbent who is paid above the range set for the job. For example, assume that an employee's current pay is $15.00 per hour due to a reassignment to a lower-level position. But the pay range for that grade is $11.00 to $14.50. Over time, management would attempt to bring the employee's rate into grade.

Several approaches can be used to bring a red-circled employee's pay into line. Although the fastest way would be to cut the employee's pay, that approach is not recommended and is seldom used. Instead, the employee's pay may be frozen until the pay range can be adjusted upward to get the employee's pay rate back into the grade. Another approach is to give the employee a small lump-sum payment but not adjust the pay rate when others are given raises; this is referred to as a red-circled bonus.

Green-Circled Employees   An individual whose pay is below the range is a **green-circled employee**. Promotion is a major cause of this situation. Generally, it is recommended that the green-circled employee receive pay increases to get him or her to the pay grade minimum fairly rapidly. Frequent increases should be considered if the increase to minimum would be substantial.

Pay Compression

Pay Compression One major problem many healthcare employers face is **pay compression**, which occurs when pay differences among individuals with different levels of experience and performance become small. Pay compression is frequently a result of labor market pay levels increasing faster than current employees' pay adjustments. Further contributing to the problem are pay freezes put in place during economic downturns. In the past, employees may not have been aware of these pay compression situations. However, young employees in the millennial generation are very open about pay matters and they widely discuss their pay with coworkers. Healthcare managers have to be prepared to address pay compression as it occurs.[36]

In response to competitive market shortages of particular job skills, managers occasionally may have to deviate from the priced grades to hire people with skills that are scarce. For example, suppose the worth of a radiological special procedures technician's job is evaluated at $48,000 to $58,000 annual salary in a hospital, but qualified individuals are in short supply and other employers are paying annual salaries of $70,000. The hospital must pay the higher rate to attract new technicians. Suppose also that several technicians who have been with the hospital for several years started at $48,000 and have received 4 percent increases to their rates each year. These current employees will still be making less than salaries paid to attract new technicians from outside with less experience, causing a significant pay compression issue between the current employees and the new hires.

ISSUES INVOLVING PAY INCREASES

Decisions about pay increases often are critical ones in the relationships among employees, their managers, and the healthcare organization. Individuals express expectations about their pay and about how much increase is "fair," especially in comparison with the increases received by other employees. There are several ways to determine pay increases.

Pay Adjustment Matrix

Many healthcare employers profess to have a pay system based on performance. But relying on performance appraisal information for making a pay adjustment assumes that the appraisals are accurate and done well, which is not always the case. Consequently, a system for integrating appraisals and pay changes must be developed and applied equally. Often, this integration is done through the development of a **pay adjustment matrix**, or *salary guide chart*. Using pay adjustment matrices, adjustments are based in part on a person's **compa-ratio**, which is the pay level divided by the midpoint of the pay range, as shown in Figure 12-13.

Such charts can facilitate an employee's upward movement in an organization, which depends on the person's performance, as rated in an appraisal, and on the person's position in the pay range, which has some relation to experience as well. Notice that as employees move up the pay range, they must exhibit higher performance to obtain the same percentage raise as those lower in the range performing at the "meets performance expectations" level. This approach is taken because the firm is paying above the market midpoint but receiving only satisfactory performance

FIGURE 12-13   Performance-Based Pay Adjustment Matrix

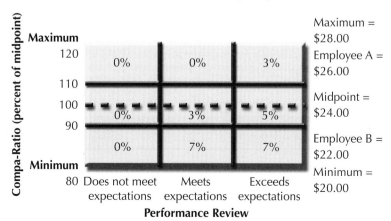

rather than above-expectations performance. Charts can be constructed to reflect the specific pay-for-performance policy and philosophy in an organization.

Seniority

Seniority, or time spent in the organization or on a particular job, can be used as the basis for pay increases. Many employers have policies that require a person to be employed for a certain length of time before being eligible for pay increases. Pay adjustments based on seniority often are set as automatic steps once a person has been employed the required length of time, although performance must be at least satisfactory in many nonunion systems.

Step systems, which use pay increases based solely on the attainment of a designated period of employment (typically 2,080 hours), continue to be a popular method of awarding pay increases in healthcare organizations, especially in states where there is significant unionization of healthcare employees. Each step represents the pay adjustment for employees as they attain one full-time equivalent year of employment (2,080 hours).

Cost-of-Living Adjustments (COLAs)

A common pay-raise practice is the use of a *standard raise* or **cost-of-living adjustment (COLA)**. Giving all employees a standard percentage increase enables them to maintain the same real wages in a period of economic inflation. Often, these adjustments are tied to changes in the consumer price index (CPI)[37]or some other general economic measure. However, numerous studies have revealed that the CPI overstates the actual cost of living.

Unfortunately, some healthcare employers give across-the-board raises and call them **merit raises**, which they are not. If all employees get the same increase, it is legitimately viewed as an across-the-board adjustment that has little to do with good performance. For this reason, employers should reserve the term *merit* for any amount above the standard raise, and they should state clearly which amount is for performance and which is the COLA adjustment.

Lump-Sum Increases

A compensation practice that has gained popularity among some healthcare organizations is to pay a lump-sum bonus in lieu of an incremental increase to an employee's base pay. As an example, employees who receive a pay increase, for either merit or seniority, may have their base pay adjusted and receive an increase in the amount of their regular monthly or weekly paycheck. For instance, an employee who makes $15.00 per hour and then receives a 3 percent increase will move to $15.45 per hour.

In contrast, a lump-sum increase (LSI) is a onetime payment of all or part of a yearly pay increase. The pure LSI approach does not increase the base pay. Therefore, in this example the person's base pay remains at $15.00 per hour. If an LSI of 3 percent is granted, then the person receives $936.00 (45¢ per hour for 2,080 working hours in the year). However, the base rate remains at $15.00 per hour, which slows down the progression of the base wages. It also allows for the amount of the "lump" to be varied, without having to continually raise the base rate. Some organizations place a limit on how much of a merit increase can

---

HEALTHCARE REFORM AND COMPENSATION PRACTICES

The Affordable Care Act (ACA) aggressively stresses the importance of primary care provision for U.S. consumers of healthcare.[38] An analysis of the cost drivers in the healthcare system clearly indicates that patients who rely on emergency rooms for their primary care or who are not routinely treated for a chronic disease add significantly to the cost of healthcare for the country. A key method of diverting patients from emergency rooms and/or receiving appropriate care for a chronic disease is for each consumer of healthcare to have a primary care doctor. However, due to the shortage of primary care doctors in the United States, the success of the ACA could be impacted. Many initiatives are in the process of being implemented to deal with this issue, including giving a limited 10 percent Medicare incentive payment to eligible primary care physicians, expanding primary care residency slots, and implementing teaching health centers that are community based. But these legislated initiatives will take time to impact the shortage of primary care providers. Innovative healthcare organizations are turning to an alternative primary care provider labor force—physician assistants (PAs).

PAs, within the scope of their practice, are able to provide a significant portion of primary care to their patients.[39] However, this new and increasing demand for PAs has created a compensation challenge for organizations that have turned to them as a significant source for delivering primary care. Part of the challenge is how much to pay them, but another part of the challenge is on what to base their pay. Should they receive base wages only? Base wages plus productivity pay, similar to their physician counterparts? Or some hybrid, unique to their practice?[40]

Healthcare HR professionals and managers will face many challenges as the healthcare industry responds to the new realities of healthcare reform. Changing work patterns and the workforce realignments as described above will require proactive and innovative compensation strategies.

---

be taken as a lump-sum payment. Other organizations may split the lump sum into two checks, each representing one-half of the year's pay raise.

EXECUTIVE COMPENSATION

Executive compensation in healthcare organizations is typically treated much differently than nonexecutive pay. Executive compensation typically includes multiple components, whereas nonexecutive compensation may include only pay and benefits.

As Figure 12-14 shows, the common components of executive compensation are salaries, annual bonuses, long-term incentives, supplemental benefits, and perquisites.

Executive Salaries

Salaries of executives vary by type of job, size of organization, region of the country, and industry segment. In healthcare organizations, especially not-for-profits, salaries make up the majority of the typical top executive's annual compensation total.

FIGURE 12-14 **Executive Compensations Components**

Perquisites
Supplemental Benefits
Long-Term Incentives
Annual Bonuses
Executive Salaries

© 2016 Cengage Learning®

Executive Bonus and Incentive Plans

Executive performance may be difficult to evaluate, but incentive and bonus compensation must reflect some performance measures if they are to be meaningful. Bonuses for executives can be determined in several ways. A discretionary system whereby bonuses are awarded based on the judgments of the chief executive officer and the board of directors is one way.[41] However, the absence of formal, measurable targets detracts significantly from this approach. Also, as noted, incentives can be tied to specific measures, such as effectively managing costs, improving patient satisfaction, or meeting revenue targets. More complex systems create incentive pools and thresholds above which payments are computed. Whatever method is used, it is important to describe it so that executives trying to earn incentives and bonuses understand the plan; otherwise, the incentive effect will be diminished.

As an example, a large orthopedic surgical practice ties the annual bonuses for its senior managers to revenue targets, patient satisfaction scores, and employee retention. The bonuses have amounted to as much as 25 percent of each senior manager's base salary.

Performance Incentives: Long Term Versus Short Term

Performance-based incentives attempt to tie executive compensation to the long-term growth and success of the organization. However, whether the emphasis is really on the long term or merely represents a series of short-term rewards is controversial. Short-term rewards based on quarterly or annual performance may not result in the kind of long-run-oriented decisions necessary for the organization to continue to do well.

Benefits for Executives

As with benefits for nonexecutive employees, executive benefits may take several forms, including traditional retirement, health insurance, vacations, and others. However, executive benefits may include some items that other employees do not receive. For example, executive health plans without copayments and without limitations on deductibles or physician choice are popular among small and medium-sized organizations. Deferred compensation offers another possible means of helping executives with tax liabilities caused by incentive compensation plans.

Executive Perquisites

In addition to the regular benefits received by all employees, executives often receive benefits called perquisites. **Perquisites (perks)** are special executive benefits—usually noncash items. Perks help tie executives to organizations and demonstrate their importance to their companies. Many executives value the status enhancement of perks because these visible symbols of status allow executives to be seen as very important persons (VIPs) both inside and outside their organizations.

Current Nature of Healthcare Executive Compensation

Healthcare executives—typically someone in the top two levels of an organization, such as CEO, administrator, president, or senior vice president—are paid very well.[42]

In most healthcare organizations, the board of directors or its equivalent in smaller healthcare organizations sets policy. For publicly traded companies covered by federal regulatory agencies, such as the Securities and Exchange Commission (SEC), the board must approve executive compensation packages. Even for many nonprofit organizations, IRS regulations require the board to review and approve the compensation for top-level executives.

In many healthcare organizations the **compensation committee of the board of directors** usually is a subgroup of the board composed of directors who are not officers of the firm. Compensation committees generally make recommendations to the board of directors on overall pay policies, salaries for top officers, supplemental compensation such as bonuses, and additional perquisites for executives.

Determining The "Reasonableness" of Executive Compensation

The reasonableness of executive compensation is often justified by comparison to compensation market surveys, but these surveys usually provide a range of compensation data that requires interpretation. Various questions have been suggested for determining if executive pay is "reasonable," including the following:

- Would another organization hire this person as an executive?
- How does the executive's compensation compare with that for executives in similar organizations in the industry?
- Are the executive's pay and benefits consistent with those for other employees in the organization?

Boards must address the need to continually link organizational performance with variable pay rewards for executives and other employees. There is certainly more controversy about executive compensation in other industries, but healthcare boards of directors must also be mindful of the reasonableness and transparency of executive pay and benefits.[43]

In the next chapter, the other key components of compensation (benefits and variable pay) are discussed. It is important that all compensation types are seen as interrelated components of a healthcare organization's total compensation program.

Gardenview Long-Term Care is a private, not-for-profit, retirement community located in a medium-sized market. It is a 50-year-old facility offering three levels of care for its elderly residents: independent living, assisted living, and skilled/full nursing care. Gardenview's administration has recently identified a strategic initiative to aggressively pursue the area of dementia/Alzheimer's care. In order to pursue this new strategic initiative, Gardenview is attempting to recruit a marketing director for the organization to market the new program.

The board of directors has contracted with an executive recruitment firm to conduct the search for the new marketing director. The first step in the recruitment firm's process was to determine a market-competitive compensation and benefits package for the position. Their market research determined the following:

- Starting salary range: $150,000 to $175,000
- Incentive bonus potential: 10 percent to 15 percent of base salary
- Special perks: travel allowance, conference funds, and expense account
- Benefits: fully paid health, dental, life, and disability insurance
- Pension: 10 percent contribution to a 403(b) plan

Questions

1. Is the package that is recommended by executive search committee typical for positions of this nature?
2. How could the board of directors be confident that the compensation package recommended by the executive search committee is market competitive?

1. Robert Grossman, "Invest in Older Workers," *HR Magazine* (August 2013), 20–25.
2. "Ways to Retain Experienced Nurses," *Trustee* (October 2009), 4.
3. Matt Bolch, "Another Brutal Year, Employers Struggle to Contain Rising Care Costs," *Managed Healthcare Executive* (September 2011), 30–32.
4. S. Farah, "Cloud Computing or Software as a Service—Which Makes the Most Sense for HR?," *Employment Relations Today* (Winter 2010), 31–37.
5. Kenneth W. Thomas, "The Four Intrinsic Rewards That Drive Employee Engagement," *Ivey Business Journal* 73 (2009), 9; Katie Kuehner-Hebert, "Can You Really Have It All?," *Human Resources Executive Online* (September 18, 2012).
6. "Hay Group Study Shows Slight Uptick in Use of Variable Pay," IOMA.com (February 2011).
7. Kathryn Tyler, "Basic Math Reveals the Reward for Rewards," *HR Magazine* (October 2011), 93–95.
8. Andrew R. McIlvaine, "Targeting Rewards," *Human Resource Executive Online* (June 2, 2009); Paul F. Buller and Glen M. McEvoy, "Strategy, Human Resource Management and Performance: Sharpening Line of Sight," *Human Resource Management Review* 22 (2012), 43–56.
9. Lin Grensing-Pophal, "Money vs. Happiness," *Human Resource Executive* (December, 2011), 14; Sanford E. Devoe, Byron Y. Lee, and Jeffrey Pfeffer, "Hourly versus Salaried Payment and Decisions about Trading Time and Money over Time," *Industrial and Labor Relations Review* 63 (2010), 627–640.
10. Vas Taras, "Direct versus Indirect Compensation: Balancing Value and Cost in Total Compensation," *Compensation & Benefits Review* 44 (2012), 24–28.
11. John M. Buell, "Shedding Light on Hidden Cost—More Savings in Labor, Supply Chain than You Know," *Healthcare Executive* (January 2011), 9–16.
12. Sanghee Park and Michael C. Sturman, "How and What You Pay Matters: The Relative Effectiveness of Merit Pay, Bonuses and Long-Term Incentives on Future Job Performance," *Compensation & Benefits Review* 44 (2012), 80–85; Tom Burke, "The New Normal in Compensation Programs," WorldatWork

(June 2011), *http://www.worldatwork.org/waw/adimComment?id=52475&from=cf_editorial_2411*.

13. "WorldatWork" (September 7, 2012), http://www.worldatwork.org/waw/aboutus/html/aboutus-waw.html.

14. Joanne Sammer, "Measure Compensation's Impact," *HR Magazine* (September 2012), 85–90; Eric Marquardt and Nick Dunlap, "Compensation Risk Assessments: A Process for Active Plan Management and Continuous Improvement," *Compensation & Benefits Review* 44 (2012), 6–11.

15. T. Weinberger, "Assessing the Situational Awareness of Employees for Pay Practice Adherence to Compensation Philosophy," *Compensation & Benefits Review* (July 2010), 215–221.

16. "Consultant Details Advantages of Pay for Performance," *Report on Salary Surveys* (October 2013), 8–9.

17. J. Smith, "The 10 Hardest Jobs to Fill in America," *Forbes* (May 31, 2011), 35.

18. F. Giancola, "Skill-Based Pay: Fad or Classic?," *Compensation & Benefits Review* (July 2011), 220–226.

19. See http://www.pennstatehershey.org/web/nursing/home/overview/professionaldevelopment/clinical ladder for more information.

20. F. Aime et al., "Legitimacy of Team Rewards: Analyzing Legitimacy as a Condition for the Effectiveness of Team Incentive Designs," *Journal of Business Research* (January 2010), 60–66.

21. A. Garreti, "Crash Course in Performance-Related Pay," *Management Today* (April 2012), 18.

22. Fay Hansen, "Having Their Say on Pay," *Workforce Management* (January 2011), 22–23; Kevin F. Hallock, "Pay Secrecy and Relative Pay," *Workspan Magazine* (April 2011), 10–11.

23. Steve Werner and Naomi Werner, "Indications Your Company Has External Inequity Issues," *Workspan Magazine* (September 2009), 67–70.

24. Melanie Trottman, "Employees Urged to Seek Wage Rights," *Wall Street Journal* (April 6, 2010).

25. Sarah E. Needleman, "As Wages Rise, Tough Choices," *Wall Street Journal* (December 1, 2011).

26. See http://livingwage.mit.edu/states/21/locations for more information.

27. Matthew J. Heller, "Quicken Verdict Gives Employers Hope on Overtime," *Workforce Management* (May 2011), 6–7.

28. "State Laws Can Trump Federal Overtime Rules," *Payroll Manager's Letter* (October 7, 2010), 26.

29. Jerry Kalish, "Worker Classification Question: Is You Is Or Is You Ain't My Employee?," *Employee Benefit News* (September 15, 2010), 44, 46.

30. "Employee Misclassification Can Lead to Big Penalties for Employers," *http://www.Americanbar.org*, July 2011.

31. Mark McGraw, "Reconsidering Worker Classifications," *Human Resource Executive* (November 2011); "Time to Settle Worker Classification Issues," *http://www.shrm.org* (November 2011).

32. See http://www.dol.gov/whd/workers/misclassification/#stateDetails for more information.

33. "Employer's Supplemental Tax Guide," IRS.gov, Publication 15-A, 2012; "The IRS's 20-Factor Analysis," U.S. Chamber of Commerce, Small Business Nation (2012).

34. Rajiv Burman, "Building a Market-Based Pay Structure from Scratch," *http://www.shrm.org* (April 10, 2012); Joseph B. Kilmartin and Andrew K. Miller, "Understanding Market Pricing," Salary.com (August 2008), 1–5.

35. "Salary Structures: An Effective Tool to Create Competitive and Equitable Pay Levels," Culpepper.com (November 2010).

36. Rebecca Manoli, "Addressing Salary Compression in Any Economy," *Workspan Magazine* (December 2009), 52–56.

37. See http://www.bls.gov/cpi/home.htm for more information.

38. See http://www.aafp.org/dam/AAFP/documents/advocacy/coverage/aca/ES-Primary-CareACA-061311.pdf for more information.

39. A. Topin, "The Doctor–Patient Disconnect," *Pharmaceutical Executive* (January 2013), 54–55.

40. A. Robeznieks, "Helping Hands: Roles and Responsibilities Are Expanding for Nurse Practitioners and Physician Assistants—but Not without Some Resistance," *Modern Healthcare* (May 23, 2011), 26–29.

41. "Hay Group Study Shows Slight Uptick in Use of Variable Pay," *Report on Salary Surveys*, BNA (December 2010), 6–7.

42. "Compensation in Healthcare Field on a Steady Rise," *Report on Salary Surveys*, BNA (June 2013), 13–15.

43. B. Hermalin and M. Weisbach, "Information Disclosure and Corporate Governance," *Journal of Finance* (February 2012), 195–234.

13 The Management of Benefits and Variable Pay in Healthcare

Learning Objectives

After you have read this chapter, you should be able to:

- Describe the challenges that confront healthcare employers in providing benefits and variable pay programs.

- Discuss why healthcare employers must offer competitive benefits programs to their employees.

- Identify various types of benefits.

- Explain the role that healthcare HR professionals must play in administering benefits.

- Compare and contrast individual and team-based incentives.

HEALTHCARE HR INSIGHTS

Annually, *Modern Healthcare* magazine publishes a list of the 100 best places to work in healthcare. A number of healthcare organizations have made the list multiple times, including Baptist Health South Florida, Holy Name Medical Center, and Palmetto Health. As part of the assessment to determine the best-places-to-work status of these organizations, these organizations' employees were surveyed on a number of criteria. The survey uncovered some noticeable differences between the 100 best places to work and all other participating organizations on key benefits and perquisites. Each of the designated 100 best scored significantly higher in the following areas; their offerings included:

- Bonuses to employees who refer new hires
- Giving paid time to employees for community service and volunteer work
- Compressed workweeks as a standard, year-round practice
- Domestic partner benefits
- Profit-sharing programs

Other points of interest about the practices of these select organizations included fun employee activities such as having an ice cream truck come to the facility to reward employees for their hard work, sponsoring theme parties (e.g., '80s prom night) for their employees, and coordinating family fun days.[1] Clearly, these organizations see a strategic importance in offering competitive benefits and perquisites to achieve employee satisfaction, resulting in high levels of employee engagement and retention.

Developing and implementing compensation strategies for healthcare organizations is important for healthcare HR professionals. But whether considered as a part of a total compensation approach or viewed separately, developing and implementing employee benefits and variable pay programs for healthcare organizations is challenging.[2]

Healthcare employers provide employee benefits to their workers for being part of the organization. A **benefit** is a form of indirect compensation. Benefits for healthcare employers often include health, dental, life, and disability insurances, educational assistance, retirement plans, vacations with pay, and other programs.

Benefits influence employees' decisions about which particular employer to work for, whether to stay or leave employment, and when to retire. However, the unique characteristics of benefits sometimes make them difficult to administer. For example, government involvement in benefits continues to expand. Federal and state governments *require* that certain benefits be offered (Social Security, workers' compensation, and unemployment insurance), and various governmental regulations apply to many of the nonrequired benefits as well (retirement, family leave, and flexible benefits).

Further, employees tend to take benefits for granted. For instance, so many organizations have offered health insurance that employees expect it. However, because benefits are also complex, many employees do not understand them, or sometimes do not even know what benefits exist. Yet benefits are costly to employers, averaging over 30 percent of employees' base pay.[3] These characteristics of benefits suggest that healthcare HR professionals should carefully consider the strategic role of benefits in their organizations.

STRATEGIC PERSPECTIVES ON BENEFITS

For many healthcare employers, providing employee benefits represents a double-edged sword. On one side, employers know that in order to attract and retain employees with the necessary training and competence, they must offer appropriate benefits that can have significant expense to the overall operation of the organization.[4] On the other side, they know the importance of controlling or even cutting costs. Too often, both managers and employees think of only wages and salaries as compensation and fail to consider the additional costs associated with benefits expenditures.

Healthcare employers find themselves on both sides of the healthcare insurance cost debate. Specifically, they must negotiate for the most cost-effective coverage possible for their employees with their insurance carriers. As providers, they must defend the highest possible reimbursement for the health services they provide, often with the same carriers.

Because of their sizable proportion of organizational costs, the compensation components of base pay, variable pay, and benefits require serious and realistic assessment and planning.

Goals for Benefits

Benefits should be looked at as part of the overall compensation strategy of the organization. For example, healthcare organizations can choose to compete for employees by providing base compensation, benefits, or variable pay, or perhaps all three. Which approach is chosen depends on many factors, such as the competition, organizational life cycle, and corporate strategy. For example, a new clinic may choose to have lower base pay, and use high variable incentives to attract new employees, but keep the cost of benefits as low as possible. Or a hospital that hires predominantly female employees might choose a family-friendly offering of benefits including on-site child care and access to full-time benefits for part-time work to attract experienced employees.

Benefits Needs Analysis

Given the current challenges healthcare employers face in recruiting and retaining skilled workers, understanding what employees want in a benefit program is critical.[5] A **benefits needs analysis** includes a comprehensive look at all aspects of benefits in an organization. Done periodically, such an analysis is more than simply deciding what benefits employees might want. To make certain that the mix of benefits is doing what it should, someone doing a benefits needs analysis might consider the following issues:

- How much total compensation, including benefits, should be provided?
- What part should benefits comprise of the total compensation of individuals?
- What expense levels are acceptable for each benefit offered?
- Why is each type of benefit offered?
- Which employees should be given or offered which benefits?
- What is being received by the organization in return for each benefit?
- How does having a comprehensive benefits package aid in minimizing turn-over or maximizing recruiting and retention of employees?
- How flexible should the package of benefits be?

Funding Benefits

Total benefits costs can be funded by both contributions made by the employer and contributions made by the employee. If the employer fully subsidizes a benefit, the cost to the employee would be zero. But if an employer chooses to pay $800 per month toward an employee's health insurance premium while the employee pays $100, then the employee contributes to covering benefits costs.

Benefit plans also can be funded by purchasing insurance from an insurance provider. Premiums to be paid reflect the predicted claims and will be adjusted based on actual claims. Some large healthcare employers choose to "self-fund" and are their own insurers—they set aside money to cover benefits costs. Self-funding by larger employers often has been effective in containing the overall costs of providing this benefit. Figure 13-1 shows how the typical benefits dollar is spent.

Tax-Favored Status of Benefits

Providing employees benefits rather than wages can be advantageous for employees. Most benefits (except for paid time off) are not taxed as income to employees. During World War II, wage and price controls were instituted to ensure appropriate use of resources and to keep inflation rates low. Wishing to attract and reward hardworking employees, companies began to offer paid fringe benefits as added incentives. Since benefits were not paid in wages, they were never taxed as income to the employee yet the company could deduct the cost as a business expense. This explains why the United States differs from many other countries in how benefits (especially health insurance) are provided to workers.

The tax-favored status means that a dollar in employee benefits is actually worth much more to an employee. For example, if Sally is an employee who is in a 25 percent tax bracket and earns an extra $400 as a special bonus, she will pay $100 in taxes on this amount (disregarding deductions). So, her

---

FIGURE 13-1 **How the Typical Benefits Dollar Is Spent**

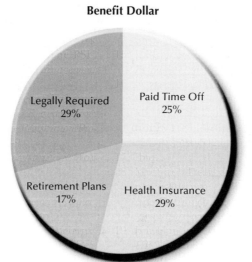

Benefit Dollar

Legally Required 29%

Paid Time Off 25%

Retirement Plans 17%

Health Insurance 29%

© 2016 Cengage Learning®

special bonus increases her total rewards by only $300. But if Sally's employer provides her with group legal insurance benefits worth $400, she receives the full value of $400 since it is not reduced by taxes. This feature makes benefits a desirable form of compensation to employees if they understand the value provided by the benefits.

TYPES OF BENEFITS

Employers offer some benefits to aid recruiting and retention, some because they are required to do so, and some because doing so reinforces the organization's HR philosophy. For example, life insurance can be purchased at a better rate if the purchaser is a large employer that qualifies for a group rate. Further, tax laws provide beneficial tax treatment of some employer-provided benefits for employees that they would not get if purchased by individuals. Figure 13-2 shows the many different benefits offered, classified by type.

Government-Mandated Benefits

There are many **mandated benefits** that employers in the United States must provide to employees by law. Social Security and unemployment insurance

FIGURE 13-2   Types of Benefits

Security	Health Care	Family Oriented
- Workers' compensation - Unemployment compensation - Supplemental unemployment benefits (SUBs) - Severance pay	- COBRA and HIPAA provisions - Medical and dental - Prescription drugs - Vision - PPO, HMO, and CDH plans - Wellness programs - Flexible spending accounts	- FLMA provisions - Adoption benefits and dependent-care assistance - Domestic partner benefits
Retirement	**Financial**	**Time Off**
- Social security - ADEA and OWBPA provisions - Early retirement options - Pension plans - Individual retirement accounts (IRAs) - Keogh plan - 401(k), 403 (b), and 457 plans	- Financial services (e.g., credit unions and counseling) - Relocation assistance - Life insurance - Disability insurance - Long-term care insurance - Legal insurance - Education assistance	- Military reserve time off - Election and jury leaves - Lunch and rest breaks - Holidays and vacations - Family leave - Medical and sick leave - Paid time off - Funeral and bereavement leaves
	Miscellaneous	
	- Social and recreational programs and events - Unique programs	

© 2016 Cengage Learning®

are funded through a tax paid by the employee and employer based on the employee's compensation.[6] Workers' compensation laws exist in all states. In addition, under the Family and Medical Leave Act (FMLA), employers must offer unpaid leaves to employees with certain medical or family difficulties. Other mandated benefits are available through Medicare, which provides healthcare for individuals who are age 65 and over. It is funded in part by an employer tax through Social Security. The Consolidated Omnibus Budget Reconciliation Act (COBRA) and the Health Insurance Portability and Accountability Act (HIPAA) mandate that an employer continue healthcare coverage paid for by the employees after they leave the organization, and that most employees be able to obtain coverage if they were previously covered in a health plan.

Voluntary Benefits

Employers voluntarily offer other types of benefits in order to compete for and retain employees. By offering additional benefits, organizations are recognizing the need to provide greater security and benefit support to workers with widely varied personal circumstances.

Benefits For Part-Time Employees

Another key design issue is whether or not to provide benefits coverage to employees who are not regular full-time employees. Many healthcare employers provide benefits to part-time employees, which is different from the practices of many non-healthcare-industry organizations. Part-time workers are an essential component of most healthcare organizations' workforces, especially 24/7 operations.

According to a study by the U.S. Bureau of Labor Statistics, only 39 percent of part-time workers are in company retirement plans, only 24 percent are eligible for health care benefits, and only 26 percent are eligible for paid sick time.[7] Part-time employees who do receive benefits usually do so in proportion to the percentage of full-time work time they provide.

SECURITY BENEFITS

A number of benefits provide employee security. These benefits include some mandated by laws and others offered by employers voluntarily. The primary security benefits found in organizations include workers' compensation, unemployment compensation, and severance pay.

Workers' Compensation

Workers' compensation provides benefits to persons injured on the job. State laws require most employers to provide workers' compensation coverage by purchasing insurance from a private carrier or state insurance fund or self-insuring the coverage.

The workers' compensation system requires employers to give cash benefits, medical care, and rehabilitation services to employees for injuries or illnesses occurring within the scope of their employment. In exchange, employees give up the right of legal actions and awards. However, it is in the interests of both employers and employees to reduce workers' compensation costs through safety and health programs.

Unemployment Compensation

Another benefit required by law is unemployment compensation, established as part of the Social Security Act of 1935. Because each U.S. state operates its own unemployment compensation system, provisions differ significantly from state to state. Employers finance this benefit by paying a tax on the first $7,000 (or more, in 37 states) of annual earnings for each employee. The tax is paid to state and federal unemployment compensation funds. The percentage paid by individual employers is based on *experience rates*, which reflect the number of claims filed by workers who leave.

Severance Pay

Severance pay is a security benefit voluntarily offered by employers to some employees who lose their jobs. Severed employees may receive lump-sum payments if the employer terminates their employment.[8]

Some healthcare employers have offered reduced amounts of cash severance and replaced some of the severance value by offering continued health insurance and *outplacement* assistance. Through outplacement assistance, ex-employees receive résumé-writing instruction, interviewing skills workshops, and career counseling.

RETIREMENT SECURITY BENEFITS

Few people set aside sufficient financial reserves to use when they retire; instead, they count on retirement benefits for a large part of their income.[9] Many healthcare employers offer some kind of retirement plan. Generally, private pensions make up a critical portion of income for people after retirement. With the baby boomer generation in the United States closing in on retirement, pressures on such funds are likely to grow.

Retirement Benefits

In the United States, the number of citizens at least 55 years or older has increased significantly in recent years, and older citizens constitute a large portion of the population. More workers are delaying retirement because of financial difficulties and decreased value of retirement savings coupled with longer life spans. Approximately 30 percent of workers surveyed had no plans to stop working or did not know when they would retire.[10]

Unfortunately, most U.S. citizens have inadequate savings and retirement benefits to fund their retirements. According to a study by the Employee Benefit Research Institute, 60 percent of workers report that they have less than $25,000 in savings excluding the value of their home.[11] While traditional pension plans that provided a defined amount for retirement at a defined age were the norm for decades, since the early 1980s fewer companies have provided these benefits. Instead, employee-funded retirement accounts have become the standard. Therefore, individuals must rely on Social Security payments, which were not designed to provide full retirement income.

Retirement benefits can be a valuable tool for attracting and retaining workers. Sixty percent of employees with less than two years of service at companies with traditional pension plans state that the pension plan is an important reason for their job choice. Further, 80 percent of workers at companies with traditional pensions plan to continue working for their employer until they retire. More than half of employees surveyed report that they would switch jobs to get better retirement benefits.[12] Therefore, the decisions a healthcare organization makes about its retirement benefits can have an important and lasting impact on talent management.

Retirement Plan Concepts

Certain rights are associated with retirement plans. One such right called **vesting** means that the employee has a benefit that cannot be taken away. If employees resign or are terminated before they have been employed long enough to become vested, no pension rights accrue to them except the funds they have contributed. If employees work for the required number of years to be fully vested, they retain their pension rights and receive the amounts contributed by both the employer and themselves.

Another feature of some retirement plans is **portability**. In a portable plan, employees can move their retirement benefits from one employer to another. Instead of requiring workers to wait until they retire to move their retirement plan benefits, once workers have vested in a plan for a period of time, such as five years, they can transfer their fund balances to other retirement plans if they change jobs.

Retirement Plans

A **retirement plan** is a program established and funded by the employer and/or employees to fund the employee's retirement years. Organizations are not required to offer retirement plans to employees beyond contributions to Social Security. There are two broad categories of retirement plans: defined benefit plans and defined contribution plans, as shown in Figure 13-3.

Defined-Benefit Pension Plans   A traditional pension plan is one in which the employer makes required contributions and the employee receives a defined amount each month upon retirement. Through a **defined-benefit plan**, employees

FIGURE 13-3   Comparison of Defined Benefit and Defined Contribution Retirement Plans

Defined Benefit	Defined Contribution
• Typically funded at least in part by employer • Amount of benefit paid at retirement is predetermined • Investment risk borne by employer • Benefit guaranteed by pension • Benefit Guaranty Corporation (PBGC) • Amount of contribution changes on the basis of actuarial assumption • Common in public sector and unionized workforces	• Typically funded by employee and employer • Amount of benefit at retirement is determined on the basis of investment performance • Investment risk borne by employee • Benefit not guaranteed • Amount of contribution is defined by employee participation level and company match • Common in private sector and non union workforces

© 2016 Cengage Learning®

are promised a pension amount based on age and years of service. Less than 10 percent of workers in the private sector are now covered by these plans. Small firms are less likely to offer defined-benefit plans than are larger firms because they are costly administer and to fund. Workers in the public sector are far more likely to have a defined-benefit plan with over 90 percent of public employers providing this benefit.[13]

Contributions are based on actuarial calculations of the benefits to be paid to employees after retirement and the formula used to determine such benefits. A defined-benefit plan gives employees greater assurance of benefits and greater predictability in the amount of benefits that will be available for retirement. These plans reward long service with a company.

Organizations that provide defined-benefit plans must comply with cumbersome and strict government rules regarding the funding of the plan. If the funding is inadequate to pay the benefits promised, the company must make up the shortfall. Therefore, many employers have dropped defined-benefit plans in favor of defined-contribution plans (discussed next) so that their contribution liabilities are known.

Defined-benefit pension plans offer greater security to employees. The benefits are guaranteed by the Pension Benefit Guaranty Corporation (PBGC). The PBGC maintains a solvency fund to pay benefits if a company goes bankrupt and cannot pay its retiree benefits. The fund is supported by employer contributions of approximately $50 per participant per year.

Defined-benefit plans may see a resurgence but in a modified form. Since so few healthcare organizations offer them to new employees, reintroducing these plans could be a source of differentiation in the labor market. However, funding risk and regulatory burdens make companies wary. Organizations may create new hybrid plans that will be attractive to employees without creating too great a liability for the employer.[14]

Defined-Contribution Pension Plans

In a **defined-contribution plan**, contributions are made to the plan by the employer and/or employee to fund an account for the employee's retirement. The key to this plan is the contribution rate; employee retirement benefits depend on fixed contributions and investment earnings.

Individual Retirement Options

The availability of several retirement benefit options makes the pension area very complex. The most prominent options are individual retirement accounts (IRAs), 401(k) and 403(b) plans, and 457 plans. These plans may be available in addition to organizational pension plans.

Individual Retirement Accounts

An IRA is a special account in which an employee can set aside funds that will not be taxed until the employee retires. The major advantages of an IRA are the ability to accumulate extra retirement funds and the shifting of taxable income to later years, when total income—and therefore taxable income—is likely to be lower. Federal law changes in 1997 authorized a special type of IRA, called the *Roth IRA*, which likely will increase the usage of IRAs.

401(k), 403(b), and 457 Plans

The **403(b)** and **457 plans** are available only to employees of nonprofit employers, while **401(k) plans** are available to both nonprofit and for-profit organizations. Figure 13-4 describes the various aspects of these defined-contribution plans. These plans allow individual employees to elect to reduce their current pay by a certain percentage, which is then used to fund a retirement plan.[15]

Since these plans hinge on the investment returns on previous contributions, employees' retirement benefits are somewhat less secure and predictable. But because of their portability and other plan features, these plans are sometimes preferred by younger, shorter-term employees.

The **401(k) plan** gets its name from Section 401(k) of the federal tax code. This plan is an agreement in which a percentage of an employee's pay is withheld and invested in a tax-deferred account. The 401(k) plan now dominates the field of employment-based retirement programs.[16] These plans are attractive to employees because contributions are made on a tax-deferred basis, so the employee pays lower income taxes during working years. Of course, taxes must be paid when funds are withdrawn during retirement. The most common

---

FIGURE 13-4   Defined Contribution Retirement Plan Types

Individual Retirement Accounts
An IRA is the most basic sort of retirement arrangement. An employer can help its employees set up and fund their IRAs. With an IRA, what the employee gets at retirement depends on the funding of their IRA and the earnings (or income) on those funds.

Traditional 401(k) Plan
Employers have discretion over whether to make contributions for all participants, to match employees' deferrals, to do both, or to do neither. These contributions can be subject to a vesting schedule (which provides than an employee's right to employer contributions become non forfeitable only after a period of time). Annual testing ensures that benefits for rank-and-file employees are proportional to benefits for owners/managers.

403(b) Plan
(tax sheltered annuity plan or TSA) is a retirement plan offered by public schools and certain charities. It's similar to a 401(k) plan maintained by a for-profit entity. Just as with a 401(k) plan, a 403(b) plan lets employees defer some of their salary into individual accounts. The deferred salary is generally not subject to federal or state income tax until it's distributed.

457 Plan
are typically offered to certain employees of state and local governments, churches, schools and hospitals. The major provisions of this plan are similar to 401(k) and 403(b) plans. However, this plan still differs substantially in some respects. The plan allows participating employees to defer a portion of their income into a tax-deferred savings plan that offers a preset selection of investment choices. Contributions grow tax-deferred until retirement, when they are either rolled over or withdrawn.

reason given by companies for offering 401(k) plans is a concern for employee financial security.[17]

There are many features that healthcare organizations may include in the 401(k) plan. A highly-valued feature is company matching contributions. Many employers contribute to the employee's account up to a percentage of pay. Employees in plans with matching contributions are more likely to contribute themselves. In a study recently conducted for a group of physician practices in the mid-west, nearly 100 percent of the practices provided an employee match.[18] Unfortunately, since employer contributions are voluntary, during economic recessions many healthcare organizations reduce or stop making their matching contributions. As the economy improves, they restore the matches but set lower limits on the company's participation in the plan.[19]

Financial education and counseling can be used to help employees understand how to manage their 401(k) and get the greatest value from the plan. People who use investment assistance earn better returns on their retirement funds than those who manage their own accounts. Employers can offer a variety of education programs designed for specific groups of employees. Over 75 percent of companies offer online education tools such as webinars, risk assessments, and retirement calculators.[20] Since companies have turned to 401(k) plans as the main retirement programs, educating employees is an important part of helping them to achieve financial security in retirement.

Cash Balance Pension Plans   Some employers have changed traditional pension plans to hybrids based on ideas from both defined-benefit and defined-contribution plans. One such plan is a **cash balance plan**, in which retirement benefits are based on an accumulation of annual company contributions, expressed as a percentage of pay, plus interest credited each year. With these plans, retirement benefits accumulate at the same annual rate until an employee retires. Since cash balance plans spread funding across a worker's entire career, these plans work better for mobile younger workers. The plans are gaining in popularity, especially among small businesses, which account for 84 percent of these plans.[21]

Legal Regulation of Retirement Benefits

Numerous laws and regulations affect retirement plans. Key regulations govern plan communications, funding, and other important aspects of retirement programs. The laws have been enacted to ensure that workers understand their plans and are assured of receiving the full value of promised benefits.

Employee Retirement Income Security Act

Widespread criticism of many pension plans led to enactment of the Employee Retirement Income Security Act (ERISA) in 1974. The purpose of this law is to ensure that private pension plans meet minimum standards. ERISA requires plans to periodically provide participants with information about the plan features (such as vesting) and funding, benefit accrual amounts, and gives participants the right to file lawsuits for violations of the law. Violations of ERISA can lead to costly lawsuits and possible disqualification of a pension plan. Employers spend considerable time to comply with the provisions of pension law.

Retirement Benefits and Age Discrimination

As a result of an amendment to the Age Discrimination in Employment Act (ADEA), generally employees cannot be required to retire at a specific age. Employers have had to develop different policies to comply with this amendment. In many employer pension plans, "normal retirement" is the age at which employees can retire and collect full pension benefits. Employers must decide whether individuals who continue to work past normal retirement age (perhaps age 65) should receive the full benefits package, especially pension credits. Possible future changes to Social Security may increase the age for full benefits past 65, so modifications in policies are likely.

Early Retirement   Historically many healthcare organizations have included pension plan provisions for **early retirement** in order to give workers opportunities to retire early from their jobs. After spending 25 to 30 years working for the same employer, some individuals may wish to use their talents in other areas.

Some healthcare employers have used early retirement buyout programs to cut back their workforces and reduce costs. Healthcare employers must take care to make these early retirement programs truly voluntary. Forcing workers to take advantage of an early retirement buyout program led to the passage of a federal law titled the Older Workers Benefit Protection Act (OWBPA).

Given the current state of healthcare staffing, some healthcare employers are rethinking incentives for early retirement. Some employers are moving to a concept referred to as **phased retirement**, defined as a program that helps employees retire in stages. These programs include options that allow employees to reduce the number of hours worked, take a different job, or be hired into a different job after retirement. This may be a very attractive option for older employees in good health who wish to stay active or for those who do not have adequate pension funds or savings to retire completely.[22]

Social Security

The Social Security Act of 1935, with its later amendments, established a system providing *old age, survivors, disability,* and *retirement benefits.* Administered by the federal government through the Social Security Administration, this program provides benefits to previously employed individuals or their dependents. Employees and employers share in the cost of Social Security through a tax on employees' wages or salaries.

Since the system's inception, Social Security payroll taxes have risen to 15.3 percent currently, with employees and employers each paying 7.65 percent up to an established maximum. In addition, Medicare taxes have more than doubled, to 2.9 percent.

HEALTHCARE BENEFITS

Many healthcare employers provide a variety of healthcare and medical benefits, usually through insurance coverage. The most common plans cover medical, prescription drug, and vision care expenses for employees and their dependents. Dental insurance is also important to many employees. Some dental plans include orthodontic coverage, which is a major expense for some families. Some employer medical insurance plans also cover mental health counseling, but many do not.

The costs of healthcare insurance have continued to escalate at a rate well in excess of inflation for several decades. Estimates are that the average healthcare cost per employee is more than $5,800 per year.[23] By the end of the 1990s, the rise in healthcare costs forced many employers to make concerted efforts to control medical premium increases and other healthcare costs. Although those cost-control efforts were successful for a while, the rate of increases in health benefits costs has risen again. The passage of the Affordable Care Act has and will have a profound impact on how employers, healthcare and others, will provide health insurance for their employees.

Affordable Care Act (ACA) Requirements

As part of the ACA, beginning in 2015 certain employers with 50 or more "full-time equivalent" employees (FTEs) who do not provide affordable healthcare coverage may be assessed a penalty if at least one full-time employee qualifies for a premium tax credit and uses it to purchase coverage in the **health insurance exchange**. A health insurance exchange is a state-provided health insurance plan that is federally subsidized. The exchanges are designed to help more people afford health insurance and spread the risk between the insurance companies and the state and federal government. Health insurance exchanges are not able to exclude people due to preexisting conditions.

Additionally, the law requires employers to provide prescribed health coverage, known as **minimum essential coverage**, while, at the same time, penalizing some employers who may fail to offer what is defined by the law as "affordable" coverage. Further, for the first time, this new law defines a full-time employee as someone who works 30 hours per week, averaged over the course of a month, rather than the traditional definition of 40 hours per week.

Only employers with 50 or more FTEs may be fined for failing to provide coverage to their full-time employees (and their dependents). In determining whether an organization has 50 or more FTEs, you must include the hours worked by your part-time employees.

A key requirement of the law is that employers must provide affordable coverage for low-income employees. Effectively, the employee's portion of the premium for individual coverage cannot exceed 9.5 percent of his or her household income. Low-income employees are defined as having household income falling between 100 percent and 400 percent of federal poverty level. In addition, to meet the requirement the employer's plan must pay, on average, at least 60 percent of the costs of covered services.

Employers who fail to provide the required level of coverage at an affordable cost may be subject to a penalty. The penalty associated with the employer mandate is often called a **"free-rider" penalty** because it is triggered when an employer's low-income employee "free-rides" on the federal government to obtain healthcare coverage. Under the law, low-income employees who do not have access to affordable employer-sponsored coverage that provides the minimum value are eligible for financial assistance from the federal government, in the form of a premium tax credit, to purchase coverage in the newly created exchange. This financial assistance will be available, as noted above, to low-income employees with income between 100 percent and 400 percent of the federal poverty level (FPL), depending on family status. (For example, a household income of $92,200 for a family of four in 2012 = 400% FPL.) The penalty amount assessed to the employer will vary based on whether the employer fails to offer any healthcare coverage at all to full-time employees or offers coverage that is not affordable and/or does not provide the minimum value required.[24]

Another key concept provided for in the ACA is **minimum essential coverage**. Starting in 2014, all nongrandfathered, insured individual and small-group health plans (covering up to 50 people) offered on and off the public health insurance marketplaces—or "exchanges" as they are commonly known—must cover the following "essential health benefits" consisting of 10 core health benefit categories:

- *Ambulatory Patient Services*—Doctor visits when you are sick or injured, or outpatient clinic visits
- *Emergency Services*—Visits to the emergency room including ambulance services or treatment at an urgent care center
- *Hospitalization*—A stay in the hospital including inpatient surgery and recovery
- *Maternity and Newborn Care*—for women who need prenatal care or help with pregnancy, complications, delivery, etc.
- *Mental Health and Substance Use Disorder Services, Including Behavioral Health Treatment*—Visits with a doctor or other health care professional, etc.
- *Prescription Drugs*
- *Rehabilitative and Habilitative Services and Devices*—Physical therapy, speech therapy, artificial limbs, and other medical equipment
- *Laboratory Services*—X-rays, MRIs, blood tests, etc.

- *Preventive and Wellness Services and Chronic-Disease Management*—Screening tests for things like osteoporosis and mammograms, and help living with long-term illnesses like diabetes
- *Pediatric Services, Including Oral and Vision Care*—Dentist checkups, routine eye doctor visits, eyeglasses, immunizations, and more[25]

Controlling Healthcare Benefits Costs

Regardless of the requirements and potential benefits of ACA, healthcare employers must aggressively seek ways to control costs associated with offering healthcare benefits. Healthcare employers are taking a number of approaches to control their costs. The most prominent ones are:[26]

- Increasing deductibles and copayments
- Instituting high-deductible plans
- Increasing employee contributions
- Using managed care
- Limiting family coverage; excluding spouses
- Switching to consumer-driven health plans
- Increasing health preventive and wellness efforts

Many of these strategies, as noted above, are subject to the requirements of the ACA.

Increasing Employee Cost Sharing A **deductible** is paid by an insured individual before the medical plan pays any expenses. Employers who raise the per-person deductible from $50 to $250 realize significant savings in health care expenses because employees use fewer health care services and prescription drugs.

Copayments are costs that an insured pays for medical treatment. For example, the health plan may require a fixed $20 copay for each physician visit. Alternatively, the copay may be based on a percentage, such as 20 percent, of medical treatment costs up to a set dollar amount. Companies can increase the fixed copay amount, increase the percentage, or increase the dollar amount on which employees share costs.

Increasing Employee Contributions

Employees are usually required to pay a portion of the monthly premium to maintain health care insurance. On average, single employees pay 18 percent of premiums, while employees with family coverage pay 28 percent of premiums. Over 50 percent of employers plan to increase the percentage that employees contribute to health plan premiums.[27]

Using Managed Care   Several other programs attempt to reduce health care costs paid by employers. **Managed care** consists of approaches that monitor and reduce medical costs through restrictions and market system alternatives.

Managed care plans emphasize primary and preventive care, the use of specific providers that charge lower prices, restrictions on certain kinds of treatment, and prices negotiated with hospitals and physicians. Preferred provider organizations (PPOs) and health maintenance organizations (HMOs) are the most common forms of managed care.

Spousal Exclusions   Spousal exclusion provisions limit access to a company's health plan when an employee's spouse works for another company that offers health insurance. Companies may charge a premium surcharge to enroll the spouse or require that the spouse enroll in his or her own employer's plan. Approximately 20 percent of employers have adopted these restrictions and more companies are planning to do so.[28]

Consumer-Driven Health Plans

Many healthcare employers are turning to health insurance plans where the employee chooses the insurance. The most widely used is a **consumer-driven health (CDH) plan** in which the employer provides financial contributions to employees to help cover their health-related expenses. The organization provides a fixed sum of money to employees and allow them to choose their medical coverage and insurer from an online marketplace. The employee can buy up the benefit level by paying the additional costs beyond what the employer contributes.[29]

CDH plans may represent the wave of the future by giving employees ownership of their healthcare dollars. Over 20 percent of large employers offer the plans and the trend is on the increase.[30] Successful implementation of CDH plans involves timely, accurate data for informed employee decisions. Communicating throughout the year and helping employees to make good spending decisions can achieve satisfied employees and cost savings.[31]

Legislation Impacting Benefits Administration

COBRA Provisions   Legal requirements in **COBRA** require that most employers (except churches and the federal government) with 20 or more employees offer extended healthcare coverage to the following groups:

- Employees who voluntarily quit, except those terminated for "gross misconduct"
- Widowed or divorced spouses and dependent children of former or current employees
- Retirees and their spouses whose healthcare coverage ends

Employers must notify eligible employees and/or their spouses and qualified dependents about COBRA within 60 days after the employees quit, die, get divorced, or otherwise change their status. The coverage must be offered for 18 to 36 months, depending on the qualifying circumstances. The individual no longer employed by the organization must pay the premiums, but the employer may charge this individual no more than 102 percent of the premium costs to insure a similarly covered employee.

For most healthcare employers, the COBRA requirements mean additional paperwork and related costs. For example, employers must not only track the former employees but also notify their qualified dependents. The 2 percent premium addition generally does not cover all relevant costs; the costs often run several percentage points more.

HIPAA Provisions   **HIPAA**, passed in 1996, allows employees to switch their health insurance plan from one employer to another to get new health coverage, regardless of preexisting health conditions. The legislation also prohibits group insurance plans from dropping coverage for a sick employee and requires them to make individual coverage available to people who leave group plans. The HIPAA legislation also established very high standards and controls for healthcare providers, insurance companies, and other organizations that have access to or knowledge of an individual's medical information, referred to as protected health information (PHI), to maintain and protect medical record confidentiality. These requirements also affect how employers deal with employees' PHI related to benefits information.

FINANCIAL, INSURANCE, AND OTHER BENEFITS

Healthcare employers may offer workers a wide range of special benefits: financial benefits, insurance benefits (in addition to health-related insurance), educational benefits, social benefits, and recreational benefits. These benefits can be useful in attracting and retaining employees. Workers like receiving special benefits, which often are not taxed as income.

Financial Benefits

Financial benefits include a wide variety of items. A *credit union* sponsored by the employer provides saving and lending services for employees. Employee *thrift savings plans* may be made available. To illustrate: in a savings plan the organization provides matching funds equal to the amount invested by the employee in the 401(k) plan. At a large family practice group, the employees receive a matched contribution of up to 6 percent of their contributions to the plan.

Insurance Benefits

In addition to health-related insurance, some employers provide other types of insurance. These benefits offer major advantages for employees because many employers pay some or all of the costs. Even when employers do not pay any of the costs, employees still benefit because of the lower rates available through group programs.

Life Insurance   It is common for employers to provide *life insurance* for employees. Life insurance is bought as a group policy, and the employer pays all or some of the premiums, but the level of coverage is usually low and is tied to the employee's base pay. A typical level of coverage is one or two times an employee's annual salary. Some executives may get higher coverage as part of executive compensation packages. Healthcare employers frequently provide their employees access to additional optional life insurance for which the employee pays the full premium but at discounted group rates.

Disability Insurance   Other insurance benefits frequently tied to employee pay levels are *short-term* and *long-term disability insurance.* This type of insurance provides continuing income protection for employees who become disabled and unable to work. Long-term disability insurance is much more common because many employers cover short-term disability situations by allowing employees to accrue sick leave granted annually. A growing number of healthcare employers are integrating their disability insurance programs with efforts to reduce workers' compensation claims. There are a number of reasons to have **integrated disability management programs**, such as cost savings and better coordination.

Educational Benefits

Another benefit used by many healthcare employees is *educational assistance programs* to pay for some or all the costs associated with formal education courses and degree programs, including the costs of books and laboratory materials. Some employers pay for schooling on a proportional schedule, depending on the grades received; others simply require a passing grade of C or above. As an example, the employees of one family practice clinic receive an annual tuition benefit of $1,700. They can use these monies to attend classes that directly apply to their work or prepare them for advancement within the clinic. Unless the education paid for by the employer meets certain conditions, employees must count the cost of educational aid as taxable income.

Social and Recreational Benefits

Some benefits and services are social and recreational in nature, such as bowling leagues, picnics and parties, employer-sponsored athletic teams, organization-owned recreational lodges, and other sponsored activities and interest groups. As interest in employee wellness has increased, more firms are providing recreational facilities and activities. But employers should retain control of all events associated with their organizations because of possible legal responsibility.

Family-Oriented Benefits and the Family and Medical Leave Act

The composition of families in the United States has changed significantly in the past few decades. The number of traditional families—in which the man is the primary or exclusive "breadwinner" and the woman stays home to raise children—has declined significantly, while the percentage of two-worker families has more than doubled. The growth in dual-career couples and single-parent households, and increasing work demands on many workers have increased the emphasis some employers are placing on family-oriented benefits. To provide assistance, employers have established a variety of family-oriented benefits, and the federal government passed the Family and Medical Leave Act in 1993.

The FMLA covers all employers with 50 or more employees who live within 75 miles of the workplace and includes federal, state, and private employers. Only employees who have worked at least 12 months and 1,250 hours in the previous year are eligible for leaves under FMLA.

FMLA Eligibility   The law requires that employers allow eligible employees to take a total of 12 weeks' leave during any 12-month period for one or more of the following situations:

- Birth, adoption, or foster-care placement of a child
- Caring for a spouse, child, or parent with a serious health condition
- Serious health condition of the employee

A **serious health condition** is one requiring inpatient, hospital, hospice, or residential medical care or continuing physician care. An employer may require an employee to provide a certificate from a doctor verifying such an illness as being covered. FMLA provides for the following guidelines regarding employee leaves:

- Employees taking family and medical leave must be able to return to the same job or a job of equivalent status or pay.
- Health benefits must be continued during the leave at the same level and conditions.
- The leave taken may be intermittent rather than in one block, subject to employee and employer agreements, when birth, adoption, or foster child care is the cause. For serious health conditions, employer approval is not necessary.
- Employees can be required to use all paid-up vacation and personal leave before taking unpaid leave.
- Employees are required to give 30-day notice, where practical.[32]

Family-Care Benefits

The growing emphasis on family issues is important in many healthcare organizations and for many workers. Many healthcare employers have a large female workforce, so adoption benefits, child-care programs, and elder programs are critical benefits for recruitment and retention purposes. Although studies indicate that men are becoming more involved in child-care responsibilities, a significant part of child-care responsibilities still rests on the shoulders of female employees. If healthcare employers wish to be competitive for skilled female employees, they must include these programs in their benefits offerings.

Adoption Benefits   As noted, healthcare employers provide maternity and paternity benefits to employees when they or their spouses give birth to children. In comparison to those giving birth, a relatively small number of employees adopt children, but in the interest of fairness, a growing number of organizations provide benefits for employees who adopt children.

Child Care   Balancing work and family responsibilities is a major challenge for many healthcare workers. Whether single parents or dual-career couples, these employees often experience difficulty in obtaining high-quality, affordable child care. Healthcare employers are addressing the child-care issue in several ways, from providing on-site day-care facilities to having referral services to aid parents in locating competent, affordable child-care providers.

Elder Care   Another family-related issue of growing importance is caring for elderly relatives. Various organizations have surveyed their employees and found that as many as 30 percent of them have had to miss work to care for an aging relative. The responsibilities associated with caring for elderly family members have resulted in reduced work performance, increased absenteeism, and more personal stress for the affected employees.

Benefits for Domestic Partners and Spousal Equivalents

As lifestyles change in the United States, employees who are not married but have close personal relationships with others are confronting healthcare employers with requests for benefits. The terminology often used to refer to individuals with such living arrangements as *domestic partners* or *spousal equivalents.*

The argument made by these employees is that if an employer provides benefits for the spouses of married employees, then benefits should be provided for employees without spouses but with alternative lifestyles and relationships. This view is reinforced by: (1) data showing that a significant percentage of heterosexual couples live together before or instead of formally marrying, and (2) the fact that more gays and lesbians are being open about their lifestyles.

The proportion of couples fitting the "traditional" definition of a family, including husband, wife, and children, is only 25 percent today. The number of Americans living in unmarried-partner households is growing much more rapidly than those living in married households. Several studies have shown that employers who offer this coverage may experience an increase in enrollment in the 1 percent to 2 percent range.

The U.S. Supreme Court in *United States v. Windsor* voted to strike down a key provision of the federal **Defense of Marriage Act (DOMA)** as unconstitutional. Specifically, the Court found that Section 3 of DOMA (which provided that only persons of opposite sex could be considered "married" for purposes of federal law) was unconstitutional. On the same day, in *United States v. Hollingsworth*, the Court refused on procedural grounds to rule on the Ninth's Circuit decision that California's Proposition 8 was unconstitutional. As background, Proposition 8 was a referendum passed by California voters in 2008 that prohibits the status of marriage for same-sex partners. As a result, a body of federal law, including tax laws and rules governing employee benefit plans, that provides spousal protections and privileges to married individuals is no longer blocked for legally married same-sex couples. These decisions have dramatically changed the way benefits are administered for married same-sex couples, giving them the same benefits and tax law rights as opposite-sex married couples.[33]

Time Off Benefits

Healthcare employers give employees paid time off under a variety of circumstances. Paid lunch breaks and rest periods, holidays, and vacations are common. But leaves are given for a number of other purposes as well. Time off benefits represent an estimated 5 percent to 13 percent of total compensation. Typical time off benefits include *holiday pay, vacation pay, or paid time off (PTO)*, and *leaves of absence*.

Medical and Sick Leave
Employers grant **leaves of absence**, taken as time off with or without pay, for a variety of reasons. Medical and sick leave and paid time off programs are closely related. Many employers allow employees to miss a limited number of days because of illness without losing pay. Some employers allow employees to accumulate unused sick leave, which may be used in case of catastrophic illnesses. Others pay employees for unused sick leave. Some organizations have shifted emphasis to reward people who do not use sick leave by giving them **well pay**—extra pay for not taking sick leave.

Paid Time Off (PTO) and Extended Illness Banks (EIBs)
Many healthcare employers have made use of **paid time off (PTO) plans** and **extended illness banks (EIBs)**.[34] PTO combines short-term sick/personal leave, vacations, and holidays, or some combination, into a total number of hours or days that employees can take off with pay. EIB programs allow employees to accrue time to be used for longer-term illness or health-related care that does not result in a disability, such as maternity care. One healthcare organization discovered that when it stopped designating a specific number of sick-leave days and a PTO plan was implemented, absenteeism dropped, time off was scheduled better, and employee acceptance of the leave policy improved. An example of PTO and EIB accrual is depicted in Figure 13-5.

Other Leaves
Other types of leaves are given for a variety of purposes. Some, such as *military leave, election leave,* and *jury leave,* are required by various state and

FIGURE 13-5   **Paid Time-Off (PTO) and Extended Illness Bank (EIB) Accrual**

Years of Service		Annual Accrual For Full-Time Employee # Hours		
		PTO	EIB	Total
Positions with 2 week (10 day) vacation allowances	1–5	176	56	232
Positions with 3 week (15 day) vacation allowances	5–12	216	56	272
Positions with 4 week (20 day) vacation allowances	20+	256	56	312

© 2016 Cengage Learning®

federal laws. Employers commonly pay the difference between the employee's regular pay and the military, election, or jury pay. Some firms grant employees military time off and give them regular pay while the employees also receive military pay. Federal law prohibits taking discriminatory action against military reservists by requiring them to take vacation time to attend summer camp or other training sessions. However, the leave request must be reasonable and truly required by the military.

Funeral or bereavement leave is another common leave offered to healthcare employees. A leave of up to three days for the death of immediate family members is usually given, as specified in many employers' policy manuals and employee handbooks. Some policies also give unpaid time off for the death of more distant relatives or friends.

BENEFITS ADMINISTRATION

Employees generally do not know much about the values and costs associated with the benefits they receive from employers. Yet benefits communication and benefits satisfaction are linked.

Benefits Communication

Many employers have instituted special benefits communication systems to inform employees about the value of the benefits they provide. The use of organizational websites and intranets are excellent benefits communication methods.

Benefits Statements   Some healthcare employers also give each employee an annual *personal statement of benefits* that translates benefits into dollar amounts. Federal regulations under ERISA require that employees receive an annual pension-reporting statement, which also can be included in the personal statements. By having a personalized statement, each employee can see how much his or her own benefits are worth. Employers hope that by educating employees about benefit costs, they can manage expenditures better and can give employees a better appreciation for the employers' payments.

Human Resources Information System (HRIS) and Benefits Communication   The advent of HRIS options linked to intranets provides additional links to communicate benefits to employees. Employee self-service for benefit administration allows employees to obtain benefits information online. Utilizing their work or home computers and other information technology allows employees to change their benefits choices, track their benefits balances, and submit questions to HR staff members and external benefits providers.

Flexible Benefits

A **flexible benefits plan**, sometimes called a *flex* or *cafeteria* plan, allows employees to select the benefits they prefer from groups of benefits established by the employer. By making a variety of benefits selections available, the organization allows each employee to select an individual combination of benefits within some overall limits. As a result of the changing composition of the workforce, flexible benefits plans have grown in popularity.

Flexible Spending Accounts   Under current tax laws (Section 125 of the IRS code), employees can divert some income before taxes into accounts to fund certain benefits. These **flexible spending accounts** allow employees to contribute pretax dollars to buy additional benefits.

The funds in the account can be used to pay for any of the following: (1) healthcare expenses, including offsetting deductibles and purchasing non-prescribed medications, such as aspirin; (2) life insurance; (3) disability insurance; and (4) dependent-care benefits. Flexible spending accounts have grown in popularity as more flexible benefits plans have been adopted by more healthcare employers.

Benefits in the Future

Employees' needs are changing. Those changes, along with the IRS code, have made benefits increasingly more complex. As a result, benefit functions are among the most outsourced in HR. Pension plans, health plan administration, or COBRA tracking are all targets for benefit outsourcing, as are benefits administration, service, financial reporting and accounting, and compliance and reporting.

Many employees also have access to Internet-based benefits support systems. For instance, use of the Internet allows employees in a growing number of organizations to check their retirement fund balances and move funds among various investment options.

Variable Pay: Incentives for Performance

Pay and benefits make up two components of compensation. The third component for many healthcare workers is **variable pay**, which is compensation that is linked to individual, team, and organizational performance. Traditionally known as *incentives*, variable pay plans attempt to provide tangible rewards to employees for performance beyond normal expectations.[35] Several types of variable pay can be used for individuals, groups, and organizations.

Types of Variable Pay

Individual incentives are given to reward the effort and performance of individuals. The most common means of providing healthcare employees variable pay are bonuses. Others include special recognition rewards, time off, and gift certificates.

When an organization rewards an entire work group or team for its performance, cooperation among the members usually increases. However, competition among different teams for rewards can lead to decline in overall performance under certain circumstances. The most common team or group incentives are *gainsharing plans*, where employee teams that meet certain goals share in the gains measured against performance targets. Often, gainsharing programs focus on quality improvement, cost reduction, and other measurable results.

Organizational incentives reward employees based on the performance results of the entire organization. This approach assumes that all employees working together can generate greater organizational results that lead to better financial performance. These programs often share some of the organization's financial gains with employees through payments calculated as a percentage of each employee's base pay. Also, organizational incentives may be given as a lump-sum amount to all employees, or different amounts may be given to different levels of employees throughout the organization. For healthcare senior managers and executives, variable pay plans often are established to provide deferred compensation that minimizes the tax liabilities of the recipients. Figure 13-6 shows some of the programs under each type of incentive or variable pay plan.

FIGURE 13-6   Types of Variable Pay Plans in Healthcare

Individual	Group/Team	Organization-Wide
- Volume rates - Bonuses - Special recognitions (trips, merchandise) - Safety awards - Attendance bonuses	- Gainsharing rewards - Quality improvement rewards - Labor cost reduction payouts	- Gainsharing budget targets - Cost reductions program - Deferred compensation - Market share or census growth achievements

© 2016 Cengage Learning®

Most healthcare employers adopt variable pay incentives in order to link individual performance to organizational goals and reward superior performance. Other goals might include improving productivity or increasing employee retention. Variable pay plans can be considered successful if they meet the goals the organization had for them when they were initiated.

The concept of rewarding healthcare workers on an incentive basis is relatively new. The great majority of the acute care hospitals in the United States are run as not-for-profits. The fact that they are a charity is an important component of their mission. One of the direct impacts of hospitals operating with a charitable mission is that paying employees incentive compensation was thought to be counter to that mission. In other segments of the healthcare industry, especially those that operate as for-profit organizations such as physician and medical clinics, there has been a greater use of incentive compensation programs. With the current shortage of healthcare workers, healthcare organizations of all types must increase their ability to link rewards to performance, as well as utilize incentives to attract and retain competent employees.

Effective Variable Pay Plans

Variable pay systems should be tied to desired performance. Employees must see a direct relationship between their efforts and their financial rewards. Indeed, higher-performing organizations give out far more incentive pay to their top performers than do lower-performing companies.

Since people tend to produce what is measured and rewarded, healthcare organizations must make sure that what is being rewarded ties to meeting organizational objectives. Use of multiple measures helps assure that various performance dimensions are not omitted. For example, a hospital's patient scheduling department sets incentives for its employees to increase productivity by lowering their time spent per call. That reduction may occur, but customer service might drop as the schedulers rush callers to reduce talk time. Therefore, the department should consider both talk time and customer satisfaction survey results.

Indeed, linking pay to performance in a healthcare setting might not always be appropriate. For instance, if the output cannot be objectively measured, management may not be able to correctly reward the higher performers with more pay. Managers might not even be able to accurately identify the higher performers. Under those circumstances, individual variable pay is inappropriate.

Individual Incentives

As noted earlier, individual incentive systems try to relate individual effort to pay.

Bonuses Individual employees may receive additional compensation payments in the form of a **bonus**, which is a onetime payment that does not become part of the employee's base pay. Generally, bonuses are less costly to the employer than other pay increases because they do not become part of employees' base wages, upon which future percentage increases are figured. Growing in popularity, individual bonuses often are used at the executive levels in organizations, but bonus usage also has spread to jobs at all levels in some firms. Whatever method of determining bonuses is used, legal experts recommend that bonus plans be described in writing. A number of lawsuits have been filed by employees who leave organizations demanding payment of bonuses promised to them.

Special Incentive Programs Numerous special incentive programs that provide awards to individuals have been used, ranging from onetime contests for meeting performance targets to rewards for performance over time. Although special programs can also be developed for groups and for entire organizations, these programs often focus on rewarding specific high-performing individuals. Some hospitals and medical centers have awarded bonuses to all employees after successful JCAHO reviews. Special incentives include special awards, recognition awards, and service awards.

Group/Team-Based Variable Pay

A group of employees is not necessarily a "team," but either group or team work can be the basis for variable compensation. The use of work teams in organizations has implications for compensation of the teams and their members. Interestingly, although the use of teams has increased substantially in the past few years, the question of how to equitably compensate the individuals who compose the team remains a significant challenge. As Figure 13-7 notes, organizations establish group or team variable pay plans for a number of reasons.

FIGURE 13-7 Why Organizations Establish Team Variable Pay Plans

Team Variable Pay =
- Enhances productivity
- Ties earning to team performance
- Improves quality
- Aids recruiting and retention of employees
- Improves employees' morale

© 2016 Cengage Learning®

Distributing Team Incentives   Several decisions about methods of distributing and allocating team rewards must be made. The two primary approaches for distributing team rewards are as follows:

1. *Same amounts of reward for each team member*—In this approach, all team members receive the same payout, regardless of job levels, current pay, or seniority.
2. *Different amounts of rewards for each team member*—Using this approach, employers vary individual rewards based on such factors as contribution to team results, current pay, years of experience, and skill levels of jobs performed.

Generally, more organizations use the first approach as an addition to different levels of individual pay. This method is used to reward team performance by making the team incentive equal, while still recognizing that individual pay differences exist and are important to many employees.

Problems with Team-Based Incentives   The difference between rewarding team members *equally* or *equitably* triggers many of the problems associated with team-based incentives. Rewards distributed equally in amount to all team members may be perceived as "unfair" by employees who work harder, have more capabilities, or perform more difficult jobs. This problem is compounded when a poorly performing individual negatively influences the team results. Also, employees working in teams have shown a relatively low level of satisfaction with rewards that are the same for all, rather than having rewards based on performance, which often may be viewed more equitably.

Successful Team Incentives   The unique nature of the team and its members figures prominently in the success of establishing team-based rewards. The employer must consider the history of the group and its past performance. Use of incentives generally has proven to be more successful where groups have been used in the past and where those groups have performed well.

Another consideration for the success of team-based incentives is the size of the team. If a team becomes too large, employees may feel their individual efforts will have little or no effect on the total performance of the group and the resulting rewards. Team-based incentive plans may encourage teamwork in small groups where interdependence is high. Therefore, in those groups the use of team-based performance measures is recommended.

Group/team-based reward systems use various ways of compensating individuals. The components include individual wages and salaries in addition to team-based rewards. Most team-based organizations continue to pay individuals based either on the jobs performed or their competencies and capabilities. The two most frequently used types of group/team incentives situations are work team results and gainsharing.

HEALTHCARE REFORM AND HR PRACTICES

The use of incentives has been introduced under various aspects of healthcare reform. As an example, an experiment under way in Massachusetts involves paying doctors for how well they care for patients, as opposed to how often. That experiment began more than two years ago between the state's Blue Cross and Blue Shield health plans and primary care doctors, specialists, or hospitals (or some combination) at eight locations. Among those that signed contracts to test the model were a primary care practice with 75 doctors and the for-profit Steward Health Care System.

The experiment, a combination of quality **incentives** and lump-sum payments for each patient, is seeking to slow the rate of healthcare spending by one-half within five years. The Boston-based system did not make radical changes and has seen quality gains and reduced medical costs thanks to the heightened focus and measurement improvements. Steward Health Care System, to ensure alignment of efforts and rewards, has invested $100 million in healthcare information technology and developed software to monitor performance for its Blues contracts.[36]

As these experiments and related demonstration projects prove successful in healthcare organizations in improving the delivery of healthcare results at lower cost, it will dramatically change how doctors and other care providers are compensated. Healthcare leaders and HR professionals will be required to develop new compensation strategies to distribute these incentive payments.

Organizational Incentives

An organizational incentive system compensates all employees in the organization based on how well the organization as a whole performs during the year. The basic concept behind organizational incentive plans is to produce better results by rewarding cooperation throughout the organization. To be effective, an organizational incentive program should include everyone from nonexempt employees to managers and executives. As an example, a large dental clinic developed an organizational incentive plan based on patient satisfaction. It used aggregated information from its patient surveys to determine a base level of acceptable patient satisfaction scores and then set goals to increase patient satisfaction. Upon attainment of the goals, the clinic awarded *all* employees a significant year-end cash bonus.

The results of variable pay plans, like those in other areas of HR, should be measured to determine the success of the programs. Different measures of success can be used, depending on the nature of the plan and the goals set for it. Regardless of the plan, the critical decision is to gather and evaluate data to determine if the expenditures on it are justified by increased performance and results.[37] If the measures show positive analyses, then the plan is truly pay-for-performance in nature.

Successes and Failures of Variable Pay Plans

Even though variable pay has grown in popularity, some attempts to implement it have succeeded and others have not. Incentives *do* work, but they are not a panacea because their success depends on the circumstances.

The positive view that many employers have for variable pay is not shared universally by all employees. If individuals see incentives as desirable, they are more likely to put forth the extra effort to attain the performance objectives that trigger the incentive payouts. One problem is that many employees prefer that performance rewards increase their base pay, rather than be given as a one-time, lump-sum payment. Further, many employees prefer individual rewards to group/team or organizational incentives.

Providing variable pay plans that are successful can be complex and requires significant, continuing efforts. Some suggestions that appear to contribute to successful incentive plans are as follows:

- Develop clear, understandable plans that are continually communicated.
- Use realistic performance measures.
- Keep the plans current and linked to organizational objectives.
- Clearly link performance results to payouts that truly recognize performance differences.

CASE

Regional Hospital, a 400-bed community hospital, was struggling with recruitment and retention issues. These issues were occurring in spite of area labor statistics that indicated that there was a sufficient supply of skilled healthcare workers to meet their needs.

Regional's HR director undertook a comprehensive analysis of the recruitment and retention issues with the support of the board and senior management of the hospital. The HR director utilized information from a recent employee satisfaction survey and exit interviews. From those sources she learned the following:

- Current employees believed that Regional's benefit program was not competitive in comparison to other hospitals and companies in the area.
- For the employees who voluntarily resigned from Regional in the last 12 months, benefit issues were critical. They reported receiving employment offers that included: lower healthcare insurance premiums, employer-paid dental insurance, higher accruals on paid time off, and sign-on bonuses.
- Regional's healthcare competitors were aware of Regional's less-competitive benefits package and would aggressively recruit Regional employees, noting the differences when interviewing Regional employees.

Questions

1. Given the findings from the HR director, what additional benefits plans should be considered by Regional Hospital?
2. What would be the advantages and disadvantages to increasing the competitiveness of the benefits plan at Regional Hospital?

END NOTES

1. Ed Finkel, "Top Workplaces Buckle Down, Cut Loose," *Modern Healthcare* (October 24, 2011), 8–38.

2. C. Roman, "The Challenge Of Funding Hospital Employee Retirement Benefits," *Healthcare Financial Management* (December 2012), 92–97.

3. "Employee Costs for Employee Compensation" (December 2013), U.S. Department of Labor, Bureau of Labor Statistics: News (March 12, 2014), 1–23.

4. "Benefit Cost Highlights," *Employee Benefits News* (December 2013), 34.

5. S. Wells, "Benefits Strategies Grow," *HR Magazine* (March 2013), 24–34.

6. See *https://faq.ssa.gov/link/portal/34011/34019/ArticleFolder/254/Employer-Wage-Reporting* for more information.

7. See *http://www.bls.gov/opub/ted/2010/ted_20100806.htm* for more information.

8. "Legal Briefs," *HR Specialist: Employment Law* (March 2014), 3.

9. N. Adams and J. VanDerhei, "Closing the Retirement Expectations 'Gap': Variations in Demographics, Sources of Information, and the Implications of a 'Bad Guess,' " *Journal of Financial Service Professionals* (January 2014), 59–71.

10. "Changes to Retirement Benefits: What HR Professionals Need to Know in 2012," *Workplace Visions—SHRM* 1 (2012).

11. Stephen Blakely and Jack VanDerhei, "EBRI's 2012 Retirement Confidence Survey: Job Insecurity, Debt Weigh on Retirement Confidence, Savings," *Employee Benefit Research Institute* (March 13, 2012).

12. Stephen Miller, "Better Retirement Plans May Prompt Job Switching," *HR Magazine* (July 2012), 11; "Reeling Them in with Retirement Bait: Retirement Benefits Shown Effective to Attract and Retain," *Employee Benefit News* (February 2011), 58.

13. Nancy L. Bolton, "Comparing Apples to Oranges," *Employee Benefits News* (July 2011), 12; John Kador, "Factoids from the Workplace and Beyond," *Human Resources Executive* (September 16, 2011), 50.

14. Joanne Sammer, "Are Defined Benefit Plans Dead?" *HR Magazine,* (July 2012), 29–32.

15. See *http://www.irs.gov/* for more information.

16. Christopher Farrell, "Fine-Tuning the 401(k)," *Bloomberg Businessweek* (April 5, 2012), 80.

17. "2012 Workplace Benefits Report," *Bank of America Merrill Lynch* (2012).

18. W. J. Flynn and Associates LLC 2014, benefits and compensation study.

19. Jilian Mincer, "Many U.S. Employers Cut 401(k) Matches," *Wall Street Journal* (March 26, 2009); Aleksandra Todorova, "No Match," *Wall Street Journal* (April 7, 2009); and Kelly Greene, "Retirement Plans Make Comeback with Limits," *Wall Street Journal* (June 14, 2011).

20. Kathleen Koster, "Online or Face Time?," *Employee Benefit News* (October 2012), 20–22.

21. "Annual Adoption of Cash Balance Plans Nearly Doubled," *http://www.shrm.org* (July 26, 2012).

22. J. Tacchino, "Will Baby Boomers Phase into Retirement?," *Journal of Financial Service Professionals* (May 2013), 41–48; Roselyn Feinsod and Allen Steinberg, "Back to the Future of Phased Retirement: Developing Flexible Retirement Programs That Work," *Worldatwork* (October 2012).

23. "Employer Health Benefits 2013 Annual Survey," *Medical Benefits* (October 15, 2013), 1–2.

24. See *http://www.hhs.gov/healthcare/* for more information.

25. A. Bianchi, "IRS, Treasury Department Issue Proposed Rules Governing Minimum Value, Affordability, and Wellness Programs," *Employee Benefit Plan Review* (July 2013), 9–12.

26. "Health-Care Costs Projected to Increase 5.3% in 2013," *Worldatwork.org* (August 29, 2012); "U.S. Employers Revamping Health Care Benefits," *HR Magazine,* HR Trendbook (2012).

27. Joanne Sammer, "Health Care Costs Likely to Jump in 2013," *Business Finance Magazine* (September 17, 2012); "Large Employers Plan Benefits Overhaul," *Employee Benefit News* (October 2011), 66.

28. David Tobenkin, "Spousal Exclusions on the Rise," *HR Magazine* (November 2011), 55–60.

29. Anna Wilde Mathews, "Big Firms Overhaul Health Coverage," *Wall Street Journal* (September 27, 2012).

30. Sander Domaszewicz, "A Considered Approach," *Human Resource Executive Online* (May 2, 2009).

31. Phillip T. Powell and Ron Laufer, "The Promises and Constraints of Consumer-Directed Healthcare," *Business Horizons* 53 (2010), 171–182; Anthony T. Lo Sasso, Lorens A. Helmchen, and Robert Kaestner, "The Effects of Consumer-Directed Health Plans on Health Care Spending," *The Journal of Risk and Insurance* 77 (March 1, 2010), 85–103.

32. See *http://www.dol.gov/dol/topic/benefits-leave/fmla.htm* for more information.

33. A. Moran and M. Leon, "Implementing New Rules for Same-Sex Spouses after the Supreme Court Decision," *Employee Relations Law Journal* (Spring 2014), 88–100.

34. "Paid-Time-Off Programs, Practices: Where Does Your Company Stand?," *Payroll Manager's Report* (September 2010), 1–5.

35. "4 Steps for Implementing a Variable Pay Program," *HR Specialist: Compensation & Benefits* (October 2010), 4.

36. Adapted from M. Evans, "Another Experiment: 1 Quality Incentive Pay Model Under Way In Boston," *Modern Healthcare* (July 26, 2011), 18.

37. Ross Levin, "Rethinking Employee Compensation," *Journal of Financial Planning* (April 2013), 30–31.

14 Safety, Health, and Security in Healthcare Organizations

Learning Objectives

After you have read this chapter, you should be able to:

- Explain the nature of safety, health, and security in the healthcare workplace.

- Identify the various aspects of Occupational Safety and Health Administration (OSHA) compliance.

- Define the components of an effective ergonomics program.

- Discuss health issues in the healthcare workplace.

- Understand the importance of dealing with workplace violence.

The American Nursing Association (ANA) aggressively advocates for states to pass legislation designed to protect healthcare workers from violence in the workplace. To date, well over 25 states have passed legislation requiring organizations, not just healthcare employers, to have preventive policies and programs designed to deal with workplace violence. However, according to the ANA the workplace violence issues in healthcare facilities suggest that healthcare workers might be more vulnerable and require specific legislation to protect them. According to the Bureau of Labor Statistics, nearly 60 percent of all nonfatal assaults and violent acts in the workplace occurred in the healthcare and social assistance industry.[1]

The ANA has developed a model "state" bill—the Violence Prevention in Health Care Facilities Act—the key components of which would include:

- All healthcare facilities would be required to establish a violence prevention program.

- Each facility would have a violence prevention committee, managers, direct care staff, and individuals with safety expertise.

- The committee would develop a violence prevention plan for each facility, monitor issues, propose remediation efforts, and provide an annual comprehensive violence risk assessment for the facility.

- Establish a postincident response system that provides, at a minimum, an in-house crisis response team for employee-victims and their coworkers, and individual and group crisis counseling, which may include support groups, family crisis intervention, and professional referrals.

- Each facility would have a policy prohibiting any retaliatory action against any healthcare worker for reporting violent incidents.[2]

Whether a bill of this nature is passed by each state, the data are indisputable: workplaces in the healthcare and social assistance industries are dangerous areas to work. Healthcare leaders and HR professionals have a critical responsibility to ensure that their facilities are safe and to protect their workers from violence and other safety issues.[3]

Most healthcare workplaces offer a unique set of safety, health, and security challenges. Not only are there the usual workplace safety, health, and security issues to contend with, but there is also the issue of protecting the patients, residents, and clients that are cared for in the workplace. Protecting both healthcare workers and the individuals they provide care for is an ongoing responsibility for the leaders of healthcare organizations.[4]

NATURE OF SAFETY, HEALTH, AND SECURITY

The terms *safety*, *health*, and *security* are closely related. Typically, **safety** refers to protecting the physical well-being of people. The main purpose of effective safety programs in organizations is to prevent work-related injuries and accidents.

The broader and somewhat more nebulous term is **health**, which refers to a general state of physical, mental, and emotional well-being. A healthy person is one who is free of illness, injury, or mental and emotional problems that impair normal human activity. Health management practices in healthcare organizations strive to maintain the overall well-being of individuals.[5] The purpose of **security** is protecting employees, patients or residents, clients and visitors, and organizational facilities. With the growth of workplace violence, security at work has become an even greater concern for healthcare employers and employees alike.

Safety, Health, and Security Responsibilities

The general goal of providing a safe, secure, and healthy workplace is attained by operating managers and HR staff members working together. As Figure 14-1 indicates, both the HR unit and operating managers must be involved in coordinating health, safety, and security efforts.

The primary safety, health, and security responsibilities in an organization usually fall on supervisors and managers. An HR manager or safety specialist can help coordinate health and safety programs, investigate accidents, produce safety program materials, and conduct formal safety training. However, department supervisors and managers play key roles in maintaining safe working conditions and a healthy workforce. For example, a dental clinic supervisor has several health and safety responsibilities: (1) reminding employees to wear the appropriate protective equipment and clothing, checking on the cleanliness of the work area; (2) observing employees for any alcohol, drug, or emotional problems that may affect their work behaviors; and (3) conducting safety orientations and in-service training.

FIGURE 14-1   Typical Division of HR Responsibilities for Health, Safety, and Security Issues

HR Unit	Operating Managers
• Coordinate health and safety programs • Develop safety reporting system • Provide accident investigation expertise • Provide technical expertise on accident prevention • Develop restricted-access procedures and employee identification systems • Assist with disaster and recovery planning efforts	• Monitor the health and safety of employees daily • Coach employees to be safety conscious • Investigate accidents • Monitor workplace for security problems • Communicate with employees to identify potentially difficult employees • Implement disaster and recovery plan

© 2016 Cengage Learning®

THE JOINT COMMISSION AND SAFETY, HEALTH, AND SECURITY

The Joint Commission on the Accreditation of Healthcare Organizations (JCAHO) has several topic areas that contain standards specifically relating to safety, health, and security. The primary topic areas are environment of care; infection prevention and control; and emergency management.[6]

Environment of Care

Healthcare organizations must provide a safe, functional, and effective environment of care (EC) for patients, visitors, medical and nursing staffs, vendors, volunteers, students, and others. The standard requires the development of plans that address safety and security; hazardous materials and waste; fire safety; medical equipment; and utilities. These plans are designed to promote a safe, secure environment. With education and ongoing supervision, staff members implement each phase of the plans. Figure 14-2 illustrates the components of the environment of care standard.

Infection Prevention and Control

All staff in healthcare organizations have some infection control (IC) responsibilities and must competently perform their assigned roles. JCAHO has a set of standards that specifically addresses the protection of patients, staff, and visitors, and focuses on identifying organizational infection risks and taking the necessary risk reduction steps. As an example, screening staff for tuberculosis, providing hepatitis B vaccinations, and implementing ongoing education regarding the importance of hand washing are risk reduction activities.

FIGURE 14-2   Components of the Environment of Care Plan

© 2016 Cengage Learning®

Emergency Management

The emergency management (EM) standards for the JCAHO require member hospitals to conduct emergency preparedness drills regularly. The Joint Commission describes four phases of emergency preparedness—mitigation, preparedness, response, and recovery. Each phase requires healthcare organizations to develop plans covering such areas as communications; providing resources and assets; staff responsibilities; and patient clinical and support activities.

The HR management implications of emergency preparedness are very significant.[7] As proven by the recent events of school shootings, terrorist bombings like what occurred at the Boston Marathon, or natural disasters, the importance of having competent, well-trained healthcare workers who have the ability and skills to provide care in times of disaster has increased in importance.

The Joint Commission's accreditation standards are relevant only to its subscribing organizations. The Centers for Medicare and Medicaid Services (CMS), which would have broader impact on this topic, has recently proposed a rule that would require all hospitals participating in Medicare and Medicaid to develop an emergency preparedness plan as described below.

- Conduct risk assessment and planning based on an all-hazards approach.
- Develop policies and procedures based on the emergency plan and risk assessment.
- Develop a communication plan that coordinates patient care within the facility, across healthcare providers, and with state and local public health departments and emergency systems.
- Develop and implement emergency preparedness testing and training programs.[8]

Regardless of the oversight body and its influence on this topic, healthcare HR professionals, along with healthcare managers and safety professionals, play key roles in preparing for disaster situations. Given the fact that healthcare organizations are both employers and care providers, disaster preparation is important for both the management of internal disasters (such as fires and hazardous chemical leaks or spills) and dealing with the patient care needs created by external disasters (such as those noted above). In both instances, healthcare workers are required to perform in extraordinary ways. Their personal safety maybe at risk or they may have to deal with the patient care needs of a high volume of critically injured or exposed patients.

LEGAL REQUIREMENTS FOR SAFETY AND HEALTH

Healthcare employers must comply with a variety of federal and state laws when developing and maintaining healthy, safe, and secure working environments. Three major legal concerns are workers' compensation legislation, the Americans with Disabilities Act, and child labor laws.

Workers' Compensation

First passed in the early 1900s, workers' compensation laws in some form are on the books in all states today. As noted in Chapter 13, under these laws employers contribute to an insurance fund that compensates employees for injuries received while on the job. Premiums paid are experience rated to reflect the accident rates of the employers, with employers that have higher incident rates being assessed higher premiums. Depending on the amount of lost time and the wage level in question, these laws often require that payments be made to an employee for the time away from work because of an injury, to cover medical bills, and for retraining if a new job is required as a result of the incident. Most state laws also set a maximum weekly amount for determining workers' compensation benefits. Figure 14-3 shows a four-year overview of the number of workplace fatalities and the rates of workplace injuries and illnesses per 100 full-time workers in healthcare and social assistance. An injury or illness is considered to be work related if an event or exposure in the work environment either caused or contributed to the resulting condition or significantly aggravated a preexisting condition.[9]

Workers' compensation coverage has been expanded in many states to include emotional impairment that may have resulted from physical injury, as well as job-related strain, stress, anxiety, and pressure. Some cases of suicide have also been ruled to be job related in some states, with payments due under workers' compensation.

Another aspect of workers' compensation coverage relates to the use of telecommuting by employees. In most situations, while working at home for employers, individuals are covered under workers' compensation laws. Therefore, if an employee is injured while doing employer-related work at home, the employer is likely liable for the injury.

Unfortunately, healthcare employers have not consistently focused as much effort on injury and accident prevention as they should. As noted in the

FIGURE 14-3   Work-Related Fatalities, Injuries, and Illness Workers in Healthcare and Social Assistance

	2009	2010	2011	2012
Fatalities				
Number of fatalities	133	155	138	120
Rate of injury and illness cases per 100 full-time workers	5.4	5.2	5.0	4.8
Total recordable cases				
Cases involving days away from work, job restriction, or transfer	2.4	2.4	2.3	2.3
Cases involving days away from work	1.4	1.4	1.4	1.3
Cases involving days of job transfer or restriction				

HR Healthcare Insights feature, the healthcare industry has some of the highest injury rates when compared to other industries. The cost of healthcare worker injuries and fatalities is calculated to be in excess of $13 billion with more than 2 million lost workdays per year.[10]

Controlling Workers' Compensation Costs   Workers' compensation costs can represent from 2 percent to 10 percent of payroll for healthcare employers. In addition to a well-designed and -implemented prevention program, a key to reducing these expenses has been *return-to-work plans*. These plans monitor employees who are off work because of injuries and illness. Also, the plans focus on returning the individuals to do *light-duty work* that is less physically demanding until they are able to perform their full range of job duties. However, in certain healthcare jobs, such as nurses or X-ray technicians where patient safety might be an issue, light-duty work might not be available.

Workers' compensation fraud is an expensive problem. It has been estimated that about one-fourth of the workers' compensation claims filed are fraudulent. False and exaggerated claims make up the bulk of the fraud—costing employers billions of dollars annually. Employers must continually monitor their workers' compensation expenditures. Efforts to reduce workplace injuries, illnesses, and fraud can reduce workers' compensation premiums and claims costs. Many of the safety and health management suggestions discussed later in this chapter can contribute to reducing workers' compensation costs.

The Family and Medical Leave Act (FMLA) affects workers' compensation as well. Because the FMLA allows eligible employees to take up to 12 weeks of leave for their serious health conditions, injured employees may ask to use that leave time in addition to the leave time allowed under workers' compensation, even if it is unpaid. Some employers have policies that state that FMLA leave runs concurrently with any workers' compensation leave.

Americans with Disabilities Act and Safety Issues

Employers that try to return injured workers to light-duty work to reduce workers' compensation costs may incur issues under the Americans with Disabilities Act (ADA). When making accommodations for injured employees through light-duty work, employers may undercut what are really essential job functions. Making such accommodations for injured employees for a period of time may require employers to make similar accommodations for job applicants with disabilities.[11]

Health and safety record-keeping practices have been affected by an ADA provision that requires all medical-related information to be maintained separately from all other confidential files. Specific access restrictions and security procedures must be adopted for medical records of all types, including employee medical benefits claims and treatment records.

Healthcare HR professionals understand the ADA guidelines as they affect physical disabilities. However, it becomes more difficult where mental illness is at issue. Employees may not be aware of the extent to which their disability may impact their performance. To the extent workplace misconduct is the issue, management should follow normal procedures. Depending on the seriousness of the complaint, it should be determined if the employee presents a risk of violence, but concerns must be based on objective facts. Although no one should ignore a threat to safety, an overreaction to odd behavior could be a liability under the ADA.[12]

Child Labor Laws

Risk management includes dealing with safety concerns that have resulted in restrictions affecting younger workers, especially those under the age of 18. Child labor laws, found in the Fair Labor Standards Act (FLSA), set the minimum age for most employment at 16 years. Individuals who are 14 or 15 years old may work no more than 3 hours per day and a total of 18 hours in a week when school is in session, and they can work only from 7 a.m. to 7 p.m. When not in school or during the summer months, individuals can work 8 hours per day and a total of 40 hours per week, and June 1 until Labor Day they can work as late as 9 p.m.[13]

Work-related injuries of younger workers are not a significant issue for healthcare employers because the industry employs very few young employees. The only exception would be long-term care employers that sometimes utilize younger workers in part-time service worker positions.

OCCUPATIONAL SAFETY AND HEALTH ACT

The Occupational Safety and Health Act of 1970 was passed to ensure that the health and safety of individuals employed in organizations would be protected. Every employer that is engaged in commerce and has one or more employees is covered by the act. Farmers having fewer than 10 employees are exempt. Employers in specific industries, such as railroads and mining, are covered under other health and safety acts. Federal, state, and local governments are covered by separate statutes and provisions.

The Occupational Safety and Health Act of 1970 established the Occupational Safety and Health Administration, known as OSHA, to administer its provisions. The act also established the National Institute for Occupational Safety and Health (NIOSH) as a supporting body to do research and develop standards. In addition, the Occupational Safety and Health Review Commission (OSHRC) has been established to review OSHA enforcement actions and to address disputes between OSHA and employers that have been cited by OSHA inspectors.

By making employers and employees more aware of safety and health considerations, OSHA has significantly affected organizations. OSHA regulations and on-site presence appear to have contributed to reductions in the number of accidents and injuries in some cases. But in other industries, OSHA has had little or no effect.

OSHA Enforcement Standards

To implement OSHA regulations, specific standards were established to regulate equipment and working environments. National standards developed by engineering and quality control groups are often used. OSHA rules and standards are frequently complicated and technical. Small healthcare employers who do not have specialists on their staffs may find the standards difficult to read and understand. In addition, the adoption of many less important minor standards has hurt OSHA's credibility.

Two provisions have been recognized as key to healthcare employers' responsibility to comply with OSHA:

- *General Duty*—The act requires that the employer has a general duty to provide safe and healthy working conditions, even in areas where OSHA standards have not been set. Employers that know or reasonably should know of unsafe or unhealthy conditions can be cited for violating the general duty clause.

- *Notification and Posters*—Employers are required to inform their employees of safety and health standards established by OSHA. Also, OSHA posters must be displayed in prominent locations in workplaces.

Hazard Communication OSHA has established *process safety management* (PSM) standards that focus on hazardous chemicals. As part of PSM, hazard communication standards require manufacturers, importers, distributors, and users of hazardous chemicals to evaluate, classify, and label those substances. Employers must also make information about hazardous substances available to employees, their representatives, and health professionals. This information is contained in material safety data sheets (MSDSs), which must be kept readily accessible to those who work with chemicals and certain other dangerous substances. The MSDSs indicate antidotes or actions to be taken should someone come in contact with the substances. If the organization employs many workers for whom English is not the primary language, then the MSDSs should be available in the necessary languages. Also, workers should be trained in how to access and use the MSDS information.

The Internet has made it much quicker and easier for companies to meet OSHA's hazard communication requirements because (1) employers can access safety information produced by vendors and suppliers on hazardous materials and chemicals and (2) information technology allows employers to use the Internet to maintain MSDSs on chemicals and workplace substances. As part of hazard communications, OSHA has established *lockout/tag-out regulations.* To comply with these regulations, health facilities must provide maintenance staff with locks and tags to use to make equipment inoperative during repair or adjustment to prevent accidental start-up of defective equipment. Only the person whose name is printed on the tag or engraved on the lock may remove the device.

Blood-Borne Pathogens The blood-borne pathogen standard resulted from a series of healthcare worker fatalities that were caused by workplace exposure to hepatitis B and HIV. The postexposure assessment of the healthcare workplaces where the exposures occurred indicated that the workers were not provided with the necessary protective equipment or clothing, nor had they been given specific instruction on how to perform their jobs in a manner to protect them from exposure. As a result of these cases, OSHA issued a standard "to eliminate or minimize occupational exposure to hepatitis B virus (HBV), human immunodeficiency virus (HIV), and other blood-borne pathogens." This regulation is designed to protect employees who regularly are exposed to blood or body fluids. Physicians and other healthcare workers such as laboratory workers, nurses, and medical technicians are at greatest risk.

As of 2010, 57 documented transmissions and 143 possible transmissions had been reported in the United States. No confirmed cases of occupational HIV transmission to healthcare workers have been reported since 1999. Under-reporting of cases is possible, however, because case reporting is voluntary. Healthcare workers who are exposed to HIV-infected blood at work have a 0.3 percent risk of becoming infected. In other words, 3 of every 1,000 such injuries, if untreated, will result in infection.[14]

Personal Protective Equipment   One goal of OSHA has been to develop standards for personal protective equipment (PPE). These standards require that employers analyze job hazards, provide adequate PPE to employees in hazardous jobs, and train employees in the use of PPE items. Common PPE items in healthcare include gowns, lab coats, surgical scrubs, masks, and gloves. Healthcare employers are required to provide PPE to all employees (at no cost) who are working in an environment that presents hazards or who might have contact with hazardous chemicals and substances on the job.[15] Figure 14-4 indicates the type of PPE required for various healthcare positions.

In addition, a recent court ruling specified that employees should be paid at the proper hourly rate for the time it takes to put on and take off protective equipment, including any potential overtime that is incurred beyond a 40-hour workweek.[16]

FIGURE 14-4   Personal Protective Equipment Requirements

POSITION	PPE
Dentist	Gowns, gloves, mask, protective eyewear
Operating room nurse	Gowns, gloves, mask, protective eyewear
Central sterile technician	Gowns, gloves, mask, protective eyewear
Autopsy assistant	Mask, protective eyewear, impermeable (metal mesh) gloves, and rubber aprons
Repair personnel	Safety glasses, hard hat, safety shoes
Cafeteria kitchen worker	Aprons, gloves, safety shoes

© 2016 Cengage Learning®

Pandemic Guidelines   In addition to regulations, OSHA issues guidelines that can help to protect people at work in matters of health or safety. One such set of guidelines can help employers to prepare for a pandemic disease. These guidelines provide information about how the organization can manage a serious disease outbreak with proper procedures and safety equipment.

Ergonomics and OSHA

Ergonomics is the study and design of the work environment to address physical demands placed on individuals. In a work setting, ergonomic studies look at factors such as fatigue, lighting, tools, equipment layout, and placement of controls. Ergonomics can provide economic value to employers as it can reduce injuries.

For many years, OSHA focused on the large number of work-related injuries that occur because of repetitive stress and repetitive motion, such as cumulative trauma disorders, carpal tunnel syndrome, and other injuries. **Cumulative trauma disorders (CTDs)** are muscle and skeletal injuries that occur when workers repetitively use the same muscles to perform tasks. *Carpal tunnel syndrome*, a cumulative trauma disorder, is an injury common to healthcare workers who put their hands through repetitive motions such as typing, dispensing medications, and suturing.

Most recently, attention has focused on the application of ergonomic principles to the design of workstations where workers extensively use personal computers, portable message devices, cell phones, and video display terminals for extended periods of time. Further, OSHA has approached ergonomics concerns by adopting voluntary guidelines for specific problem industries and jobs, identifying industries with serious ergonomic problems, and giving employers tools for identifying and controlling ergonomics hazards. Among the industries receiving guidelines are nursing homes.

Work Assignments and OSHA

The rights of employees regarding work assignments have been addressed as part of OSHA regulations. Two primary areas where work assignments and concerns about safety and health meet are reproductive health and unsafe work.

Work Assignments and Reproductive Health Work Assignments and Reproductive Health   Related to unsafe work is the issue of assigning employees to work in areas where their ability to have children may be affected by exposure to chemical hazards, biomedical waste, or radiation. Women who are able to bear children or who are pregnant have presented the primary concerns, but in some situations, the possibility that men might become sterile also has been a concern.

In a court case involving reproductive health, the Supreme Court held that an employer's policy of keeping women of childbearing capacity out of jobs that might involve lead exposure violated the Civil Rights Act and the Pregnancy Discrimination Act.[17] However, the duties of many healthcare occupations may pose a threat to a healthcare worker's ability to conceive, maintain pregnancy, or deliver a healthy baby. Consistent with the Supreme Court ruling, healthcare organizations cannot bar workers from these occupations to protect the health of the fetus.

However, healthcare employers need to protect themselves from liability from the effects of workplace exposure. Although there is no *absolute* protection from liability for employers, the following actions are suggested:

- Maintain a safe workplace for all by using the safest methods of working.
- Comply with all state and federal safety laws.
- Inform employees of any known risks.
- Document employee acceptance of any risks.

Refusing Unsafe Work   Both union and nonunion workers have the right to refuse to work when they considered the work unsafe. In many court cases, that refusal has been found to be justified. The conditions for refusing work because of safety concerns include the following:

- The employee's fear is objectively reasonable.
- The employee has tried to have the dangerous condition corrected.
- Using normal procedures to solve the problem has not worked.

This may pose a serious issue for healthcare employers when an employee's concern over unsafe work resulting in his or her refusal to perform the work jeopardizes the delivery of patient care. Healthcare managers and HR professionals must proceed cautiously in this area in effecting the appropriate balance between their employee's rights and providing safe care to patients. As an example, at a large medical center a pregnant nurse in the oncology unit was responsible for administering antineoplastic drugs, which are used to treat some forms of cancer. She was aware that exposure to these drugs could have an adverse impact on her unborn fetus; consequently she refused to administer these drugs. The nurse manager, in consultation with her HR representative, decided to reassign the nurse to other duties and had another nurse administer the drugs.

OSHA Record-Keeping Requirements

Employers are generally required to maintain a detailed annual record of the various types of injuries, accidents, and fatalities for inspection by OSHA representatives and for submission to the agency. OSHA guidelines state that facilities where accident records are below the national average rarely need inspecting. But those with high "days away from work scores" may get letters from OSHA and perhaps an inspection.[18]

Reporting Injuries and Illnesses   Four types of injuries or illnesses are defined by the Occupational Safety and Health Act. They are as follows:

- *Injury- or Illness-Related Deaths*—Fatalities at workplaces or caused by work-related actions (must be reported within eight hours)
- *Lost-Time or Disability Injuries:* Job-related injuries or disabling occurrences that cause an employee to miss regularly scheduled work on the day following the accident

- *Medical Care Injuries:* Injuries that require treatment by a physician but do not cause an employee to miss a regularly scheduled work turn
- *Minor Injuries:* Injuries that require first aid treatment and do not cause an employee to miss the next regularly scheduled work turn

The record-keeping requirements for these injuries and illnesses are summarized in Figure 14-5. Notice that only very minor injuries do not have to be recorded for OSHA. For example, a hospital maintenance employee was repairing a monitor when his hand slipped and hit the sharp edge of the monitor's frame. His hand was cut and he received five stitches and was told by the doctor not to use his hand for three days. This injury was recorded and reported to OSHA because the stitches and restricted duty required that it be recorded.

OSHA Inspections

The Occupational Safety and Health Act provides for on-the-spot inspections by OSHA representatives, called compliance officers or inspectors. In *Marshall*

FIGURE 14-5 **Guide to Recordability of Cases under the Occupational Safety and Health Act**

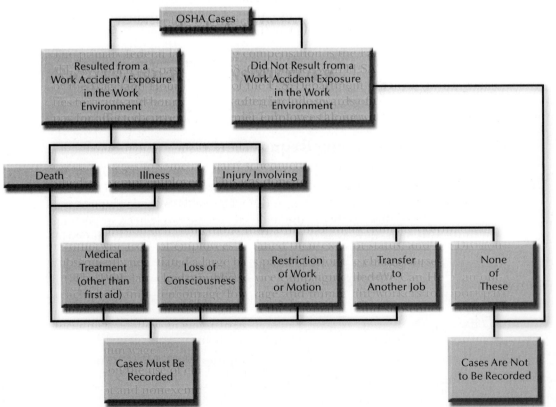

v. Barlow's, Inc., the U.S. Supreme Court held that safety inspectors must produce a search warrant if an employer refuses to allow an inspector into the plant voluntarily. The Court also ruled that an inspector does not have to show probable cause to obtain a search warrant. A warrant can be obtained easily if a search is part of a general enforcement plan.[19]

Dealing with an Inspection   When an OSHA compliance officer arrives, managers should ask to see the inspector's credentials. Next, the company HR representative or safety professional should insist on an opening conference with the compliance officer. The compliance officer may request that a union representative (if appropriate), an employee, and a company representative be present while the inspection is conducted. During the inspection, the officer checks organizational records to see if they are being maintained and to determine the number of accidents that have occurred. Following this review of the safety records, the officer conducts an on-the-spot inspection and may use a wide variety of equipment to test compliance with standards. After the inspection, the compliance officer can issue citations for any violations of standards and provisions of the act.

Citations and Violations   Although OSHA inspectors can issue citations for violations of the act, whether or not a citation is issued depends on the severity and extent of the problems, and on the employer's knowledge of them. In addition, depending on the nature and number of violations, monetary penalties can be assessed against employers. The nature and extent of the penalties depend on the type and severity of the violations as determined by OSHA officials.

Many types of violations are cited by OSHA. Ranging from the most severe to minimal, including a special category for repeated violations, the most common are as follows:

- *Imminent Danger*—When there is reasonable certainty that the condition will cause death or serious physical harm if it is not corrected immediately, an imminent-danger citation is issued and a notice posted by an inspector. Imminent-danger situations are handled on the highest-priority basis. They are reviewed by a regional OSHA director, and the condition must be corrected immediately. If the condition is serious enough and the employer does not cooperate, a representative of OSHA may obtain a federal injunction to close the facility until the condition is corrected. The appropriate labeling on volatile chemicals is one example of an imminent danger.

- *Serious*—When a condition could probably cause death or serious physical harm, and the employer should know of the condition, OSHA issues a serious-violation citation. Examples of serious violations would be the failure to repair a safety latch on a steam sterilization autoclave.

- *Other than Serious*—Violations that could impact employees' health or safety but probably would not cause death or serious harm are called "other than serious." Having frayed electrical cords on a piece of medical equipment might be classified as an other-than-serious violation.

- *De Minimis*—A *de minimis* condition is one not directly and immediately related to employees' safety or health. No citation is issued, but the condition is mentioned to the employer. Lack of doors on toilet stalls is a common example of a *de minimis* violation.

- *Willful and Repeated*—Citations for willful and repeated violations are issued to employers that have been previously cited for violations. If an employer knows about a safety violation or has been warned of a violation and does not correct the problem, a second citation is issued. The penalty for a willful and repeated violation can be high. For example, if death results from an accident that involves such a safety violation, a jail term of six months can be imposed on the executives or managers who were responsible.

Consider a case in which a dental practice instructed its employees to utilize equipment differently than usual when OSHA conducted an inspection. It also hid pieces of equipment, and management lied about its usual practices. These actions led to a willful violation and large fines for numerous violations, primarily because the dental practice tried to cover up its noncompliance.

Critique of OSHA

OSHA has been criticized on several fronts. Since the agency has so many work sites to inspect, employers have only a relatively small chance of being inspected. Figure 14-6 depicts the total number of OSHA inspections in 2012 and the number that were conducted at hospitals.[20] As the figure suggests, considering the dangers that exist in healthcare facilities, this relatively small number of inspections is noteworthy.

Some suggest that employers pay little attention to OSHA enforcement efforts for this reason. Labor unions and others have criticized OSHA and Congress for not providing enough inspectors. For instance, it is common to find that many of the work sites at which workers suffered severe injuries or deaths had not been inspected in the previous five years.

Employers, especially smaller ones, continue to complain about the complexity of complying with OSHA standards and the costs associated with penalties and with making changes required to remedy problem areas. Larger healthcare employers typically hire safety and health specialists and establish

FIGURE 14-6 Inspections in FY 2012

TOTAL INSPECTIONS	HOSPITAL INSPECTIONS	HOSPITAL INSPECTIONS AS % OF THE TOTAL
Federal OSHA: 46,869	208	.44
State OSHA: 56,121	368	.66

© 2016 Cengage Learning®

more proactive programs. However, smaller organizations, like physician groups or small rehabilitation facilities, cannot afford to do so but still have to comply with the regulations, meaning that managers need to be more involved in safety management.

SAFETY MANAGEMENT

Effective safety management requires an organizational commitment to safe working conditions.[21] But well-designed and -managed safety programs can reduce accidents and the associated costs, such as workers' compensation and possible fines. Further, accidents and other safety concerns do decline as a result of an effective safety management program with a number of components.

The organizational characteristics that achieve a safety culture include:

- Leaders demonstrate a commitment to safety.
- The organization must have organizational processes in place that identify, evaluate, and address safety problems promptly.
- Each employee must be responsible for safety.
- The organization must plan and control work activities to maintain safety.
- The organization must be committed to continuous learning around safety.
- Safety must keep pace with dynamic and evolving work environments.
- All employees should feel empowered to raise safety concerns.
- The organization must facilitate effective safety-related communications.[22]

The Organization and Safety

At the heart of safety management is an organizational commitment to a comprehensive safety effort. This effort should be coordinated from the top level of management to include all members of the organization. It also should be reflected in managerial actions. There are three different approaches that employers such as these use in managing safety. Figure 14-7 shows the organizational, engineering, and individual approaches and their components. Successful programs may use all three in dealing with safety issues.

Safety and Engineering

Healthcare employers can prevent many accidents by designing processes, using equipment, and maintaining work areas so that workers who perform potentially dangerous jobs cannot injure themselves and others. Providing safety equipment, ensuring appropriate maintenance and repair, installing emergency switches and safety rails, keeping aisles clear, and maintaining adequate ventilation, lighting, heating, and air conditioning can all help make work environments safer.

FIGURE 14-7 **Approaches to Effective Safety Management**

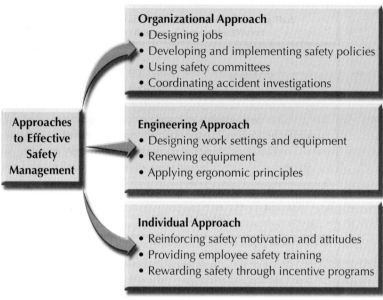

© 2016 Cengage Learning®

Individual Considerations and Safety

Engineers approach safety from the perspective of redesigning the equipment, processes, or work area; industrial psychologists and human factors experts see safety differently. They are concerned with the proper match of individuals to jobs and emphasize employee training in safety methods, fatigue reduction, and health awareness. Experts have conducted numerous field studies with thousands of employees that looked at the "human factors" in accidents. The results show a definite relationship between emotional factors, such as stress, and accidents. Other studies point to the importance of individual differences, motivation, attitudes, and learning as key factors in controlling the human element in safety.

Attitudinal variables are among the individual factors that affect accident rates because more problems are caused by careless employees than by equipment or employer negligence. At one time, workers who were dissatisfied with their jobs were thought to have higher accident rates. However, this assumption has been questioned in recent years. Although employees' personalities, attitudes, and individual characteristics apparently have some influence on accidents, exact cause-and-effect relationships are difficult to establish.

Work schedules can be another cause for accidents. The relationship between work schedules and accidents can be explained as follows. Fatigue based on physical exertion sometimes exists in today's healthcare workplace. But boredom, which occurs when a person is required to do the same tasks for a long period of time, is rather common. As fatigue of this kind increases, motivation is reduced; along with decreased motivation, workers' attention wanders, and the likelihood of accidents rises.[23] A particular area of concern in healthcare is *overtime* in work scheduling. Overtime work has been consistently related to accident or patient care incidents. Further, the more overtime worked, the more severe accidents appeared to be. The healthcare industry has been especially concerned about the fatigue factor for employees who work 10- and 12-hour shifts, or who may be required to work double shifts. Consider the implications of an intensive care unit nurse who works a physically demanding and emotionally draining 10-hour shift being asked to stay on and work a double. The nurse's ability to render safe care could clearly be impacted.

Another area of concern is the relationship of accident rates to different shifts, particularly late-night shifts. Since there often are fewer supervisors and managers working the 11 P.M. to 7 A.M. shift, workers tend to receive less training and supervision. Both of these factors can lead to higher accident rates.

Safety Policies, Discipline, and Record Keeping

Designing safety policies and rules and disciplining violators are important components of safety efforts. Regularly reinforcing the need for safe behavior and frequently supplying feedback on positive safety practices are also effective ways of improving worker safety. Such safety-conscious efforts must involve employees, supervisors, managers, safety specialists, and HR staff members.

For policies about safety to be effective, good record keeping about accidents, causes, and other details is necessary. Without records, an employer cannot track its safety performance or compare benchmarks against other employers, and therefore may not realize the extent of its safety problems.

Safety Training and Communication

Safety training can be conducted in various ways to effectively reduce accidents. Training and orientation are especially critical in healthcare organizations. A significant percentage of errors occur in health facilities due to inadequate employee training.[24] Regular sessions with supervisors, managers, and employees are often coordinated by HR staff members. Communication of safety procedures, reasons why accidents occurred, and what to do in an emergency is critical. Without effective communication about safety, training is insufficient. To reinforce safety training, continuous communication to develop safety consciousness is necessary. Merely sending safety memos is not enough. Producing newsletters, changing safety posters, continually updating bulletin boards, and posting safety information in visible areas are also recommended.

It is frequently difficult to convince healthcare employees to focus on safety standards while performing their jobs. Often, employees think that safety measures are bothersome and unnecessary until an injury occurs. For example, it might be necessary for employees to wear safety glasses in a laboratory most of the time. But if the glasses are awkward, employees may resist using them, even when they know they should have eye protection. Also, some employees who may have worked without wearing the glasses and never sustained an injury might think this requirement is a nuisance. Because of such problems, safety training and communication efforts must address safety issues in such a way that employees view safety as important and are motivated to follow safe work practices.

Healthcare employers may need to communicate in a variety of media and languages. Such efforts are important to address the special needs of workers who have vision, speech, or hearing impairments; who are not proficient in English; or who are challenged in other ways. Many approaches might be needed in training to enhance individual learning, including the use of role-playing and other active practice exercises, behavioral examples, and extensive discussion.

Employee Safety Motivation and Incentives

To encourage healthcare employees to work safely, many healthcare organizations have used safety contests and have given employees incentives for safe work behavior. As an example, a community hospital in Wisconsin awards extra time off to the employees of departments that do not incur a loss-time injury during the calendar year. Unfortunately, there is concern that employees and managers may not report accidents and injuries so that they can collect on the incentive rewards. This concern about safety incentives was also raised by OSHA.

Effective Safety Committees

Employees frequently participate in safety planning through safety committees, often composed of workers from a variety of levels and departments.[25] A safety committee generally meets at regularly scheduled times, has specific responsibilities for conducting safety reviews, identifies risks, and makes recommendations for changes necessary to avoid future accidents. Usually, at least one member of the committee comes from the HR department. Both OSHA and the Joint Commission recognize the importance of safety committees to drive organizational safety agendas. In approximately 32 states, all but the smallest employers may be required to establish safety committees. From time to time, legislation has been introduced at the federal level to require joint management–employee safety committees. But as yet, no federal provisions have been enacted.

Companies must take care to ensure that managers do not constitute a majority on their safety committees. Otherwise, they may be in violation of provisions of the National Labor Relations Act, commonly known as the Wagner Act. That act, as explained in detail in Chapter 11, prohibits employers from "dominating a labor organization." Some safety committees have been ruled to be labor organizations because they deal with working conditions.

Inspection, Investigation, and Evaluation

It is not necessary to wait for an OSHA inspector to check the work area for safety hazards. Regular inspections should be done by a safety committee or by a company safety coordinator. Problem areas should be addressed immediately to prevent accidents and keep work productivity at the highest possible levels. Also, OSHA inspects organizations with above-average rates of lost workdays

FIGURE 14-8   Phases of Accident Investigation

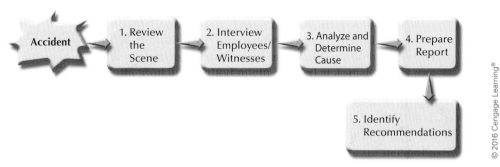

more frequently. Therefore, reducing accidents can lower the frequency of on-site OSHA visits.

The phases of accident investigation are shown in Figure 14-8. Identifying why an accident occurred is extremely useful.

Closely related to accident investigation is research to determine ways of preventing accidents. Employing safety engineers or having outside experts evaluate the safety of working conditions may be useful. If many similar accidents seem to occur in an organizational unit, a safety training program may be necessary to emphasize safe working practices. As an example, a medical center reported a greater-than-average number of back injuries among employees who lifted heavy patients. Installation of patient-lifting devices and safety training on the proper way to use them was initiated. As a result, the number of worker injuries was reduced.

Measuring Safety Efforts

Healthcare organizations should monitor and evaluate their safety efforts. For those organizations that subscribe to the Joint Commission, it is a requirement to meet the standards as described earlier in this chapter. Just as organizational accounting records are audited, an organization's safety efforts should be audited periodically as well. Accident and injury statistics should be compared with previous accident patterns to identify any significant changes. This analysis should be designed to measure progress in safety management.

Various safety efforts can be measured. Common metrics are workers' compensation costs per injury/illness; percentage of injuries/illnesses by department, work shifts, and job categories; and incident rate comparisons with industry and benchmark targets. Regardless of the specific measures used, it is critical to track and evaluate safety management efforts using relevant HR metrics.

Employers in a variety of industries have found that emphasizing health and safety pays off in many ways. Lower employee benefits costs for healthcare, fewer work-related accidents, lower workers' compensation costs, and more productive employees can all be results of employer efforts to stress health and safety.

HEALTHCARE REFORM AND HR PRACTICES

Although not a direct result of healthcare reform as legislated by the ACA, the nature of healthcare delivery today and the demands on the healthcare system are causing workplace safety issues throughout the industry. The high demand for health services, and the associated issues of declining reimbursement and related economic pressures, has created staffing shortages that are felt by hospitals and other healthcare organizations. These shortages place an incredible burden on healthcare workers.

As noted throughout this chapter, the very nature of healthcare delivery carries with it many health, safety, and security issues. Adding staff shortages to the mix exacerbates the problem. Recognizing that staff shortages impact not only the safe delivery of patient care but also the health of workers, the American College of Healthcare Executives (ACHE) has developed a series of recommendations designed to deal with these issues. Many of the recommendations have direct implications on workplace safety and health, including:

- Maintaining workloads and expectations that strive to alleviate and prevent burnout
- Creating systems for job assignments and backup coverage that ensure responsibilities are appropriately matched with qualifications
- Responding to potential disasters that would significantly impact staff availability over sustained periods, requiring multilevel backup capacity
- Conducting employee opinion surveys and exit interviews, using the results to identify steps to improve job satisfaction
- Analyzing departments or units with high turnover rates to determine whether management shortcomings, working conditions, and/or other factors may be contributing to staff morale problems
- Closing units or diverting patients if shortages become severe to ensure that patient care is not compromised and high-quality care is maintained[26]

On the face of it, these recommendations are very practical and clearly provide a logical way to address staff morale, burnout, and related problems. However, many healthcare organizations fail to develop and/or implement recommendations of this nature. Healthcare HR professionals can provide leadership in this area, and in many healthcare organizations they have been effective advocates for dealing with worker shortage issues.

HEALTH

Employee health problems are varied—and somewhat inevitable. They can range from minor illnesses such as colds to serious illnesses related to the jobs performed. Some employees have emotional health problems; others have alcohol or drug problems. Some problems are chronic; others are transitory. But all these issues can affect organizational operations and individual employee productivity.

Healthcare Workplace Health Issues

Healthcare employers face a variety of workplace issues. Previously in this chapter, cumulative trauma injuries, exposure to hazardous chemicals, and blood-borne pathogens have been discussed because OSHA has addressed these concerns through regulations or standards. But there are a number of other key health issues for healthcare workers, including substance abuse, emotional and mental problems, indoor air quality, latex allergies, inadvertent needle sticks, and slips and falls.

Substance Abuse Substance abuse is defined as the use of illicit substances or the misuse of controlled substances, alcohol, or other drugs. There are millions of substance abusers in the general workforce, and they cost employers billions of dollars annually. In the United States over 70 percent of substance abusers hold jobs; one worker in four, ages 18 to 34, used drugs in the past year; and one worker in three knows of drug sales in the workplace. Substance abusers increase risk of accident, lower productivity, raise insurance costs, and reduce profits.[27]

Healthcare workers are at an increased risk for developing chemical dependencies because they have easier access to controlled substances than does the general population. Also, healthcare workers experience unique stressors (e.g., regular exposure to death and individuals experiencing trauma or emotional suffering) that contribute to chemically assisted coping. As an example, the prevalence of substance abuse among nurses is believed to parallel that in the general population, approximately 10 percent. Figure 14-9 depicts the common signs of alcohol and drug abuse.

The Americans with Disabilities Act (ADA) affects how management can handle substance abuse cases. Currently, illegal drug users are specifically excluded from the definition of *disabled* under the act. However, those addicted to legal substances (alcohol, for example) and prescription drugs are considered disabled under the ADA. Also, recovering alcoholics are considered disabled under the ADA.

FIGURE 14-9 Common Signs of Substance Abuse

- Fatigue
- Slurred speech
- Flushed cheeks
- Difficulty walking
- Inconsistency
- Difficulty remembering details
- Argumentative behavior
- Missed deadlines
- Many unscheduled absences (especially on Mondays and Fridays)
- Depression
- Irritability
- Emotionalism
- Overreacting
- Violence
- Frequently borrowing money

© 2016 Cengage Learning®

Preemployment alcohol and drug testing is used by many healthcare employers. Testing is also done following an accident or for reasonable cause, or as part of a random testing program instituted by employers.

To encourage employees to seek help for their substance abuse problems, a **firm-choice option** is usually recommended and has been endorsed legally. In this procedure, the employee is privately confronted by a supervisor or manager about unsatisfactory work-related behaviors. Then, in keeping with the disciplinary system, the employee is offered a choice between help and discipline. Treatment options and consequences of further unsatisfactory performance are clearly discussed, including what the employer will do. Confidentiality and follow-up are critical when employers use the firm-choice option.

As a profession, nursing has been very aggressive in managing workplace substance abuse issues. According to the American Nurses Associations (ANA) Code of Ethics, addicted nurses may have difficulty remaining accountable to themselves and others for their own actions or in assessing self-competence. It is the responsibility of management and coworkers to respond to questionable practices as an advocate for patients. The ANA suggests ensuring that an impaired nurse "receives assistance in regaining ability to function appropriately."[28]

Emotional/Mental Health Concerns Many individuals today are facing work, family, and personal life pressures. These pressures are managed successfully by many people. But some individuals have difficulties handling these demands. Also, specific events, such as death of a spouse, divorce, or medical problems, can affect individuals who otherwise have been coping successfully with those pressures. As noted earlier, a variety of emotional/mental health issues arise at work that must be addressed by employers. It is important to note that emotional/mental illnesses such as schizophrenia and depression are considered disabilities under the ADA. Therefore, employers should be cautious when using disciplinary policies if diagnosed employees have work-related problems.

Stress is one concern, when individuals cannot successfully handle the multiple demands they face. All people encounter stress, but it is when *stress overload* hits that work-related consequences can result. HR professionals, managers, and supervisors must be prepared to handle employee stress; otherwise, employees may burn out or exhibit various unhealthy behaviors, such as abusing alcohol, misusing prescription drugs, demonstrating outbursts of anger, or other symptoms. Healthcare employees are especially vulnerable to stress overload due to the nature and pace of their work. Beyond effects on communications and relieving some workload pressures, it is generally recommended that supervisors and managers contact the HR staff, who may intervene and may refer the affected employees to outside resources through employee assistance programs.[29]

Depression is another common emotional/mental health concern. Estimates are that 20 percent of individuals in workplaces suffer from depression. One indicator of the extent of clinical depression is that the sales of prescription drugs, such as Prozac and Zoloft, covered by employee benefits plans have risen significantly in the past several years. The effects of depression are seen at all levels, from nursing units and business offices to executive suites. Carried to the extreme, depression can result in employee suicide. That guilt and sorrow felt by those who worked with the deceased individuals must be dealt with by

HR staff, often aided by crisis counselors. To deal with depression, it is recommended that HR professionals, managers, and supervisors be trained in recognizing the symptoms of depression and knowing what to do when symptoms are indicated in employees. Employees can be guided to employee assistance programs and helped with obtaining medical treatment.

Workplace Air Quality   An increasing number of employees work in settings where air quality is a health issue. One cause of poor air quality occurs in "sealed" buildings where windows cannot be opened when air flows are reduced to save energy and cut operating costs. Also, inadequate ventilation, as well as airborne contamination from carpets, molds, copy machines, adhesives, and fungi, can cause poor air quality and employee illnesses.[30]

Latex Allergy   For years, natural rubber latex allergies have been an employee concern. These rubber products, typically in the form of gloves, are used to protect employees from the spread of infection. Latex allergies were originally recognized in the 1970s but did not become a major concern until latex products began to gain wider use in response to the Centers for Disease Control's 1987 recommendation that blood and body fluids should always be approached as if potentially infectious. In 1992, OSHA established the blood-borne pathogens standard requiring the use of barrier protection. Consequently, the use of latex gloves by healthcare workers increased dramatically.

OSHA estimates that 6 percent to 17 percent of exposed healthcare workers are allergic to natural rubber latex. The allergic employee experiences a simple irritation reaction. Although uncomfortable, usually it is not a serious problem in itself. However, it can lead to more serious and detrimental allergic reactions, including serious health problems. Some argue that as more healthcare workers began to use latex gloves, the sheer increase in wearers statistically increased the number of people who might develop an allergy to latex.

Healthcare employers have attempted a number of actions to help allergic workers, such as providing cotton glove liners for use with the latex glove, placing allergic workers in non-patient-care positions, or stocking latex-free carts on patient units. As an example, a major health system uses vinyl gloves as the standard examination glove.

Inadvertent Needle Sticks   Healthcare workers run the highest risk of disease transmission from injury by contaminated devices. Needles or syringes most frequently cause injury; about 20 percent of needle sticks fall into high-risk exposure to such blood-borne diseases as hepatitis B and C viruses and HIV. Estimates are that 500,000 needle stick injuries occur annually among healthcare workers in the United States. Nurses sustain the majority of these injuries, but other employees are also at risk, including physicians, nursing assistants, and environmental services personnel.[31]

To address this concern, the Needle Stick Safety and Prevention Act (NSPA) was passed by Congress in November 2000. The NSPA mandated that OSHA revise the blood-borne pathogen standard to integrate the act's requirements. This act focuses attention on safer medical devices, such as needle-less medical devices for withdrawing fluids or administering medications and the incorporation of these devices in an organizational exposure control plan. The act also requires employers to solicit input from nonmanagerial healthcare workers regarding the identification, evaluation, and selection of safer medical devices.[32]

Slips and Falls   Slips and falls result in 15 percent of all accidental workplace deaths and 16 percent of accidents resulting in disability. Slips result in head or back injuries, lacerations, fractures, pulled muscles, and contusions, and cost employers billions of dollars annually.

The healthcare workplace can offer its share of hazards, including wet floors, inclines, stairways, and cluttered passageways. Given the often-cluttered and busy nature of the healthcare workplace, protecting workers from slips and falls is a challenging task. Safety experts recommend the establishment of a comprehensive slip-prevention program focusing on risk assessment, good housekeeping, the use of slip-resistant flooring, and appropriate footwear. Employee awareness and safety training is also important.

Health Promotion

Healthcare employers who are concerned about maintaining a healthy workforce must move beyond simply providing healthy working conditions and emphasize employee health and wellness in other ways. **Health promotion** is a supportive approach to facilitate, encourage, and help employees to enhance healthy actions and lifestyles. Going beyond just compliance with workplace safety and health regulations, organizations engage in health promotion by encouraging employees to make physiological, mental, and social choices that improve their health.

Health promotion efforts can range from providing information and enhancing employee awareness of health issues to creating an organizational culture supportive of employee health enhancements, as Figure 14-10 indicates. The first level is useful and may have some impact on individuals, but much is left to individual initiatives to follow through and make changes in actions and behaviors. Employers provide information on such topics as weight control, stress management, nutrition, exercise, and smoking cessation. Although such efforts may be beneficial for some employees, employers who wish to impact employees' health must offer second-level efforts through more comprehensive programs and efforts that focus on the lifestyle "wellness" of employees.

FIGURE 14-10   Health Promotion Levels

LEVEL 1 Information and Awareness	LEVEL 2 Lifestyle Wellness	LEVEL 3 Health Emphasis
• Brochures and materials • Health risk screenings • Health tests and measurements • Special events and classes	• Wellness education program • Regular health classes • Employee assistance programs • Support groups • Health incentives	• Benefits integrated with programs • Dedicated resources and facilities • Continuous health promotion • Health education curriculum

© Cengage Learning®

Wellness Programs   Employers' desires to improve productivity, decrease absenteeism, and control healthcare costs have come together in the wellness movement. **Wellness programs** are designed to maintain or improve employees' health before problems arise. Wellness programs encourage self-directed lifestyle changes.

There are a number of ways to assess the effectiveness of wellness programs. Participation rates by employees are one way. The participation rates vary by type of activity, but generally 20 percent to 40 percent of employees participate in the different activities in a wellness program. Although more participation would be beneficial, the programs have resulted in healthier lifestyles for more employees. Cost–benefit analyses tend to support the continuation of wellness programs as well.[33]

Employee Assistance Programs (EAPs)   One method that organizations are using as a broad-based response to health issues is the **employee assistance program (EAP)**, which provides counseling and other help to employees having emotional, physical, or other personal problems. In such a program, an employer establishes a liaison with a social service counseling agency. Employees who have problems may then contact the agency, either voluntarily or by employer referral, for assistance with a broad range of problems. Counseling costs are paid for by the employer, either in total or up to a preestablished limit.

EAPs are attempts to help employees with a variety of problems. Generally, EAP counselors find that the most common employee issues dealt with are: (1) depression and anxiety, (2) marital and relationship problems, (3) legal difficulties, and (4) family and children concerns. Other areas that also are commonly addressed as part of an EAP include substance abuse, financial counseling, and career advice. Critical to employee usage of an EAP is preserving confidentiality. That is why employers outsource EAPs to trained professionals, who usually report only the numbers of employees and services provided, rather than details on individuals using the EAP.

Organizational Health Culture   A number of employers, both large and small, have recognized that an organizational culture that emphasizes and supports health efforts is beneficial. Common to these employers is an integrative, broad-based effort supported both financially and managerially. Development of policies and procedures supporting health efforts, establishing on-site exercise facilities, and consistently promoting health programs all contribute to creating a health promotion environment throughout the organization.

SECURITY

Traditionally, when healthcare employers have addressed worker health, safety, and security, they have been concerned about reducing workplace accidents, improving workers' safety practices, and reducing health hazards at work. However, over the past few decades, providing security for employees' patients, residents, or clients has grown in importance. Incidents of workplace violence occur regularly in hospitals, clinics, and nursing homes. The domestic problems of patients, residents, or clients and their family members can erupt in verbal or physical assaults. Healthcare workers can easily get caught in the middle of these issues or may be required to attempt to manage them.

Workplace Violence

Workplace violence is violent acts directed at someone at work or on duty. For example, physical assault, threats, harassment, intimidation, and bullying all qualify as violent behaviors at work. Workplace violence can be instigated by several individuals:

- *Criminal*—A crime is committed in conjunction with the violence by a person with no legitimate relationship with the business (e.g., robbery, arson, trespassing).
- *Customer*—A person with a legitimate relationship with the business becomes violent (e.g., patients, students, inmates, customers).
- *Coworker*—A current or past employee attacks or threatens another employee (e.g., contractor, temp).
- *Domestic*—A person who has no legitimate relationship with a business but has a personal relationship with the victim commits some form of violence against an employee (e.g., family member, boyfriend).

Workplace Violence Warning Signs   There is reason to believe that some people might downplay the risks associated with violent colleagues.[34] However, there are warning signs and characteristics of potentially violent persons at work that should be recognized by employees. Individuals who have committed the most violent acts have had the profile depicted in Figure 14-11. Someone with some of these signs and characteristics may cope for years until a trauma pushes that person over the edge. A profound humiliation or rejection, the end of a marriage, the loss of a lawsuit, termination from a job, or other sources of stress may make a difficult employee turn violent.[35]

Workplace Incivility and Bullying   Workplace incivility occurs when rude behavior by ill-mannered coworkers or bosses makes the targets of incivility feel annoyed, frustrated, or offended. Most employees do not find incivility serious

FIGURE 14-11   Profile of Potentially Violent Employees

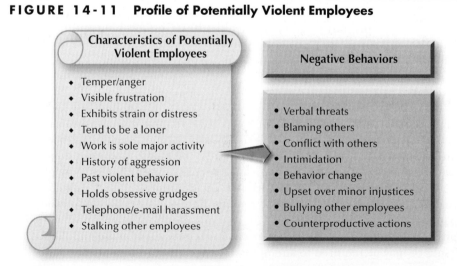

enough for formal action.[36] But incivility can escalate into bullying, which is more likely to require action.[37]

Bullying is a behavior that the victim perceives as oppressive, humiliating, threatening, or infringing on his or her human rights that occurs over an extended period of time. Bullying, especially by supervisors, can result in damage to the employee and to the organization, leading to increased turnover.[38] Research exploring a random sample of 45 bullying cases that were heard in U.S. courts found that almost 20 percent of situations contained violence were often precipitated by a manager, and that public organizations experienced a majority of the problems. Just over one-third of organizations had crafted an antibullying policy.[39] This finding suggests a need for management attention to the problem through training, policies, and codes of conduct.[40]

Domestic Causes of Workplace Violence   Too often violence that begins at home with family or friends can spill over into the workplace. Many abused women report being harassed frequently at work, by telephone or in person, by abusing partners. Such behavior can disrupt the workplace and create a negative work environment for all parties involved.

Domestic violence can harm work attitudes and, even worse, put the well-being of employees in jeopardy. One survey determined that 21 percent of workers claimed that they had suffered from domestic abuse, and well over half indicated that this violence adversely impacted them on the job. Another study found that approximately 10 percent of surveyed employees claimed that they were currently dealing with domestic violence, with 19 percent of those claiming that the abuse was taking place on the job.[41] The fact that 70 percent of employers have not developed workplace violence policies, and of those that do, only 30 percent focus on domestic abuse at work, tends to make matters worse. Organizations need to be proactive about teaching supervisors about the dangers of such misconduct and get victims proper counseling and assistance.[42]

Domestic violence is particularly troubling as HR professionals find it difficult to take action because of concerns over personal privacy.[43] A reaction by employers is to sometimes ignore obvious signs of domestic violence. In fact, some employers have been sued and found liable for ignoring pleas for help from employees who later were victims of domestic violence in company parking lots or on employer premises.

Dealing with Workplace Violence   The increase in workplace violence has led many healthcare employers to develop policies and practices for trying to prevent and respond to it. Policies can identify how workplace violence is to be dealt with in conjunction with disciplinary actions and referrals to EAPs. Training of managers and others is an important part of successful practice. As an example, nurses routinely receive training on dealing with violent behaviors. An appropriate organizational climate can also mitigate concerns about workplace bullying and other counterproductive behaviors.

One application of these policies is a *violence response team.* Composed of security personnel, key managers, HR staff members, and selected employees. This team functions much like a safety committee but with a different focus.

Such a team conducts analyses, responds to and investigates employee threats, and may even help to calm angry, volatile employees.

Employers must be careful because they may face legal action for discrimination if they discharge employees for behaviors that often precede violent acts. For example, in several cases, employees who were terminated or suspended for making threats or even engaging in physical actions against their coworkers then sued their employers, claiming they had mental disabilities covered under the Americans with Disabilities Act.

Postviolence response is another part of managing workplace violence. Whether the violence results in physical injuries or death or just intense interpersonal conflicts, it is important that employers have plans to respond afterward. Their response must reassure employees who may be fearful of returning to work or who experience anxiety and sleeplessness, among other reactions. Providing referrals to EAP resources, allowing employees time to meet with HR staff, and arranging for trained counselors on-site are all possible elements of postviolence response efforts.

Security Management

A comprehensive approach to security management is needed to address a wide range of issues, including workplace violence. HR managers may have responsibility for security programs or may work closely with security managers or consultants.

Security Audit   A **security audit** is a comprehensive review of organizational security. Sometimes called a *vulnerability analysis*, such an audit uses managers inside the organization (e.g., the HR manager and the facilities manager) and outsiders (e.g., security consultants, police officers, fire officials, and computer security experts) to assess security issues and risks.

Typically, a security audit begins with a survey of the area around the facility. Factors such as lighting in parking lots, traffic flow, location of emergency response services, crime in the surrounding neighborhood, and the layout of the buildings and grounds are evaluated. The audit may also include a review of the security available within the firm, including the capabilities of guards. Another part of the security audit reviews disaster plans, which address how to deal with events such as earthquakes, floods, tornadoes, hurricanes, and fires.

Controlled Access and Monitoring   A key part of security involves controlling access to the organization and monitoring activities in such areas as elevators, stairwells, and other low-traffic areas. Many workplace homicides occur during robberies. Therefore, employees who are most vulnerable can be provided bulletproof partitions and restricted access areas.

Many healthcare organizations limit access to facilities and work areas by using video surveillance, electronic access, or keycard systems.[44] Areas such as emergency rooms and nurseries are typically monitored utilizing these types of systems. Although not foolproof, these systems can make it more difficult for an unauthorized person to enter the premises.

Controlling computer access may be an important part of securing information technology (IT) resources. Coordination with IT resources to change passwords, access codes, and otherwise protect company information may also be important. The inappropriate use of information resources is a common problem in companies today. A recent study determined that making employees aware of security measures, providing instruction that heightens understanding of security, and monitoring the use of computers could reduce improper use of information systems through tougher and more certain perceived punishments.[45]

Violence Training   Managers, HR staff members, supervisors, and employees should be trained on how to recognize the signs of a potentially violent employee and what to do when violence occurs.[46] During training at many organizations, participants learn the typical profile of potentially violent employees and are trained to notify the HR department and to refer employees to outside counseling professionals. Such training requires observers to notice verbal and nonverbal reactions by individuals that may indicate anger or hostility, and to listen to individuals exhibiting such reactions.

Specific suggestions addressed in training for dealing with potentially violent employees typically include the following:

- Ask questions requiring explanations and longer answers that allow individuals to vent.
- Respond calmly and nonthreateningly to individuals' emotions, acknowledge concerns, and demonstrate understanding about how the individuals feel.
- Get assistance from others, perhaps a manager not directly affected by the situation being discussed.
- Indicate the need for time to respond to the concerns voiced, and then set up another time for follow-up.
- Notify security personnel and HR staff members whenever employees' behaviors change dramatically or when job disciplinary action may provoke significant reactions by employees.

Employee Screening and Selection

A key facet of providing security is screening job applicants. HR management is somewhat limited by legal constraints on what can be done, particularly regarding the use of psychological tests and checking of references. However, healthcare organizations that do not screen employees adequately may be subject to liability if an employee commits crimes later. For instance, an individual with a criminal record for assault was hired by a home healthcare agency to assist clients in their homes. The employee assaulted a client; consequently, the home healthcare agency was held responsible for not doing an adequate background check. When selecting employees, employers must be careful to use only valid, job-related screening means and to avoid violating federal EEO laws and the Americans with Disabilities Act.

Security Personnel

Providing adequately trained security personnel in sufficient numbers is a part of security management. Many large healthcare organizations such as hospitals and medical centers maintain their own security staff or contract with firms specializing in security. If security is handled in-house, security personnel must be selected and trained to handle a variety of workplace security problems, ranging from dealing with violent behavior by an employee to taking charge in natural disasters.

CASE

Hemmingway Nursing Care is a home healthcare agency providing in-home care to elderly and special-needs patients. Many of Hemmingway's patients would be considered vulnerable adults due to their diagnoses. Hemmingway, consistent with state law, routinely conducted criminal background studies on applicants that had received a conditional offer of employment. If the applicant had a disqualifying record, the offer for employment would be withdrawn.

Recently, the HR director had been informed that one of Hemmingway's long-term nursing aides with an exemplary record of performance and attendance had been arrested and charged with domestic abuse. If the nursing aide is ultimately convicted on the charge, Hemmingway will be required to terminate that person based on state law.

Questions

1. What is the purpose of state laws that require certain types of employers, especially healthcare employers, to conduct criminal checks on workers?
2. Should Hemmingway terminate the employment of the nursing aide if the individual is convicted of domestic abuse regardless of his or her work record?

END NOTES

1. See *http://www.bls.gov* for more information.
2. See *http://nursingworld.org/workplaceviolence* for more information.
3. Sheena Harrison, "Health Care Providers Face Up to Workplace Violence," *Business Insurance* (November 4, 2013), 47.
4. A. Jenkins, "Worker Safety in the Health Care Industry," *Risk Management* (March 2014), 8–9.
5. Shawn Galloway, "Establishing a Sustainable Safety Culture," *EHS Today* (August 2011), 22–26.
6. "Comprehensive Accreditation Manual," *The Joint Commission* (2013).
7. Tamura Lytle, "Rising from the Rubble," *HR Magazine* (September 2011), 65–69.
8. "CMS Proposes Rule to Strengthen Emergency Preparedness," Health Facilities Management (February 2014), 7; see *http://www.federalregister.gov/a/2013-30724* for more information.
9. See *http://www.bls.gov/iag/tgs/iag62.htm#fatalities_injuries_and_illnesses* for more information.
10. See *http://www.bls.gov* for more information.
11. S. Johnson and A. Bleeker, "Common Mistakes Employers Make When Considering ADAAA Accommodations," *Employee Benefit Plan Review* (October 2013), 26–28.
12. Robert Fisher, "Legal Implications of Mental-Health Issues," *Human Resource Executive Online* (May 2, 2009), *http://www.hreonline.com*, 1–3.
13. Alice Andors, "Keeping Teen Workers Safe," *HR Magazine* (June 2010), 76–80.
14. See *http://www.cdc.gov/hiv/risk/other/occupational.html* for more information.
15. OSHA Standard 1910.132—Personal Protective Equipment.
16. Amy Onder, "Donning and Doffing Protective Gear Was 'Work' Under FLSA," *HR Magazine* (September 2011), 113.
17. *United Autoworkers v. Johnson Controls, Inc.*, 111 S. Ct 1196 (1991).
18. "OSHA Flags High Injury and Illness Rates," *HR Magazine* (June 2009), 24.
19. *Marshall v. Barlow's, Inc.*, 98 S. Ct. 1816 (1978).
20. See *https://www.osha.gov/pls/imis/industry.html* for more information.

21. K. McCarthy, "More than Mere Compliance," *Industrial Safety & Hygiene News* (November 2013), 47.
22. Adapted from "Nine Values for Safety Culture," *Professional Safety* (November 2013), 37.
23. "Fatigue-Related Incidents Are Preventable," *Professional Safety* (May 2013), 58.
24. A. Tucker et al., "Organizational Factors That Contribute to Operational Failures in Hospitals," Working Paper, Harvard Business School Division of Research (January 2013), 1–32.
25. "Tips for Strengthening Safety Committees," *Professional Safety* (December 2012), 57.
26. Adapted from "Ethical Issues Related to Staff Shortages," *Healthcare Executive* (July/August 2013), 94–95.
27. "Can You Tell If Your Workers Are Using Drugs?," *Safety Compliance Letter* (June 2012), 7–12; D. Epstein, "Extinguish Workplace Stress," *Nursing Management* (October 2010), 34–37.
28. See *http://www.nursingworld.org/codeofethics* for more information.
29. K. Koster, "EAPs Unite to Combat Alcohol Problems," *Employee Benefit Adviser* (August 2010), 8.
30. "Sick Buildings Linked to Migraines," *Safety Compliance Letter* (April 2013), 11.
31. J. Akridge, "Sharpening Safety Skills; Products, Techniques Reduce Needlestick Injury," *Healthcare Purchasing News* (December 2013), 20–28.
32. See *https://www.osha.gov/needlesticks/needle-faq.html* for more information.
33. "Wellness Matters!," *HR Magazine* (April 2014), 62–63.
34. Frank S. Perri and Richard G. Brody, "The Sallie Rohrbach Story: Lessons or Auditors and Fraud Examiners," *Journal of Financial Crime* 18, no. 1 (2011), 93–104.
35. Pamela Babcock, "Workplace Stress? Deal with It!," *HR Magazine* (May 2009), 67–70.
36. Lilia Cortina and Vicki Magley, "Patterns and Profiles of Responses to Incivility in the Workplace," *Journal of Occupational Health Psychology* 14 (2009), 272–288.
37. Brad Estes and Jia Eang, "Integrative Literature Review: Workplace Incivility," *Human Resource Development Review* 7 (2008), 218–240.
38. Vincent Roscigno et al., "Supervisory Bullying, Status Inequities, and Organizational Context," *Social Forces* 87 (2009), 1561–1589.
39. William Martin and Helen LaVan, "Workplace Bullying: A Review of Litigated Cases," *Employee Responsibilities and Rights Journal* 22 (2010), 175–194.
40. Jack Howard, "Employee Awareness of Workplace Violence Policies," *Employee Responsibility and Rights Journal* 21 (2009), 7–19.
41. Dori Meinert, "Out of the Shadows," *HR Magazine* (October 2011), 50–55.
42. Ibid.
43. Ibid.
44. "High-Tech Tracking: Good Business Practice or Orwellian Nightmare?," *HR Focus* (May 2013), 1–3.
45. John D'Arcy, Anat Hovav, and Dennis Galletta, "User Awareness of Security Countermeasures and Its Impact on Information Systems Misuse: A Deterrence Approach," *Information Systems Research* 20, no. 1 (2009), 79–98.
46. Carol Hymowitz, "Bosses Have to Learn How to Confront Troubled Employees," *Wall Street Journal* (April 23, 2007), B1.

GLOSSARY

401(k), 403(b), and 457 plans Retirement plans that allow employees to elect to reduce their current pay by a certain percentage, which is then used to fund a retirement plan.

A

Absenteeism Any failure by an employee to report for work as scheduled or to stay at work when scheduled.

Adult learning "the training design must consider that all the trainees are adults, but adults come with widely varying learning styles, experiences, and personal goals"

Affirmative action Beneficial steps taken to remedy present, past and continuing discrimination.

Affirmative action program (AAP) Proactive steps the organization will take to attract and hire members of underrepresented groups.

Applicant pool All people who are actually evaluated for selection.

Applicant population A subset of the labor force population that is available for selection using a particular recruiting approach.

Arbitration Arbitration can be conducted by an individual or a panel of individuals; a neutral third party makes a decision.

Assessment considers employee and organizational performance issues to determine if training can help.

Assessment centers A series of evaluative exercises and tests used for selection and development.

Authorization cards Requires employees to sign the card that authorizes the union to seek a representation election that could formalize the union's role in negotiating labor contracts on behalf of the employee group.

B

Balanced scorecard "The balanced scorecard is a framework organizations use to report on a diverse set of performance measures."

Base pay Basic compensation that an employee receives, usually as a wage or salary.

Behavioral event interview An interview in which applicants are required to give specific examples of how they have handled a problem or situation in the past.

Behavioral modeling involves copying someone else's behavior and it particularly appropriate for skill training in which the trainees must use both knowledge and practice.

"Behaviorally anchored rating scale" In a behaviorally anchored rating scale (BARS), examples of employee job behaviors are "anchored" or measured against a scale of performance levels.

Behavior-based criteria "Identification of behaviors that may lead to successful job performance."

397

Benchmark jobs Jobs that are found in other organizations and performed by several individuals who have similar duties that require similar KSAs.

Benchmarking Benchmarking is the process of comparing the business metrics and outcomes to an industry standard or best practice.

Benefit An indirect reward given to an employee as a part of organizational membership, regardless of performance.

Blended learning Learning that combines short, fast-paced, interactive computer-based lessons and teleconferencing with traditional classroom instruction and simulation.

Board of inquiry A board appointed by the FMCS Director to investigate, report, and recommend solutions to resolve contractual disputes.

Bona fide occupational qualification (BFOQ) A legitimate reason why an employer can exclude persons on otherwise illegal bases of consideration.

Bonus Receiving additional compensation payments.

Broadbanding The practice of using fewer pay grades with much broader ranges than in traditional compensation systems.

Burden of proof The responsibility placed on a defendant to prove or disapprove an arguable fact .

Business necessity A practice required for safe and efficient organizational operations.

C

Cash balance plans Pension plans that are a hybrid of defined-benefit and defined contribution plans, based on a hypothetical account balance.

Central-tendency raters Managers who tend to rate all of their employees within a narrow range

Certify Designation by the NLRB that a union has met the required conditions and received the necessary votes to become the bargaining representative of an employee group.

Closed shop A provision which requires individuals to join a union before they can be hired.

Coaching Training and feedback given to employees.

Cognitive ability tests Tests that measure an individual's thinking, memory, reasoning, verbal, and mathematical abilities.

Collective bargaining The process whereby representatives of management and workers negotiate over wages, hours, and other terms and conditions of employment.

Compa-ratio The pay level divided by the midpoint of the pay range.

Compensable factor A factor that identifies a dimension that is part of every job and can be rated for each job.

Compensation committee of the board of directors A subgroup of the board composed of directors who are not officers of the firm who determine and recommend the compensation components and levels of executive pay to the full board.

Competencies Basic characteristics that can be linked to enhanced performance by individuals or teams.

Competency approach Method of job analysis that focuses on the competencies that individuals need in order to perform jobs, rather than on the tasks, duties, and responsibilities that compose a job.

Complaint An indication that shows the dissatisfaction of an employee.

Conciliation A provision that allows the third party to assist union and management negotiators to reach a voluntary settlement, but makes no proposals for solutions.

Concurrent validity Method for establishing the validity associated with a predictor.

Constructive discharge Situation when an employer creates impossible working conditions that force an employee to resign.

Consumer-driven health (CDH) plan Employer provides financial contributions to employees to help cover their health-related expenses (HSAs and HRAs).

Contaminated Measurement process that includes irrelevant criteria.

Contrast errors Situation in the performance review process in which a manager compares employees to each other rather than to job-performance standards.

Copayments Costs that an insured pays for medical treatment.

Core competencies "A core competency is a unique capability that creates high value and at which a healthcare organization excels."

Cost-of-living adjustment (COLA) A standard raise based on an economic measure, such as the consumer price index.

Cultural competence The ability to communicate with people of different cultures and backgroups in an effective manner.

Cumulative trauma disorders (CTD) Problems that occur when workers repetitively use the same muscles to perform tasks, resulting in muscular and skeletal injuries.

D

Decertify Designation by the NLRB that employees have met the required conditions to remove a union as their representative.

Deductible Amount paid by an insured individual before the medical plan pays any expenses.

Deficient Measurement process that omits significant criteria.

Defined-contribution plan Pension plan in which the employer makes an annual payment to an employee's account.

Department A distinct grouping of organizational responsibilities.

Disparate impact It occurs when there is substantial underrepresentation of protected-class members as a result of employment decisions that work to their disadvantage.

Disparate treatment It occurs when protected-class members are treated differently from others.

Drug- Free Workplace Act of 1988 Law enacted to make workplaces free from the use of drugs or controlled substances.

Due process A method of questioning a disciplinary action.

Duty A larger work segment comprised of several tasks that are performed by an individual.

Early retirement To retire early from jobs.

Employee assistance program (EAP) A program which provides counseling and other help to employees having emotional, mental, or other personal problems.

Employee development A process that focuses on individuals gaining new capabilities useful for both current and future jobs.

Employee engagement The level of employee commitment to the organization's goals and values and the employee's sense of well-being in their job.

Employee leasing A concept where the employer "leases" its employees from the leasing company, which then writes the paychecks, pays the taxes, provides benefits, prepares and implements HR policies, and keeps all the required personnel records.

Employee relations philosophy A philosophy that describes the relationship the employer wishes to have with its employees.

Employment- at-will provisions Provisions in employment agreements and handbooks that states that employees may be terminated at any time for any reason.

Employment brand The view both employees and outsiders have of healthcare organizations.

Employment contract Formal agreement between an employer and an employee contractually defining the working relationship.

Employment Practices Liability Insurance (EPLI) Insurance that protects employers against lawsuits initiated by their employees.

Environmental scanning "The process of studying the environment of the organization to pinpoint opportunities and threats."

Equal employment opportunity A broad concept holding that individuals should have equal treatment in all employment related actions.

Ergonomics The study and design of the work environment to address physiological and physical demands a position.

Essential job functions The fundamental job duties.

Exempt employees Employees who hold positions for which employers are not required to pay overtime.

Exit interview An interview of those who are leaving the organization to determine the reasons for their departure.

Extended illness banks Program that allows employees to accrue time to be used for longer-term illness or health-related care that does not result in a disability, such as maternity care.

F

Feedback systems Three components of performance appraisal: collecting data, evaluating data, and taking action based on the data.

Flexible spending accounts (FSA) A plan that allows employees to contribute pre-tax dollars to pay for additional benefits.

Forced distribution Appraisal method of ranking employees and using statistics to sort all employees along a bell curve.

Forecasting "Using information from the past and present to identify expected future conditions."

Free-rider penalty A penalty associated with the employer mandate

Funeral or bereavement leave Time off to attend to the arrangements and funeral after the death of an immediate family member.

G

Gap analysis "Process that identifies the distance between where an organization is with its employee capabilities and where it needs to be."

Garnishment Occurs when a creditor obtains a court order that directs an employer to set aside a portion of an employee's wages to pay a debt owed to the creditor.

Glass ceiling Discriminatory practices that have prevented women and other protected class members from advancing to executive level jobs.

Good faith and fair dealing A provision that tells that the employer and the employee have entered into a relationship whose objective is treating each other fairly.

Graphic rating scale A scale that allows the rater to mark an emplyee's performance on a continuum.

Green-circled employee An incumbent who is paid below the range set for the job.

Grievance A complaint formally stated in writing whether or not a union is involved.

Grievance arbitration A third party settles disputes arising from different interpretations of a labor contract.

H

Halo effect Situation in the performance review process when a manager rates an employee high on all job standards based on one characteristic.

Health A general state of physical, mental, and emotional well-being.

Health insurance exchange A marketplace for individuals and businesses to compare, choose, and buy health insurance.

Health promotion A supportive approach to facilitate and encourage employees to enhance healthy actions and lifestyles.

Hostile environment Actions such as commenting on appearance or attire, telling jokes that are suggestive or sexual in nature, allowing revealing photos and posters to be displayed, or making continual requests to get together after work that create an environment of hostility in the workplace.

HR Otherwise known as Human Resource.

HR Analytics "HR analytics is an evidence-based approach to making HR decisions on the basis of quantitative tools and models."

HR metrics HR metrics are specific measures of HR practices.

Human capital "Human capital is the collective value of the capabilities, knowledge, skills, life experiences, and motivation in an organization's workforce."

Human resource planning "Human resource planning is the process of analyzing and identifying the need for and availability of people so that the organization can meet its strategic objectives."

I

Illegal issues Issues that require either party to take illegal action.

Immediate confirmation "Training concept that people learn best if reinforcement and feedback are given as soon as possible after training."

Impasse Situation in which negotiating parties cannot come to an agreement.

Implied contracts Unwritten agreements between employers and employees, which suggest that an employee will be employed indefinitely or as long as the employee performs the job satisfactorily.

Independent contractors Workers who perform specific services on a contract basis.

Individual incentives Pay given to reward the effort and performance of individuals.

Intangible rewards Differs among employees and it cannot be easily measured or quantified.

Integrated disability management programs Integrating disability programs with workers' compensation programs to reduce costs and coordinate claim processing.

Interest-based bargaining A style of negotiating contracts based on identifying and meeting the parties' mutual interests.

Internal recruiting Focusing on recruiting current employees.

J

Job A grouping of common tasks, duties, and responsibilities.

Job analysis A systematic way to gather and analyze information about the content and human requirements of jobs and the context in which jobs are performed.

Job criteria Identifies factors employees must meet for satisfactory job performance.

Job description Summary of multiple criteria that defines a job.

Job design Organizing tasks, duties, and responsibilities into a productive unit of work.

Job evaluation A systematic basis for determining the relative worth of jobs within an organization.

Job family A grouping of jobs with similar characteristics.

Job posting and bidding Method for recruiting employees, whereby the employer provides notices of job openings and employees respond by applying for specific openings.

Job responsibilities Obligations to perform certain tasks and duties.

Job satisfaction A positive emotional state resulting from job experiences.

Job sharing Two part-time employees perform the work of one full-time job.

Job specification It lists the knowledge, skills, and abilities (KSAs) an individual needs to perform a job satisfactorily.

L

Labor force population All individuals who are available for selection if all possible recruitment strategies are used.

Labor–management committees Committees that are jointly sponsored by management and the union. Their purpose is to identify common problems, interpret contract language, and resolve the issues.

Leadership standards The level of quality required by a person to be a leader.

leaves of absence Time off with or without pay.

Lenient raters Managers who give all of their employees high ratings.

Living wage Wages that are supposed to meet the basic needs of a worker's family.

Lockout Management shuts down operations to prevent union members from working and also avert possible damage or sabotage to the facility or injury to employees who continue to work. It also gives management leverage in negotiations.

Loyalty Defined as being faithful to an institution or employer.

M

Managed care Approaches that monitor and reduce medical costs through restrictions and market-system alternatives.

Management by objectives Specifies the performance goals that an employee and manager agree to complete within a defined period.

Management rights Clauses that vary from contract to contract and give management the exclusive right to manage, direct, and control its business.

Mandatory issues Issues identified specifically by labor laws or court decisions that relate to wages, benefits, nature of jobs, and other work-related subjects.

Marginal job functions Duties that are part of a job but are incidental or ancillary to the purpose and nature of the job.

Market pricing An analysis which uses market pay data to identify the relative value of jobs based on what other employers pay for similar jobs.

Mediation Dispute resolution process in which a trained mediator assists the parties in reaching a negotiated settlement.

Mentoring A relationship in which experienced managers aid less experienced individuals in the earlier stages of their careers.

Merit raises Raises based on performance.

Minimum essential coverage The type of coverage an individual must have to meet the individual responsibility requirement under the Affordable Care Act. This includes individual market policies, employer provided insurance, Medicare, Medicaid, and certain other coverage.

N

Non-compete provisions Contract provisions that specify that employees will not compete with the organization if they leave.

Nonexempt employees Employees who hold positions for which employers are required to pay for overtime.

O

Ombuds Employees outside the normal chain of command who act as independent problem solvers for both management and employees.

On-the-job training (OJT) Planned training that uses a supervisor or manager to teach and show the employee what to do.

Open shop A provision in Right-to-work laws which indicates workers cannot be required to join or pay dues to a union.

Open-door policy A policy that allows workers, who have a complaint, to talk directly to someone in charge.

Organization chart A chart that depicts the relationships among jobs/departments in an organization.

Organizational commitment "The degree to which employees believe in and accept organizational goals and desire to remain with the organization."

Organizational culture "A pattern of shared values and beliefs giving members of an organization meaning and providing them with rules for behavior."

Organizational incentives Compensation given to reward people based on the performance results of the organization.

P

Paid time off plan A time off program that combines short-term leave, vacation, and holiday pay into one bank.

Panel interview Several interviewers interview the candidate at the same time.

Pay adjustment matrix A salary guide chart in which adjustments are based in part on the person's pay, divided by the midpoint of the pay range.

Pay compression Shrinking the pay differences among individuals with different levels of experience and performance.

Pay equity Idea that pay for jobs requiring comparable levels of knowledge, skill, and ability should be similar, even if actual duties differ significantly

Performance appraisal The process of evaluating how well employees perform their jobs when compared to a set of standards, and then communicating that information to employees.

Performance Management A series of activities designed to ensure that the organization gets the performance it needs from its employees.

Performance standards Standards that tell what the job accomplishes and how performance is measured in key areas of the job description.

Perquisites (perks) Special executive benefits, usually noncash items, that help to retain executives to organizations and demonstrate their importance to their companies.

Person– organization fit The congruence between people and companies.

Person–job fit A concept of matching characteristics of people with characteristics of jobs.

Phased retirement A program that helps employees retire in stages over time.

Physical ability tests Tests that measure an individual's abilities such as strength, endurance, and muscular movement.

Placement Fitting a person to the right job.

Portability Ability to move pension funds from one company to another.

Position A job performed by one person.

Predictive validity A method where test results of applicants are compared with their subsequent job performance.

Predictors of selection criteria Measurable or visible indicators of those positive characteristics (or criteria).

Prevailing wage Rate paid for a job by a majority of the employers in a particular geographic area.

Privacy Act of 1974 Law that issues regulations that affect human resource record-keeping systems, policies, and procedures.

Progressive discipline A discipline process that includes a series of steps before an employee separation can occur.

Psychological contract The unwritten expectations that employees and employers have about the nature of their work relationships.

Psychomotor tests Tests that measure a person's dexterity, hand–eye coordination, arm–hand steadiness, and other factors.

Public-policy violation A provision under which an employee can sue an employer if the employee was discharged for reasons that violate a public policy.

Q

Quid pro quo Harassment in which employment outcomes are linked to granting sexual favors.

R

Ranking Appraisal method that compares employees, against each other.

Rater bias "Situation in the performance-review process when a manager has a bias against a certain employee or employee group based on the manager's own values or prejudices."

Ratification Occurs when union members vote to accept the terms of a negotiated labor agreement.

Realistic job preview (RJP) Part of a job selection process that is designed to inform job candidates of the organizational realities of the job so they can evaluate their own job expectations.

Reasonable accommodation A modification or adjustment to a job or work environment that enables a qualified individual with a disability to have equal employment opportunity.

Recruiting Identifying where to recruit, whom to recruit, and what the job requirements will be.

Red-circled employee An incumbent who is at or above the maximum of the range set for the job.

Reinforcement Concept of training based on the law of effect.

Resource (float pools) Workers specifically hired to be available (float) to various units when the needs are higher than core staff can meet.

Results-based criteria Process that identifies behavior based on results that are easy to identify and evaluate.

Retaliation It occurs when employers take punitive actions against individuals who exercise their legal rights.

Retention agreement A contract agreement that is designed to retain key employees during mergers, consolidations, or changes in the organizational leadership.

Right-to-sue letter A letter initiated by the Equal Employment Opportunity Commission that notifies the complainant that he or she has 90 days in which to file a personal suit in federal court.

Right-to-work laws A provision that allows a person the right to work without having to join a union.

S

Sabbatical An opportunity provided by some companies for employees to take time off the job to develop and rejuvenate, as well as to participate in activities that help others.

Safety Protecting the physical well-being of people.

Salary Compensation based on a fixed amount, regardless of hours worked.

Security Protecting employees, patients/residents/clients, and visitors.

Security audit Conducting a comprehensive review of organizational security; sometimes called a vulnerability analysis.

Selection criterion A charactistic that a person must have to do the job successfully.

Self-efficacy Refers to a person's belief that he or she can successfully learn the training program content

Separation agreement A provision in which an employee who is being terminated agrees not to sue the employer in exchange for specified benefits, such as additional severance pay or other "considerations."

Serious health condition Health condition that requires inpatient, hospice, or residential medical care or ongoing physician care.

Severance pay A security benefit voluntarily offered by employers to some employees who lose their jobs.

Sexual harassment Unwelcome verbal, visual, or physical conduct of a sexual nature that is severe and affects working conditions or creates a hostile work environment.

Simple majority A process that requires employees, without help from their employer, to obtain signatures from at least 30 percent of the employees who are union members.

Situational judgment tests Tests that measure a person's judgment in work settings.

Status-blind Decisions are made without regard to applicants' personal characteristics (i.e., age, sex, race, and so on).

Statutory rights Existing laws, legislation, and evolving case law that protect employees' rights.

Step systems Pay system in which employees' wages are adjusted based on how long they have been with the organization.

Strategic HR management "Strategic HR management maximizes the effectiveness of employees and results in the achievement of an organizational mission and a competitive advantage in the market."

Strict raters Managers who in the performance-review process, give all of their employees low ratings.

Strike When employees believe their interests are not being adequately considered by managers, organizations or politicians picket or demonstrate outside the place of business by carrying placards and signs.

Succession planning A process of identifying a longer-term plan for the orderly replacement of key employees.

T

Tangible rewards Includes base pay and variable pay; it can be measured, and it is possible to calculate the monetary value of each reward.

Task A distinct, identifiable work activity comprised of motions.

Temporary employees Workers who are hired on a rate-per-day or per-week basis as needed.

Total rewards The package includes all forms of compensation, the monetary and non monetary rewards provided by an organization to attract, motivate, and retain employees.

Training A process whereby people acquire capabilities to aid in the achievement of organizational goals.

Trait-based criteria Process that identifies subjective personal traits that may contribute to job success.

U

Undue hardship A significant difficulty or expense imposed on an employer in making an accommodation for individuals with disabilities.

Union A formal association of workers that promotes its members' interests through collective bargaining.

Union membership rate The percentage of wage and salary of workers who were members of unions.

Union security provisions Clauses in union contracts that recognize the exclusive right of a union to bargain on behalf of the employees.

V

Variable pay Compensation linked directly to individual, team, or organizational performance.

Vesting Nonforfeitable ownership by an employee of the retirement benefits they have earned.

W

Wage survey A collection of data on compensation rates for workers performing similar jobs in other organizations.

Wages Compensation paid on an hourly basis or salary.

Wellness programs Programs designed to maintain or improve employee health before problems arise by encouraging personal lifestyle changes.

Work sample tests An applicant performs a simulated task that is a specified part of the target job

Work–life balance Achieving the appropriate balance between one's work commitments and their personal lives.

Forced distribution, 236–237
Forecasting, 54–55
401(k) plan, 342
403(b) plan, 342
457 plan, 342
"Free-rider" penalty, 346
Free speech, employees' right
  to, 259–260
Funeral leave, 354

G

Gainsharing plans, 356
Gap analysis, 194
Gardenview Long-Term Care
  case, 330
Garnishment, 317
Gender discrimination, 75–79
  breaking the glass, 78–79
  equal pay and pay equity,
    76–77
  glass ceiling, 78
  job evaluation and gender
    issues, 320
  pregnancy discrimination,
    75–76
Gender in workforce, 59
General/generic
  competencies, 101
Genesee Health Plan, 3
Genesys Health System (Flint,
  Michigan), 3
Genesys Physician Hospital
  Organization, 3
Genetic bias regulations, 86
Genetic Information
  Nondiscrimination Act
  (GINA), 86
Geographic labor markets,
  125
GINA. *See* Genetic
  Information
  Nondiscrimination Act
  (GINA)
Glass ceiling, 78
Glass elevators, 78
Glass walls, 78
Global and cultural
  effectiveness, 22
Good faith, 252
Governmental factors, 50–51
Government-supported job
  training, 204
Graphic-rating scale, 234, 235
Green-circled employees, 324

Grievance arbitration, 296
Grievance management,
  295–297
  employee grievance process,
    297
  procedures, 295–296
  responsibilities, 295
  steps in, 296–297
Griggs v. Duke Power (1971), 67

H

Halo effect, 240
Hanson Rehabilitation
  Hospital case, 183
Hazard communication, 372
Hazards in healthcare work,
  17
Health. *See also* Occupational
  Safety and Health Act
  (OSHA); Safety
defined, 366
  healthcare workplace health
    issues, 385–388
    emotional/mental health
      concerns, 386–387
    inadvertent needle sticks,
      387–388
    latex allergy, 387
    slips and falls, 388
    substance abuse, 385–386
    workplace air quality, 387
  health promotion, 388–389
  Hemmingway Nursing Care
    case, 394
  Joint Commission and,
    367–368
  legal requirements for,
    367–371
    Americans with Disabilities
      Act and, 370–371
    child labor laws, 371
    workers' compensation,
      369–370
nature of, 365–366
promotion
  Employee assistance
    programs (EAPs), 389
  levels, 388
  organizational health
    culture, 389
  wellness programs, 389
reproductive health,
  374–375
responsibilities, 366

Healthcare
  access to, 7
  current state of, 7–8
  disparities in, 9
  distribution of positions, 5, 7
  employment in, 4–5
  future of, 8–9
  HR management function
    in, 15–17
  insurance coverage, 7
  legal risk management and,
    7
  position hierarchy, 6, 7
  projected growth in, 9–12
  reform implications, 8
  types of jobs, 5–7
  worker shortages, 8
Healthcare and HR practices
  Seven C's in, 58
Healthcare compensation
  approaches, 303
Healthcare occupations
  independent practice,
    11–12
  managing change in, 12–13
  projected growth of, 9–12
Healthcare organizational
  charts, 26, 27
Healthcare organizations
  managing change in, 12–13
  nature of, 4–7
  types of, 4
Healthcare reform and HR
  practices, 14, 35–36
Health insurance exchange,
  345
Health Insurance Portability
  and Accountability Act
  (HIPAA), 96, 115, 249,
  349
  financial, insurance, and
    other benefits, 349–354
  educational benefits, 350
  family-oriented benefits,
    350–351
  financial benefits, 349
  insurance benefits,
    349–350
  social and recreational
    benefits, 350
  healthcare legislation, 349
Health issues of employees, 17
HealthPartners (Minnesota),
  3
Health service businesses, 11